DIALOGUES BETWEEN
FAITH AND REASON

DIALOGUES
BETWEEN FAITH
AND REASON

The Death and
Return of God in
Modern German Thought

JOHN H. SMITH

CORNELL UNIVERSITY PRESS
Ithaca and London

First published 2011 by Cornell University Press

Printed in the United States of America

Library of Congress Cataloging-in-Publication Data

Smith, John H., 1954–
    Dialogues between faith and reason : the death
and return of God in modern German thought /
John H. Smith.
        p. cm.
    Includes bibliographical references and index.
    ISBN 978-0-8014-4927-7 (cloth : alk. paper)
    ISBN 978-0-8014-7762-1 (pbk. : alk. paper)
    1. Death of God theology.   2. God (Christianity)—
History of doctrines.   3. Theology, Doctrinal—
Germany—History.   4. Philosophical theology—
Germany—History.   5. Atheism—Germany—History.
I. Title.
    BT83.5.S65   2011
    231.0943'0904—dc22   2011000861

Cornell University Press strives to use environmentally
responsible suppliers and materials to the fullest extent
possible in the publishing of its books. Such materials
include vegetable-based, low-VOC inks and acid-free
papers that are recycled, totally chlorine-free, or partly
composed of nonwood fibers. For further information,
visit our website at www.cornellpress.cornell.edu.

Cloth printing   10 9 8 7 6 5 4 3 2 1
Paperback printing   10 9 8 7 6 5 4 3 2 1

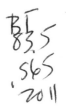

❧ Contents

🦋 PREFACE

In 1966, the death of God made the front cover of *Time* magazine—on Good Friday, no less. We have here not so much a case that confirms Nietzsche's madman's point that it will take a while for the news of God's death to reach the masses. Rather, what sparked the cover story was in fact the return of theology in the form of a North American movement called "death-of-God theology." In a more academic forum—namely, his extensive study of atheistic philosophies and Christian apologetics in the seventeenth century—Hans-Martin Barth begins with a reference to the disappearance and return of discussions about God's existence:

> In the Preface to the first edition of his complete works in 1846 Ludwig Feuerbach wrote: "The question of whether God exists or not, the opposition of theism and atheism, belongs to the eighteenth and seventeenth centuries, not to the nineteenth." Not to mention the twentieth—, one could logically conclude. Amazingly, however, the question of God has been the focal point of an intense theological discussion for nearly a decade. What a philosopher of the last century could consider over and done with for at least a century, appears to have found its way, with considerable delay, back into the field of vision of contemporary theology. (13)

What Barth has in mind with this "return" of the question of God's existence in "contemporary" discourse is, in fact, the same "death-of-God theology" that made the cover of *Time,* for he encountered it during his studies in the United States (at Harvard Divinity School) in the late 1960s. And so this professor of systematic theology at the famed University of Marburg, which had been part of a new movement to "save" Protestant theology and rethink philosophy after the demise of Judeo-Christian values in the wake of Nietzsche and World War I, himself must engage with a new movement that takes as its explicit starting point the death of God. The goal of this book is to provide a broad historical and intellectual context for these amazing phenomena—the death(s) of God and his return(s).

The divide between believers and nonbelievers, theists and atheists, has been, and continues to be, perhaps the deepest one separating individuals and groups. As we learned from the 2004 U.S. presidential election, in the United States today the main predictor of voting patterns turns out to be regular church attendance. "Red" and "blue" depict not just party affiliation by state but, more fundamentally, the divide between those who see faith as central to all aspects of their lives and those who consider it a private, if not irrelevant, matter. Certainly the opposition, both real and politically hyped, between religious believers—such as "Christian" versus "Muslim" or "Fundamentalists/Orthodox" versus "modernists/liberals"—can be deadly serious. But the conflict *within* the realm of faith is different from that between the secular and the devout. After all, for nonbelievers, there is always a "pox-on-both-your-houses" sentiment lurking in the background, a sense that the real problem lies with religion, or at least monotheisms, per se. And, of course, for the religious nothing could be worse than those who profess to challenge the foundation of religion as such.

The goal of this book, however, is not to take sides in this debate, as there are enough polemics promoting proofs for the existence or nonexistence of God.[1] It is not my interest either to support radical skepticism or to "displace the secular economy" with a new theology.[2] Rather, I will be arguing that the two positions have in fact been historically interconnected for at least four centuries. Specifically, I will be retracing the course of a "slippery slope" that has led from belief to unbelief, from God to the death of God, resulting not so much from attacks from the "outside" of religion as from intellectual and philosophical developments *within* modern Christian theology. Many thinkers along this path who intended to support or at least grasp the essence of Christian faith with reason ended up undermining it. Paul Ramsey wrote in the preface to Gabriel Vahanian's *The Death of God* in 1961 that "every revival of Christianity in the past three hundred years has revived less of it" (xxiv), a claim I will be applying to mostly well-intended theological and philosophical "revivals." We know where the best intentions are said to lead. The goal is to show how a certain logic in modern thought about Christianity brought about both its own undoing and the seeds for

---

1. Hence, I will not take up Bertrand Russell's call to atheism, "Why I Am Not a Christian," as does William Connolly in his *Why I Am Not a Secularist*. Nor will I address the strident new atheists Daniel Dennett, Richard Dawkins, Sam Harris, and Christopher Hitchens (or even less strident earlier ones such as Michael Martin).

2. See Phillip Blond's introduction to *Post-Secular Philosophy* (5).

a revival of faith from a new perspective. Stated in political terms, I'd like to show people in the "red" state of mind how those in the "blue" came to think as they do; and those in the "blue" how their position grew out of "red" soil.

The notion of an ongoing "dialogue" over the past five hundred or so years of Western (esp. German) thought between reason and faith presumes two things about the very nature of dialogue. First, despite the contentiousness of the exchanges and despite the call from both sides to break off all communication with the other, the past existence of a dialogue between the two means that some form of common language must be possible. Within the tradition of Christian theology and philosophy that is the focus of this book that common basis resides in the very notion of *logos,* a rich term variously translated as word, discourse, speech, reason, or calculation. It forms the precondition of dialogue, a term derived from the Greek *dia-logos,* from *dia-legein,* meaning to speak through or across, to speak alternately. After all, as we will see, *logos* is both the very foundation of Western conceptions of rationality and, thanks to the early melding of Jewish and Greek thought, the very beginning of Christian conceptions of God. Hence, in these times of conflict between secularism and religiosity, Enlightenment and piety, we can, I hope, benefit from the exploration of historical sites of interaction, the attempts to "think through faith" (an intentionally ambiguous formulation).

Second, it is valuable to recall an essential feature of all genuine conversation or dialogue that the philosopher Hans-Georg Gadamer highlighted in his major study on hermeneutics as the art/science of achieving understanding. He argued, namely, that partners in a dialogue who are interested in generating new knowledge, as opposed to merely repeating what is already known or to speaking past each other, do not so much lead the conversation as they are led by it.[3] If in a dialogue we are mutually open to what the other is trying to say, we end up—hopefully—at a new place because we allow the matter under discussion (*logos*) to set the direction. In this case, the dynamic of the "slippery slope" guides attempts within modern (German) Christian thought to use reason to justify faith. I hope to encourage readers, even or

---

3. Gadamer writes on conversation: "To conduct a conversation means to allow oneself to be conducted by the subject matter to which the partners in the dialogue are oriented. . . . What emerges in its truth is the *logos,* which is neither mine nor yours and hence so far transcends the interlocutors' subjective opinions that even the person leading the conversation knows that he does not know. The art of conducting a conversation, dialectic, is also the art of seeing things in the aspect of unity" (*Wahrheit und Methode,* 367–68).

especially those allied with one side or the other, to jump into this ongoing process because its movement should not leave us unchanged.[4]

The entire book can be viewed as an elaboration on the historical developments summarized in the following passage from Max Horkheimer:

> We see after the Renaissance a process whereby the more science rises up and extends its mode of thinking in opposition to theology, the more philosophy takes upon itself the task of supporting Christian doctrine, or at least its key postulates, through rational methods that are related to the sciences. The concept of God as creator, law-giver, and judge, and especially the religious regulations that were most important for the functioning of society—these were to be reinterpreted as rational truths and thus harmonized with the sciences. Postulates once derived from revelation were decoupled from that endangered concept and allowed to stand on their own as eternal beliefs arrived at through autonomous reflection. Diverse philosophical systems were in agreement on this basic endeavor. The motivation to save European culture in the face of ever-widening knowledge of the world, led to both Humanism and the development of modern philosophy. The latter, even more than the former, is intricately bound up with the thought that morality, the immortality of the soul, and social life itself cannot survive without God. As much as Descartes and Leibniz, and indeed also Kant, were committed to the most rigid scientific methods, the legitimation of religious principles by identifying them with the concept of reason still forms a decisive motive of their thinking. (231–32; my translation)

I will be tracing this deep-seated irony of modern thought, the complex conversation between (Christian) faith and reason, from Humanism through to the present.

This book is the fruit of a series of courses that I have taught at the University of California, Irvine, both for undergraduates and for local school teachers as part of the project UCI-Santa Ana Teachers Institute. The motivation for those courses brings me to the present writing and is fourfold: (1) religion

---

4. Gadamer also calls for a broader "dialogue" between these different modes of understanding in "Mythos und Vernunft." The contemporary philosopher and theologian Kurt Hübner calls for a future cultural form in which science and myth learn to relate to each other (*Die Wahrheit des Mythos,* 410; cited in Hans Weldenfels, "Mythos und christlicher Logos," in Scheffczyk, *Rationalität,* 253–86, here 263).

plays a central role in the lives of many of our students, and if education is to be "relevant" for them, that issue must be addressed; (2) and yet we in the academy (with the exception of religious studies programs) have focused over the years on a variety of components of identity formation—basically, the powerful and nontrivial mantra of race, class, gender, and sexuality—but we have all too often left religion out, thereby giving our students critical tools to analyze so much of the world around them, just not one defining aspect;[5] (3) hence, many of the students—again, both believers who get their religion from churches, mosques, temples, and synagogues and nonbelievers who often have had no contact with religious traditions at all—lack the kind of critical relationship to religious issues that we have, I believe, so successfully tried to introduce in other areas; and finally, (4) the reason academic approaches to religion in the classroom have probably been avoided (outside of religious studies departments) is that they bring along problems that have not been satisfactorily addressed (among them: Does a teacher "out" him- or herself as an atheist or believer? Can we honestly say that a "critical analysis" of religion is not a "critique" since reflection on faith undoubtedly influences it? How do we introduce religion without opening the door to proselytizing? That is, does dealing with religion academically not involve an element of bad faith vis-à-vis one's audience since the claim of "distance to the material" necessarily must be undermined insofar as religion poses direct challenges to identity?).[6] I confess that the first times I taught these courses I was nervous again at the front of the classroom as I hadn't been for many years, even after having addressed all the other "difficult" issues of identity politics.

My way of answering the motivational impulses that arose in the classroom formed the rudimentary core of the present book. As a Germanist specializing in German intellectual history, I realized that the German philosophical and theological tradition—to make an understatement—has had something important to say about religion.[7] In particular, one can trace a development

---

5. This situation in U.S. colleges and universities has been addressed since the 1980s by George Marsden, William Connolly, and Stanley Fish (in a variety of op-ed pieces and blog entries).

6. As important as religious studies departments are, I would argue that it is also important that religion not be "ghettoized" but, rather, should be considered—like race, class, gender, and sexuality—inseparable from other material and thus introduced into nonspecialized classes.

7. Albert Schweitzer claimed: "When, at some future day, our period of civilization shall lie, closed and completed, before the eyes of later generations, German theology will stand out as a great, a unique phenomenon in the mental and spiritual life of our time" (1). In pursuing this tradition, I am working at the intersection of a number of disciplines: the philosophy of religion (which tries to explain the nature of religious behavior and experience); theology (reasoning or discourse about the nature of God); philosophy; and intellectual history.

from Luther and Erasmus on free will, through the Enlightenment introduction of historico-philological biblical exegesis and moral reinterpretations of Christianity, to the powerful nineteenth-century critiques of religion ending in Nietzsche's bold proclamation of the death of God. This tradition is in its own way profoundly *religious;* that is, it grows out of attempts to provide strong grounds for religious understanding and offers us (and our students) insights into the background of the kinds of arguments they or others might use to justify belief. At the same time, with a fascinating inexorable logic, this very tradition propels itself down that slippery slope and many an attempt to put the brakes on actually turns out to push the runaway sled faster toward the nadir of a godless world. At which point the stage is set for a dramatic return of and to God, albeit in a new guise. By teaching this material, I found that both believers and nonbelievers saw the origins of the chasm separating them and the ways various authors strove to bridge it, with greater or lesser success, over the course of some four centuries. Because so many students responded by saying that they simply never had known this tradition of critical thought existed, I address much of the following book to them.

A word of gratitude to Klaus and Jutta Beversdorf-Burghard for helping create the optimal conditions under which this book was first written; to the Humboldt Foundation and Professor Rolf-Peter Horstmann (Humboldt University) for their support; to my many colleagues and friends in Berlin and at the University of California, Irvine, for encouragement, conversations, and shared manuscripts; and to Jane, for accompanying me up and down these slopes. I dedicate the book to my daughter, Jordan, who matured along with the manuscript.

 DIALOGUES BETWEEN
FAITH AND REASON

Introduction

Logos, *Religion, and Rationality*

> Looking back over the dramatic history of reason and
> faith in modernity, which has led to the elimination
> of God from politics and science, the observer cannot
> avoid a conflicted impression: To what extent was this
> history "necessary," to what extent not? Is this histori-
> cal process towards de facto godlessness irreversible,
> has it run its course once and for all? Or does belief
> in God have a future after all, indeed, under the con-
> dition of and acknowledging the modern process of
> secularization and emancipation, a new future?
>
> —Hans Küng, *Existiert Gott?*

> `Εν ἀρχή ἦν ὁ λόγος, καί ὁ Λόγος ἦν πρός τόν Θεόν, καί
> Θεός ἦν ὁ λόγος. (In the beginning was the *logos*, and
> the *logos* was with God, and God was the *logos*.)
>
> —John 1.1

One can wonder, as did Erasmus, Lessing, and
many others, whether this darkly profound sentence is in fact a good beginning for theological understanding of the nature of faith and Christianity.
Its ambiguity and metaphorical richness have certainly encouraged two mil-
lennia of philosophical reflection, but clarification of meaning will hardly
be forthcoming.[1] However, if we are to understand how thinking about
religion has unfolded over at least the past five hundred years, we must come
to an appreciation of how this opening to the Gospel according to John has

---

1. In his article on *logos* for the third edition of *Religion in Geschichte und Gegenwart,* Ernst Fuchs
goes so far as to claim: "Ohne den johanneischen Satz . . . gäbe es trotz Paulus wahrscheinlich keine
christliche Theologie." R. Alan Culpepper comments that "by any standard the prologue to the Gospel of John is one of the most profound passages in the Bible. As simple as its language and phrases
are, its description of Jesus as the Logos has exerted a lasting influence on Christian theology" (110).
See Kelber, *Logoslehre* for a full history of this doctrine.

introduced a contradiction into the very foundation of Western/Christian religious discourse that will set it on a trajectory of debate and conflict.[2] My claim in this book is that the "death of God" is in a crucial sense inscribed into this Christian identification of God with *logos,* an identification that, by definition, makes theo-logy and critical/rational reflection on the divine an inherent necessity.[3] That "death," therefore, does not come to Him from "outside" Christian tradition but from within. It occurs through the different ways in which that *logos* comes to be identified over time, the different discursive spheres that bring their own "logics" to bear on understanding (the Christian) God.[4] Because that *logos* is not *one*—that is, it takes the form, among others, of philology, natural science, ethics, Idealist philosophy, anthropology, ideology, existentialism, and ontology—the long process of God's death also contains a constant returning to religion and of religion, as different thinkers again and again take on the task, ironically, not of killing but of understanding God with *logos.*

Conversely, the identity posited so directly here by the evangelist has the consequence of injecting (the Christian) God into the heart of the Western concept of *logos.*[5] Historically, from this point on, the exercise of reason associated with philosophy can never be practiced in isolation from theology. The relationship may be positive, with rational argument coming to the aid of theism, or negative, with reason attempting to demarcate a line of difference from its religious other. But in either case, *logos* is with God, or, at least, in communication with God. This means that philosophy will return again and again to the question of God and religion will return again and again, finding in philosophy new sources of life even after it might seem

---

2. Generally, "religion" throughout the following refers to "Christianity." That is the object of the dialogues between faith and reason that will follow. Undoubtedly, the dialogue would have taken a different form if other religious traditions had entered in as an equal partners, and the opening up to them is one of the main desiderata of our time. But even for that to happen, an understanding of the nature of the relatively "closed" dialogue between Christianity and rationality is necessary.

3. See Ludger Honnefelder, "Wissenschaftliche Rationalität und Theologie," in Scheffczyk, *Rationalität* (289–314). Scheffczyk also points out that this relationship between faith and reason is part of the New Testament as a whole (379). Of course, there is also considerable tension, as Scheffczyk also explains (381), esp. in Paul's critique of Greek knowledge/*logos* in 1 Corinthians 2, a tension to which I will return in chapter 10.

4. Schulte, in Scheffczyk, *Rationalität,* points out that theology is always bringing new "Denkformen" to bear on belief (317).

5. This opening verse is quite radical for another reason as well. If one considers how *logos* stands in opposition to *mythos,* i.e., how Western and Christian *logos* can be seen as largely responsible for the downfall of earlier mythic belief systems, then the positing of that very *logos* always already at the beginning rewrites mythic history, or, more precisely, rewrites universal history in such a way that myth no longer exists in prehistory (since *logos* was there "from the beginning").

that logic leaves no room for faith. This "essential complementarity" is at the heart of the contemporary efforts of both Pope Benedict XVI and the "Radical Orthodoxy" theologians to analyze our "postsecular" age. The neo-Marxist critical theorist Max Horkheimer formulates this relationship as a dialectical paradox: "Even if playing a new role, religion . . . survived the nineteenth century as an element of individual bourgeois life. Thanks not least to forces of atheism. . . . Indeed, the [atheistic] antithesis, in its radical or softer form, depended so heavily on its thesis, the spirit of the gospels, that it tended to deepen rather than eradicate religion" (*Zur Kritik der instrumentellen Vernunft* [*Critique of Instrumental Reason*], 221; my translation). The *logos* in God has led over centuries to His death and the God in *logos* has led time and again to His return. To better grasp this irony, which is at the heart of the unfolding of the Western tradition and our own contemporary situation, we need to pursue the consequences of the identification of God with *logos*.[6]

While it would be impossible to provide a full discussion of this prologue to John's Gospel, which has been the object of hundreds of biblical commentaries, we see here the origins of a paradox, or at least a rich dialogue, at the heart of Christian doctrine. To begin with, the context of this opening line contains references to many traditions. The echo of the Hebrew Bible connects *logos* to the *tyvarb* of Genesis 1:1 ("God said") and *yhla rmayw* or *memra*, the "Word" of God that often is used to refer to God Himself or as an intermediary. But John is certainly also influenced by the Hellenic tradition.[7] In Greek philosophy *logos* means the "world-soul," the all-pervading force and rational principle, and goes back at least to Heraclitus, who said it "always exists" and that "all things happen according to this *logos*" (frag. 2). The Hellenistic Jewish thinker, Philo of Alexandria, used it often to characterize the Platonic notion of a heavenly realm of archetypes.[8] And the Stoics developed this idea the furthest, seeing *logos* as the "eternal Reason" that pervaded the universe. They saw it as a force and principle, not as person/God.

---

6. The next section of John's opening deals with the concept of *kenosis* and the becoming-flesh, or incarnation, of the *logos*. This further central doctrine of Christianity can also be incorporated into the kind of historical argument I am making. (For example, for Vattimo in *Belief*, precisely the incarnation of God means his rejection of transcendence and hence the necessity of a human condition thrust upon a never-ending process of interpreting *logos*.)

7. Benedict XVI makes the claim that the Septuagint, the Greek translation of the Hebrew Bible, "brought about this encounter [of traditions] in a way that was decisive for the birth and spread of Christianity. A profound encounter of faith and reason is taking place here" (*Regensburg Lecture,* 136–37).

8. The classical philologist Werner Jaeger demonstrated that Plato was the first philosopher to use the term $\theta\varepsilon o\lambda o\gamma\acute{\iota}\alpha$ (see Weischedel, 14).

Hence, the evangelist is using a term that has a deep philosophical tradition and also is a common word for speech/discourse/word.

Traditionally, the Greek *logos* has been rendered "Word": "In the beginning was the Word, the Word was with God, and the Word was God." The Vulgate (Latin) version of the New Testament translates *logos* as *verbum*, "word," while Erasmus used the alternative *sermo*, "speech," to convey a greater sense of the spoken or active nature, as opposed to the lexical fixity, of this divine Word. And yet this is not the only possibility. Consider, for example, Faust's bold, if not blasphemous, decision in Goethe's famous play to render the holy original not as "Word" but as "Sense/Meaning" (*Sinn*), then "Force" (*Kraft*), and finally "Deed" (*Tat*)—at which point the devil (Mephistopheles) makes his appearance, as if called into being by this forced (mis)translation (*Faust* ll.1224–37). In fact, however, considering other meanings of *logos* (from which we get "logic"), it would not be philologically incorrect to interpret this most famous opening of John's Gospel in yet another way, namely, as positing the identification of God and rationality—"in the beginning was reason (*ratio*)."[9] How blasphemous is this rendition? Is it perhaps the most appropriate? And if we entertain its possibility, what kind of demand does such a view of God as *logos* place on man, the "rational animal" (the *zoion logon echon,* according to Aristotle)?[10] That is, what happens when we inject the claims of reason and rational discourse into the very nature of God? What kind of faith is called forth when reason is inherently implicated? And what kind of reason is this that attains a divine status?

In the history of Christian theology, the first great and sustained effort to unite rationality and faith, i.e., to bring powers of reasoning to bear on religious belief in order to support it, came with Scholasticism around the thirteenth century.[11] Thomas Aquinas argued against positions that would separate God from the powers of the human intellect, insisting that God is in Himself supremely knowable, even if only indirectly (as the sun can be visible, but not directly). Hence, Thomas sought to develop a systematic analysis of the created world in order to grasp the nature of the creator. Moreover, in

---

9. W.R. Inge summarizes this history of translation in the article on *logos* in the *Encyclopedia of Religion and Ethics:* "The Greek word λόγος has no exact equivalent in any other language. . . . Latin theology wavered between *Verbum, Sermo,* and *Ratio* before accepting *Verbum,* the least satisfactory, perhaps, of the three."

10. See the excellent summary of *logos* as speech vs. reason in the chapter "Isocrates and the Power of Logos" in Ijsseling (18–25).

11. On Thomas, see Georges Gottier, "Intellectus und Ratio," in Scheffczyk, *Rationalität* (229–50). See also Scheffczyk's own contribution, "Die Rolle der Ratio im Glauben und in der Theologie," 377–400, esp. 382–89 on the early Christian church. The Jewish tradition has had its own history of various strands of both irrationalist mysticism and rationalist Torah exegesis.

the England of Henry of Ghent (1217–93) and Duns Scotus (1266–1308), a "natural theology" developed that, in the critically tinged formulation of Phillip Blond, involves "the surrender of theology to secular reason's account of nature" (6). And yet, if God Himself is, from the beginning, *logos,* then is "surrender" the right word here? As opposed to the mystical traditions of, say, a Meister Eckehart, these efforts insisted on the application of logical and empirical investigations in order to glean from the world an understanding of the essence of God, legitimated by the intimate association of God and rationality.

That tradition of theological rationalism achieved its apex in the Age of Enlightenment. In his study of religious and scientific thought in the seventeenth and eighteenth centuries, Thomas P. Saine reports an incident from Johann Christian Edelmann's (1698–1767) autobiography, in which this rationalist critic of Lutheranism, indeed, one of its "most famous heretics," had a major insight concerning biblical translation: "At the beginning of the Gospel of St. John, the Greek word *Logos* should not be construed as 'Word,' but rather as 'Reason': 'God is reason'" (207).[12] Edelmann was not just returning to an older Stoic tradition but was drawing the logical conclusion of his own *Age of Reason.* This would mean for Edelmann that it must be the intention of God that humankind use its reason in all things, including the very study of God. That such an "inspiration" would lead future thinkers to the verge of beliefs that would challenge the very significance of theology and all institutions of worship—since what does a God identified with Reason need of praise or fear-inspired awe?—is the paradox at the heart of the story I wish to tell. My story is as much about the history of thinking about God—different proofs of His existence or arguments against it, claims about the relationship between philosophy and theology—as it is about the very history of a "modern logic," i.e., of the *logos* inherent in Western modernity as such, that guides the ongoing dialogue between faith and reason. Indeed, these two strands of the story cannot be separated.

Of course, *logos* does also mean "word," "speech," "discourse," and so we need likewise to address the relationship connecting religion, language, philosophy, and reason. As Jacques Derrida, father of late twentieth-century

---

12. This reappears in the contemporary commentary by M.G.J. Beets, who translates John 1 as: "In the beginning was reason (logos) and reason was with the god and god was reason." He means by this a Kantian notion of "Vernunft" as "the faculty of the purely formal" (129), what Beets calls a wordless voice that guides us always already (hence, "in the beginning") toward the basic unity of thought and being. "It has a clear meaning; the indivisible, ubiquitous god . . . is present with its whole being, as 'reason', in the individual mind to guide it back into the unity of being from which it has severed itself" (129–30).

poststructuralism, writes: "Now if, today, the 'question of religion' actually appears in a new and different light, if there is an unprecedented resurgence, both global and planetary, of this ageless thing, then what is at stake is language, certainly—more precisely the idiom, literality, writing, that forms the element of all revelation and of all belief" (*Religion,* 4). Just as the identification of God and reason inserts "in(to) the beginning" a contradiction that the history of Western thought attempts to resolve again and again, so, too, the idea that God is Word raises the demand that He be approached as language itself. Of course, gods in many religions express themselves to humankind in different ways that need to be interpreted. One can think of Apollo's tragically ambivalent oracles at Delphi. But if the Christian God is Word itself, then would love of God not involve the practice of "philology"? And if that is the case, would He not have to succumb to the same fate as any "text" that becomes all the denser, richer, more polyvalent, the more the tools of the historically critical philologist are applied? And do these tools, brought to bear out of the inner necessity, not then generate yet more words about words, a layering of human language upon the divine? Or does the final turn of the opening to John's Gospel—"And the Word was God"—not lead time and again lovers of words to discover underneath the layers of human language/*logos* a "divine" element, i.e., something within human reason and language that can only be "divined"?

These considerations of the implications of the linguistic nature of the Christian God/*logos* connect my book to the project undertaken by Jürgen Habermas "to take account of the conditions of modern postmetaphysical thought under which an ontotheologically insulated discourse with God cannot be continued."[13] I take Habermas's statement to mean not that the process we have come to call "modernity" has made God irrelevant or removed discussion of God from the world. Rather, if we place emphasis on the phrase "ontotheologically insulated," we realize that what has been "killed off" has been the possibility of a realm—linguistically, a discursive sphere—in which talk with or about God can be presumed to be of a character totally and essentially different from other discourses.[14] In a variation of Ludwig Feuerbach's analysis of the essence of Christianity, which we will explore below, Habermas is saying here not so much that God is to be pulled back to the realm of man but that the *language* of religion/God

---

13. Cited in Eduardo Mendieta's introduction to Habermas, *Religion and Rationality,* 12. Originally in *Philosophical Discourse of Modernity,* 406–7 n. 46.

14. The exploration of the decline of such discourse about the divine is undertaken by Charles Taylor in his monumental *Secular Age.*

cannot be separated out from other forms of language. "In the beginning was *logos*" might have meant for the Gospel a primal divine Word different from all others. But for us it comes to mean, according to Habermas, that the divine is always implicated in a process of using language, or, in his term, "linguistification" (and vice versa).[15]

The reason, therefore, we need to pursue the relationship between philosophy and religion in the Western tradition is not because of a fundamental division in principle between faith and knowledge, reason and belief, but because these two discursive realms have been the most closely, even if often polemically, interrelated. That is, to read the philosophico-theological tradition of the "death of God" is to examine neither "secularization" as a sociological process nor the victory of modern rationality over superstition, but, instead, to explore the sites where dominant discourses of the West tried (in vain) to define their insularity and where the rational and public discussion of religion tried (in vain) to isolate forms of religious experience as irrational and private.[16] Ironically, as we will see in the next chapter, the figures of Erasmus and Luther, who stand at the beginning of these developments, in many ways saw in advance what the stakes were and what was to come. This process has significant implications for both sides, i.e., for the competing discursive spheres of a logico-scientific philosophy and an ever more privatized and silenced religiosity. The mutual "contamination" of these spheres— and I use that term advisedly, although the very nature of the sacred and the profane does make it appropriate—means that talk with and about God that would attempt to maintain its isolation will find itself increasingly speechless, i.e., self-contradictory (and often, therefore, forced to nonlinguistic gestures of force), and, at the same time, talk that would imagine itself so "enlightened" as to have left religion behind will not be aware of its own implication in the process by which the religious entered into discourse. In the beginning, and the end, was *logos*.

---

15. Despite its radically divergent discursive strategy, Jacques Derrida's analysis of religion can be seen in the same light. Benjamin D. Crowe makes much the same point about Wilhelm Dilthey's approach to religion: "While Dilthey's position certainly parallels the general trends in post-Kantian philosophy of religion, there are some important qualifications. The first of these is a general theoretical commitment that might be termed 'expressivism.' On this Dilthey seems to agree with James. For Dilthey religious experience, in order to become communicable and to find a place within intelligible discourse, must 'express' itself in ways that are understandable. As Dilthey describes the process, religious experience must, in order to achieve 'clear consciousness,' explicate itself in terms of the 'representational nexus' of nature, which, with its categories of 'space, time, substance, and causality,' is universally accessible" (270–71).

16. See Schrey, *Säkularisierung* for an overview of approaches. As will be clear from the argument that follows, my "dialogical" approach diverges from the "secularization thesis."

Habermas seems to share three basic assumptions with major figures from Enlightenment philosophical theology like Lessing and Kant (who will be discussed in chapter 3): (1) confronted with a plurality of religions, each one (esp., in their cases, Christianity) must recognize the simultaneity of a particularity of practices and a universality of principles ("the religious"); (2) that universality is grounded in moral principles that must be defended rationally (or for Habermas, discursively); and (3) individual and collective human development involves a progression through modes of relating to the absolute (e.g., mythological, traditional, religious, philosophical). However, Habermas (and here he does seem to overlap with Derrida, even if their justifications would differ) points to the inability of morality to ground itself fully in terms of secular philosophy since it must rely on preconceived identifications of the community, i.e., on the binding/bonding force that is associated with religion. Because he also does not want to go as far as Horkheimer, who claimed that it was "futile . . . to seek an unconditional meaning without God,"[17] the question of the possibility of a postmetaphysical philosophy, then, boils down to the possibility of a binding *logos* that is not in the beginning and the end "with God."

The contemporary Italian, post-Heideggerian philosopher Gianni Vattimo addresses this same problem in his many writings on religion and hermeneutics—for example, in his contribution to the volume *Religion,* edited by Derrida and Vattimo, which grew out of a small conference on the island of Capri attended by, among others, Derrida and Gadamer. According to Vattimo: "It is (only) because metaphysical meta-narratives have been dissolved that philosophy has rediscovered the plausibility of religion and can consequently approach the religious need of common consciousness independently of the framework of Enlightenment critique" (*Religion,* 84). What we have here is an inversion of the graffiti often seen in academic bathroom stalls. There we read: " 'God is dead'—Nietzsche . . . 'Nietzsche is dead'—God"; and here we might imagine: " 'Religion is dead'—Philosophy . . . 'Philosophy is dead'—Religion." We will see in the chapters that follow that it is precisely the attempt of reason and philosophy to define a rational God and then to define themselves *as* that God, followed by the perceived failure of that endeavor, that has opened the way to a return of religion to replace the binding force lost by the collapse (or, in Max Horkheimer's and Martin Buber's term, "eclipse") of reason. However, the notion of the need for a living conception of a "common consciousness"

---

17. See Habermas's essay with this title in *Religion and Rationality,* and Horkheimer, *Zur Kritik der instrumentellen Vernunft* (*Critique of Instrumental Reason*) where this statement occurs (227).

that is not grounded in metaphysical concepts does not necessarily entail a "return" to religion. Habermas's continuation of the Enlightenment project would try to locate the nature of that common consciousness in other features of humanity that *also* account for the function of religion in community formation. We might restate the problem by questioning whether the postmetaphysical philosophical (*and nonphilosophical, i.e., popular*) need for a common consciousness really must involve a religious turn "independently of the framework of Enlightenment critique." But to decide that, we must develop more fully the history of the Enlightenment critique of religion.[18]

Specifically, what I hope to show is the way in which the intellectual development of thought about religion and its critique did not unfold in a uniformly progressivist sense. This means both that the story of the decline of the idea of God involves many actors who did not see themselves contributing to that plot and that the (long) death of God has always been accompanied by various modes of resurrection, for example, in heavenly geometry and infinitesimal calculus, in morality, in a dialecticized spirit, in the necessity of ritualized practices, in capitalism, or in variously defined spheres of "otherness."[19]

Derrida, Habermas, and Vattimo are just a few of the many contemporary thinkers who are attempting to work through a dense core of intertwined conceptual issues involving religion. A sample of those issues would include the relationship between reason and religion, or thinking and feeling in grounding religious belief; the particularity and plurality of religious systems vs. the universality of "the religious"; the uniquely binding/bonding force that religions (as *re-ligare*) exert on communities; the historicity of the great scriptures underlying the Abrahamic religions vs. their transtemporal claims; the status of transcendence as utopian necessity, or ideological mask, or anthropological drive. I will be addressing these issues through an intellectual history of (predominantly German and Protestant) philosophico-

---

18. Indeed, this will also involve an interrogation of the very notion of rationality, although in a sense different from Wolterstorff, who explores how some Protestant and Catholic traditions have come to define a form of "rationality" that is inseparable from religious starting points, i.e., is not the same as a rationality defined in terms of Enlightenment autonomy *from* religion.

19. John Charles Cooper's *Roots of Radical Theology* contains a number of historical sketches on thinkers that are also dealt with below. But since he is not aiming at "completeness," and neither am I, we tend to complement each other with different characters in our stories. (He barely touches on Erasmus, skips the seventeenth century, and looks to a very different "afterlife" in the twentieth.) Moreover, his intention is different insofar as he traces the background to a specific theological movement whereas I want to see how the ideas unfolded, following one upon the other. Finally, although I would agree with some of his characterizations (of Kant and Feuerbach, for example), I would like to demonstrate in greater detail their actual argumentation.

theological debates. I approach these questions from this perspective for two reasons: first, there is a preponderance of appeals in much contemporary writing to general concepts like "philosophy" or "the religious," a tendency that I hope to counter by attaching specific arguments to positions (Luther on faith, Erasmus on biblical philology, Lessing on human education, Kant on morality, Feuerbach on transcendence, Nietzsche of value formation, etc.). Second, by telling a story about the historical unfolding of these issues, I hope to provide readers the kind of background that will make other discussions more concrete and comprehensible.

Derrida deserves special mention here at the outset since his essay on religion, "Faith and Knowledge" (in *Religion*), functions as an explicit and implicit dialogue partner throughout the following project.[20] In a key passage, Derrida asks rhetorically whether one can really understand the phenomenon of religion or the return of the religious "*today* if one continued to oppose so naively Reason *and* Religion, Critique or Science *and* Religion, technoscientific Modernity *and* Religion" (28). He goes on to imply that the one cannot remain "within a *certain* tradition of the Enlightenment, one of the many Enlightenments of the past three centuries (not of an *Aufklärung,* whose critical force is profoundly rooted in the Reformation) . . . [this] single ray a *certain* critical and anti-religious vigilance, anti-Judeo-Christiano-Islamic, a *certain* filiation 'Voltaire-Feuerbach-Marx-Nietzsche-Freud-(and even)-Heidegger'" (28). He calls for us to go "beyond this opposition and its determinate heritage" in order to understand "how the imperturbable and interminable development of critical and technoscientific reason, far from opposing religion, bears, supports and supposes it" (28). This intermingling of faith and techno-*logos,* which has spread its reach globally, he names with the neologism *mondialatinisation* ("this strange alliance of Christianity, as the experience of the death of God, and tele-technoscientific capitalism," 13). His goal is to deconstruct the opposition by showing that reason and religion have the same source, namely, "the testimonial pledge of every performative, committing it to respond as much *before* the other as *for* the high-performance performativity of technoscience" (28). As powerful as this bold claim is, I would argue that we need to consider it more carefully. First, it is odd that Derrida would develop one "filiation" of the Enlightenment but then oppose it to a potentially more critical or forceful one, an *Aufklärung* rooted in the Reformation. One point that I will make is that these "Enlightenments" themselves cannot be so neatly separated and that

---

20. Hent de Vries, esp. in *Philosophy and the Turn to Religion,* provides an extensive reading of Derrida's many explicit and implicit treatments of religion.

the German heritage Leibniz-Lessing-Kant-Hegel-Feuerbach-Nietzsche is more complex than the simplifying strands Derrida would isolate in this passage. For this reason, second, the very tradition he would brand as "antireligious" is itself at the same time closely allied to its dialogical partner. Finally, by showing this intellectual-historical interrelationship, we can modify the notion of the "common source" of reason and faith. My intention is to focus on the specific historical sources in specific arguments where the religious and antireligious are discussed. My reason for doing so is to limit what I perceive as a considerable danger when the broader claim leads to a view that "in principle"—in their appeal to the performative—religion and reason are "the same." The historical turn allows us to pursue both connections and distinctions, to show the dialogues between faith and reason that allow them to relate without reducing their difference.

Modernity, Religion, *Logos*

How can God return from the death of God? What is the relationship between religious belief and what "reasonable people" might believe, and how did rational arguments play a role in religion and religious arguments in rationality? Isn't it the nature of modernity to have supplanted religion? It is important to address such questions in a historical context, extending the range of investigation historically to cover a longer discussion on the nature of God rather than looking at isolated thinkers or periods. In this way, I hope to present a different perspective that shows a paradoxical *re-ligio* and logic, or *ratio,* at work in modern Western thought.

The relationship between faith and reason, and the tensions inhering within the Christian *logos,* need to be related to the processes of secularization and modernization. According to the most widespread view, those two processes are inextricably linked, such that the failure to secularize society—or to relegate the religious to the private sphere—indicates a failed or incomplete modernization. This is the argument often used, of course, in contemporary discussions (or critiques) of the role of Islam in the Middle East. The underlying assumption of such a theory consists in a more-or-less linear view of historical development that accepts setbacks, to be sure, but nonetheless hopes to measure the progress of something called modernization by the degree of secularization and privatization of religion. This model of the process of secularization has its roots in the nineteenth- and twentieth-century sociology of Max Weber and Émile Durkheim.

But this notion of a "secularization" thesis has come under considerable critique over the past decades, so much so that I would align my own position with the approaches to our present age that characterize it as "postsecular." This "post," like the much-discussed one that is attached to "modernism," refers less to a radical break with the past—as if we have made a turn, or even return, back to the religious—than to a new possibility for reinterpreting the past in a more dialectical way. When Bruno Latour proposed that "We Have Never Been Modern," he wanted to disrupt a narrative that claimed a victory for one-sided Enlightenment values of rationality, objectivity, and science. Similarly, the claim that we are now writing from a "postsecular" perspective means that we must abandon the accepted, long-dominant thesis of the teleologically framed history that would see a gradual movement, beginning in the sixteenth century, from a religious to a nonreligious Weltanschauung. (Even Charles Taylor's comprehensive and nuanced study follows this trajectory.) The problem with this narrative of secularization is that it does not take into account the dialogical nature of the relation between faith and reason throughout the long history of Christianity and Western philosophy. Instead, it casts some figures—from the seventeenth century, through the Enlightenment and nineteenth century, to the present—as agents of secularization, and others (positively or negatively) as religious resisters to the inevitable undermining of religion.[21]

Two contemporary thinkers have, from quite different perspectives, also addressed the dangers involved when secular worldviews do not take into account their own religious roots or the religious discourses around them. William Connolly, in *Why I Am Not a Secularist,* explores how unself-reflexive secular conceptions have the tendency to become "religious" in nature, i.e., turn into isms (hence, "secularism"). He associates the rise of secularism with a formation of "a public sphere in which reason, morality, and tolerance flourish" (3), but which, in pushing the "religious" into the realm of the private, loses "the very resources needed to foster a generous pluralism" (3). He calls for a reworking or "refashioning" of secularism—not its abandonment—which would go back through the history of the modern, Western encounter between theistic and non- or a-theistic discourses in order to tell a different story. In doing so, he hopes to address one of the main needs of today, as he sees it, namely, "to cultivate a public ethos of *engagement* in which a wider variety of perspectives than heretofore acknowledged inform and restrain each other" (5). That is, as I try to emphasize throughout

---

21. Earlier challenges to the secularization thesis came from Hans Blumenberg, *Legitimacy of the Modern Age* (37–52) and Peter Berger. Benjamin Lazier refers to Gershom Scholem, who "inverted" the secularization thesis, arguing "for secularization from within rather than from without [religion]" (3), a position with which my approach is deeply aligned.

the present book, only an attempted dialogue between faith and reason can prevent the double and mutually reinforcing dangers—what Connolly calls the "old game plan" (6)—of a dominant secular perspective that is blind to its own indebtedness to religious discourse and of a minoritized theism that is cornered into irrationalism (see also Connolly, 19).

However, although Connolly indicates a historical narrative of the rise of secularism that could stress how elements *within* Christianity ironically paved the way for "secularist conceptions of mastery over a disenchanted nature" (21), indeed, although he says that such a story is indispensable to the kind of deep and internal discursive engagement between the limited poles of "religious faith" and "secular argument," his focus is largely on the makeup of the public sphere and not on the conceptual developments. He does point out the significance of the way Kant combined the conceptions of a "rational religion," a university with academic freedom, and a public use of reason unhindered by the church—a pivotal turning point in the formation of modernity that I will address below in chapter 3—but the wider ironic story of the entanglements between faith and reason around complex forms of *logos* remains largely untold.

Talal Asad has also offered one of the most sweeping and insightful challenges to the theory of modernization as ever-increasing secularization.[22] His two major books, *Genealogies of Religion* and *Formations of the Secular* detail the ways in which the secular and the religious are complexly linked in the formation of the "modern West." Interested in a dialectic not unlike Hegel's involving "pure (rationalistic) insight" and "faith" (*reine Einsicht* and *Glaube*),[23] which also presaged Theodor Adorno and Max Horkheimer's "dialectic of Enlightenment," Asad investigates, for example, how the modern secular state needs religion as its other in order to define itself and how religious modes of experience persist—indeed, expressed more strongly, *must* persist—in secular societies to respond to unaddressed needs.[24] Thus for him both the radical forms of religious movements as well as the liberal forms are accommodations to the modern state. The necessary simultaneity of the religious and the secular within the modern plays itself out on many levels, as we can read every day in the newspaper, from the political to the pedagogical, from the social to the scientific, from the emotional to the intellectual.

---

22. Here he is closer to Connolly's *Political Theory and Modernity* and John Milbank's *Theology and Social Theory*.

23. See *Phenomenology*, and below, chapter 4.

24. In this he is not unlike Habermas, who in *Dialectics of Secularization* points out that, so long as there are not alternatives to deal with certain experiential needs, religion will fulfill that function.

While I will not attempt to provide anything like an alternative sociohistory of religion, I do hope to untangle one of the strands, specifically that of the philosophical debate, which is interwoven into the discursive formation of the "modern West." This strand reveals *both* the movement attributed to the process of modernization (hence, the "death of God") *and* an internal dialectic that, rather than driving forward toward a final *Aufhebung,* maintains a contradiction at the heart of our world and allows for God's repeated return. This contradiction is both productive and destructive. The conflict between the drive toward secular interpretations of all aspects of public life and the "return of religion" haunts the West, serving as a reminder of the inherent presence of something other than reason within secular *logos*—as well as the presence of something other than *religio* (namely, the logico-scientific demand to provide "sufficient reason") within religion. I am not privileging the philosophical as an origin of these developments (as if the ideas determined monodirectionally the course of history). But the arguments and theological debates that I will be presenting in the following chapters do capture the tensions that have come to define the "modern West" as it worked through a seemingly inexorable process of secularization (or even "atheization") driven in large measure by the very same thinkers who were out to "save religion" in its essence.

We might take as a typical example an argument from Gotthold Ephraim Lessing (who will be dealt with in more detail in chapter 3), who gave some of the most powerful formulations to the Enlightenment efforts to salvage faith *by means of* a rigid critique of religious appeals to biblical fundamentalism. He wrote in the *Gegensätze* (*Counter-Propositions,* 1778), one of his many responses to those who considered his historico-philological approach to the Bible an attack on Christianity itself: "The letter is not the spirit, and the Bible is not the religion. Consequently, objections against the letter and against the Bible are not the same thing as objections against the spirit and against the religion" (*Philosophical and Theological Writings,* 63). Such an argument, as much as it defends a rationalist undermining of religious orthodoxy, prepares the ground for a return of religion as the return of the spirit out of the death of the letter. That is, the focus on the *language* of God that occurs with Luther (*sola scriptura*) and the interpretation of God as *logos* make possible a philo-logical approach to the Bible (beginning with Erasmus and going through Spinoza, Reimarus, and Lessing) that would then seek to remove the letter/word and resuscitate the spirit. But in so doing, the foundation of Lutheran Christianity has been removed. The shift from *logos* as Word to Spirit to (ethical) Deed is a slippery slope. We have here not only the traditional Pauline sentiment that "the letter killeth" but the more complex dialectic that insists on killing/critiquing the letter—even if (or because?) it had been the representative of religious belief—in order to salvage faith. *Logos* (reason) must be used to expose the letter/Word (*logos*) philologically so that the Spirit (*logos*) can emerge, albeit transformed. By bringing out Christianity's inherent *logos,* this approach would save religion from and for itself—by attacking it. Not only do we still need to plumb the depths of this dialectic in order to understand the conditions of our "modernity," but we also might be able to find in it potential ways for grappling with our contradictory predicament. (We will see how Kant's, Hegel's, Feuerbach's, and even Nietzsche's arguments do offer ways to *address* religious concerns critically—a necessity if we are to avoid the crass and destructive dialectic that would emerge by *avoiding* religion.)

Given this view of the interrelationship of religion and the *logos* of Western modernity, I would be sympathetic to a claim that *any* thinker of that *logos* needs to be investigated for the theological import of his or her ideas and, conversely, that all theological discussions, no matter how "insulated" from other discourses, participate in the unfolding of our historical form of rationality. But because not everyone and everything can be included, the question arises: Why have I chosen these thinkers in particular? At the most general level, each tries to rethink religion and God, taking up different discourses from a variety of spheres—philology, natural science and mathematics, ethics, dialectics, anthropology, economics, sociology, phenomenology—in order to apply their modes of argumentation to theological concerns. They are all concerned with the nature of God as *logos,* but each will provide a different conception and evaluation of what *logos* entails. With some exceptions throughout the text, I have not focused on the two (diametrically opposed) groups that often come to mind in terms of the question of God and religion, namely, the theologians, who are motivated by faith, and the social scientists, who have a strictly functionalist and reductionist model for the role of religion in society (i.e., those who present a version of the argument that "religion is nothing but X"). While it is the case that three important figures for my study, Feuerbach, Marx, and Nietzsche, are all engaged in radical critique, they are still trying to explain something about the "essence" of religion as opposed to attempting to understand *other* phenomena (the history of capitalism or social interactions), whereby religious issues are just epiphenomena. Indeed, like Max Weber, even these radical critics of religion continued to believe in the powerful and lasting impact of that essence of religion on all realms of modern life. Moreover, the figures I have chosen serve as illustrative protagonists in a story, allowing connections and threads to emerge over the four hundred years covered, without restricting the sequence to direct influences.

The more specific question could be raised concerning my choices: Why the concentration on European, indeed "old European," ideas and thinkers? Ironically, this focus emerged for me as all the more important *because* I write this largely for a *U.S.* audience. Certainly there are many books in English that address the history of religious thought in the United States from the Puritans to the present. And judging from contemporary *cultural* relations between (old) Europe and the United States, it might seem that there is little room for dialogue: Europeans, for example, just do not understand how "religion" could have played such an influential role in the 2004 presidential elections, and many in the United States consider European secularism a dead end in the historical course of values. These mutual (mis)understandings are prevalent in the main media. But for me, the present lack of dialogue across traditions makes it all the more imperative that there be a more serious engagement between them. My intention and hope is that readers from the U.S. context will see that there is a related but alternate mode of thinking about religion. The core of the roots in the Protestant Reformation is common to both traditions. But the developments experienced on the European continent, at least within the intellectual history I trace here, are not familiar to many U.S. readers. Indeed, the developments within German philosophy are not as such *opposed* to the roots of the tradition but, seen in a certain way, consequences of it. Moreover, like living in a foreign country, examining a foreign tradition provides a certain amount of "alienation" that allows U.S. readers to see their own perspective differently and to engage in a mode of reflection along different lines. The point is not to produce a "conversion to atheism" experience, a celebration of the "death of God," but to present one side of the story, in all its ironic complexity, in a way that is nonetheless both accessible and thus available for knowledgeable discussion and critique.

Thus, an important goal of this book is to explore ways to find a common discourse in which such matters can be discussed. In an increasingly polarized environment, it is crucial that attempts be made (difficult though they may be) to have some grasp of the other's position. The point is not to offer "rational" arguments that would/should convince "believers" or to adopt the religious perspective so that nonbelievers will be convinced by "proofs" of the existence of God. Rather, the thinkers and the traditions explored in the chapters to follow are all fully engaged with *both* sides. In fact, what makes them so interesting is that they genuinely inhabit the positions of "faith" and "knowledge." The irony of the "slippery slope," the fact that, in using one kind of discourse to defend religion and God, thinkers in the modern

West often undermined traditional faith, makes them all the more "useful" as examples of efforts to bridge the gap. I myself, in writing about them, must also straddle discursive spheres.

This "bringing to discourse" is the "political" intention behind this book. In my preface I referred to my experiences in the classroom. Both my religiously motivated and agnostic students responded to this material in general with surprise: "We never knew that these kinds of discussions existed!" I think they were basically saying that they never knew that religion could be talked about in these different ways. They were able to recognize that the formulation in language ("linguistification") of their thoughts on and experiences with religion would lead to new debates and perhaps challenges, and it would force them to put into discourse their responses to the discursive critiques that confronted them. This did not necessarily mean that they were expected to abandon their faith (or lack of faith). Had I taken such an approach in the classroom, it would have led to pedagogical failure. The comparison I often used is the following: just as critical media studies do not expect students to stop participating in Hollywood culture, even as they do offer different modes of analyzing it "critically," so, too, a study of the traditions of debates about the existence of God (many of which tried to *defend* religion) makes available to (religious) students a language different from the only one they might otherwise receive from their religious practice. In this way, there is the possibility of finding a middle ground, of making nondiscursive religious belief take on a form that is possible for public life while showing secular post-Enlightenment intellectuals that they are themselves the products of a long debate about religion.

In many ways my project here has been motivated by developments and experiences similar to those that have inspired George Marsden's studies of the relationship between religious scholarship and universities in the United States. He writes about the historical process through which U.S. universities transformed into professional institutions serving "an emerging technological society," an inevitable process of secularization that led to the estrangement of the academy and the church(es). Ironically, he argues, liberal Protestant theologians contributed to this process. He critiques the "virtual exclusion of religious perspectives from the most influential centers of American life" and calls for the reintroduction of religious thinking as one of the many aspects of pluralism. However, I do think that the longer tradition of dialogues between faith and reason needs to be traced if the background of this specific institutional process is to be understood. (See chapter 3 on Kant, where the role of the university will be discussed in the context of this longer tradition.)

This is not to say that any of the particular positions presented below is to be held up as right or worthy of a "return." Rather, it is the entire enterprise of retracing a history of discourse on religion that is important. Given this emphasis on a historical investigation of treatments of Christianity, my project can be understood in terms of Martin Heidegger's introduction to lectures on the Phenomenology of Religion that he delivered in Marburg in the winter semester, 1920–21 (see below, chapter 7). He argues that it is an inherent tendency of human life experience (*faktische Lebenserfahung*) that it "degrades" into an objectifying and scientifistic/positivistic relationship between "man" and "world" seen as two separate realms instead of as co-constitutive. In wondering whether there is any hope, especially for philosophy, of bringing about a turn or transformation in this development, he decides not to explore the conditions of the lifeworld itself, but, rather, he approaches this question through the "more comfortable path" (*bequemeren Weg*) of looking at the history of past and recent *philosophies* of religion to see how *they* have defined man, God, and world in terms that turn them into objects, and to isolate these "objects" from each other, and to determine how they might offer clues to a different mode of thinking. The overall argument of my own book follows a similar course (although I am not sure I can vouch for how "comfortable" it will be). Rather than undertaking a sociological, anthropological, or political-economic study of the role of religion in society, I trace historically different philosophies of religion and the way they engage with their discursive environments—natural science, historical philology, Enlightenment institutions, capitalism, "modernity" itself. We will see a complicated relationship: on the one hand, they strive to tie discussion of God to the discursive conditions of the day (making Him relevant to their environment); but this process brings with it an objectification, a splitting off of the theological from the realm of lived experience and hence a kind of positivistic death. The "return" of God and religion can be seen as an attempt to retie the connection of and to the *Lebenswelt,* an attempt on the part of society to reestablish its sense of cohesive, constituting history (*re-ligare*) and on the part of theory to "reread" (*re-legere*) such that it also no longer exists in a rarified, abstract realm. I am not saying that the history of ideas offers a necessarily privileged way to explore these developments; but it is an appropriate way (among others).

With Hans Küng, the contemporary Catholic theologian, who provides the epigraph to this introduction, I ask: Is there a lesson to be drawn from this history of the "death of God" for the present? Even an "optimistic" one? Consider the following: in many ways I am tracing the steps of modernity that lead "inevitably" to Nietzsche and Heidegger. Each step of the way is an attempt to "secure" God and hence to secure the anchor that would bind together (*ligare*) a world of values. But each act of "securing" is ultimately a step toward absolutizing the world of human values, turning them into "fixtures" that must be maintained at all costs. The result of this process is what Nietzsche calls "nihilism" or the claim "God is dead." That is, we can trace a development very clearly that insists on security, i.e., on positing values and justifying belief in God—but in so doing undermines both. The lesson for today: Could it be that the insistence on security, God, and values is a last desperate gasp, the final form that nihilism takes before we wake up and recognize that we need to think differently about these things? That we cannot base our lives on security? That the positing of values as the prime aspect of human life ends up devaluing the world? That each insistence on denying or justifying God performs the ultimate act of injustice? The originary proposition of Christianity—"In the beginning was *logos* and *logos* was with God"—sets a historical dynamic in motion that attempts to secure God through *logos* and to secure for *logos* its own sense of divinity. This dynamic, as the course of modern Western (German) thought on God and theology shows, leads to both an end ("God is dead") and the sense of an endless conflict between "faith" and "reason" (thereby guaranteeing a return). It is crucial that we retrace this development so that we might start to imagine an alternative to an either/or, namely, the possibility of reaching an understanding that sees both a rational core to faith (i.e., its inherent drive to express itself in a language of reasons) and an unfathomable and self-transcending aspect to rationality and language (i.e., their inherent drive to their own limits and their reliance on ungrounded assumptions).

I ought to lay my cards on the table, although I hope to show that the complications of my position on these matters in fact implicate me in the very processes I am investigating. Having learned and lived with this other German/European critical tradition, I have come to identify with it. I cannot deny that part of me is taken by the dramatic story line of this book, namely, the encroachment of an irresistible *logos* into the sphere of religion (or the growth of this enemy from within) and the resultant collapse of belief or faith when confronted with the demand to give reasons.[25] The irony that this gradual corrosion of traditional religion occurred in large measure thanks to the influence of those who would have saved it, makes the story all the more interesting for atheists like myself. There is an undeniable delight in the "cunning of history" that would turn the brilliant efforts

---

25. Henri de Lubac, *The Drama of Atheist Humanism,* also traces a story of modern philosophy, but more critically.

of a Leibniz, Lessing, Kant, or Hegel to justify the existence of God into yet another nail in the coffin. However, because the story and its reception are even more complex, I have to meet them on different terms as well. Like characters in a long novel who refuse to die, God and religion return again and again in modern Western discourse, and their uncanny forms—for they change over time—turn out then to be integral to the tale being told. That is, once we recognize that there is no simple opposition between the "march of modernity" and the "resistance of religion," but that, instead, these are both components of the same complex history, we realize how important it is to deal with both seriously. Here I agree with Talal Asad, who also makes the argument that tradition and modernity are not really mutually exclusive states of culture or society but different aspects of the West's development; their opposition is not "necessary" but is itself often the function of other forces (like nation formation). The story of how Western thought/*logos* has addressed (critically) the question of God, and how Christianity and *logos,* theology and philosophy, are tied together in a centuries-old dialogue, tells us much about the function of religion within our culture and often gives us clues as to how we might deal with its return in "secular" modernity.

Because the many stations along the road that leads to the "death of God" are marked by attempts to understand religion, indeed to offer an explanation of the essence of Christianity through the discursively defined *logos* of its time, we can look to them to discover possibilities for talking about religion. That is, because none of the thinkers treated below considered it an option to simply *avoid* religion/Christianity, and because avoidance is likewise not an option for *us,* they give us signals of different modes of understanding the recurrence of religious/Christian phenomena. Faith returns from and through its encounters with reason for a number of reasons.

First, to the extent that the dialogue between reason and faith unfolds dialectically, there is a historical dimension such that each side tends at times to drift away from the other in opposition to it, only to be brought back into relation. Here we can learn from Hegel's explorations of the dialectic of Enlightenment. On the one hand, religion within this dynamic can take on the form of the emotional or experiential side of human life in opposition to a reason that sets itself up as pure instrumentalism. The turn to subjectivism in religion, be it Luther's or Schleiermacher's or Kierkegaard's, in the face of a dominant rationalism, or the pope's call for religion to lay the foundation of an emotionally rich communal bonding in the midst of alienating individualism, as in contemporary late-capitalist societies, can serve as examples. But on the other hand, we see a division between private and public spheres, with religion occupying the former and reason the latter. However, as in a genuine dialectic, each side comes to be defined by the other that it would negate or oppose, leading us to wonder if the opposition was legitimate from the beginning.

Kant offers a second way of understanding how religious faith must recur dialectically in the face of reason. Given the inherently dualistic nature of human beings—body and spirit, nature and reason, causal determination and freedom—which is captured in the very essence of our will, we know rationally what we "ought" to do and yet experience influences that contravene our rational intentions. This fundamental conflict within human existence means that we will always have need of nonrational means to provide motivations for actions that are rationally justified. That is, while no act that is justified by anything other than rational means can be moral for Kant, we are unlikely to act according to the dictates of our reason unless there are other, nonrational motivations. Religion makes up one of the spheres where we derive such motivations. Of course, this sphere has a necessary limitation in its function; it can never offer *reasons* for actions (or, as the title of Kant's main book on religion states, he hopes to relegate it to a place "within the limits of mere or pure reason"). But it is also unavoidable. Its "positivity," that is, its externally given images, traditions, and stories (including the Bible), is a necessary component so long as all exercise of human will stands "at the crossroads" between reason and nature.

In Feuerbach and Nietzsche we find a third critical understanding of religion that goes beyond a merely reductive critique (as rejection), by looking to the function of transcendence. The philosophical-anthropological-psychological turn beginning in the nineteenth century has a familiar "debunking" side according to which religion is "nothing more" than the human, all too human, drive to interpret aspects of the world in escapist terms. According to the reductive versions of these theories, our capacity for infinite reasoning gets represented pictorially (Hegel call this "mere" thinking in images, *Vorstellungsdenken*) as a heaven beyond this realm of limitations, our failings and hopes get transformed into projections of a perfect being, our existential dependence ("debt") gets rationalized in terms of a guilt to a personalized God. But the core thought behind these philosophies is anything but reductive. It captures the way that the human condition is indeed always striving beyond itself, captured in the very capacity of most languages to express a subjunctive mood: It is not raining, but if it *were*. . . . Or: Although it is not the case, let us imagine a world *as if it were*. . . .[26] These expressions voice a longing, a utopian possibility, a

---

26. See, e.g., Vaihinger, *Die Philosophie des Als Ob.*

"principle of hope" (Ernst Bloch) that insists on expanding horizons. It is important that this transcendental impulse is itself neither rational nor irrational. It moves both reason and faith. This means that both reason and faith in their own way express this impulse and both can become either rational or irrational in their expressions. The "irrationality of reason" is what Adorno and Horkheimer termed the "dialectic of Enlightenment," and Hegel indeed saw it first take form in the conflict of insight and faith (or critical enlightenment and religious superstition).[27]

What we have today are competing forces that would co-opt this transcendental tendency for a variety of social, economic, and political ends, thereby channeling it into limiting forms, the narrowly "technoscientific" and the "religious." These opposites meet not because they are the "same," but because functionally they serve the same role in terms of their constraining impact. My hope is that by returning to different sites of exchange where, in the beginning, *logos* meets faith, we can avoid the dangers inherent in turning rationality into a faith or in using an appeal to faith in an attempt to deny the force of reason. Our salvation—which can be understood both spiritually and materialistically—depends on the dialogue between these registers of our human existence.

---

27. Karl Jaspers develops a theory of transcendence in order to deal with the phenomenon of religious faith (as opposed to what he terms "philosophical faith" that unfolds in open and universalizing acts of communication). "Transcendence" has a variety of synonyms in his work, for it can only be pointed at and marked by "*Chiffren*" (ciphers, signs, or figures) that make it intuitively experienceable but never present or knowable conceptually. See his *Chiffren der Transzendenz,* and Kurt Salamun, "Zum Verhältnis von Vernunft und Religion bei Karl Jaspers," in Breuninger and Welsen, 103–24 (here 111–14).

 CHAPTER 1

Erasmus vs. Luther

Philo-logos *vs. Faith*

> It is certainly not by chance that the first fundamen-
> tal exchange between Reformation Protestantism
> and the spirit of modernity, namely, the exchange
> between Luther and Erasmus, was over the issue of
> predestination.
>
> —Friedrich Gogarten, afterword to Luther,
>   *Vom unfreien Willen*

Throughout the 1520s, Erasmus of Rotterdam
(1466–1536) and Martin Luther (1483–1546) engaged in one of the most
heated and central debates of the early modern period. Given the occasional
vehemence of its tone, this exchange, which the authors referred to under
the rhetorical genre of "diatribe," pushed the limits of what could even
be considered a dialogue. It set out the basic arguments that separated a
form of Christian Humanism from the more radical views of the Protestant Reformation.[1] The topic of the debate was the status of the free will,
with Erasmus claiming in the opening salvo, *De libero arbitrio* (*On the Free
Will,* 1524), that the actions of human beings do contribute to the possibility of their eternal salvation or damnation, and Luther responding in his
De servo arbitrio (*On the Enslaved Will* [*On the Bondage of the Will*], 1525)
and his *Catechism* (1529) that only God's grace determines the fate of our

---

1. As we will see in the following chapters, esp. chapter 8, the conflict between Erasmus and
Luther played itself out in many ways again in the early twentieth century. Already in the sixteenth-
century reception of Erasmus by Melanchthon, the ideas of a unity of faith and culture and of the
unfolding of salvation within human history had entered into Protestantism, ideas that were to be
picked up by the "liberal theologians" in the nineteenth century (e.g., Ernst Troeltsch). Precisely
these ideas were rejected by the dialectical theologians. Hence, it is not by chance that Friedrich
Gogarten published and supplied the afterword to a translation of Luther's *Vom unfreien Willen* (On
the Unfree Will) in 1924.

soul.[2] Erasmus brought his part of the "diatribe" to a conclusion with his *Hyperaspistes diatribae adversus "servum arbitrium" Martini Lutheri* (*The Diatribe "Hyperaspistes" against Martin Luther's "Enslaved Will"*) in 1526 and 1527.[3] Major academic and political figures of the day were drawn into the debate, from Melanchthon to Henry VIII of England and Emperor Charles V (both of whom came to Erasmus's defense). Erasmus and, especially, Luther thought that these works were some of the most important contributions they had made to theological discussions, and their positions on the topic of free will continue to resonate in modern Western thought on the status of subjectivity and agency. But the debate also brought forth competing visions of biblical exegesis, the role and value of rationality and philosophy in theological matters, and the very meaning of certainty (intersubjective consensus vs. personal and divinely granted faith). In all of these areas we will see that Erasmus represents a "modern" or "enlightened" position, one that corresponds to a nuanced academic discussion, while Luther insists on an uncompromising stance that both ridicules his opponent's hairsplitting and warns against the potential danger of introducing critical thinking into matters of belief. The opposition between "faith" and "knowledge," or "reason" and "religion," whether or not it can be in principle dialectically or deconstructively challenged, was given its primary form through this debate. Despite the force of Luther's arguments, in many ways Erasmus carried the day by laying the foundation for historico-philological biblical criticism—and so Luther's warnings, as some religious figures and communities stress to this day, were all too accurate, since Erasmus's Humanism did set the ball rolling down a problematic slippery slope toward nonbelief.

The background to the debate can be painted by brief reference to important points in the biographies of the two thinkers:

The early years of Erasmus (Desiderius, of Rotterdam) are shrouded in uncertainty, including the exact date of his birth, October 28, 1466 or 1469. Although born out of wedlock, he was cared for by his parents until their death in the plague, when he was then sent to a series of monastic schools where he received a solid education. From early on he was oriented toward a

---

2. Erasmus was responding to the thirteenth of Luther's forty theses from his *Heidelberger Disputation* (April 26, 1518) and Luther's response to the denunciatory papal bull of Leo X (in Latin, November 29, 1520, published shortly afterward in German).

3. The very title, "Hyperaspistes," gives an indication of the kind of philological play and bitter sarcasm that often permeated these exchanges. The term derives from the adjective meaning "protected by a shield" and implies that the work is Erasmus's self-defense. However, there is more to the term than that. Luther had occasionally referred to Erasmus as a "viper" (*vipera* in Latin, ἀσπίς in Greek), and Erasmus seems to imply that he is playing the role of a "super snake."

religion of personal devotion and tended to resist the stricter monastic rules. He entered the Augustinian order, and after 1495 lived and studied in Paris. During his years there he attained a reputation as a Humanist. After a stay in Italy (1506–9) and then contact with Thomas More, he developed an ideal of *humanitas christiana,* a synthesis of spiritualism and Humanism. In 1516 he published the first edition of the New Testament in Greek, including an important methodological introduction, "Ratio verae theologiae." From 1521 to 1529 he lived in Basel, a neutral city, where he tried to find a middle way between the Reformation and the Catholic Church. Here he published his critique of Luther and other Protestant views (e.g., on the symbolic interpretation of the Last Supper). Once Basel itself became Protestant, he moved to Freiburg im Breisgau (1529–35). His political ideal was formed by the notion of a *respublica christiana,* and he remained attached to the tradition of the church fathers and even Scholasticism, although he focused on the scriptures as well. Of course, with the split of the church during his lifetime, this ideal combining Catholicism, Humanism, and Reformation *scriptura* became impossible. The core of his theological thought he traced back to Christ's Sermon on the Mount, rather than Paul.[4] This led him to both a more ethically oriented faith not a system but a more general notion of a good life—and a belief in the (at least partial) goodness of (human) nature, despite original sin. Salvation of individuals and humanity as a whole is modeled on a Greek conception of education (*paideia*) rather than conversion or transformation. He used the methods of historico-philological criticism, satire, and "diatribe" (dialogical exchange) to challenge especially the ossified versions of medieval Scholasticism, but also to work toward a broader consensus. The consensus was not to be. And his middle-of-the-road position became reviled by both sides as his books were later placed on the index and banned by the Catholic Counter-Reformation, even though Luther developed some of his most deeply rooted views in staunch opposition to Erasmus.

Luther was born on November 10, 1483, making him nearly twenty years younger than Erasmus. Raised in a family of nine children (his father worked in nearby mining), he went at the age of seventeen to study in Erfurt. There he received a solid foundation in the humanistic-rhetorical tradition, and even though his teachers likely criticized the Scholastic efforts to harmonize Aristotle and the teachings of the church, he did get a good dose of Aristotle. Often tormented by a sense of sin and fears for his salvation, during a

---

4. Paul is central for Luther, early twentieth-century Protestant theology (Karl Barth, Rudolf Bultmann), Heidegger, and contemporary thinkers (e.g., Alain Badiou). As we will see in chapter 10, the Catholics (e.g., Pope Benedict XVI [Joseph Ratzinger]) lean toward John the Evangelist.

thunderstorm in 1505 he made the oath to enter the monastery. He became an Augustinian monk and continued his studies in theology. Even after a trip to Rome and as he then became a professor of theology in Wittenberg, he was constantly plagued by the thoughts of divine justice. In 1517 he posted the Ninety-Five Theses on the door of the Wittenberg cathedral, in which he (not for the first time) criticized the church, most notably for its practice of selling indulgences. After a series of public disputations, the differences between Luther and the Catholic Church in Rome reached the point of a break, and Luther concluded that the individual must stand up for scripture even if it meant challenging the authority of the church. The years 1518–20 saw a tremendous outpouring of major writings reinterpreting the role of the church, and Wittenberg became a new center also for Humanists (e.g., Melanchthon). Once the church imposed the Edict of Worms on Luther, he, thanks to his supportive prince, withdrew to the Wartburg Castle. In eleven weeks during 1521 he translated the New Testament into German (using both the Vulgate and Erasmus's recently published Latin version). He also addressed a number of more "worldly" issues, the question of marriage and especially the sharpening of the division of the two spheres, whereby the Christian must show obedience to the political order but could disobey religious authority in matters of faith and conscience. He used this reasoning in his writings against the revolutionary reformer Thomas Münzer and against the attempts of the peasants to rebel using religious arguments. In the middle of this period of crisis, Luther fell ill and, fearing his death might be near, married. Until his death on February 18, 1546, he continued writing under political conditions of relative peace but also suffering continually from physical illness and emotional-psychological depressions.

Let us turn to the debate and compare the positions on four major points: exegesis, intersubjectivity, philosophy-reason-theology, and the will's relation to divine grace. Each of these issues sets the basic paradigm in which modern Western treatments of religion, faith, rationality, and agency unfold.[5]

Exegesis

The opening line of Erasmus's text is startling not so much because of the claim it makes about the will but because of the implications it makes concerning the Bible. He writes: "Among the many difficulties encountered

---

5. Even if one argues, as does the contemporary sociologist of religion Alan Wolfe (*The Transformation of American Religion*), that recent evangelical, pentecostal, or fundamentalist movements in the United States are not in any direct way carrying on a tradition of Lutheranism, it is nonetheless

in Holy Scripture—and there are many of them—none presents a more perplexed labyrinth than the problem of the freedom of the will" (*Discourse*, 3).[6] Despite the genuine demeanor of calm and reasonableness that Erasmus expresses throughout his writings, both in this essay and in general, the radical nature of this claim should not be underestimated. Without a doubt Erasmus sees the Word of God whenever he opens up the holy scripture. For him, too, in the beginning was *logos*, and that *logos* is divine. However, the message of that *logos* does not emerge clearly out of the written words before him. Instead, he is confronted with "difficulties," a "perplexed labyrinth," and "problems." This will lead to the obvious need for an apparatus of philology, i.e., of rhetorical analysis, including levels of figurative language, distinctions between the more or less comprehensible passages, and a community of scholars working together to generate the most plausible interpretations. But before exploring these consequences, and without going into detail on Luther's conception, we should at least have the contrast between the two positions present to mind. Luther writes in his response: "We should adhere everywhere to the simple, pure and natural meaning of the words, according to the rules of grammar and the habits of speech which God has given unto men. . . . For me this is a serious cause. . . . The Word of God must be taken in its plain meaning, as the words stand." (128–29). That is, we are confronted with the contrast between a hermeneutics of difficulty and a hermeneutics of clarity. The former struggles to unpack and interpret comparatively, the latter would merely allow the words and meanings to "speak for themselves." As Erasmus says explicitly: "We are not involved in a controversy regarding Scripture. The same Scripture is being loved and revered by both parties. Our battle concerns *the sense* of Scripture" (15; emphasis added). Thus, the controversy concerns hermeneutics, the art/science of interpretation and understanding.

Erasmus's reading of the Bible on the issue of the free will provides us with an introductory course in philological and rhetorical techniques.[7] He finds himself forced into a figurative mode of interpretation on the basis of a relatively straightforward implicit syllogism: (1) there are many places in the Bible where one finds conflicting ideas about the role of human choice

---

crucial that the Erasmus-Luther debate sets out a discursive framework and a rich semantic pool from which contemporary movements draw.

6. Unless otherwise noted, I will cite Erasmus/Luther, *Discourse on Free Will,* trans. and ed. Ernst Winter, because of accessibility. The edition by Rupp and Watson is more complete.

7. He begins his exegesis by showing off his philological knowledge a bit, comparing the editions (*Discourse*, 31).

and divine grace; (2) yet "the Holy Spirit does not contradict himself" (59); therefore, (3) "one must find an interpretation which resolves this seeming contradiction" (59). Such an interpretation involves reading some passages as metaphors (e.g., he unpacks a verse from Ezekiel on God's ability to remove our "stony heart": "This is a metaphor" [58]). He often points out that "one should not accept [a passage] literally" (e.g., on Jacob and Esau, 53).[8] And he is drawn to the many parables that "are very instructive, but are not applicable in all instances," that is, they cannot be taken at face value; instead, "let us interpret the parable" (56).

Furthermore, Erasmus reads the Bible for the meaning implied by particular words. One consistent point he makes grows out of the interpretation of conditional sentences. In order to justify the notion that human beings have some free will in determining the fate of their souls, Erasmus lists the many places where a condition is set for us to follow God's will—on the logic that it cannot be *only* a question of divine will *if* some other terms need to be met. Specifically, then, wherever the word "if" appears,[9] he stresses, there is an implicit option offered, as in the passage from Matthew (19:17): "If thou wilt enter into life, keep the commandments," about which Erasmus claims: "The word 'if' does not at all imply necessity" (38).[10]

All this demonstrates an attention to linguistic detail that, like the graininess of an enlarged photographic image, makes the scriptures all the more ambiguous and perplexing the more closely its Word is loved and the more exhaustively it is examined. Erasmus moves from the level of the passage, through the sentence and image, down to the individual lexical item ("will," "blame," "exhort," "command," etc. [32–36]), and even the preposition (esp. 71)[11] and the original Greek in the case of the New Testament (also 72, 77). At one point, he even indicates that, because of the manuscript tradition, differences of interpretation will hinge on a letter.[12] Hence,

---

8. Also: "I know that this is a mode of figurative expression" (*Discourse*, 43).

9. One example of many: "'Si diligitis me, mandata mea servate'. Quanta apud Ionnem inculcatio mandatorum? Quam male coniunctio: 'si', congruit merae necessitati? 'Si manseritis in me et vera mea in vobis manserint. Si vis perfectus esse'" (*De libero arbitrio*, in *Ausgewählte Schriften*, 2:74). ("'If you love me then follow my commandments.' How emphatic is the impression of the commandments according to John? How badly the conjunction 'if' would fit with the idea of necessity. 'If you remain in me and my words remain in you' and 'If you want to be perfect.'")

10. Also: "Free choice is implied in 'If thou shalt separate'" (*Discourse*, 33).

11. "The preposition 'from' points to the origin and source, and therefore Paul distinctly states 'of ourselves' as 'from ourselves,' i.e. 'out of ourselves'" (*Discourse*, 71). The translator's note is particularly useful: "Erasmus distinguishes in his text *a nobis* from *ex nobis*, Paul using the former, by explaining with the Greek ἀφ' ἑαυτων ὡς ἐξ ἑαυτων."

12. As where he refers to different editions and indicates that "probably one ought to read *poietai* instead of *poiesai*" (*Discourse*, 31).

Erasmus's simple-sounding advice—"I believe it to be an excellent key to the understanding of Holy Scriptures, if we pay attention to what is meant in each passage" (74)—opens up onto not a "fundamentalist" acceptance of the scriptures but an exegetical demand for ever-deepening interpretation within an ever-widening tradition of interpretations. Thus he concludes: "It is a fact that Holy Scripture is in most instances either obscure and figurative, or seems, at first sight, to contradict itself. Therefore, whether we like it or not, we sometimes had to recede from the literal meaning, and had to adjust its meaning to an interpretation" (93–94).

Luther, in contrast, attacks Erasmus brutally precisely for "adjusting" the biblical passages to fit a mistaken interpretation: "[His interpretation] twists all the words of divine promise and declaration, just as it pleases, by discovering a figure of speech in them" (128). He imagines that Erasmus applies "tricks" and "tacks on" metaphors and similes, in short, a "trope" to what would be otherwise "the clearest and simplest passages." The entire rhetorical tradition is disdained, and Erasmus tainted by his association with it: "You ooze Lucian from every pore" (104), Luther says, associating him with the second-century CE Greek author and rhetorician. Instead, Luther would ban figurative language from the Bible: "Let this be our sentiment: that no implication or figure is to be allowed to exist in any passage of Scriptures" (128). For this reason his opening functions not as a self-deprecating act of modesty and compliment toward Erasmus, but as a backhanded insult: "I concede to you openly, a thing I have never done before, that you not only surpass me by far in literary prowess and intellectuality (which we all grant to you as your due, and the more so, since I am a barbarian occupied with the barbarous), but that you . . . artfully debate this matter with wonderful and continuous restraint" (97).[13] Although Luther himself made reference to Erasmus's philological work in completing his translation of the Bible, he removes himself from the classical tradition, identifying himself only with the vernacular ("barbarian") and the artless as a matter of pride.

What does this mean for actual interpretation? "What and whom shall we believe?" Luther asks, and then answers without hesitation: "Scriptures, [because] they are called a way and a path, doubtless because of their perfect certainty" (117). His rejection of the application of rhetorical *techne* to the study of biblical language and hermeneutics would isolate the sphere

---

13. The tone of Luther's piece, once he gets past the moderately polite, if condescending, opening paragraphs, is brutal. He says he had to overcome his "sheer disgust, anger, and contempt" for Erasmus's work in order to write his response at all.

of religious discourse from the logic into which Erasmus implicates himself. In addressing Erasmus's attempt to deduce an element of choice from such phrases as "if thou wilt" or "if thou shalt do," or from the linguistic implications of divine threats, exhortations, promises, etc., Luther recognizes that such an argument is based on an assumption that "the nature of words and the common use of language among men seem to require it," i.e., it is a matter of "the customs and things of men" (125). By disassociating the *logos* of the Bible from the realm of human language, however, Luther can allow for another logic at work in these words, one different from the connections made necessary through custom. If we assume, as he does, that scripture is "nothing else than the word that offers the Spirit and grace for the remission of sins" (126), then exhortations, promises, conditionals—i.e., all speech acts and performatives—must be traced back to a single intention that is not grounded in tradition and convention and thus has no historical dimension or confirmability. While we might agree that in a certain sense both Erasmus's and Luther's interpretations of biblical speech acts are based on a faith—in the continuity of the interpretations of the church and church fathers, on the one hand, and in the Holy Spirit's bestowal of grace, on the other—they still operate on two different levels. That is, there is no ultimate grounding for speech acts or *logoi* that could be "pointed to," since even that ground would have to be accepted and the very act of "pointing" interpreted. However, given this uncertainty, Erasmus and Luther respond in two radically different ways: the former by appealing to the shaky and ever-widening field of traditional authority, concrete texts, and figures that can at least be shared, while the latter puts an end to uncertainty by an act of faith established in a subjectively immediate relation to meaning.[14]

Intersubjectivity (Authority and Tradition)

One crucial consequence of the opposing conceptions of the Word offered by Erasmus and Luther is their opposing understanding of the status of the community of biblical scholars. Given the "difficulties" of the text, Erasmus can never claim to have immediate access himself to meaning but must

---

14. Hegel refers to "the great form of the World Spirit . . . the principle of the North and, from the religious point of view, Protestantism,—subjectivity in which beauty and truth are represented in feelings and attitudes, love and understanding. Religion builds its altars and temples in the heart of the individual, whose sighs and prayers seek a God whose vision is denied to it because it is a danger to the understanding, for which anything envisioned is reduced to a thing, like a forest reduced to firewood ("Glauben und Wissen" ["Faith and Knowledge"], 289–90).

time and again turn to the interpretations of others, especially the church fathers, to gain insight into the possible sense of passages. Meaning emerges for him as the result of intersubjective exchange. The radically dialogical nature of human beings and the radically complex nature of the Bible make us dependent on others in a search for comprehension. Significance results from consensus secured in part by the tradition and authority of previous interpretations. Not, of course, that they cannot be wrong and that we ought not to challenge the past with better efforts. After all, it was Erasmus who returned to the Greek version of the New Testament to revise the Vulgate. However, no individual can claim independent access to meaning. Luther, in contrast, rejects this entire line of reasoning: "But that there are in Scriptures some things abstruse and not quite plain, was spread by the godless Sophists, whom you echo, Erasmus" (103). Those who would rely on each other for a shared approach to interpretation are thus linked with the sophists, those bogeymen held up by all antirhetoricians to keep readers away from the haunted house of consensualism.

Erasmus turns to others for guidance, therefore, as a matter of both practice and principle. He claims, with an implicit criticism of Luther:

> This then I want to reply to those who discard without hesitation the old interpretation of sacred books, and instead submit their own, as if an oracle had proclaimed it. . . . Even though Christ's Spirit might permit His people to be in error in an unimportant question on which man's salvation does not depend, no one could believe that this Spirit has deliberately overlooked error in His Church for 1300 years, and that He did not deem one of all the pious and saintly Church Fathers worthy enough to be inspired, with what, they contend, is the very essence of all evangelical teaching. (19)

That is, the possibility that any *one* individual could be wrong on a particular interpretive point (Erasmus included: "How can I also possess the certainty?" [18]) means that we are necessarily thrust upon a community of interpreters, "the entire long list of most erudite men who have enjoyed the approval of many centuries up to the present day" (13). This includes drawing the reader as well into this developing tradition: "Hence, I want the reader to consider whether he thinks it is fair to condemn the opinion offered by the Church Fathers, approved for so many centuries by so many people" (94). Erasmus's claim to be a "disputer" (5, 94) entails an opening up of dialogue that would not deny the truth of the Word of God but would demand a collective search for its meaning. Of course, he knows the obvious objection to this dependence on consensus: "What can large numbers contribute to an understanding of the Spirit?" and offers the equally obvious response: "What can a small number of people?" (17).

Luther faces scripture on his own. Of course, this approach is grounded in his conception of *sola scriptura,* i.e., the view that the Bible and only the Bible is the source of God's message to the faithful. It allows him to reject the authority of the tradition of the church fathers and all previous interpretations for the sake of a direct confrontation with the Bible. But rather than rehearse that position and its complications,[15] I will focus on Luther's association of the very activity of debate itself with skepticism. In the same passage where he attacks Erasmus by associating him with the rhetorician Lucian, he charges: "You swill Epicurus [and his antisupernaturalist skepticism] by the gallon" (104).[16] He quotes Erasmus's claim that he so dislikes "assertions" that he would prefer the views of the skeptics when there is not complete clarity on the scriptures and, while granting Erasmus some points for his "charitable mind," nonetheless feels that he must attack him and anyone else for such an erroneous view (100). "The Holy Spirit is no skeptic, and what He has written into our hearts are no doubts or opinions but assertions, more certain and more firm than all human experience and life itself" (103). This means that "not to delight in assertions is not the mark of a Christian heart. Indeed, one must delight in assertions to be a Christian at all!" (100). Rather than debate, therefore, the Lutheran Christian engages in "a constant adhering to and affirming of your position, avowing and defending it, and invincibly persevering in it" (100–101). No genuine intersubjective contact becomes possible, because no genuine risk is involved. Luther "asserts" not in order to expose a fallible claim to interpretation and counterargument but to proclaim the righteousness of his position. Others are needed (as, in this case, Erasmus is for Luther) only to provide the opportunity to strengthen one's own asserted position.[17]

This is not to say that there is no community. But the turn to others does not generate the possibility of arriving at the truth for Luther; instead, only those who have already "received the Spirit" could be considered useful sources.[18] And by definition, the only thing they teach us can be a

---

15. For the view that this is not a straightforward doctrine regarding hermeneutics and/or translation, see Jane O. Newman, "Word Made Print."

16. For a summary of Epicureanism and an indication of its threat to the Christian worldview, see Saine, 25ff.

17. "Therefore," Luther writes, "I shall be even more grateful if you gain greater certainty through me, just as I have gained in assurance through you" (98).

18. This notion of "election" by God as the basis of community becomes crucial for Calvin and later for Max Weber's analysis of the importance of sects in the establishment of capitalism in the

"confirmation of the doctrine of Christ" (115). Of course, even Luther must "admit that many passages in Scriptures are obscure and abstruse. But that is due to our ignorance of certain terms and grammatical particulars, and not to the majesty of the subject" (103). In mentioning this, however, is he not opening the door to dependence on others? Here he can only repeat the argument, which we will see more developed below, separating the realms: in matters of man, grammar and intersubjective exchange are necessary for clarity; in matters of the Word of God, only faith.

Philosophy-Reason-Theology

The very meaning of "knowledge" and the status of rationality in theological matters are at stake. Erasmus never hesitates to bring *logos* to bear on *logos,* logical reasoning as a tool to understand the Word. This means that his aim is "illuminating, if this be possible, in the subsequent clash of scriptural passages and arguments, the truth, the investigation of which has always been the most reputable activity of scholars" (6). The only "tool" or "fighting equipment" (15) at his and his opponent's disposal is the public use of reason, the open exchange of ideas through oral and written communication that can be compared on the basis of established rules of logic and rhetoric. Erasmus refers to this ability in human beings as "our power of judgment—whether we call it *nous,* i.e., mind or intellect, or rather *logos,* i.e., reason" (22). Its public nature is guaranteed by the fact that it must express itself, indeed only exists in its expression. For this reason, it is interesting to note that Erasmus's Latin translation of the opening passage of John's Gospel departed from the traditional "In the beginning was *verbum,*" to yield "In the beginning was *sermo.*" The difference reveals his rhetorical nature since as opposed to the "dead" *verbum* (that can be a mere lexical entry), the "living" *sermo* thrives in its spokenness. Hence, the limits of Erasmus's efforts are the limits of reason: "But let us cease reasoning," he writes near the end of his disputation as he imagines an exchange between God and one of those who would deny free will, "with those devoid of reason" (89).[19]

By introducing the rhetorical logic of language into the *logos* of the scripture, Erasmus not only opens up theology to analysis and makes scholarly

---

United States because recognition of members of one's own community/sect means a shared faith or belief, and hence credibility and monetary creditworthiness. Derrida also exploits the Latin roots of belief and credit (*credo*) in "Faith and Knowledge" (in *Religion*).

19. We will return to this emphasis of the spokenness of the Word when we discuss Franz Rosenzweig and Martin Buber in chapter 9.

dispute a quasi-divine enterprise; he also implies that the very Word of God cannot but follow the laws of human hermeneutics. Let us look at a passage where Erasmus takes one of the passages from Paul that most challenges his thesis and unfolds a reasoning that, in Derrida's term, is like a machine. After quoting Romans 9:11–13, which seems to state straightforwardly that God dictates a purpose to man in advance, Erasmus claims that "it is obviously contradictory that God, who is not only just, but also merciful, should have hardened the heart of a man," making him evil before all deeds or free will (47). There is a logic, in other words, that even God cannot escape, one lodged within the very meaning of words ("just," "merciful"). To resolve the contradiction he turns then to Origen's commentary, specifically to the original Greek (which he quotes at length in the original). The examples in scripture (Paul's use of an Old Testament passage [Malachi 1:2]) give way to Origen's own analogies, figurative expressions "customary in popular sermons" ("just as after the same rain"; "just as wax becomes soft and clay hard under the same sun"). Only via the mediation of other interpretations can Erasmus and the reader reinterpret the original Epistle. Think through the language, Erasmus seems to be saying, for though it leads into other networks of texts and thought, the combined force of its tradition will not lead astray.

Luther lambastes all efforts to introduce reasoning, rhetoric, and philosophy into biblical interpretation. "We should indeed be content with the words of God and simply believe what they say," he writes, "for the works of God are utterly indescribable" (129). The fact that even he himself engages in rational argumentation with Erasmus he considers merely the necessity to "humor Reason, i.e., human folly" that counts for little more than "act[ing] the fool . . . and babbling" (129). Where Erasmus would introduce laws of rationality that bind even the Holy Spirit (who cannot contradict himself), Luther rejects the notion of any *ratio*/measure/reason that could ever be used to judge God's will, since that will is itself the ultimate *ratio*. Hence, he writes, "God is God" is the only version of the law of noncontradiction that he is likely to accept. And he continues: "For whose will no cause or reason may be laid down as its rule and measure. For nothing is on a level with it, not to speak higher. It is itself the measure of all things. If any rule or measure, or cause or reason existed for it, it could no longer be the will of God. What God wills is not right because He ought to or was bound to so will. On the contrary, what takes place must be right, because He so wills it" (130).[20]

---

20. The Latin of this passage makes clear that for Luther, there is no identification of God and *logos* as *ratio:* "Deus est, cuius uoluntatis nulla est caussa nec ratio, quae illi cue regula (et) mensura

It is not surprising, then, that Luther would disparage Erasmus's use of "Lady Reason," who becomes a whore to sophistry: "[You are employing] Arguments of Lady Reason. . . . Reason, by her conclusions and syllogisms, interprets and twists the Scriptures of God whichever way she likes. I shall enter upon this dispute willingly and with confidence, knowing that her babblings are folly and absurdity, especially when she attempts to make a show of her wisdom in divine matters" (125).[21] Nearly a century before Francis Bacon captures the spirit of burgeoning modernity in the simple equation of knowledge and power, Luther warns against the seductive nature of knowledge. Where for Erasmus, we must employ our reason to interpret the divine law and choose to act accordingly, for Luther the law is dictated to give us knowledge only of our sin and inability, on our own, to live up to it. "This knowledge is not power, nor does it bring power, but it teaches and shows that there is no power here, but great weakness" (126). Reason undermines itself as it yields to the force of faith, by whose light the "blindness of reason" is revealed (126). Thus, while the Age of Enlightenment does indeed in part grow out of the "forms" of "subjectivity" (as in the subtitle of Hegel's "Glauben und Wissen" ["Faith and Knowledge"], "The Reflective Philosophy of Subjectivity in the Totality of its Forms") that the Reformation unleashes, in part against all tradition and authority, the opposition between faith and reason operating here still prohibits any illumination emanating from the fallen state of mankind.[22]

Free Will

We can now turn to the actual topic of the debate. It is not by chance, as the early twentieth-century Lutheran theologian Friedrich Gogarten stated

---

praescribatur, cum nihil sit illi aequale aut superius, sed ipsa est regula omnium. Si enim esset illi aliqua regula uel mensura, aut caussa aut ratio, iam nec Dei uoluntas esse posset" (*Studienausgabe,* 281). Some additional passages by Luther attacking philosophy, rhetoric, and dialectic (the three basic modes of reasoning) are cited in Oesterreich ("'Allein durchs Wort': Rhetorik und Rationalität bei Martin Luther," in Breuninger and Welsen, *Religion und Rationalität,* 31–50), for example: "Nam credite mihi, diabolus est dialecticus, rhetor, philosophus" (32).

21. In the Latin Luther refers either to *"Ratio humana"* or *"Ratio domina."*

22. This is not to say that Luther is strictly speaking an irrationalist. Oesterreich (n. 20 above) argues that Luther did introduce powerful versions of both rhetoric and rationality into Protestantism. According to Oesterreich, just as Luther is looking for a religious rhetoric (that is not just an independent tool that can be used for evil), so, too, does he formulate a kind of religious dialectic/philosophy/*ratio.* That is, he wants a hermeneutic (rhetoric and dialectic) that emerges *from* the Bible, not one that is separate and applied *to* the Bible. Luther thus sees the Holy Spirit as the highest orator (purveyor of the divine Word) and philosopher: "Ceterum spiritus sanctus optimus Rhetor et dialecticus est" ("Moreover, the Holy Spirit is the best rhetorician and dialectician") (35).

in the passage that serves as an epigraph to this chapter, that the issue of free will is at the heart of the matter.[23] If, according to Luther, Erasmus's way of reading the Bible (introducing uncertainties and the need to interpret collectively) would lead to the kinds of doubts that raise the specter of radical skepticism, so, too, Erasmus's notion of the free will (introducing the possibility of human agency and the contribution of mankind to its ultimate fate) would lead to radical autonomy and the blasphemy or heresy of hubris. Luther is onto something. We will see that here Luther unfolds the more consistent argument, even if, as he himself admits, it is more difficult to adopt in its entire rigor because of the way it undermines our sense of self-control.

True to the spirit of compromise that dominates his essay, Erasmus strives to find a middle ground between the extremes of the determinists (Luther, Calvin, Wycliffe) and a more radical Humanist position that places all emphasis on the powers of mankind. For the latter position one can take the famous passage from Pico della Mirandola (1463–94), whose *Oration on the Dignity of Man* puts the following words into God's mouth:

> We have given you, Oh Adam, no visage proper to yourself, nor any endowment properly your own, in order that whatever place, whatever form, whatever gifts you may, with premeditation, select, these same you may have and possess through your own judgment and decision. The nature of all other creatures is defined and restricted within laws which We have laid down; you, by contrast, impeded by no such restrictions, may, by your own free will, to whose custody We have assigned you, trace for yourself the lineaments of your own nature. I have placed you at the very center of the world, so that from that vantage point you may with greater ease glance round about you on all that the world contains. We have made you a creature neither of heaven nor of earth, neither mortal nor immortal, in order that you may, as the free and proud shaper of your own being, fashion yourself in the form you may prefer. (7)

The issue revolves around the ability of human beings to redeem themselves in their post-Fall state. While they are by definition in a condition of sin, what does it take to achieve salvation? Can they contribute to their own salvation themselves?

Erasmus defines his stance by offering a modified version of the Pelagians, i.e., the followers of the late fourth- to early fifth-century Celtic

---

23. Gogarten, one of the central figures in the new "dialectical theology" of the 1920s, will be discussed in more detail in chapter 8, together with Karl Barth and Rudolf Bultmann.

monk, Pelagius, who "taught that no new grace was needed once grace had liberated and healed the free will of man . . . [and that] the free will of man by itself was deemed sufficient to achieve eternal salvation" (26). That is, while Erasmus grants that no individual can in any literal sense "save himself," since that would amount to a challenge to God and a debasement of "true piety if man relies solely on his own strength" (28)—as if one could stand before the gates of heaven and demand entry on the basis of good deeds accomplished—he nonetheless believes that once God has granted a general "healing" of mankind, it is up to each individual to choose to turn toward or away from salvation. He writes: "By freedom of the will we understand in this connection the power of the human will whereby man can apply to or turn away from that which leads unto eternal salvation" (20). The will allows us to take certain steps in the right or wrong direction. However, that direction is defined by the presence or absence of the grace and mercy of God. No salvation without light, but we can move toward or away from it. The will takes a position between two instances of the gift of grace, the original healing grace and the final one of salvation.[24] He would like to see "will and grace together" (28) or "our virtuous endeavors [uniting] with divine grace in order to reach perfection gradually through righteous deeds" (44).

In order to develop this modified position, Erasmus does indicate the two opposing camps. He characterizes Augustine, through his reading of Paul, as giving "greater stress to the role of grace" (28), while versions of the Pelagians stand in for the heresy of human insubordination. He engages in a variety of arguments defining different kinds of grace and versions of causality in order to distinguish the kinds of effect that each one can have, lest he be forced to choose himself between one and the other. And he is a master at providing parables or images of how it might be possible for both aspects to be at work. Consider, for example, the way Erasmus first reasons in the spirit of the Scholastics, differentiating between will and grace in terms of differing causal relationships ("grace being the principal cause and will a secondary"), and then provides parables—comparing the will to eyesight or the father educating a child—by way of explanation (86–87).

Confronted with the charge of extremism, Luther goes on the offensive. His basic argument is that there is no compromise possible and that one must ultimately choose between absolute freedom of will (and in essence

---

24. "But since all things have three parts, a beginning, a continuation and an end, grace is attributed to the two extremities, and only in continuation does the free will effect something" (*Discourse*, 85).

denial of God) or denial of free will completely. For all the rhetorical brutality that Luther brings to bear on Erasmus for avoiding the clearness of
this choice, on which, for Luther, everything hinges, he does have a strong
position. We can isolate three major questions and issues that drive Luther's
argument (obviously leaving out the differences in biblical exegesis discussed
above). First: Does it make sense to be a "semi-Pelagian"? Can the will be
"partially" free in principle? Here Luther knows that it hardly makes sense
to speak of a "partially free will." The ability to determine one's fate, if one
believes in such an ability, may certainly be hindered or incapacitated, but the
assumption that it exists entails its power to effect a change. In characteristic
condescension, Luther demonstrates the "carelessness and sleepy stupidity"
of Erasmus's position: "If there is so much good in free will that it could
apply itself unto good, it would have no need of grace" (123). After all, the
notion of meeting God's grace halfway, which Erasmus proposes as such a
reasonable compromise, already assumes that the steps taken *toward* grace can
be taken without it. For this reason, Luther sides with Augustine against the
philosophy of Pelagius, seeing in it a hidden prioritizing of the human over
the divine will, or at least a clear statement of the former's autonomy. Indeed,
to ascribe such power to the will would, for Luther, be "plainly to ascribe
divinity to free will!" (121). In short, Erasmus might as well "go to extremes"
and "attribute all and everything to free will, as the Pelagians do" (133)—or
abandon his position in favor of Luther's.

The second point is a far-reaching philosophical one that Luther never
makes fully or explicitly but nonetheless underlies some of his sharpest critiques. It involves the groundlessness of the will, which has two classic formulations. The one, made famous by Buridan, imagines the free will like
a donkey faced with a choice between two equal feed buckets equally far
away; the donkey would starve, he claims, unless it had some inherent drive
to move toward one or the other bucket, just as the will must always already
have something pushing it, since by itself it would have no motive/reason
(it is groundless) actually to overcome its freedom and to choose. The other
formulation of the free will's inherent contradiction is the infinite regress
in which one gets trapped when one recognizes that to will X, the will had
to first will to will X, and before that, to will to will to will X, etc. Luther
never develops these formulations in detail but he does refer to the notion of
"the necessity of immutability" of the will, i.e., "that the will cannot change
itself" (111).[25] In his version, one who wills evil cannot then will good, since

---

25. This may be what Luther is getting at in his somewhat Scholastic treatment of Erasmus's
more contorted argumentation: "I suppose, then that this 'ability of the human will' means a power,

by definition the will was willing evil. For the will to change, something else (e.g., "the sweet influence of the Spirit of God") must step in to effect a radical transformation that the will can thenceforth follow. Likewise, in a kind of phenomenology of willing *avant la lettre,* he critiques a free will (like Buridan's ass) because it would be "a sort of mere abstract willing, pure and simple, either upward unto God by grace, or downwards unto evil by sin" (124)—the problem being that such an abstract willing can never be real willing, "because desire must strive and aim for something" (125), i.e., must have its directionality from its very inception.

Finally, Luther takes one of the most perplexing questions of Christian theology head on and cuts the knot with a bold assertion. Namely, he does not try to skirt the issue of how God's foreknowledge of our actions could hamper our free will (how could I be free to choose X if God already knows that I've chosen it?) but, rather, claims that precisely the notion of divine omniscience shatters the possibility of free will. He avoids the contradiction not by challenging God's preknowledge, nor by attempting to split hairs (e.g., God's knowledge vs. mine); instead he abandons free will: God's prior knowledge of my actions *does* in fact mean that I am predestined. He has it easier than Erasmus who tries to finesse the classic dilemma of whether or not Judas could have changed his mind and *not* betrayed Jesus. Erasmus, wanting to have it both ways, claims that "Judas could have changed his will . . . [but] even then God's foreknowledge would not have been wrong and his will not hindered, because in such a case he would have known and willed that change also" (52). Such an endeavor to employ "Scholastic subtlety" seems to skirt the issue that foreknowledge entails necessity and causation, as Luther rants: "Let the Diatribe invent and go on inventing, let it cavil and cavil again, [and yet the fact is that] if God foreknew that Judas would be a traitor, Judas became a traitor of necessity, and it was not in the power of Judas, nor of any creature,

---

or faculty, or disposition, or aptitude to will or not to will, to choose or refuse, to approve or disapprove, and to perform what other actions belong to the will. Now, what it means for the same power to 'turn toward' or to 'turn away,' I do not see, unless it be the very willing or not willing, choosing or refusing, approving or disapproving, that is, the very action of the will itself. Thus we must suppose that this power is a kind of something that comes between the will and the action itself, something by which the will itself elicits the action of willing or not willing, or by which the action itself of willing or not willing is elicited. It is impossible to imagine or conceive of anything else. If I am mistaken, blame the author who gave the definition, and not me who examines it" (*Discourse,* 120). His critique seems to state that the will leads us to action, but what elicits the will? If that is itself an act of willing, then the regress begins. If the will requires some other power to "elicit" it, then it is not free. We will see a version of this argument later in Schelling, who recognizes the groundlessness of the will, its inability to ground itself, and hence the "abyss" (*Abgrund*) underlying human freedom of the will. God needs to be grasped as this unfathomable *Unwille* (or *Ur-sein*). For modern treatments of the will, see Smith, *Dialectics of the Will.*

to alter it, or change his will from that which God had foreseen" (131). Now Luther knows, and had himself experienced, the "offense" (131) that such a view offers to individuals who would naturally resist the sense of living out of nothing but divine necessity. But in a way that will foreshadow Kierkegaard, he turns this "deepest abyss of despair" into a "healthgiving" one (131) that provides the metaphysical consolation that he is in the hands of grace. Indeed, he goes so far to claim that "I should not want free will to be given me, even if it could be, nor anything else be left in my own hands to enable me to strive after my salvation" (135). Like a swimmer who has grown exhausted struggling against a current, he learns to allow it to carry him to safety/salvation.

Of course, Luther recognizes that we possess an intuitive sense of free will that cannot be denied. To deal with this, he develops a version of his conception of "two realms."[26] The claim that we have no choice does not apply to things of "this world" (like whether we should get up to get a drink of water), but only to matters of the soul. As he says to Erasmus, "You are perhaps right in assigning to man a will of some sort, but to credit him with free will in the things of God is going too far" (119). This division has a paradoxical consequence: he is claiming that in worldly matters we can affect our choice and are in a sense free, while in the important spiritual realm our fate is determined. However, this distinction, seen from another perspective, leads to its opposite, namely, the fact that in worldly matters our decisions can be affected by empirical realities while our conscience (our God-given will) remains forever free. Thus, he states: "A good theologian teaches that the common people should be restrained by the external power of the sword when they do evil. . . . But their conscience must not be fettered by false laws. . . . For consciences are bound by the law of God alone" (107). This enslavement of the will to divine law constitutes the radically subjective "Christian liberty, in order that we may not be ensnared into bondage by human traditions and human laws" (109).[27]

---

26. Charles Trinkaus shows how Erasmus and especially Luther were part of the separation of the moral or religious and economic-commercial-political spheres. This was the major legacy of the Renaissance. He stresses the "paradox that the limitation of free will both reinforced the amoralism and determinism of social and natural science and led to ultimately greater human powers of control over the external environment. Free will was thereby acquired in the very area in which it was most vigorously denied, but not for moral ends" ("Problem of Free Will," 58–59). What we have here is both a "dialectic of enlightenment" (with a small "e") operating in the sixteenth century, a Horkheimerian or Habermasian notion of the rise of instrumental rationality, ironically because reason was banned from theology. This also seems to be a more historical version of Derrida's notion of the way religion and technoscience work hand in hand.

27. The Lutheran view is, of course, profoundly influential and is rooted in a view of original sin that fundamentally corrupts the human soul. Thomas Saine cites the *Formula of Concord,* which,

As their biographies and the tone and content of this exchange on the status of free will in relation to salvation make clear, Erasmus and Luther differed not only in terms of theological doctrine and exegetical practice but also in terms of temperament. Erasmus sought to compromise in order to save the "corporate" structure of the church and was interested in establishing peace between Roman Catholics and Reformers; Luther, on the other hand, was a ruthless defender of what he considered the truth and was willing to sacrifice all peace (and friendship) to it. Erasmus is the rhetorician, Luther the dogmatist. Hence, Erasmus opens his discourse with the statement: "Nobody should therefore consider it unseemly if I should openly disagree with him [Luther], if nothing else, as one man from another. It is therefore by no means an outrage to dispute over one of his dogmas, especially not, if one, in order to discover truth, confronts Luther with calm and scholarly arguments" (5). And he concludes with the statement: "I have come to the end. It is for others to judge" (94). Luther responds directly to Erasmus: "You make it clear that this peace and tranquility of the flesh are to you far more important than faith, conscience, salvation, the word of God, the glory of Christ and God himself. Therefore, let me tell you, and I beg you to let it sink deep into your mind, I am concerned with a serious, vital and eternal verity, yes such a fundamental one, that it ought to be maintained and defended at the cost of life itself, and even though the whole world should not only be thrown into turmoil and fighting, but shattered in chaos and reduced to nothing" (107–8).[28] And Luther concludes with a radically different turn to his audience, not an openness to collective interpretation but an imposition of doctrine: "In this book of mine, I have not made comparisons, but have asserted and still do assert. I wish none to become judges, but urge all men to submit!" (138).[29]

I mention this difference of temperament and style not just because, as Nietzsche stresses in his own view of philosophy, each system of thought bears the stamp of an individual with a particular mode of living in the

---

he says, "ended the period of controversies after Luther's and Melanchthon's deaths and was also regarded as a binding doctrinal statement . . . : 'Again we believe, teach, and confess, that original sin is not a simple corruption, but rather such a profound corruption of human nature that nothing of the body or soul, of man's inner or external powers has remained whole or healthy'" (Saine, 199; article 1, third affirmation).

28. Consider also his Thesis 95: "And let them [the people] thus be more confident of entering heaven through many tribulations rather than through a false assurance of peace."

29. This is not to say that Erasmus could not be forceful, bitterly sarcastic, and downright rhetorically overwhelming in his own right. His response to Luther's response, the "Hyperaspistes," takes on a sharper and more unforgiving tone than his earlier essay. Part 1 (published in 1526, evidently written in ten days after he read Luther's essay) was some three times longer than Erasmus's original

world. More important, we see here that approaches to the question of faith and rationality are often accompanied by an entire ethos, a bearing that one has to the world, a sense of one's security or insecurity and the means for living with either one. It is not too extreme to say that these two personal styles met their matches in the movements of Humanism and Protestantism, and live on as both individual styles and movements today that represent opposing modes of being in the world.

Following from this emphasis on ethos, we see in this "dialogue" the introduction of contrasting approaches to moral/ethical arguments concerning the status of God, faith, and human responsibility. Erasmus, in addition to being conciliatory, was more utilitarian. He was deeply concerned with the ethical life as *imitatio Christi*. This concern meant, for example, that he would reject notions like predestination (or at least still hold on to the Catholic notion of a "mystery") not just because it could not be defended philosophically and exegetically but, more important, because it did not help men behave better. Erasmus was horrified by the thought that the notion of a lack of free will would lead to indolence and loss of hope. For this same reason, Erasmus could not hold to Luther's distinction between the mundane and the divine (free in the former, not in the latter) since even our actions in this world influence and are important for salvation. This opens the possibility of an "ethical" "measure" for judging beliefs. Thus, for Erasmus, those parts of the Bible are clearest that offer "the precepts for a morally good life. This is obviously the word of God which one does not have to fetch down from high heaven, or a distant sea, but which one rather finds near at hand, namely in our mouths and in our hearts" (10). Indeed, these moral precepts are contained in "the Law of Nature, carved deeply into the minds of all, tell[ing] Scythians as well as Greeks that it is unjust to do to another what one does not wish to suffer himself" (14). Because of its universality, the ethical principle provides a test in exegetical matters as well. For example, in a case of conflicting interpretations, each side might lay claim to the truth because they each bear "the mark of the Holy Spirit." One way to adjudicate this

---

(even though it addresses only Luther's critiques of the introduction), and part 2 (1527) was some six times longer. After Luther's personal attacks on Erasmus, Erasmus also partakes in his share of ad hominem argument, accusing Luther of catering to his blind followers, suffering from mental illness, and wrapping himself in a cloak of infallibility that tolerates no contradiction. But Erasmus brings all his powerful philological weight to bear as well, pointing out both weaknesses in Luther's use of Scholastic categories and all the biblical passages where there are contradictions or textual variations. Finally, however, the conclusion takes a turn to direct pastoral concerns of the church, whereby the issue of freedom of the will is handled as more than an academic or dogmatic one. Erasmus's humane concerns for the betterment of believers come clearly to the fore.

would be to look closely and decide whether one sees or misses "among them a conduct of life commensurate with the Spirit" (18).

Luther rejects this general ethical approach. He is, to begin with, not concerned with the edification of individuals by religion; his goal is not to provide individuals the conciliatory doctrines that might help them be better people. "You say: Who will endeavor to reform his life [if there is no free will]? I answer: Nobody! No man can! God has no time for your self-reformers, for they are hypocrites. The elect who fear God will be reformed by the Holy Spirit. The rest will perish unreformed" (110). The notion, therefore, that there could be values applying to all human beings, which all might use to work toward salvation, is anathema to Luther who opens up a cataclysmic divide between the saved and the unsaved. He writes of such universalism: "You draft for us a list of those things which you consider sufficient for Christian piety. Any Jew or Gentile utterly ignorant of Christ could easily draw up the same, because you do not mention Christ in a single letter. As though you thought that Christian piety is possible without Christ, if God be but worshipped with one's whole heart" (104). He fears, rightly in a sense to be established as theological thought unfolds in the following centuries, that this "essence of Christianity . . . without Christ," which Erasmus proposes to prevent the schism and conflagration of the Reformation, will lead to the gradual decline of Christian religious faith.

Finally, related to the status of the ethical is the problem of evil, which they also address in diametrically opposed ways.[30] Erasmus cannot accept the thought that if man is not free to choose evil, and if God is omnipotent, then it means that God is willing man to commit sin and be damned. Without a notion of free will, he believes, "there is no telling how the problem of divine justice and mercy could be solved" (84). Only if it is left up to man to commit evil could God be considered just according to the principle that justice is an evaluation of rational choice. Despite his fundamental disagreement with Augustine on the freedom of the will, Erasmus does seem to concur with the notion that evil is not an alternative principle that exists and acts upon man (the basic tenet of Manichaeanism), but rather, evil arises from man's deprivation of good or the "turning away" from the divine. Consequently, humans have the freedom to make this basic decision. God's mercy comes from the possibility in man to be able to choose the good and from the option of salvation offered to those who do choose it. Justice is so to

---

30. The problem of justifying evil will continue to be a central issue for the Christian thinkers we will deal with in the following chapters (esp. Leibniz and Kant).

speak a secondary principle enacted in response to man's actions. The final conclusion that Erasmus sees arising from the denial of free will would be that evil deeds are ultimately *caused* by God (31).

Luther is willing to take the step of accepting the reality of both good and evil in the world. Man does not choose between them but is chosen to be one or the other. In one of his most extreme images: "Thus the human will is like a beast of burden. If God rides it, it wills and goes whence God wills. . . . If Satan rides, it wills and goes where Satan wills. Nor may it choose to which rider it will run, nor which it will seek" (112). Because Luther, too, needs to avoid the heresy of the Manichaeans, he must in the end trace even evil back to God. His point is that there is no such thing as good or evil forces (since God is the motive force moving all things); but there is also no such thing as a "neutral" entity that could, on its own, take upon itself good or evil characteristics. Rather, each person "according to his nature" is an "instrument" of good or evil through which God works as they are "carried along by that motion of Divine Omnipotence" (130). Both what it is and whatever turn it should take (to continue in sin or to repent and be saved) are determined by God. While the ultimate reality of good is thereby guaranteed, the reality of evil as a thing's/person's *essence* and as a course (of life) that cannot be changed (by the person him-/herself) is likewise made absolute in this world. Justice emerges not as a secondary response to choice but as the inner principle to which, through faith, we hand ourselves over. Hence, the Bible verse that most grounds Luther's theology—"For in it [the Gospel] the justice of God is revealed, from faith unto faith, as it is written, *He who is just lives by faith*" (Romans 1:17, emphasis added)—allows faith to define justice rather than a system of rewards and punishments for actions. Radical good and radical evil are therefore "justified" by God.[31]

---

31. Leopold Damrosch's essay "Hobbes as Reformation Theologian" provides a useful transition to the next chapter insofar as it indicates unintended consequences of the Luther-Erasmus debate in the seventeenth century. Having established the radical opposition between reason and faith, we should consider what happens when the opposition is revealed to be less stable. In Damrosch's reading of Hobbes's "Questions concerning Liberty, Necessity, and Chance" and the debate with Bishop Bramhall, Hobbes introduces a new threat to "semi-Pelagians" who might want, like Erasmus, to maintain the validity of human reason and free will. Namely, Hobbes's "determinism rests on irrefutable and impersonal proofs," not "faith alone" (345). "Thus, Hobbes preserves a version of familiar Christian belief, but with its spiritual vitality drained away. His God is a *deus absconditus* with a vengeance: Reformation voluntarism stressed God's ever-present power, Hobbes his omnipotent remoteness" (345–46). The conclusion is ironic: Luther attacked Erasmus for introducing reason in order to justify a notion of free will, an introduction that he saw leading to the denial of God; here, however, Hobbes introduces reasoning in order to justify Lutheran determinism, leading to a radical theism bordering on atheism.

✍ CHAPTER 2

God and the *Logos* of Scientific Calculation (Descartes, Spinoza, Leibniz, Pascal)

> That You are, O Lord, my God, I must think though I did not believe.
>
> —Anselm, from the *Proslogium* (*Alloquium Dei*)
>
> Ergo est Deus. Q. E. D.
>
> —Jacob Wilhelm Schwartz, "Demonstratio Dei contra Spinosam"
>
> Two extremes: to exclude reason, to admit reason only.
>
> —Pascal, *Pensées*
>
> From this it is now wonderfully clear how in the very origination of things a certain Divine mathematics or metaphysical mechanics is employed, and how a determination of the maximum holds good.
>
> —Leibniz, "On the Ultimate Origination of Things"

Luther, as we know, had his way. He insisted on promoting his "vital and eternal verity" and thereby brought about what he was prepared to endure: "even though the whole world should not only be thrown into turmoil and fighting, but shattered in chaos and reduced to nothing" (*Discourse on the Will,* 108). A century of religious war and bloodshed ensued. But not only the Thirty Years' War between Protestants and Catholics created the sense of chaos. The fragmenting within Protestantism and the generation of competing sects also brought about a profound sense of doctrinal confusion and conflict. The influential Jansenist Antoine Arnauld, for example, wrote a letter of May 13, 1686, to the Prince of Hessen-Rheinfels that captures the course of the post-Reformation, in this case the variety of disputes within Protestantism itself on the question of the free will:

> This Lutheran minister of whom Your Highness speaks must have good qualities, but it is something incomprehensible and marking an

extremely blind prejudice that he can regard Luther as a man destined by God for the Reformation of the Christian religion. He must have a very low idea of true piety to find it in a man like him, imprudent in his speech and so gluttonous in his manner of living. I am not surprised at what this minister has said to you against those who are called Jansenists, since Luther at first put forward extreme propositions against the co-operation of grace and against the freedom of will so far as to give to one of his books the title *De servo arbitrio,* Necessitated Will. Melanchthon, some time after, mitigated these propositions a great deal and since then the Lutherans have gone over to the opposite extreme so that the Arminians have nothing stronger to oppose to the Gummarists than the doctrines of the Lutheran Church. There is no cause then for astonishment that the Lutherans of to-day, who occupy the same positions as the Arminians, are opposed to the disciples of Saint Augustine. For the Arminians are more sincere than are the Jesuits. They grant that Saint Augustine is opposed to them in the opinions which they have in common with the Jesuits but they do not think themselves obliged to follow him.[1]

Given these conflicting positions, no wonder people wanted a rational solution that would bring these often bloody arguments to rest on first principles. Where could they turn?

In fact, not all was chaos. In the midst of perhaps the greatest unleashing of violent disruption that the European social order had ever seen, scientists were working out the systematic and natural laws that brought a clockwork regularity into the universe. For many, this scientific rationality offered a safe harbor from the ravages of religion. Indeed, it invited claims or charges of "atheism," as thinkers from many schools—Aristotelian, Stoic, Epicurean, or Spinozist—allowed the concept of an orderly "Nature" to take over the role once played by God.[2] But it became also a new source for a different kind

---

1. From Leibniz, *Discourse on Metaphysics,* 101. Arnauld (1560–1619) is in many ways a linchpin connecting most of the figures dealt with in this chapter, Descartes, Pascal, and Leibniz. Pascal wrote his eighteen letters published as *Les provinciales* (1656–57) in defense of Arnauld and the Jansenists (who challenged the Jesuits and the Catholic Church on precisely the issue of the free will, taking up St. Augustine's position against the Pelagians). His *Port-Royal Grammar* (1660) and *Port-Royal Logic* (1662) were both based on Descartes' *Regulae* and showed influences by Pascal (whose method Arnauld introduced). Early in his life he conducted a voluminous correspondence with Leibniz.

2. See Hans-Martin Barth's excellent monograph for a different approach to the theological debates of the seventeenth century, namely, the charges and claims of "atheism" and the Christian "apologetics." The philosophers I am dealing with in this chapter to varying degrees were caught up in both sides (that is, often could be considered atheists—esp. Descartes and Spinoza—and yet were providing what they saw as support of theism via the new scientific thinking rather than returning to orthodoxy).

of religious thought in turn. That is, what concerns us is not so much the opposition between scientific knowledge and religious faith, secularism and sectarianism, as, rather, the way the calculability (i.e., *ratio* or *logos*) associated with scientific thinking was brought to bear on theology. Thomas P. Saine summarizes developments in the seventeenth and eighteenth centuries as follows: "Thinkers attempted to harmonize the results of modern science with traditional theological concepts, so as to save as much as possible of the old God in the new age" (187). The irony turns out to be that the very tools used to slow down the progress of Western thought toward a god-less world would end up hastening it and making it more final in the end. That is, those who "attempted to harmonize" a scientific reason and faith *within* a religious framework may have done more damage—at least from one perspective—to that framework than those who rejected it outright. While in this and the next chapter I will be covering the same period and some of the same thinkers as Saine, I will concentrate on certain main lines of thought (and not the numerous interesting and relevant "secondary" intellects that Saine investigates). And my emphasis will be slightly differ-ent as I also prepare for the following chapters. The point, as Saine shows, is that once (some) intellectuals get taken in by the powers of science (esp. Newton) and scientific reasoning, they cannot but help bring it to bear on theology. Hence, I wish to show the historical connections between mechanistic technoscientific rationality and theological argumentation that Derrida works with in strictly conceptual terms. That is, if we consider the quotation from Leibniz that serves as an epigraph to this chapter, the issue for me is to show how the seventeenth century ushered in a new kind of *logos* modeled on the natural sciences (esp. physics) and mathematics, locat-ing it at the very origin or *arche* of (Judeo-Christian) religious thinking. It is worth recalling, in fact, that one of the basic meanings of *logos* has to do with (mathematical) calculation. It is not by chance that we will see a return to the ontological proofs for the existence of God, since in a way not unsimilar to Anselm (as quoted also above), major thinkers like Descartes, Spinoza, and Leibniz would stress the attempt to *think* God (necessarily) even in the absence of *belief,* thereby establishing a new ground for belief. The outcome of this turn in theological discourse is anything but "wonderfully clear," as it merely sharpens and transforms traditional paradoxes rather than solving them. Although Leibniz will be the main focus of this chapter, we need to begin with a discussion of Descartes, who laid the foundation for the course of theological thought in the seventeenth and eighteenth centuries. He insisted on the inherence of reason, in the form of mathematical *ratio,* within faith, and hence the grounding—if not displacement—of the latter by the former. As a result of his modern philosophy, new tensions arose, however, between reason and faith (with Pascal, who will be treated at the end of this chapter, offering one of the most innovative and paradoxical relationships between them).[3]

René Descartes was a young man in the most tumultuous, indeed violent times Europe had ever seen. Not only the wars of religion, which he experienced firsthand during his travels to Germany, but also, more specifically for him as an intellectual, Giordano Bruno's execution as a heretic by burning in 1616, the incarceration of Tommaso Campanella for his anti-Aristotelian (even atheistic) views, and the condemnation of Galileo in 1633, created an environment of danger for those who might challenge traditional views. Hence, it is not by chance that Descartes waited a number of years before he published his physical and mathematical theories. If he insisted on absolute certainty in his philosophy, it was also a matter of life and death. In his *Discourse on Method* (1637) he provides a brief autobiography because he took as one of his basic principles, given the doubts and confusions and conflicts he saw around him among other academics, to acquire his knowledge only from the "book of the world" and the "book of his own self." For this reason, he needed to have clarity about his own development and reveal it openly to his public so that others as well could see how he came to his views. The traditional authorities—the church, Aristotelian philosophy, the Bible—could no longer play the primary role in the formation of knowledge. Instead he read widely in the book of the world by traveling extensively across Europe (in part pursuing the career of an army officer) and gained a firm grounding in the mathematics and physics that he saw as the most powerful of the day (Copernicus, Galileo, Kepler). In his first unpublished and unfinished philosophical work, the *Regulae ad directionem ingenii* (*Rules for the Direction of the Natural Intelligence*), composed in 1628, he lays out his ideas for the attainment of true knowledge:

> Rule One, On Wisdom and Science: The goal of studies should be the direction of the natural intelligence toward the formation of solid and true judgments about all the things that occur to it (65).
>
> Rule Two, On science and knowledge: We should attend only to those objects for whose certain and indubitable cognition our natural intelligence seems to suffice (71).

---

3. For a very brief summary of this development, see Alasdair MacIntyre's discussion of the "first crisis of theism" in *The Religious Significance of Atheism* (9–14). My goal is to unfold it in greater detail (he mentions only Newton and Pascal, and then jumps to a second crisis of theism in the nineteenth century).

Rule Three, On intuition and deduction: Concerning proposed objects, one has to investigate, not what others may have felt or what we ourselves conjecture, but what we can clearly and evidently intuit or certainly deduce—for knowledge is acquired in no other way (77).

Rule Four, On method, mathematics, and 'mathesis universalis': A method is necessary for investigating the truth of things (85).

If mathematics, or more precisely, the kind of deductive reasoning found in geometric proofs (see below on Spinoza), was to provide the method, and if the objects of study were to be given by observation, Descartes nonetheless needed to ground his science in something more certain than the opinions of others. That he found in himself. For, he argued, that is certain which cannot be doubted, and the one and only thing that he could not doubt was the fact that he finds himself doubting, i.e., the fact that he exists as a doubting (and thus more generally *thinking*) being. *Cogito, ergo sum.*

But he hesitated to publish his ideas. The *Discourse* appeared in French in 1637 and the Latin *Meditations on First Philosophy* appeared in 1641. And in fact, especially the latter led to both the victory of his philosophy in many circles as well as to dangerous charges of skepticism, Pelagianism, and even atheism. Ironically, however, Descartes was still interested in using his new method of reasoning in order to provide a proof of God's existence that also could not be doubted. Indeed, so that he could connect the certainty of his own existence to the knowledge he developed about the real world extended around him, he *needed* the idea of a perfect being who would have created the perfect "fit" between the existing world and his "clear and distinct ideas" about it. Hence, we should turn first to Descartes' proof; Leibniz's response to it will be discussed below.

Descartes had given the "ontological proof" for the existence of God its most powerful modern formulation and made it the touchstone of his rationalism.[4] Of course, the ontological proof had existed long before the seventeenth century. Anselm developed the proof based on the concept of God as the "being than which no greater can be conceived." The argument runs, basically, that a contradiction arises if we were to say that such a being does not exist, for then we could conceive of a being greater than it—a contradiction in terms—because it would, in addition, also exist.[5] There is something suspect about such an argument, for it seems to follow from an arbitrary definition and has a vicious circularity to it (i.e., I define a being

---

4. For a good review of ontological arguments, see Oppy, *Ontological Arguments*.
5. See Bencivenga, *Logic and Other Nonsense*, for a contemporary perspective on Anselm.

as perfect such that it must exist and then conclude that it exists). Thomas Aquinas refuted Anselm's argument for this and other reasons and for many centuries seemed to put it to rest. My goal here is not to review the literature and the wide array of different arguments. Indeed, there is some dispute on just how organized a collection of such arguments are. My main aim here is to show how in the seventeenth century there was renewed interest in a certain mode of argumentation (*logos*) for dealing with the existence of God. That *logos* is associated with *rationalism,* and the "ontological proofs" are significant because they would formulate a *reason* to accept the existence of God that depends on nothing else but the workings of human *Reason,* a Reason that supersedes historical particularities. Such proofs, like mathematical truths, would be accessible to anyone capable of the use of reason (and conceptual language) regardless of confession or background. Hence, they would be the best tools for putting an end to the violent disputes of the post-Reformation.

Descartes developed the most famous proof in his *Meditations,* returning to the argument dismissed by Aquinas. As he says in the introduction, addressed to the "Dean and Doctors of the Faculty of Sacred Theology of Paris," he is explicitly trying to find a common, indeed universal, ground, so that not only people of different religious opinions but even believers and nonbelievers could come to a rational agreement on God's existence (61–63).[6] Whereas Erasmus and Luther conducted their diatribe over conflicting interpretations of scripture, Descartes knows that those without faith find such an appeal would "proceed in a circle" (62). They require an appeal to "rational reason." While he is resuscitating a form of proof that had been in many ways dismissed after Aquinas's critique, there is an important difference in Descartes' conception of the proof. Not only does it have a simplicity that should make it appealing to any philosophically unprejudiced mind, it has the power of a *mathematical* proof. This is a point that Descartes mentions numerous times. This last point is crucial for the self-understanding of the theologians/ philosophers in the seventeenth century. The way to guarantee belief in God's existence was to use mathematical reasoning. In fact, when Descartes raises the "proof" in the Fifth Meditation, he does so as if he were merely extending the solid reasoning from mathematics into the realm of theology. He asks:

> But if the mere fact that I can produce from my thought the idea of something entails that everything which I clearly and distinctly perceive to belong to that thing really does belong to it, is not this a possible basis

---

6. The page numbers for the *Meditations* refer to Descartes, *Discourse on Method and the Meditations,* trans. John Veitch.

for another argument to prove the existence of God? Certainly, the idea of God, or a supremely perfect being, is one that I find within me just as surely as the idea of any shape or number. And my understanding that it belongs to his nature that he always exists is no less clear and distinct than is the case when I prove of any shape or number that some property belongs to its nature. (106)

The rhetorical nature of his question demonstrates that a key inversion has, of course, already taken place because the way he places philosophical insight and mathematical certainty as "a possible basis for another argument to prove the existence of God" implies their foundational status over and against theology. In fact, it would be more correct to say that both geometric/mathematical truths and divine ones rest on the same principle of "clear and perceptive ideas." Once I have, through meditation, attained such an idea, it has the firm status of truth. Such is the nature of the truth of a necessarily existing, supremely perfect being. He writes:

Whatever method of proof I use, I am always brought back to the fact that it is only what I clearly and distinctly perceive that completely convinces me. Some of the things I clearly and distinctly perceive are obvious to everyone, while others are discovered only by those who look more closely and investigate more carefully; but once they have been discovered, the latter are judged to be just as certain as the former. In the case of a right-angled triangle, for example, the fact that the square on the hypotenuse is equal to the square on the other two sides is not so readily apparent as the fact that the hypotenuse subtends the largest angle; but once one has seen it, one believes it just as strongly. But as regards God, if I were not overwhelmed by philosophical prejudices, and if the images of things perceived by the senses did not besiege my thought on every side, I would certainly acknowledge him sooner and more easily than anything else. For what is more manifest than the fact that the supreme being exists, or that God, to whose essence alone existence belongs, exists? (108)

The point here is that he is working not from a definition of God, a "mere" concept, but from a clearly perceived idea.[7] Or more precisely, Descartes' goal is to develop the art of meditation, i.e., the ability in all rational beings to cast

---

7. This can be considered his answer to Aquinas: God's existence is not self-evident to everyone, only to those who have developed a clear and distinct idea of the perfect being through proper meditation. See Nolan, "Descartes' Ontological Argument."

away that which is doubtful (by confronting it) and then, beginning with only those "clear and distinct ideas" that remain, move through a chain of reasoning to other secure truths. The fact that such a process of meditation leads the meditator to this "proof," or actually to the direct intuition that God exists as a necessary being because that idea follows "self-evidently" (*per se notam*) from the notion of a perfect being (seen "clearly and distinctly")—this resulting insight is almost an afterthought, God an outcome of intuitive logic.

Before turning to Leibniz, we should consider briefly the work of the other philosopher who hoped to present his ideas on theology, man, and world using the rigor of the "geometrical method"—even though he came to radically different views on the nature of God—namely, Spinoza. He seemed to adopt the paradoxical position of on the one hand defending Christianity while on the other denying the existence of God (as a being independent from nature).[8] Baruch (Benedikt, "the blessed") Spinoza, whom Hans Küng called the "most derided" (*meistbeschimpfter*) philosopher of the early modern period (160), began his studies in rabbinical school in Amsterdam.[9] However, his interests in Latin, literature, and philosophy soon established him as an independent thinker. A follower of Descartes, he early on developed an understanding of natural laws as an order inherent within nature itself. His metaphysics of a thoroughly dynamic universe attempted more than any other of the time to take into account the new scientific understanding of nature. He was banned from the Amsterdam Jewish community in 1656 (the same year that Pascal's *Les provinciales* was condemned). Instead of accepting an academic position at the University of Heidelberg (offered to him by the brother of Elizabeth of the Palatinate, to whom Descartes dedicated his *Principles of Philosophy*), Spinoza withdrew to the countryside where he supported himself as a lens grinder as he pursued his philosophical writing. The *Tractatus theologico-politicus* (*Theological-Political Treatise,* 1670) was the only work he published during his lifetime (although under a pseudonym and listing a fictitious press). His *Ethica ordine geometrico demonstrata* (*Ethics Demonstrated by the Geometric Method*) appeared shortly after his death in 1677.

We can summarize Spinoza's contribution to the theological discussions of the seventeenth century (and beyond) in terms of three important ideas:

1. His philosophical, philological, and historical approach to biblical criticism extended Erasmus's exegesis and laid the foundation for the

---

8. Barth, *Atheismus,* 232–36, summarizes the disputes of Spinoza's contemporaries.

9. Spinoza's impact on the late eighteenth century, esp. in Germany, was significant (Lessing, Jacobi, Goethe, Hegel, et al.) and led to the so-called *Pantheismusstreit,* which involved major Enlightenment and Idealist thinkers. See Beiser, 44–108.

kinds of radical questioning that emerged in the following century (see the next chapter on Reimarus and Lessing). Indeed, the Bible for him was not so much an error-free book of the direct Word of God as a contradictory text containing the expression of human (Jewish) faith. It is open to interpretation and misinterpretation. His *Theological-Political Treatise* opens with a discussion of superstition, a phenomenon that has led to a lack of consistent reason that "has been the cause of many riots and ferocious wars" (5), as well as despotism and tyranny. To rid the world of the kinds of religious disputes that threaten to extinguish the sparks of both reason and genuine faith, he "resolved in all seriousness to make a fresh examination of Scripture with a free and unprejudiced mind, and to assert nothing about it, and to accept nothing as its teaching, which [he] did not quite clearly derive from it" (8–9). This means, on the one hand, comparing the teachings of the Bible with what our "universal understanding" tells us, i.e., what "is very simple and can be easily grasped by all," and, on the other, exploring historically how diverse teachings entered into the Bible (so that anything contradicting natural reason could be explained away).

2. As indicated in the subtitle of his *Ethics,* the method with which he hoped to demonstrate the truth of religiously founded morality was based on mathematics. In this he was inspired by Descartes, who wrote in part 2 of his *Discourse on Method:* "Those long chains of reasoning, quite simple and easy, which geometricians use in order to achieve their most difficult demonstrations, had given me occasion to imagine that all things which can be known by man are mutually related in the same way" (see Leibniz, *Philosophical Writings,* xxiii). For Spinoza this means ordering his argument through three levels. Part 1, "Concerning God," has eight definitions that state what is immediately present to our intuition, seven axioms that follow immediately from the definitions, and thirty-six propositions (with corollaries) that require proofs based only on what has preceded them as defined or proven. Through this method he has not only "explained the nature and properties of God" but also "endeavored to remove any prejudices which might impede the good understanding of my propositions" (*Ethics,* 31).

3. His conception of God, developed in the first part of the *Ethics,* made Him identical with the very being of the world/Nature.[10] He offers

---

10. Hans-Martin Barth (234) points out that this identity was not new with Spinoza; it could be found in the Kabbalah and in Stoicism (which, as we saw, already entered into early Christianity with the notion of *logos* as the all-pervasive ordering force of the cosmos).

the following as his sixth definition: "BY GOD, I mean a being absolutely infinite—that is, a substance consisting in infinite attributes, of which each expresses eternal and infinite essentiality." His proposition 11 states: "God, or substance, consisting of infinite attributes, of which each expresses eternal and infinite essentiality, necessarily exists." His logic strove to provide the same kind of absolute "proof" of the existence of God that we saw in Anselm or Descartes. But his definition introduced a radically new (and for many, dangerous) vision of a universe—metaphysically speaking, all that is—as a single entity (substance) expressing itself in infinitely diverse ways (modes and attributes) with the necessity of natural laws. God does not exist here as the creator of the universe either in the biblical (engaged) or deistic (distant) sense. Rather, he saw God as a *causa immanens non transiens,* an immanent not transcendent cause. The phrase *"Deus sive natura"*—God or Nature—often repeated in Spinoza's work, captured this profound belief in an impersonal God as the basic substance of Nature. The idea that one could substitute "God" *or* "Nature" as the name for all that exists with an eternal and infinite necessity came to be associated not so much with pantheism as with atheism.[11]

These three major ideas that Spinoza contributed to modern thinking about God did not go down easily with any of the religious communities of his day; not only was he excommunicated from the Jewish community of Amsterdam, but his books were placed on the index of forbidden works by the Catholic Church. And yet the force of his logic was something that the great minds of his time could not avoid. Hegel claimed later in his lectures on the history of philosophy: "When one begins to philosophize, one must be a Spinozist. The soul must bathe in this ether of the one substance in which everything that is true has been submerged. It is this negation of all particularity to which each philosopher must attain. It is the liberation of the spirit and its absolute foundation" (*Vorlesungen über die Geschichte der Philosophie,* 19:376). It was Leibniz who in part began to philosophize in such "ether" and yet who strove to bring such ideas, which could be branded as atheist and fatalist, back into communion with religious thought.

Leibniz felt that he had solved some of the problems—mathematical, philosophical, and theological—that consumed his great predecessors, especially

---

11. On the impact of Spinoza, via Goethe, on German Idealism, see Smith, "*Die Gretchenfrage.*"

Pascal, Descartes, and Spinoza. This status of Leibniz in the history of theological debates will be decisive. To the extent that Leibniz sees himself not
as the modern rationalist who *clears away* traditional approaches and proofs
of the existence of God but as the one who provides the necessary logic to
secure them, he sees himself as bringing metaphysical theology to its logical
conclusion in a way that both completes and, in fact, overcomes it. It will be
possible at the end of the eighteenth century for Kant to challenge an entire
discursive regime and *logos*-God association by challenging the Leibnizian
(and Wolffian) line.[12]

Born in 1646, just two years before the Treaty of Augsburg concluded
the Thirty Years' War, Georg Wilhelm Leibniz came of age in a period of
relative stability compared to the violent upheavals and dangers that reigned
during the early lives of others like Descartes and Spinoza. The awareness of the conflicts of the past and the experience of a possible peace in
Europe combined to instill in him both the desire for and an optimistic
belief in a universally acceptable rational-metaphysical ground for faith. In
1669, at the end of a work by one Gottlieb Spizel, Leibniz anonymously
published a "Confessio naturae contra atheistas," in which he indicated his
early engagement with theological matters.[13] Rather than pursue a university
career, Leibniz entered the employ of the Baron of Boineburg, a minister
to the Elector of Mainz. In his service Leibniz spent four years (1672–76)
in Paris. Through his contacts with Nicolas Malebranche, Arnauld, and the
Dutch physicist Christiaan Huygens, he was introduced to the ideas of the
intellectual elite of Europe—including, for example, Pascal's mathematical papers (on the basis of which he constructed an improved calculating
machine). This introduction to higher mathematics led him to his famous
discovery of the tool of the infinitesimal calculus independent of Newton
in 1675 (although Newton waged a major campaign against Leibniz for
proprietorship of this discovery). We will deal with the metaphysical under-
pinnings of this mathematical principle in Leibniz's thought below. After his
stay in Paris, Leibniz entered the service of the Duke of Hannover where he
stayed until his death in 1716 (apart from influential trips abroad to Italy and
visits to Berlin). The guiding thread of his thought in general was the belief
in the systematic nature of knowledge and the possibility of developing a
clear language ("calculus" in the wider sense) for presenting it. The suc-

---

12. The fact that Leibniz was translated into the idiom of the Enlightenment by the likes of
Christian Wolff and Johann Christoph Gottsched is brought out by Saine. My concern here is less
with the process of mediation than with the overall consequences of this line of thought.

13. Cited often in Hans-Martin Barth, e.g., 239.

cess of such a project would "replace controversy by calculation" (Leibniz, *Philosophical Writings,* xxiii), i.e., conflictual debate of the kind that tore apart Europe could be ended through the introduction of a new technoscientific *logos* or *ratio.* But it is crucial to recognize that his goal was not to supplant or dismiss the earlier (Christian, religious) foundation of Europe. Rather, as he wrote in one of his early letters to Jacob Thomasius (1669), he hoped to reconcile Cartesianism with Aristotelianism and hence Scholasticism. "He collected ideas from the prominent philosophical traditions and then attempted to combine them in a way that would solve all the problems, and please everyone."[14]

To be Leibnizian about our approach to Leibniz (in a way that will be immediately obvious), we can gain entry into this problem in any number of ways, each affording a particular perspective.[15] I will start with Leibniz's notion that a "substance" is something that has a "complete concept." Leibniz's view of propositions is the following (as developed in the "Discourse on Metaphysics" and "The Nature of Truth"): the predicate of a proposition "X is Y" does not add anything new to the subject but is already fully contained within it. This would also imply, using the commutative principle, that any predicate Z that fits the proposition "Y is Z" would also be contained in X. Any "contingent truth" would thus consist of the infinite number of propositions that would be needed to fully confirm the initial proposition. (A "necessary truth" would be a mathematical one that can be demonstrated by a finite number of steps, like a geometrical proof.) An individual substance would be an object that is referenced by a concept and would thus itself be part of an infinite chain that would connect it to the infinity of other objects. "Radiating out" from the substance is an infinite array of propositions, the totality of which would be the entire universe (known in its totality only by God, but accessible in a limited fashion to our reason by following the chain of logical/causal associations). To modify an example of Leibniz (he uses Alexander): "Caesar was killed by Brutus" is interpreted by Leibniz to mean that the predicate, "was killed by Brutus," is "contained" in the concept "Caesar." Likewise, "Brutus is husband of . . ." is also contained in the original concept, as is "Brutus was criticized in a speech by Mark

---

14. In her 2001 book on Leibniz's early development, Christia Mercer (here 471) argues that Leibniz was "a collector of ideas," who was successful in building "an original and sublime philosophical edifice out of recycled materials" (53). He developed a "conciliatory" methodology in response to the chaos he saw around him, to the attempts of others to find solutions, and to the desire for a religiously "ecumenical" philosophy.

15. Unless otherwise noted, all citations for Leibniz refer to essays contained in *Philosophical Writings.*

Antony," etc., etc.[16] Carrying this process out infinitely, one would say that "Caesar" contains all other predicates about the universe.

One peculiar consequence of this approach is that one could likewise start the chain in any other place: "Brutus killed Caesar," for example, would "radiate out" infinitely, capturing the same totality of concepts and connections, but from a different perspective. This means that, in a crucial way, "Brutus" never actually affects "Caesar." Depending on where one starts, Brutus is contained in Caesar (as the latter's murderer) or Caesar is contained in Brutus (as his victim). If we use Leibniz's other terminology, we would say that the individual substances (Brutus, Caesar, etc.), each with its complete concept (the infinite array of propositions radiating out from it), is a "monad." Each one in a literal sense is or contains the entire universe (or the entire universe of propositions). Each is "windowless" because it exists on its own as a "self-contained" world ("self-contained" in quotes because it contains an infinite number of associated propositions and concepts about other substances).[17] One might imagine a Cartesian plane and say that any of its infinite points could be the starting point (0,0) to which any other point could be related, but depending on where one started, the universe would "look" slightly different (even though one would have all the same true propositions). As Leibniz says in a famous image capturing his perspectivism: "Every substance is like an entire world and like a mirror of God, or of the whole universe, which each one expresses in its own way, very much as one and the same town is variously represented in accordance with different positions of the observer" ("Discourse on Metaphysics," § 9:20).

Now, wouldn't it be awkward if these perspectives clashed? That is, if one started out with Brutus, came across the proposition that Brutus killed Caesar, but then also started out with Caesar, and did *not* find the proposition that he was killed by Brutus? What kind of world would that be, in which Brutus killed Caesar but Caesar was killed by, say, Alexander the Great? In principle that would be possible according to Leibniz because such propositions as "Brutus killed Caesar" or "Caesar was killed by Brutus" are, we saw, *contingent* truths, not necessary ones. Hence, it is not *necessary* that they mesh or, in Leibniz's terms, "harmonize." But the fact that they *do* harmonize turns

---

16. In Leibniz's example: In the individual notion of Alexander is "the foundation of and reason for all the predicates which can truly be stated of him —as, for example, that he is the conqueror of Darius and Porus. . . . Therefore, when one considers properly the connexion between things, one can say that there are in the soul of Alexander, from all time, traces of all that has happened to him, and marks of everything that will happen to him—and even traces of everything that happens in the universe—though no one but God can know all of them" ("Discourse on Metaphysics" § 8:19).

17. "Monads have no windows, by which anything could come in or go out" (*Monadology,* § 7).

out to be a new "proof of the existence and the majesty of God" (Saine, 70). Or actually, more accurately stated, one should say not that Leibniz saw or assumed the existence of this, "the best of all possible worlds," and then concluded from that the necessity of God's existence; rather, the existence of God as the final reason for/ground of the universe who harmonizes all substances and propositions (monads) leads us necessarily to conclude that this is the best of all possible worlds. God, seeing the infinite possibilities or infinite worlds that could have been created (actually, it is an infinity of infinities, since each of the infinite substances contains an infinite array of possibilities), created the *one* arrangement in which the perspectives of each of the substances matches. As Leibniz says in the *Monadology:* "And this is the means of obtaining as much variety as possible, but with the greatest order possible; that is to say, it is the means of obtaining as much perfection as possible. . . . It is this hypothesis alone . . . which properly exalts the greatness of God"—esp. against skeptics and critics like Pierre Bayle (§§ 58, 59).

The kind of *logos* or *ratio* that Leibniz sees here at the beginning, then, is a master organizer of the discursive or propositional order. Man's task, as "rational animal" (*zoon hen logikon*), would be to trace out the logic of this discursive order, to begin at any stage and follow the infinite number of infinitely intricate connections—for there are no gaps—as far as possible given our finite existence. "We have knowledge of a tiny part of that eternity," Leibniz writes, "which stretches out immeasurably" ("On the Ultimate Origination of Things," 142). Mankind's partial perspective of the infinite divine order provides not just a metaphysical and epistemological theory, but also a systematic practice. Although the grounding is radically different, Leibniz's philosophy provides, that is, a mission, indeed a *project* of research (in the sense of "Manhattan Project") that is not unlike that proposed by Francis Bacon nearly a century earlier. This project involves bringing together as many researchers as possible to share their "perspectives" (discursive discoveries) so that we might fill out our picture of the universe with ever-greater detail and ever-widening associations. (On this endless task of cultivation, see "On the Ultimate Origination of Things," 144). According to this view, God's *ratio* is embedded in the universe—"God acts like the greatest geometer, who prefers the best construction of problems" ("A Specimen of Discoveries about Marvellous [*sic*] Secrets of Nature in General," 76n)—and collective scientific investigation becomes a religious enterprise. The groundwork is laid here for a fusion of theology and technoscience.

Let us approach this same concern—namely, Leibniz's conceptions of God, man, and the universe as tied together by means of a technoscientific *logos*—by considering his "proof" for the existence of God based on the principle of sufficient reason. It is a proof that Kant will subsume (and critique) under the title "cosmological," since it presumes to make a statement about the "whole world." Arguing like a good scientist and logician, Leibniz points out that each individual thing and each state of the world must have prior to it a reason sufficient to explain how it came about. While one can trace this chain of reasons infinitely, "you will never find in those states a full reason why there should be any world rather than none and why it should be such as it is" ("On the Ultimate Origination of Things," 136). That is, when one considers the world as a whole, one can only conclude that "the reasons of the world then lie in something extramundane, different from the chain of states, or series of things, whose aggregate constitutes the world" (137).[18] The key here is that it is not a matter of *faith* that leads Leibniz to this proof, but the insistence on the pursuit of "reasons." As he says in the later essay "Some Metaphysical Consequences of the Principle of Reason" (1712), after arguing for the analogy of the universe and an organic body organized by God, "we can arrive at the same point [the common cause, i.e., God] in a more general way by returning to our fundamental principle" (174). By tracing the chain of causes we must conclude "that the reason for the existence of contingent things must eventually be sought outside matter and in a necessary cause; namely, in that whole reason for existing is not outside itself. This, therefore, is spiritual . . . and is also the most perfect mind" (174).

In this regard, Leibniz positions himself between the traditional and the modern. He himself knows, for example, that his concept of "substance" seems to "restore the rights of citizenship to substantial forms, which have practically been banished" ("Discourse on Metaphysics," 21). However, he justifies his approach by going on the offensive and arguing that precisely by studying both modern science and the Scholastic tradition, he uniquely sees the need to employ both:

> I have thought carefully about modern philosophy, and . . . I have devoted much time to physical experiments and to geometrical demonstrations. I was for a long time persuaded of the emptiness of these entities [from Aristotelian and Scholastic metaphysics], and was finally obliged to take them up again despite myself, and as it were by force. This was after I had myself conducted some researches which made me recognize that our modern philosophers do not do enough justice to St. Thomas and to other great men of that era, and that the views of

---

18. It is precisely this notion of "considering the world as a whole" that Kant will reject in the "antinomies" of the *Critique of Pure Reason*.

the Scholastic philosophers and theologians have much more sound-
ness than is imagined, provided that one uses them in a proper way and
in their proper place. ("Discourse on Metaphysics," 21–22)

That is, the idea of God as the ultimate source of existence relies on a concept of substance that echoes Aristotle but is derived from good scientific
principles.

According to Christia Mercer, Leibniz's engagement with these proofs
played a major role in the formation of his metaphysics (see esp. her part 3,
on "The Metaphysics of Divinity"). Let us consider some ways in which
Leibniz drew a rationalistic theology to its highpoint.

Leibniz responds, first, to Descartes by calling for the reworking of the
ontological proof because it lacks the demonstration of a premise. Thus,
while Leibniz praises Descartes for resuscitating the ontological proof of
Anselm (i.e., a proof that unfolds a priori and not from divine effects) after
the Scholastics had mistakenly rejected it as a "paralogism," he critiques its
incompleteness. Descartes argues that the existence of God follows necessarily from the idea of a supremely perfect being. However, according to
Leibniz, one would first have to show that such a being is even possible. He
claims to fix this flaw in Descartes' argument by supplying the proof that a
supreme being is *possible*. Something is possible, he says, if its *non*existence
cannot be shown to be *im*possible. This is the case with God (see "Discourse
on Metaphysics," 32–33). Once he has shown this, he can then accept the rest
of Descartes' proof. Again, our interest in this debate is less in the actual proof
than in the motivation and reasoning behind it. Leibniz insists that Descartes' is an imperfect demonstration for "it is assumed without proof that a
most perfect being does not involve a contradiction," and such an unproven
assumption would be inappropriate if one is working with a God who, we
saw, "acts like the greatest geometer, who prefers the best constructions of
problems" ("A Specimen of Discoveries about Marvellous [*sic*] Secrets of
Nature in General," 76).

Leibniz provides an extended proof of the existence of God in the *Monadology* (§§ 31–60), a late work that summarizes his philosophical position. He
arms himself with some basic distinctions (between "necessary" and "contingent" truths, between truths of "reasoning" and truths of "fact") and with
two basic tools (the law of noncontradiction and the principle of sufficient
reason). His actual argument begins (§ 37) not with the abstract or necessary
but with the basic fact of our variegated and differentiated contingent world:
"All this differentiation involves only other prior or more differentiated contingent things, all of which need a similar analysis to explain them." If we

stay at the level of contingency, "we are no further advanced." Rather, we are forced to accept that "the ultimate reason of things must lie in a secondary substance," namely, a "source" of the existence of all contingency as such; "and this is what we call *God*" (§ 37; emphasis here and in the following passages in original). But such a conception is still empty. Hence he must go on to show that "*there is only one God and this God is enough*" (§ 39, because every contingent truth is connected with every other so that it only takes one necessary reason to be the reason of the entire world of differentiated things); that God is "*perfection*" (§ 41, because there is nothing that could limit the existence of this necessary reason); and that God is the "*power*" and "*knowledge*" that creates the differentiated world of monads (§§ 47–48, because the existence of these two realms demands the possibility of a divine will that bridges the infinite/infinitesimal gap between them). Of course, as we saw above, "God's choice" in creating this universe (§ 53) must itself involve a necessary reason, thereby making this universe the only and the best one. Hence, Leibniz hopes to avoid the pure immanence and apparent fatalism of Spinoza's theory of God as substance, even as he maintains the rigor of the reasoning.

These proofs of the existence of God by Descartes, Spinoza, and Leibniz are, of course, the source of endless debate among philosophers, and they raise fundamental questions in the fields of ontology and linguistic analysis. We do not need to be concerned about their actual effectiveness or deal with the details of their different arguments. The key is that these three figures of the seventeenth and early eighteenth century put all their theological eggs in the basket of a scientific-mathematical reasoning. If for Anselm the ontological proof seemed to follow from the concept of "that than which nothing greater can be conceived," the seventeenth century derives God from the kind of truth that guarantees geometry. But already John Locke provides an early warning, namely, the problem that could arise when this one kind of proof, which even Descartes admits depends on an individual having a "clear and distinct" idea of the essence of a supreme being, muscles out all others. Locke warns those who "out of an over-fondness of that darling invention [i.e., the ontological proof], cashier, or at least endeavor to invalidate, all other arguments, and forbid us to hearken to those proofs, as being weak or fallacious, which our own existence and the sensible parts of the universe offer so clearly and cogently to our thoughts, that I deem it impossible for a considering man to withstand them" (*Essay concerning Human Understanding*, book 2, chap. 10, § 7). As we will see in the next chapter, Kant picks up on this warning and demonstrates its seriousness; by critiquing this proof and removing what some saw as firmest basis for belief in God, he shows that one had better have some other ground to stand on.

A final problem that Leibniz feels he has solved is the vexing one of the free will (and the related problem of the source of evil). Here he has two broad opponents: Spinoza's "pantheistic" Idealism and a materialism that we could associate with Hobbes. In response to the latter, he wants to "raise the minds of our philosophers from exclusively material considerations to nobler meditations" ("Discourse on Metaphysics," § 23:32). He injects a vital force into the world that allows for a unique dynamism in such a harmonious order. In response to Spinoza, he uses his distinction between "contingent and necessary truths" to argue that the foreknowledge of God about the universe, as well as its preestablished harmony, through the divine will, do not *necessitate* (by definition) a contingent action through *my particular* will.

The seventeenth century was not only dominated by the attempts to develop strictly rational grounds for faith. Already at this time—in a way that will return again in later chapters when we look at alternatives to Hegel's rationalist philosophy of religion—Pascal stood out as someone who turned from the *logos* of the mathematical natural sciences to a conception of faith based on feeling and nonrational experience. In his approach he was associated with Arnauld, who rejected the very nature of the reasoning Leibniz engaged in, writing in his letter of March 13, 1686, to Count Ernst von Hessen-Rheinfels: "Would it not be better for him to leave those metaphysical speculations which can be of utility neither to himself nor to others, in order to apply himself seriously to the most important matter he can ever undertake, namely, to assure his salvation, by entering into the Church from which new sects can form only by rendering themselves schismatic?" It is not so much the particular doctrine as the effort that Arnauld sees in Leibniz not just to employ reason alongside the church (custom, tradition) and faith, but to raise "metaphysical speculation" to new heights. (Arnauld objects that Leibniz's theory that each substance contains the entire universe would take away *divine* free will.)

Pascal had already attained an international reputation as a brilliant mathematician in the mid-1600s, having developed proofs already as a sixteen-year-old on the nature of conic sections (including the famous "mystical hexagram"). He did work on probability theory that laid the foundation of the field. In the margins of one of his hastily drafted papers on roulette Pascal made the first notes on his ideas concerning differential calculus.[19] As a physicist he made important observations on acoustics and experimented

---

19. Saine connects Pascal and Leibniz: Leibniz quotes Pascal on the infinite (from *Pensées,* § 72) and argues that if Pascal had the concept of preestablished harmony and the notions of the interconnectedness that leads to the understanding of monads mirroring the entire universe, he would

with air pressure (exploring the possibility of the existence of a vacuum, an idea that would challenge Cartesian theories). He developed a computing machine that could help his father, a tax officer in the service of Cardinal Richelieu. In all these ways he belonged to the same modern spirit as Descartes, with whom he had lukewarm contact in Paris in the 1640s. However, he was not consumed completely by the methodical drive of science. Sickly as a youth and raised at home, he suffered the first of many breakdowns as a twenty-one-year-old after working on the computing machine. In the words of Hans Küng, Pascal "is in life as in science a *man of pathos:* pathos in the original, broad sense of deep life experience, patience, suffering, and passion" (69). Moreover, unlike his other colleagues, when he witnessed the religious controversies of his time and especially the severe attacks on Jansenism (which affected his immediate circle), he did not respond by appealing to a universal reason in order to settle matters of faith. Rather, on the basis of a mystical experience he records from the night of November 23, 1654, he turned to a highly spiritual and personalized relation to God. In his famous line from the *Mémorial,* the brief notes he wrote down about his experience (including precise dating and timing) and that he carried with him for the rest of his life, he says that he no longer was interested in the "God of the philosophers" but instead returned to the "God of Abraham, Isaac, and Jacob."[20] What characterizes this relationship?

One important aspect is that the relationship to God is not one that is fixed once and for all. Rather, although the path to God is left open by divine grace, man is always approaching, feeling his way. As such, it might be compared to the method of science as developed by someone like Francis Bacon: not systematic yet nonetheless rational.[21] Trial and error, rather than deductive necessity, drives scientific investigation.

Pascal stressed the need to rely on a deeply *felt faith* because reason cannot provide the truth of first principles but can only argue logically from them

---

have come to the same conclusion (76–77). See Leibniz, *Kleine Schriften zur Metaphysik,* "Infinité," 373–85.

20. Ironically, the Heidegger student Wilhelm Weischedel will develop some three hundred years later a positive notion of the "God of the Philosophers." It is not unlike Pascal's in many ways. According to Weischedel, Pascal characterizes the human condition as an "intermediary thing between nothing and everything" ("Mittelding zwischen nichts und allen"); Weischedel, in turn, speaks of our state of "suspension" (*Schweben*). And both depend on the idea of God's absence and ungraspability to ensure an open, hermeneutic relation. The difference is that, thanks to Heidegger, Weischedel can call precisely this approach that involves constant questioning and skepticism "philosophy" as such, whereas Pascal opposes matters of the heart to philosophy.

21. Note also the similarity in the aphoristic styles of Bacon and Pascal. See Pensées § 98 on prejudice.

to deduce valid propositions. Thus, given the tradition of thinking we have been exploring in this chapter, he was an early skeptic concerning the proofs of the existence of God based on Nature. As he says in the *Pensées* (preface to the second part, § 242), those who already have faith will see God "in the smallest things which surround them [and in] the course of the moon and planets," while those without it will only think even less of the arguments in favor of God's existence if this is the best they can provide. (More trenchant criticism of such "physicotheology," i.e., seeing God's work in the order of Nature, will be presented in the next chapter dealing with Hume and Kant.) Indeed, Pascal embraces the notion from Isaiah 45:15 that God does not reveal himself through the world: "*Vere tu es Deus absconditus*" ("Verily, thou art a God that hidest thyself") (*Pensées,* § 242).[22] Because of his fundamental conception of God as hidden, he rejects any mode of belief that would claim an absolutely certain knowledge about God and embraces the Judeo-Christian tradition because it alone is willing to state clearly God's absence from the epistemic reach of the mind.

Pascal has four brief yet highly critical aphorisms on Descartes in part 1 of the *Pensées.* They indicate his dissatisfaction with the strictly scientific *logos* that would attempt to grasp divine nature or the human spirit. He writes:

76. To write against those who made too profound a study of science: Descartes.
77. I cannot forgive Descartes. In all his philosophy he would have been quite willing to dispense with God. But he had to make Him give a fillip to set the world in motion; beyond this, he has no further need of God.
78. Descartes useless and uncertain.
79. *Descartes.*—We must say summarily: "This is made by figure and motion," for it is true. But to say what these are, and to compose the machine, is ridiculous. For it is useless, uncertain, and painful. And were it true, we do not think all Philosophy is worth one hour of pain.

The study of science alone would merely lead to the kind of deism that might as well "dispense with God" in the long run. But more important,

---

22. "Instead of complaining that God had hidden Himself, you will give Him thanks for not having revealed so much of Himself; and you will also give Him thanks for not having revealed Himself to haughty sages, unworthy to know so holy a God" (§ 288).

the last line appeals to a different register completely, for he looks at human beings as endowed with feeling, not just reason. Indeed, as he says, "The human heart is endowed with reasons that reason shall never know." Hence, he must himself approach God with a broader understanding of how people behave. And although he is never an explicit point of reference for Schleiermacher, Pascal lays the foundation here for a Romantic approach to God that displaces divine and human *logos* in favor of *pathos*.

In the *Pensées* Pascal addresses the relationship between knowledge and faith that helps explain this wider context: "There are three sources of belief: reason, custom, inspiration. The Christian religion, which alone has reason, does not acknowledge as her true children those who believe without inspiration. It is not that she excludes reason and custom. On the contrary, the mind must be opened to proofs, must be confirmed by custom and offer itself in humbleness to inspirations, which alone can produce a true and saving effect. *Ne evacuetur crux Christi* ['Lest the cross of Christ should be made of none effect,' 1 Cor. 1:17]" (§ 245). And again: "Faith is different from proof; the one is human, the other is a gift of God. *Justus ex fide vivit* ['The just shall live by faith,' Rom. 1:17]. It is this faith that God Himself puts into the heart, of which the proof is often the instrument, *fides ex auditu* ['Faith cometh by hearing,' Rom. 10:17]; but this faith is in the heart, and makes us not say *scio* ['I know'], but *credo* ['I believe']" (§ 248).

Pascal attempted to work with scientific methods of *logos* even as he developed a notion of faith that is grounded differently. We can see this fascinating yet uneasy fusion of two modes of "reasoning" in two arguments. The first concerns the "proof of the machine" (§§ 246–52). While this might sound like a typical tool of the new technoscientific age, Pascal does something quite different with it. He sees human beings consisting of both intellect and automaton (§ 252). While the intellect must be persuaded by proofs, the automaton is moved by custom. Once the automaton accepts something as true, it "bends the mind" and becomes more firmly embedded than any demonstrated truth. Phenomenologically speaking, it becomes the background, part of our *Lebenswelt*, the basis on which we can even begin to judge other arguments. For this reason, the role of positivity or "the external" in religions, i.e., custom and habit, is significant even if not sufficient for faith; for "the external must be joined to the internal to obtain anything from God" (§ 250). Here Pascal points to a rich conception of religiosity that reflects his "transitional" status, conjoining the Augustinian (Lutheran) emphasis on submission and faith, the Catholic emphasis on tradition and practice, and the neoscientific emphasis on rationality. *Logos* thus takes on the varied meanings of word (even letter), spirit, reason, and *ratio* as *regulae, rules.*[23] Indeed, it is the ultimate act of (theological) reason or rational theology for reason to abandon itself, or more precisely, to follow its own judgment and submit to a force greater than itself. As he says: "There is nothing so conformable to reason as this disavowal of reason" (§ 272), or again: "All our reasoning reduces itself to yielding to feeling" (§ 274).

Hence, for all of Pascal's focus on rationality, there is always the turn to the "heart," the ultimate foundation of faith: "It is the heart which experiences God, and not the reason. This, then, is faith: God felt by the heart, not by the reason" (§ 278). And he continues in a passage reminiscent of Luther himself: "Faith is a gift of God; do not believe that we said it was a gift of reasoning. Other religions do not say this of their faith. They only gave reasoning in order to arrive at it, and yet it does not bring them to it" (§ 279). Pascal argues back to first principles and recognizes that the acceptance of them is itself an act of faith.

A second famous passage, Pascal's "wager," is likewise an intriguing mixture of faith and reason.[24] He sets up the wager as follows. The choice is simple: believe in God's existence or not. Once the wager is posed, it is impossible not to make a decision, since even to reject the wager is to choose one side. What is on the line for us in this wager is our eternal happiness (if we win) or "error" in this life (if we lose). It is crucial that the fundamental act of deciding does not rest at all on our reason. Like the later "leap of faith" developed by Kierkegaard or the kind of "decisionism" that is associated with forms of existentialism, the very nature of a decision by an individual means that it does not merely "follow" from any other chain of reasoning. A decision is not a conclusion. And yet, if we recall that one important meaning of *logos* is "calculation" (also in a mathematical sense), then Pascal the mathematician also does not leave *logos* out of the picture. The calculation he offers is: the probability strictly speaking of God's existing or not is fifty-fifty. However, the comparison between what could be gained and what could be lost contains "an infinite difference"—this finite life vs. eternal life. Given that we *have* to choose anyway, and given this infinite difference, it would not be in keeping with our reason, he says, if we were not to choose to believe. As

---

23. "The Christian religion alone is adapted to all, being composed of externals and internals. It raises the common people to the internal, and humbles the proud to the external; it is not perfect without the two, for the people must understand the spirit of the letter, and the learned must submit their spirit to the letter" (§ 251).

24. Hans-Martin Barth (293ff.) gives the background of Pascal's wager in the late seventeenth century. Many thinkers offered arguments on "balancing the risks" of believing or not believing in God. Pascal (at least in the reception he received beginning in the nineteenth century) added, however, the "existentialist" element of the decision.

he says, this argument is not itself a "proof," but it does possess tremendous nonrational force based on a rational, even mathematical calculation: "And therefore our offer possesses an infinite force if one has to wager the finite in a game that gives one an equal chance to win or lose and the reward for winning is the infinite." The wager is thus both absolutely logical (why not take the chance if there's everything to gain and nothing to lose, since my finite life is lost anyway?) and yet the choice for it can only be made on the basis of a decisive leap across an infinitesimal gap toward faith. *Logos* of the sciences, therefore, serves faith without becoming its foundation, for in order to have faith, an infinite and groundless decision must be made, a decision for "first principles" that rests as much on feeling as on rationality.

Pascal seems to know that the rationalist line in Christianity will have to play itself out, both "positively" in the (vain) effort to provide the ultimate proofs and also skeptically, as reason points out its own failure to account for real faith. As we will see in the following chapters, these positions unfold in Kant, Hegel, and Hegel's critical successors (Feuerbach and Marx). We will also look to those who pick up again Pascal's arguments not *against* reason but for the necessary supplements to *logos:* feeling, will, and decision.

 CHAPTER 3

Kant

The Turn to Ethics as Logos

Now we reach one stage further in what I shall call
the intellectual descent that the Theists have made
in their argumentations, and we come to what are
called the moral arguments for the existence of
God. You all know, of course, that there used to be
in the old days three intellectual arguments for the
existence of God, all of which were disposed of by
Immanuel Kant in the *Critique of Pure Reason;* but
no sooner had he disposed of those arguments than
he invented a new one, a moral argument, and that
quite convinced him. He was like many people: in
intellectual matters he was skeptical, but in moral
matters he believed implicitly in the maxims that he
had imbibed at his mother's knee. That illustrates
what the psychoanalysts so much emphasize—the
immensely stronger hold upon us that our very early
associations have than those of later times.

—Bertrand Russell, "Why I Am Not a Christian"

All across the theological spectrum the great reversal
had taken place. Interpretation was a matter of fitting
the biblical story into another world with another
story rather than incorporating that world into the
biblical story.

—Hans Frei, *The Eclipse of Biblical Narrative*

I open this chapter on Enlightenment theol-
ogy and critique with two brief references to twentieth-century discussions
in order to provide a contemporary context for the historical analyses to
follow. At issue is the key relationship between religion and ethics. While
for many, religion forms an indispensable foundation for ethics, Kant, we
will see, inverts this priority to ground religious faith on rationalist moral
principles.

First, in his debate with a group of contemporary theologians, Jürgen
Habermas discusses the need for theology in a "postmetaphysical" world

like our own to "translate" the language of religious discourse into that of philosophy. While he recognizes the possibility of failure given postmodern challenges to philosophy in general ("in these moments of its powerlessness, argumentative speech passes over beyond religion and science into literature" [*Religion and Rationality,* 75]), he nonetheless pushes for his version of "methodical atheism" (75ff.) that would reevaluate basic religious categories in terms of his theory of communicative action. Much of this discussion looks like a version of Feuerbach's anthropological reinterpretation of religious experience in the mid-nineteenth century (as we will see in chapter 5). But what interests me here is the point where, according to Habermas, some of the theologians resort "to an experience *accessible only in the language of the Christian tradition,* interwoven inseparably with religious discourse" (80; his emphasis). For theologians like Helmut Peukert and Charles Davis, "a secular hope without religion cannot affirm with certainty . . . a future fulfillment" or "expectation" (cited by Habermas, 81, 80) and hence would be, in a way that Habermas rejects, "indispensable in order that we would endeavor to act according to moral commands and ethical insights" (81). Habermas refers to the basic question raised by David Tracy as a motivation to move beyond philosophy, which (according to Tracy) cannot answer it, namely, "why be moral at all?" (81). With this exchange between Habermas and the theologians we are in the middle of a debate that already had its say over two hundred years ago in the last quarter of the eighteenth century. The goal of this chapter is not to reduce the present debate to "nothing but" a rehashing of the earlier one; in fact, Habermas and the others must introduce a new paradigm to account for the decline of metaphysics that has intervened. However, we need nonetheless to see the origins of this discussion to understand its terms and implications.

Second, Derrida succinctly summarizes Kant's basic premise in his introductory comments to his essay on religion and points to the irony that Kant might already be in part responsible for the death of God in a strong sense: "Is this not another way of saying that Christianity can only answer to its moral calling and morality, to its Christian calling if it endures in this world, in phenomenal history, the death of God, well beyond the figures of the Passion? That Christianity is the death of God thus announced and recalled by Kant to the modernity of the Enlightenment?" ("Faith and Knowledge," in *Religion,* 12). While, as we will have to wait to see, this *salto mortale* is not taken ultimately until Nietzsche, the core of this chapter will involve a discussion of Kant's philosophical theology and key positions that laid the foundation for his thought so that the claims made by these two very different contemporary theorists can be better evaluated. Are Kant's profound

Christianity and his turn to "practical reason" (morality) to support God's existence responsible for a major acceleration down the slippery slope to atheism?

The chapter is divided into three basic discussions: (1) Kant's rejection of the other "proofs" of the existence of God and the "moral" proof he provides as a saving alternative; (2) the way this shift toward a practical approach to religion nonetheless contains a view of "radical evil" that is the inevitable "return of the letter" of religion, i.e., the unavoidability of "positivity" (understood specifically as the insistence on modes of representation); (3) hence the need for Kant to grapple with institutional questions, esp. ones related to the university, to resist what he sees as a constant "conflict" with the forces of religiosity. We will see that Kant does occupy a special position on our slippery slope. He, along with other Enlightenment figures like Lessing and Hume, attacks aspects of traditional religion, but does so in the interest of saving a unique function for God, namely, as the guarantor of rational morality. However, in doing so, Kant inverts the order of dependence—since now God appears as a need or result of *our* ethics and rationality—and thereby exposes God to a final coup de grâce (in the form of Nietzsche's later critique of the ethical on which God has come to stand).

We need to look at the developments of the 1780s and 90s to understand the origins and political significance of Kant's formulation of the conflict between faith and Enlightenment.[1] Ernst Cassirer, the twentieth-century intellectual historian, points out that most of Kant's late work addresses all those instances of "religious and state corruption" (*Kants Leben,* 403) that Kant saw around him. Kant's problems began when Frederick William II, the nephew of Frederick the Great, rose to the Prussian throne. Already as a young man Frederick William had been drawn to Christian mysticism. One can certainly be skeptical of the "Enlightened despotism" of Frederick the Great, but there clearly was a difference between a ruler who corresponded with Voltaire and one who talked directly to invisible higher powers. Kant's former student, Johann Gottfried Kiesewetter, who became a house tutor to the royal family, wrote numerous letters to his teacher in Königsberg with news and intrigue from Berlin. On June 14, 1791, for example, he described his ruler as follows: "The Lord Jesus has already appeared to the king a number of times, and people say he's going to build a new church to the Lord in Potsdam. He's weak in body and soul, sitting for hours crying" (*Briefe,*

---

1. See Saine, chapter 9, for a fine summary of this period in Prussia and its impact on particular intellectuals of the day (Karl Friedrich Bahrdt, Johann Heinrich Schulz). Saine mentions Kant only in passing.

10:78). Frederick William quickly had the Baron von Zedlitz, to whom Kant had dedicated the first *Critique,* removed from his office as head of the Ministry for Spiritual Affairs for being a "free-thinker and enemy of the name of Jesus" (Schmidt, 35 n. 41). In his place the king appointed his advisor, Johann Christoph Woellner, who began a campaign to stamp out the Enlightenment in Berlin. Woellner's major instrument was the infamous *Religionsedikt* that imposed censorship on all writings in Prussia. (Ironically, it generated well over one hundred responses!) According to the *Religionsedikt,* religious freedom is guaranteed so long as each subject "quietly performs his duties as a good citizen of the state and so long as he keeps any peculiar opinion to himself and carefully guards himself from spreading it or persuading others, making them uncertain in their faith or leading them astray" (Gregor in Kant, *Conflict,* x). Theological archconservatives and radically anti-Enlightenment lackeys were put in charge of censorship and educational matters. As per a *Kabinettsordre* of the king from October 19, 1791, it was decreed that from now on all monthly journals, periodicals, and occasional pieces, all library and pedagogical writings, including all brochures with philosophical and moral content, as well as major theological and moral books, must be submitted for censorship. Soon after publishing two essays on religion in Berlin, Kant himself was no longer able to get his ideas past the censor and had to collect his pieces into a single volume and send it to a publisher beyond the reach of the king.

The fact that Kant found a way to publish his work on *Religion innerhalb der Grenzen der bloßen Vernunft* (*Religion within the Bounds of Mere Reason,* 1793) outside Prussia, thereby circumventing the censors, did not make a real difference for him. He in fact received a letter from the king telling him to cease teaching and publishing on theological matters—a blow that we should not underestimate. He seriously anticipated the end of his publishing career (see letter from May 18, 1794, 10:240). Kant, ever the good subject, had even agreed to go along with the imposition of censorship, at least so long as the king lived. Fortunately, he did not live long. But, as we will see below, this collision with the Prussian reaction also led to an institutional impact on the university as itself a primary site of conflict between theology and philosophy.

Given these unpleasant confrontations and the complexity of the *Kritik der reinen Vernunft* (*Critique of Pure Reason,* 1781/1787), one might wonder why Kant did not make a long career out of simply unpacking its ontological and epistemological nuances. Why the insistent turn to religion, especially in a way that must challenge the state church? There seem to be three answers that lead us to some basic claims about the content and consequences of his philosophy. The first arises out of the inner necessity of his philosophical priorities, the second involves a dialectic concerning the nature of evil (see below, 87), and the third is institutional, involving the university (see below, 90).

Religion's Place in the System

As important as the *Critique of Pure Reason* has been, especially for the analytical Anglo-American tradition, one can argue that the *practical or ethical* aspects of Kant's philosophy, his moral concerns, were truly central to thinkers in the last decades of the eighteenth century. The establishment of human beings as autonomous moral agents was Kant's goal, and the "critique" of, i.e., the "limit" placed on, theoretical reason served to ensure that that autonomy went untouched. After all, the first *Critique* established that the kind of knowledge I have of objects-appearing-in-the-world is limited to them, i.e., to phenomena, and does not apply to noumena or things-in-themselves, and so my agency, my will as a thing-in-itself, my inner sense of what I *ought* to do *in spite of* what I might sensually want to do as a physical being in the world, is thereby separated out once and for all from the world of causal determinism. Practical reason attains a special status. This absolute grounding of morality was bound to lead to a confrontation with religion, the institution that had traditionally provided the moral direction to individuals and society.

Kant (as well as his important early interpreters, such as Carl Leonhard Reinhold) knew immediately that his critical philosophy would have an impact on theology. The major places where Kant develops his ideas on religion are *Religion within the Bounds of Mere Reason* (1793) and his *Vorlesungen über philosophische Theologie* (*Lectures on Philosophical Theology,* given in the late 1780s). There is also an extensive discussion of his proof for the existence of God at the end of the *Kritik der Urteilskraft* (*Critique of Judgment,* esp. §§ 86–91; 1790). The germs of this argument can be found in the *Critique of Pure Reason* (A632–42 = B660–70, and A604–19 = B832–47; 1781/1787) and the *Kritik der praktischen Vernunft* (*Critique of Practical Reason*) (part 1, book 2, section 2, chapters 5–9; 1788). The core of his argument in all these works derives both from the doubts he raises concerning most historical and rational proofs for God's existence and from his belief that ethics could provide the more secure foundation for theology.

In his lectures, as Bertrand Russell points out in the epigraph to this chapter, Kant outlines and destroys the three major traditional proofs: (1) the ontological, (2) the cosmological, and (3) the physicotheological. Kant summarizes the ontological proof for the existence of God, which we saw earlier in our discussion of Descartes, as follows: "An *ens realissimum* [most real being] is something which contains all realities in itself. But existence is also a reality. Hence, the *ens realissimum* must necessarily exist. Thus if someone were to assert that God does not exist, he would be negating in the predicate something which is included in the subject, and this would be a contradiction" (*Lectures*, 58). That is, the very concept of God is that he is the highest, most perfect being that contains all reality within him; there is no reality outside of him. Furthermore, the argument goes, it would be illogical to say that God is absolutely perfect and real—with one exception, that he lacks existence. Kant argues, however, that "existence" is not an additional predicate that adds something to the subject and could thus be lacking from it. The subject is a concept and the concept can be grasped whether there is a corresponding existing object or not. (In Kant's example, cited also in the *Critique of Pure Reason* [A598–600/B626–28], my *concept* of one hundred taler is not changed or increased by knowing they exist. Hegel cites this in his *Science of Logic*.)[2] Of course, we might also wonder about a particular concept that we have in our minds whether or not I might be able to get that knowledge confirmed through experience (or, in Kant's terms, a posteriori), e.g., the way a scientist might need to know whether a conclusion from a theory can be corroborated by experimentation. But here's the crux for Kant: precisely such an approach goes against the very concept of God that we are trying to prove to begin with, namely, a pure concept that cannot be the object of any experience.[3] We are left with only the *possibility* of God's existence. Because I can conceive of the possibility of a highest being, it is impossible to then deny its possibility, and radical atheism, the denial of God, should be put to rest.[4]

---

2. Hegel in *Logic* on one hundred taler (*Wissenschaft der Logik*, 86–90): He would introduce a different set of distinctions—not "concept" vs. "existence" but, rather, "being" vs. "determinate being"—but they are parallel. The first in both pairs is purely abstract, a self-relation or an "identity-with-self" that has a radical "indifference" because it bears no relation to any other (88). In Hegel's terms, such abstract Being is the same as Nothing. Hence, we would also reject a proof that relies on this notion, though for different reasons. Hegel: "Just as little as I can extract from the possibility of the hundred *taler* their actuality, just as little can I extract from the Notion of God his existence" (89). On the other hand, Hegel will also bring back a kind of ontological proof (making sure that God is not viewed as a determinate being like one hundred taler) (90).

3. In Kant's terms: "Whatever our concept of an object may contain and however much it may contain, we must still go beyond it if we are to impart existence to the object" (*Lectures*, 59). But that "going beyond the concept" to confirm its existence (namely, by means of a posteriori sense data and its synthesis with the original concept) is exactly what the ontological proof—which proceeds from the mere concepts—would be trying to avoid.

4. "Hence the edifice of the dogmatic atheist falls to the ground. For if he wishes to deny God's existence and assert that there absolutely is no God, the atheist must first demonstrate the impossibility of God. But here reason forsakes him" (*Lectures*, 57).

But a move like Leibniz's of positing the actual, indeed necessary existence of God is also not grounded: "Leibniz should have concluded, however, only that my idea of such a thing [as the *ens realissimum*] is possible. For the fact that there is nothing contradictory in my concept of a thing does prove that it is the concept of something possible, but it does not yet prove the possibility of the object of my idea" (*Lectures*, 56). In two senses, then, the ontological proof does not deliver what it promises. It neither guarantees the existence of God with logical necessity nor provides us with anything like qualities we would associate with a wise, just, merciful, etc., being.[5] Rather, it leaves us with the "modest but correct knowledge," according to Kant (*Lectures*, 80), that God contains nothing but the most abstract conceptions of this highest reality. Otherwise, he leaves us with the startlingly cold statement: "With objects of pure thought, however, there is no means of knowing their existence." Kant has thus led us away from the entire trend of the seventeenth century, which strove to give us a "scientific" knowledge, indeed certainty, of God's existence. On the contrary, Kant shows that, because we should not treat God (by definition) as a possible object of experience, we should never expect a posteriori confirmation of his existence, and hence we should not confuse scientific thinking and theology. God is not to be associated anymore with the *logos* of science.

Kant's treatment of the cosmological proof uses some aspects of the ontological proof, but comes to a startling and unsettling conclusion. In essence Kant critiques Leibniz's proof of the existence of God based on sufficient reason. The cosmological proof builds on an inference from experience— "the law of causality, which says that everything contingent has a cause" (*Lectures*, 60)[6]—extending it to the *regressus in infinitum*, forcing the conclusion that there must be "an absolutely necessary being" (60), a foundational and first cause. It is called "cosmological" because it depends on the nature of any "object of possible experience," all of which make up the notion of *world* or cosmos (60–61). Because it does not depend on the specific constitution or ordered nature of this world, it differs from physicotheology (see below). But once I have worked through experience in general to the point where I posit a necessary cause/being, the question remains whether I can say anything about "what attributes a necessary being must have" (61).

---

5. In fact, according to Kant, such abstract proofs put "us in a position to remove from our knowledge of God everything sensible inhering in our concepts" (*Lectures*, 80). He thereby avoids simple anthropomorphisms, but the proof cannot accomplish its real aim.

6. He actually deals with the cosmological proof in the section on ontotheology; in the section with the heading "cosmotheology" he deals with the issue of divine knowledge (based on Alexander Baumgarten). See also *Kritik der reinen Vernunft*, A605–6/B633–34.

Since such a being does not belong to the realm of experience, "reason searches only among concepts" (61) for such attributes. In this search, Kant leads us literally into a "dizzying" (64) exchange, a *mise en abyme* in which the idea of a necessary being and the most real being turn out to be mutually dependent and hence cancel each other out. He argues two points: first, it is not enough for this proof of the existence of God to say merely that there must be a necessary first cause; we also want to know that this necessary being is also the *ens realissimum* that is God. The argument seems to be that the only way of defining a necessary being would be as something that cannot be contradicted. But if we imagine all contradictions, the only aspect uniting them is the aspect of reality. Hence, the idea of a necessary being would be the same as the *ens realissimum* from the ontological proof, since everything else besides its reality would not be necessary; but in this case, the cosmological proof fails for the same reason as the ontological, namely, we are left with a completely empty being.[7] By moving back and forth between the ontological and cosmological proofs, Kant shows that they are mutually dependent and hence mutually canceling, since if they can be shown to be connected and one fails, then so does the other. Kant's second point is that a necessary being would be one whose nonexistence would be impossible; but human reason cannot grasp such a concept. One might say (as do Wolff and Descartes)[8] that if a triangle exists, then it is impossible that three angles do not exist. But I have no reason to presume that the triangle exists necessarily in the first place. "Thus I cannot form the least concept of a thing which would leave a contradiction behind if it were canceled along with all its predicates. . . . Hence in this case it is possible that God does not exist. It costs speculative reason nothing at all to cancel God's existence in thought" (64). We therefore seem to need the notion of a necessary being but cannot "rest content" because of our inability to prove it. The result: "This absolute necessity which we need indispensably as a final ground [*Grund*] for all things is the true abyss [*Abgrund*] for human reason" (64). While speculative reason is thus drawn to the notion of a necessary being, it discovers there not a proof of God's existence but a fateful groundlessness.

The discussion of physicotheology, the third traditional proof that Kant attacks, is somewhat more complicated since by the late eighteenth century, many thinkers had come to question its status even though, as we saw, it emerged from the seventeenth century as one of the strongest and most

---

7. This argument is not unlike the famous opening of Hegel's *Logic,* where being, pure being, is so indeterminate as to be—nothing.

8. See footnote to *Lectures,* 63 n. 11.

appealing proofs. It relies on a correspondence, or a logical connection, between the order of the physical world and the nature of the being that must have created it. More precisely, Kant defines it in terms of "reason's attempt to infer the supreme cause of nature, and the properties of this cause, from the *purposes* of nature (which we can cognize only empirically)" (*Critique of Judgment,* § 85).[9] And because the scientific and mathematical discoveries of the modern age had been so successful in demonstrating a clockwork order in the world, its case for a rational and benevolent creator seemed all the more convincing. (It has resurfaced in the late twentieth and early twenty-first centuries in the form of so-called intelligent-design alternatives to Darwinian models of evolution.) Prior to Kant, David Hume had offered the most devastating attack on the physicotheological proof.[10]

Hume ensured that his *Dialogues concerning Natural Religion* (1779) would not be published until three years after his death, undoubtedly because they presented a challenge to both orthodox believers and rational theologians. In them he presents three positions, which he has a fictional character introduce as "the accurate philosophical turn of Cleanthes," "the careless skepticism of Philo," and "the rigid inflexible orthodoxy of Demea." By the "accurate philosophical turn" of Cleanthes Hume means the best possible case for the physicotheological "proof" (or the argument by design):

> Look around the world, contemplate the whole and every part of it: you will find it to be nothing but one great machine, subdivided into an infinite number of lesser machines, which again admit of subdivisions to a degree beyond what human senses and faculties can trace and explain. All these various machines, and even their most minute parts, are adjusted to each other with an accuracy which ravishes into admiration all men who have contemplated them. The curious adapting of means to ends, throughout all nature, resembles exactly, though it much exceeds, the productions of human contrivance—of human design, thought, wisdom, and intelligence. Since therefore the effects resemble each other, we are led to infer, by all the rules of analogy, that the causes also resemble, and that the Author of nature is somewhat similar to the mind of man, though possessed of much larger faculties,

---

9. Although Kant discusses this proof in numerous places, I will concentrate on the discussion in the *Critique of Judgment* because of its basic clarity and the importance of teleology in both the context of that book and the proof. In the *Lectures,* the section on physicotheology merely follows Baumgarten's *Metaphysica* on the divine will.

10. Hans-Martin Barth (251–80) provides a good summary of seventeenth-century physicotheological arguments, as well as early critiques and indications of weaknesses.

proportioned to the grandeur of the work which he has executed. By this argument *a posteriori,* and by this argument alone, do we prove at once the existence of a Deity and his similarity to human mind and intelligence. (*Dialogues,* 109)

The danger of relying on "this argument alone" is that if it is shown to fail, the believer would seem to have no firm ground to stand on. This is exactly what Philo does in demonstrating that the analogy of the world-as-machine—in this case, a ship—allows for no conclusion about the exalted nature of the "creator":

If we survey a ship, what an exalted idea must we form of the ingenuity of the carpenter who framed so complicated, useful, and beautiful a machine? And what a surprise must we feel when we find him a stupid mechanic who imitated others, and copied an art which, through a long succession of ages, after multiplied trials, mistakes, corrections, deliberations, and controversies, had been gradually improving? Many worlds might have been botched and bungled, throughout an eternity, ere this system was struck out; much labour lost, many fruitless trials made, and a slow but continued improvement carried on during infinite ages in the art of world-making. (*Dialogues,* 130)

The deist conception of the great watchmaker seems, for Hume, to be no more reasonable than this skeptical idea of a bungling apprentice with no master design at all. If *that* was the one and only argument, then the faithful are in trouble.

Kant accepts the Humean critique of the problematic analogy made in the physicotheological proofs between a condition in/of nature and a being that could have created it. But the basic gesture of Kant's argument is different. In fact, in the *Lectures* he explicitly accuses Hume of sophistry (101) and refuses to accept as reasonable the hypothesis that mere fecundity or blind accidents could have produced the world as we now find it. Kant rejects Hume's extreme skepticism because he *does* see the reasonableness of assuming a "divine understanding" as the ultimate purpose of the universe. The key to Kant's response to physicotheology, however, lies in a shift in focus; i.e., it contains *in nuce* the very essence of the epistemological or "Copernican" turn his philosophy takes in general, a turn, namely, that considers not things in themselves but things as they must appear to us given our cognitive faculties (in this case, that "thing" is the "ultimate purpose," or God). According to Kant, teleological thinking or judgment, i.e., the search for the purposes of existing entities in nature, is as indispensable as the (Leibnizian) principle of sufficient reason. "We can, and must, follow the teleological principle in many of our investigations of nature" (*Critique of Judgment*, § 85:324)—esp. organic nature, where bodies are organized by the subsumption of parts to a purposive or functional whole. And once we begin to follow this principle, there is nothing to stop us from either proceeding infinitely or wondering if there is some purpose to the whole of nature as such. Indeed, the first consideration is absolutely essential as we conduct our (scientific) investigations, since we would be employing "lazy reason" (a term that comes up a couple of times in the *Lectures*) if we stopped at any point and threw up our hands without continuing to wonder what the purpose of a given thing was. Likewise, it is a tendency of reason (explored and "critiqued" in the first *Critique,* esp. the second antinomy) to go from the chain of events/entities *within* the world to propose statements about the *entire* world as itself an event/entity. But note how the emphasis has now shifted in Kant's argument. We are no longer talking about the *object* of such physicotheological queries but, rather, the nature of our reasoning faculties that they should (have to) make such association. "Hence," Kant writes, "even if we expand physical teleology as far as possible, we must surely keep to the principle . . . that, *in view of the character and principles of our cognitive power* [my emphasis], the only way we can conceive nature as regards what purposive arrangements we have come to know in it is by conceiving nature as the product of an understanding to which it is subjected" (*Critique of Judgment*, § 85:330). Physicotheology therefore *does* reveal something, not about God but about the nature of our own faculty of teleological judgment—that it tends toward and depends on an infinite reflection on purposes. However, it "cannot determine [the concept of a deity] any further" or produce a "concept of a deity" that is "adequate" (§ 85:325, 328). "By following principles of the merely theoretical use of our reason," on which physicotheology is based, "we can therefore never provide a determinate (*bestimmt*) conception of God (§ 85:328–29).[11] That is, once we focus our attention on our own cognitive procedures, we can recognize where the desire for "intelligent design" or a purpose in nature comes from but cannot allow our judgments to transgress their limits and fill that desire with cognitive content.

---

11. In the words of the *Lectures:* "Our reason urges us on to such a being as a *hypothesis* which is subjectively necessary for us to assume, because otherwise we could provide no ground for the possibility of anything in general. But if it is a true need of our speculative reason to assume a God, nevertheless from the fact that men cannot prove this apodictically nothing follows except that such a proof transcends our faculty of reason" (100).

The key result is that Kant's attacks on the traditional proofs would seem to lead to atheism. Kant, however, hoped to show the failure of these traditional arguments for God's existence must be demonstrated in order to *strengthen* faith. True, he says, *if* one must base one's belief in God on any or all of these speculative, theoretical proofs, and *if* they are found wanting, then one's faith would be shaken. Given the validity of the second premise (they *are* weak "proofs") and given Kant's absolute rejection of the conclusion (i.e., he rejects atheism), the first premise must be wrong. Indeed, he says, precisely in order to avoid the conclusion of atheism one *must* reject those weak proofs and base one's belief in God on some other principle. Like Lessing (as we saw in the introduction above), Kant would differentiate between a critique of the proofs and a critique of the thing supposedly proven. His goal in attacking the proofs is, he claims, to clear the ground so that he can in fact provide the best proof. What good does it do us to rely on bad proofs? Having thus removed weak proofs, he locates a more secure foundation in the realm of ethics, providing what he claims is the proof of "moral theism." Kant summarizes his point:

> Thus all speculation [i.e., traditional proofs] depends, in substance, on the transcendental concept. But if we posit that it is not correct, would we then have to give up the knowledge of God? Not at all. For then we would only lack the scientific knowledge that God exists. But a great field would still remain to us, and this would be the belief or faith [*Glaube*] that God exists. This faith we will derive a priori from *moral principles*. Hence if in what follows [i.e., in his lectures] we raise doubts about these speculative proofs and take issue with the supposed demonstrations of God's existence, we will not thereby undermine faith in God. Rather, we will clear the road for practical proofs. We are merely throwing out the false presumptions of human reason when it tries from itself to demonstrate the existence of God with apodictic certainty. But from moral principles we will assume a faith in God as the principle of every religion. (*Lectures*, 39)

With Kant's announcement of the insufficiency of all but the moral proof for the existence of God, he—together with his fellow Enlighteners—has swept aside centuries of debates. Everything now rests on deriving a conception of God from a rational understanding of morals. "Moral theism is, of course, critical, since it follows all the speculative proofs for God's existence step by step and knows them to be insufficient. Indeed, the moral theist asserts without qualification that it is impossible for speculative reason to demonstrate the existence of such a being with apodictic certainty. But he is nevertheless firmly convinced of the existence of this being, and he has a faith beyond all doubt from practical grounds" (*Lectures,* 40).

Here, too, Kant was not the first to declare that speculative or theoretical reason, i.e., the *logos* of the natural sciences, must give way to practical or ethical reasoning if we are to provide a stable and universal conception of God. For example, Kant's contemporary (at least until he died at the age of fifty-two in 1781, the year the first edition of the *Critique of Pure Reason* was published) Gotthold Ephraim Lessing had been engaged in an infamous public debate on theological matters and defended an approach to understanding God that highlighted the moral core of all religions. How did Lessing come to make this turn to morality?

Although Lessing—like so many of the great German thinkers in philosophy and religion, the son of a Lutheran pastor—went off from his small birth town of Kamenz to Leipzig to study theology, he ended up shifting his goals radically when he became interested in the theater. From his years in Berlin (he went there in 1748), where he experienced the center of German and European Enlightenment with the likes of Friedrich Nicolai, Moses Mendelssohn, Voltaire, and Frederick the Great, through his years writing the famous essays and reviews of drama in Hamburg (*Die Hamburgische Dramaturgie*), Lessing became arguably the greatest playwright of the eighteenth century. In the 1760s he lived in Breslau, where he produced one of the most famous German comedies, *Minna von Barnhelm,* and engaged in intense studies of Spinoza and Leibniz.[12] However, after theorizing about and writing major exemplars in the genre of German bourgeois tragedy, he was drawn into a major theological controversy in the last decade of his life. Beginning in 1769 Lessing took the position of librarian and archivist for the Duke of Braunschweig in Wolfenbüttel, Lower Saxony. At the time (perhaps revealing his earlier roots in theology), Lessing expressed concern about the "present enemies" of Christianity (*Theological Writings,* 64). In coming to the defense of religion he is not a completely typical figure of the Enlightenment, and in fact many of his Enlightenment friends were dismayed that he got involved

---

12. His short fragment from 1763, "On The Reality of Things outside God," although still in the language of the Enlightenment philosophy of Wolff, betrays a turn to Spinoza's radical notion of divine immanence. The opening line reads: "However I may seek to explain the reality of things outside God, I must confess that I can form no idea of it" (*Theological Writings,* 102). Posthumously Lessing became the center of the huge controversy over the role of Spinoza in the last quarter of the eighteenth century. Friedrich Heinrich Jacobi reported that, shortly before his death, Lessing confessed to being a follower of Spinoza. Moses Mendelssohn responded by critiquing Spinoza and attempting to distance his friend from that position. All major German thinkers—Goethe, Jacobi, Fichte, Schelling, Hegel—were involved directly or indirectly in this dispute.

in theological debates later in his life. And yet, we will see, his "defense" took a form that led religious authorities to see *Lessing* as the enemy. Hence in Lessing we have a typical case of someone who had every intention of *strengthening* religious faith—as opposed to Enlightenment atheists—and yet who might have contributed to the opposite.

Who are these "enemies" that Lessing was concerned about? The case that caused the most problems for Lessing involved Hermann Samuel Reimarus, a professor of "Oriental" languages, whom Lessing had met in Hamburg. Reimarus died in 1769 and left behind a voluminous manuscript entitled *Apologie oder Schutzschrift für die vernünftigen Verehrer Gottes* (*Apology for Rational Worshippers of God,* not published in complete form until 1972). As part of his orders from the duke to publish holdings from the library, Lessing printed sections of Reimarus's work as the "Fragmente eines Ungenannten" ("Fragments of an Anonymous Author"). They contained very strong historical critiques of the Bible, pointing out logical and philological contradictions, and a rejection of literal readings of miracles and prophecies. Reimarus took the basic position on the New Testament that Christ must be understood as a teacher of a rational ethical religion, and so anyone who adopts rational ethical principles should be treated with the same tolerance as "Christians." Clearly Lessing was interested in these arguments and must have wanted them to be considered by his readership; but he was by no means celebrating them *because* they critiqued the Bible and Christian doctrine. And yet the publication of the "Fragments" had an unexpectedly negative impact on Lessing himself when Johann Melchior Goeze, the head of the congregation (*Hauptpastor*) in Hamburg, attacked Lessing as if he were himself an enemy of Christianity. Goeze wondered: How could one publish such a historical critique and still be a believer? That becomes the key question that Lessing attempts to answer. That is, in a series of short (and occasionally sharp and witty) exchanges with Goeze, Lessing attempted to show that it was necessary to publicize and criticize *bad arguments* for (or against) Christianity, but that this does not mean rejecting Christianity as such.

One of the key strategies, which opens the essay "Über den Beweis des Geistes und der Kraft" ("On the Proof of the Spirit and of the Power," 1777), employs the basic Leibnizian distinction between two kinds of truths, which Lessing calls *historical (accidental)* and *necessary (rational)* truths. The historical aspects of the Bible, the reports of prophecies and miracles, for example, are only "*accidental truths of history [and] can never become the proof of necessary truths of reason*" (*Theological Writings,* 53; his emphasis). Just because Lessing (and Reimarus) might critique those historical aspects does not entail a rejection of the Bible and its teachings. It just means that "I accept [them] on other grounds" (53). He needs "arguments more appropriate to my age" (52) in order to accept the basic teachings. If historical truths are *only* historical truths, if we do not expect too much of them (indeed, we *must* not expect too much of them), then we might accept or reject them, and they might be helpful to us in some edifying ways, but if they become a burden, we can drop them without fear. In this way he can be a skeptic about the historical grounds of Christianity.[13] This leaves the question, then, how the truths of Christianity are to be grounded more solidly.

Lessing offers a hint at how he might support what he would call true Christian belief even after the historical critique of the Bible when he states: "What does it matter to me whether the legend [i.e., tales of miracles, etc.] is false or true? The fruits are excellent" (55). Here he is not making a pragmatic argument in the style of Hume or the empiricists; rather, he is pointing to the core of an *ethical* argument.[14] At issue is not whether Christ performed miracles but whether "[his] teachings themselves" (55) are in keeping with basic ethical values that I can establish with my reason (and common sense).[15] At issue is not the Bible as a collection of complex philosophical or even divinely inspired doctrines but as a set of simple ethical ideas. In taking an *ethical* approach to theology, that is, in using ethical norms as the measure (*ratio,* or *logos*) for religious belief, Lessing was picking up on the tradition that we saw initiated by Erasmus's call to consider the "precepts of the morally good life" that are written "in our mouths and in our hearts" (*Discourse on the Free Will,* 10)—and against which Luther so vehemently warned for leading away from a strictly *Christian* and biblically grounded religion. Hence, in a satirical dialogue between a "He" (Goeze) and "I," Lessing defends an apocryphal statement attributed to John the Baptist over the Gospel according to John. This dialogue, entitled "The Testament of John," gives a sense of Lessing's style of writing and thinking.

I: Augustine relates that a certain Platonist said that the beginning of John's Gospel, "In the beginning was the Word," etc., deserves to be

---

13. Saine considers Lessing's introduction of historical arguments to be his greatest contribution (258).

14. This appeal to "fruits" of our beliefs and behavior is also at the core of Lessing's last great play on religious tolerance, *Nathan the Wise* (1779). He wrote it after the duke stepped into the dispute with Goeze and forbade Lessing from publishing any more on theological issues. At the center of the play is a famous "parable of the rings" in which the main character, the Jew Nathan, makes clear to the Muslim Saladin that the three major Western monotheisms are basically the same at heart. The only sign of a "true" religion should be in the ethical behavior of its believers.

15. Here again we see Lessing's Spinozist roots, since this kind of argument appeared in the preface to the *Theological-Political Treatise.*

inscribed in letters of gold in all churches in the most prominent places.

HE: Of course. The Platonist was quite right. Oh, the Platonists! Quite certainly Plato himself could not have written anything more sublime than these opening words of John's Gospel.

I: That may be. At the same time I, who do not make much of the sublime writing of a philosopher, think that it would be far more appropriate if what was inscribed in letters of gold in all our churches in the most prominent places was the Testament of John.

HE: Hm!

I: "Little children, love one another."

IIE: Yes, yes.

I: It was by this Testament of John that formerly one who was of the salt of the earth used to swear. Now he swears by the Gospel of John, and it is said that since this change the salt has become a little stale. (*Theological Writings,* 59–60)

Lessing is explicitly replacing the *logos* at the beginning of the Christian tradition with a simple call for ethical love. And given his prioritizing the unwritten law of the heart over the written Word, Lessing also makes a case for the so-called *regula fidei,* the rule or measure of faith that the early Christian community established and followed until it was superseded by the New Testament. He writes in the brief "Notwendige Antwort auf überflüssige Fragen" ("Necessary Answer to a Very Unnecessary Question of Herr Haupt-Pastor Goeze in Hamburg," 1778) that the *regula fidei* has an authenticity and divine nature that "can be proved far more easily and correctly than the authenticity of the New Testament writings" (*Theological Writings,* 63). Why? Because it holds up Christ as a "practical teacher" (as he says in § 58 of the *Erziehung des Menschengeschlechts* [*Education of the Human Race*], *Theological Writings,* 92). Unlike either the *regulae* of Descartes with their scientific rationality or the complications of the New Testament *logos* (which philologists are able to point out), the basic ethical norm of the *regula fidei* would be immediately evident to anyone employing reason. However, at this point Lessing himself stops. Both the censorship imposed by the duke and his own untimely death prevented him from ever really *showing* how these ethical truths work. He says that we are heading toward a time of "perfection" when people will recognize their ethical *duty,* i.e., to "do right because it *is* right" (*Theological Writings,* 96). But how we get to this perfection, how we define duty, how we recognize the "authenticity" of ethical rules—to these questions Lessing never provided answers. We see, therefore, that Lessing leads us up to the point where we need an ethical *argument*. He cleverly and often wittily offers pronouncements about the importance of morals, but it is up to Kant to give this turn to ethics philosophical rigor.

How does Kant in fact carry out the moral proof? We might initially point out that it would not be possible for Hume, whose concept of ethics was not based on reason but on human sympathies and the desire for well-being, an empirical basis from which only ground rules could be tentatively laid out but out of which no absolute principle (not to mention absolute being) could be derived. Ethics, according to Kant, however, rests solely on the basis of human autonomy, "the whole system of duties, which is known a priori with apodictic certainty through pure reason" (*Lectures,* 40). As strict as this is, and as extreme as Kant's occasional formulations are, there is also something commonsensical about it. After all, do we really say that someone performed an ethical act when the person has ulterior motives? Reasons like "because it felt good," or "because if I didn't, I'd break some law and be punished," or "because some higher authority wanted me to" might be common, but they do seem to compromise the ethical motivation (not to mention that they imply that, were those external conditions lacking, the person wouldn't have performed the action). Hence, the only real ethical reason to do something is because it's the right thing to do, and the only way to know what's right is to consult our own reason (via the categorical imperative, according to Kant), even if it goes against our feelings. All unethical, i.e., nonautonomous, motivations put us in a "passive" (*leidend*) state and are thus literally (etymologically) "pathological" (see *Critique of Practical Reason, Werke,* 5:32).

According to Kant, the moral law is derived analytically from the very idea of a rational agent. (Like "unmarried man" from "bachelor.") "This absolutely necessary morality of actions flows from the idea of a freely acting rational being and from the nature of action itself" (*Lectures,* 40). To be a rational agent means I fulfill the following three criteria:

1. I give myself my reasons for action from my reason. (Since otherwise I would be accepting reasons from outside that are not necessarily rational.) Those reasons cannot be reduced to my individual well-being, but must be in accord with universal reason. (In the same way that a rational scientific explanation must be repeatable.)
2. Also, if my reason (and the reason of any other individual for that individual's actions) is to be the grounds for my actions, then I can never be the means for another, but must be my own end.
3. My actions must be considered systematic as if they were a system of natural laws.

Kant also argues from the principle of noncontradiction. (This is another way of formulating the notion of "analytical" derivation.) My knowledge cannot contain contradictions. So, too, my actions can never be willed in violation of the law of noncontradiction. It is not enough that my prudent actions be consistent (since those actions contain lots of contingent factors, like my physical state, etc.). Rather, I must be sure that even my general maxims that guide such prudent behavior are universalizable without contradiction. In this way he arrives at the "categorical imperative" that serves as the sole basis for an ethical system: "Act as if the maxims of your will can at any time also be valid as a principle of universal legislation" (first formulated in the *Critique of Practical Reason, Werke,* 5:30) This statement contains nothing but a formal means for ensuring the rationality of my agency based on the three criteria just listed.[16]

Because Kant knows that we are contingent, physical beings, we cannot attain the Idea of perfectly rational, free, moral agents. Hence, the Law of Autonomy strikes us as a commandment, an imperative that is "imposed" on us. Hence, he says, we can never be "holy" but only "virtuous" insofar as we are engaged in an infinite "Progressus" of striving (*Critique of Practical Reason, Werke,* 5:32). Here we can understand "holy" ("*heilig*") also in a literal sense of "whole" ("*heil*"); human beings are by definition split between their spiritual and physical nature and must struggle against themselves rather than being at one with the law. But the only condition under which we would strive for virtue is because of the moral and theological idea of a highest good.

The fact that Kant derives his interest for theology from his (ethical) philosophy has two consequences for theology, the one immediate and negative, the other more mediated and ironically positive (even if somewhat forced). First, Kant does not hesitate to include ecclesiastical or scriptural pronouncements among the "external" motivations that cannot ground ethical behavior. It is precisely the attempt to impose or motivate actions primarily "because the Bible as a revealed text says so" that undermines and "corrupts" all ethics (which must be based on autonomous internal recognition of the morally good and not on "pathological" passivity). Such attempts to introduce external doctrines as the basis of good acts receive a number of negative terms in

---

16. It is formal because it contains itself no statement about what we should or should not do. Instead, it allows us to subject "maxims" ("Do not lie or steal . . .") to a process of reflection: What happens if we universalize this maxim? The ways we might formulate the universal lead to three versions of the categorical imperative, for example, as if your maxims were natural laws, or so that no human being ought to be a means to an end (see the *Groundwork for the Metaphysics of Morals* [*Grundlegung der Metaphysik der Sitten*], in *Werke,* 4:421, 429).

Kant's writings, esp. in *Religion within the Bounds of Mere Reason:* "dogma"; "*Afterdienst*" (a difficult term to translate; Allen Woods calls it "counterfeit service," and reminds us that "*After*" in fact means "anus"; perhaps we could think of it as "anal service" since that would capture the repetitive obsession with detail); "church" or "eclesiastical faith" (which emphasize the priority of community, ritual, litany); and "*Pfaffentum*" (clericism). Revelation ("*Offenbarung*") by definition falls into this category as well since it comes to us from outside ourselves. Here Kant, like Lessing, is extending the Protestant critique of historical "positivity" of religion into the very history of Protestantism itself.

The second, more mediated, indeed in some respects surprising, consequence is that Kant does not stop with this explicit rejection of the external, repetitive, representational aspects of belief but instead uses his ethics to bring them back for a significant rerun. Kant argues that a rational ethics based on the categorical imperative would turn irrational in a world that did not presume the possibility for an ethical person to be capable of receiving just deserts for his or her actions. Not that rewards or punishments may be the motivation for action (that would compromise them). But were "nice guys" *really* to "finish last," there would be no reason to be a nice guy. Now, it sure *seems* as if nice guys finish last. But that's where *seeming* must be distinguished from *things in themselves*. The world as we see it, as it seems to us, cannot be the only one, for otherwise our rationality would not make sense—and under such contradictions, quite literally, all hell would break loose. Hence, the only way to save our rationality and ethics is to imagine a creator who has endowed the world with an ethical order. God thereby emerges with certain ethical qualities out of the need ("*Bedürfnis*") for our practical reason to maintain itself: God is holy, good, all-powerful, and just—because He *must* be, for us (*Religion innerhalb*, 139).[17]

Finally, in one last twist to his reintroduction of religion for philosophical reasons, Kant connects religion in an essential way to aesthetics. Because we

---

17. Bertrand Russell's version of this argument debunks it roundly: "Then there is another very curious form of moral argument, which is this: they say that the existence of God is required in order to bring justice into the world. In the part of this universe that we know there is great injustice, and often the good suffer, and often the wicked prosper, and one hardly knows which of those is the more annoying; but if you are going to have justice in the universe as a whole you have to suppose a future life to redress the balance of life here on earth. So they say that there must be a God, and there must be Heaven and Hell in order that in the long run there may be justice. That is a very curious argument. If you looked at the matter from a scientific point of view, you would say, 'After all, I only know this world. I do not know about the rest of the universe, but so far as one can argue at all on probabilities one would say that probably this world is a fair sample, and if there is injustice here the odds are that there is injustice elsewhere also'" (*Why I Am Not a Christian*, 10).

lack knowledge of God in any conceptual, theoretical sense, and yet need Him to save our rationally grounded ethics, we can say only that we act "*as if*" God were a certain kind of being that would secure our ethics and the ultimate goal of a kingdom in which deeds are rewarded justly (what he calls the "Kingdom of Ends"). Kant stresses this many times, pointing out that the truth of the Bible rests in its moral content while all other aspects must be adopted by our reason *as if* they were true to the extent that they lead us to live better lives: "The divinity of [the Bible's] moral content justifies this statement: that the Bible deserves to be kept, put to moral use, and assigned to religion as its guide *just as if (gleich als ob) it is a divine revelation*" (*Conflict*, 118/119; Kant's emphasis).[18] As Cassirer points out, the human need for such an *as if*, the need to imagine and depict the moral order as the result of a creator, is ultimately an appeal to *aesthetic consciousness*.[19] Religion and art would meet in this "*Grundtendenz*" to re-present via the "schematism of analogy" (*Kants Leben*, 408). This helps explain the emergence of the third *Critique* not out of mere systematic necessity but out of Kant's explanation of the human need for a religious imagination.

Religion and Radical Evil

The second important reason Kant has for dealing with religion has to do not just with his fundamental interest in regrounding theology through morality but relates to a dialectic that emerges out of the tension between his rationalist ethics and the reality of human (bodily) existence, a dialectic that will raise the question of evil in new ways that have significant institutional consequences. The dialectic can be formulated as follows: in order to be ethical, human beings *must not* appeal to external motivations, and yet in order to be ethical, human beings *must also* appeal to some kind of external "schematization" or representation to provide motivation for their rational behavior. We need not only the singular statement of the law but the iteration of its visualizable application. The danger inherent in that secondary, though necessary repetition is that the schematization always threatens to assert itself as foundational, i.e., it might become dogmatic in a way that undermines ethics. This dialectic takes on two forms: on the one hand it can be conceived of as a simultaneity, a co-necessity of these two poles,

---

18. Because this edition is bilingual with facing pages, I give both the German (verso) and English (recto).

19. See the *Lectures*: "Man acts according to the idea of freedom, he acts *as if* he were free, and *eo ipso* he is free" (105).

the internal and the external, such that one never dissolves into the other. Viewed in this way, we can understand why Kant, in spite of the rigors of his Enlightened rationalist ethics, never abandons the need for appeals to religion, church, and scripture. They provide the necessary "mode of representation" (*Vorstellungsart*) without which reason's insights would be without influence (*Religion innerhalb*, 41). Kant locks the two poles—reason and religion, abstraction and representation, singularity and repetition— inextricably together. On the other hand, the dialectic can be conceived of temporally, i.e., as an unfolding conflict or *Kampf* of these two interactive poles, with the impossible (or better, eternal) goal being the victory of the rational over the dogmatic. The telos of "universality and unity of the essential articles/maxims of faith" (*Conflict*, 52/53) must be understood only as a regulative ideal and not as an existent or ever existing condition, providing only a measure (*Maßstab*) and directionality to deal with the "conflict that originates from what is inessential (or literally, beyond the essential)" ("Streit, der von dem Außerwesentlichen herrührt," ibid.). Religion is always becoming, again and again, what it is in its essence, namely, rational, but as *becoming* never *is* that essence. The issue is in large measure one of communicability and universalizability. The "religion of reason" can be communicated and shared (*mitteilen*) with all beings who partake of the same rational faculties, as opposed to the statutes of revealed religions, which are historical and empirical and thereby incapable of universal transmission.[20] The fact that some religions have experienced more or less universal or at least broad acceptance is merely a historical fact. Hence, the religion of reason and revealed religions, or philosophy and theology, speak different languages, or, more precisely, only the former speaks the truth of the latter. And the coexistence of two conflicting discourses and modes of exegesis leads to the institutional *Streit der Fakultäten* (*Conflict of the Faculties*, 1798).

And again we might want to compare Kant's conception of the inherent force of "positivity," the tendency of external and fixed forms of representation to emerge out of pure rationality, to Lessing. For, as was indicated above, Lessing's introduction of history into the very unfolding of religion (particularly, but not only, Christianity), is a complex dialectic. We have here not merely the rejection of the letter for the sake of the spirit. In the *Gegensätze* (counterpropositions of the editor), where he responds to his somewhat orthodox opponent (Goeze) and defends his publication of Reimarus's historical-philological critiques of the Bible, he seems to play

---

20. See *Religion innerhalb*, 114.

out a simple opposition: "The letter is not the spirit, and the Bible is not the religion. Consequently, objections against the letter and against the Bible are not the same thing as objections against the spirit and against the religion" (*Philosophical and Theological Writings*, 63). But this is actually more complicated for two reasons. First, it is not enough merely to turn to the spirit but, rather, there is a necessary double negation of the letter; there is no escaping history except by passing through history. Second, this could be why there is an irony in Lessing's most direct statement of a pure ethical religion, namely, the supposed "testament of John," by which he means not the Gospel but the simple phrase "Children, love one another" that captures the ethical core ("Das Testament des Johannis"). And yet, Lessing says, John *repeated* the phrase over and over, thereby enacting the re-petition of re-ligion, and the "I" says it is so divine that it should have been "inscribed in letters of gold in all our churches in the most prominent places" (*Theological Writings*, 60). The dialectic between the rational/natural/ethical spiritual core and the positive/dogmatic/literal representation is itself a part of the historical and living nature of religion.[21] This is the thrust of Lessing's argument in the *Education of the Human Race*, according to which different historical periods demand a different mode of representation (religion) to make the rational truths accessible in the first place.[22]

To get a sense of the force of this dialectic in Kant between reason and religion, between purity and corruption, abstract universality and repetitive representation, we should look at his discussion of evil in *Religion innerhalb der Grenzen der bloßen Vernunft* (*Religion within the Bounds of Mere Reason*). There Kant insists that humans have a "natural disposition" to "inversion" and "perversion" (*Verkehrung, perversitas*), a "turning" back or "reversal" of moral dictates. This disposition is such a part of us that "the mind's attitude is thereby corrupted at its root" (30). As the final section of this work makes clear, such a tendency to turn the dogma and rituals into the grounds of faith, i.e., to make a positive religion or church out of "natural" reason and morality, is at the heart of the actions of the clergy (and "higher faculties" at the university). But because this evil is as "natural" to us as our reason, we can only be engaged in an endless battle: "This evil is *radical*, since it corrupts

---

21. An insight that the young Hegel develops in his theological manuscripts on the "Positivity of the Christian Religion" during the 1790s. See the *Frühe Schriften*.

22. In *Theological Writings* (82–98). See also "On the Proof," referring to the true "teachings themselves": "Eighteen hundred years ago they were so new, so alien, so foreign to the entire mass of truths recognized in that age, that nothing less than miracles and fulfilled prophecies were required if the multitude were to attend to them at all" (*Theological Writings*, 55).

the ground of all maxims; as natural propensity, it is also not to be *extirpated* through human forces. . . . Yet it must equally be possible to *overcome* this evil, for it is found in the human being as acting freely" (37). Out of the very core of human reason arises the propensity and need both to rely on external representations ("positive" laws and religions) and to guide them back to their underlying ideals. The critique of religion is therefore never "done" since neither religion, nor its propensity toward positivity, nor the very effort of critique to "be done" with religion, can be eradicated. Ironically, the best we can hope for is to overcome this repetition compulsion— again, and again. Religion and rationality are caught in a dialectical dance, circling back on each other even as they (hopefully, for Kant) move forward toward a resolution at the end of time. Such a model has tremendous force in helping us understand how each of these poles is constantly reasserting itself at different moments of a society's or institution's development.

Religion and the University

The third, not unrelated, reason why Kant had to turn to discussions of religion is more directly pedagogical and political—it is a matter of what and how people are to be *taught* in order to produce freely acting, rational agents, or, more precisely and contradictorily, subjects. Christianity, he argues in *Religion within the Bounds of Mere Reason,* cannot demand absolute, i.e., unquestioned, belief, for then it would be *fides servilis,* "obedient belief" (164). Rather, it must be "taught" (*gelehrt*). But Kant sees a dangerous possibility here: "The small number of scriptural scholars (clerics), who might even not be lacking in secular knowledge, would drag [*schleppen*] along a long train of the uneducated (the laity), who don't understand scripture (among them worldly regents)" (164–65). In order to avoid such anti-enlightened tutelage at the hands of the clerics, "universal human reason . . . must be recognized and taught as the highest ordering principle in Christian doctrine" (165), while the doctrines of revelation, "upon which a church is founded and which require the scholars to interpret and preserve them, are to *be loved and cultivated as mere, but highly treasured, means*" (*als bloßes, aber höchst schätzbares Mittel;* 165, my emphasis). As in Lessing's *Education of the Human Race,* revelation becomes a helpful instrument of learning, a kind of primer allowing people to grasp the truths of reason more easily, only to be discarded once reason has in fact taken hold (*Theological Writings,* 87, 91, and 93). The clerics have been put in their place—but they *do* have their place. Yet things won't stay put for long, since religion has the habit, essentially, of returning.

What were the institutional consequences of this line of thought about religion and reason? The "Prussian reaction" instituted not only the censors but also controls on the university faculty since they did not like the sense that their authority was being challenged. Things reached a head in the middle of 1794. The university was not safe because the conservative, anti-Enlightenment ministers, Gottlob Friedrich Hillmer and Hermann Daniel Hermes, sat on the directorate (*Obercollegium*) and could thus place examiners on the boards for those seeking a degree in theology or philosophy. Hence, Kant had to deal with real issues "since they have gained influence in the universities, dictating how and what is to be taught there" (letter dated April 10, 1794; *Briefe*, 10:497). (Indeed, it seems that, unfortunately, precisely these kinds of battles at the university are destined to repeat themselves!) Given this "external" influence, Kant responded to a request for an essay with the idea for the *Streit der Fakultäten* (*Conflict of the Faculties*).

Kant's text is a compilation of three essays and a preface written between 1794 and 1798 in direct response to the battles he had with the Prussian censors. The three essays vary considerably in tone and content and are united only by an overarching architectonic order. The essays are intended to mirror in some sense the structure of the university, which was divided into the "lower" faculty—philosophy—and the three "higher" ones—theology, law, and medicine ("higher" because they are closer to extra-academic authority and power). Hence, each essay involves a conflict between philosophy and one of its disciplinary others. Moreover, the entire work deals with the relationship between the university and the public/political sphere.

Kant's first attempt at a solution to the conflict is, even on his own terms and given his own experiences, wholly inadequate. He seems to propose that the faculties simply keep their distance. The government's job, he states explicitly, is to control the population (*Conflict*, 20/21f). In order to do this, the authority of government (the monarch) issues a "pure command" from "on high" as it were (like the divine revelation behind the Bible), that establishes a canon (*Kanon*) of what is right and wrong. It is the job of those academics closest to the government, i.e., those in the "higher faculties"—theologians, jurists, and doctors—to interpret this canon, to make it an "organon" for the maintenance of authority and control "at the behest of the government" (28). It is therefore in their interest as the "businessmen" "(*Geschäftsmänner*) of the university, as well as in the interest of philosophers, to avoid any mutual contamination (he uses *anstecken*, 24) or miscegenation (*Mißheirath*, 22) between philosophy and the other faculties. And yet, what makes Kant particularly interesting and fruitful is that this split turns out to be ultimately less a separation than an "internal split," or, as Slavoj Žižek calls it, following Lacan, a "crack in the universal." That is, the point where a wished-for isolating separation is called for becomes in fact the site of conflict and contestation. We might visualize these relationships with the simple diagram in figure 3.1.

Herein lies the inherent dynamic that guarantees the continuation of conflict between the faculties. On the one hand, Kant argues, so long as "the people" desire "simple" solutions, they will find the power-hungry "higher faculties" willing to oblige them, challenging the very right of philosophy to speak at all. Such a conflict, consisting of and "resolved" by pure power plays that leave nothing to an Althusserian or Foucauldian imagination, Kant calls "illegal" (*gesetzwidrig*), and it has the potential of being "eternal" (*ewig*) and "an essential and irreconcilable" one (30/31). On the other hand, the very nature of the arbitrary dictates of authority brings them as such in conflict with the critical functioning of reason (54/55). This conflict, according to Kant called "legal" because it arises from the very nature of power, "cannot and should not be settled by an amicable accommodation (*amicabilis compositio*), but (as a lawsuit) calls for a verdict, that is, the decision of a judge (reason)" (54/55). In both cases, the split nature of the institutional and political will results in the inevitability, indeed desirability, of conflict. Kant writes: "[This conflict] can never end, and it is the philosophy faculty that must always be prepared to keep it going. . . . Consequently, the philosophy faculty can never lay aside its arms in the face of the danger that threatens

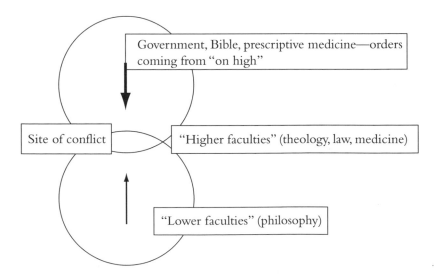

FIGURE 3.1. Site of conflict and contestation.

the truth entrusted to its protection, because the higher faculties will never give up their desire to rule" (54/55).

We can see how this model of conflicting institutional wills functions in Kant's analysis of the interaction between philosophy and theology (the institutional form of the general relationship between reason and religion). There is no doubt that Kant would put the biblical theologians in their place given the fact that the goal—eternal life—depends on a moral life, which can only be lived by following one's own reason, and not the dictates of others: "The biblical theologian says: 'Search the Scriptures, where you think you find eternal life.' But since our moral improvement is the sole condition of eternal life, the only way we can find eternal life in any Scripture whatsoever is by putting it there. For the concepts and principles required for eternal life cannot really be learned from anyone else: the teacher's exposition is only the occasion for him to develop them out of his own reason" (62/63). Kant so far seems to be adopting the antireligious strain of the Enlightenment, giving all priority to the internal voice of reason over the repetitive representations of the church. And Kant wondered why he had troubles with the ecclesiastical censors?

And yet Kant was not being disingenuous when he said that there was no reason for the church or state to be concerned with his teachings because the dialectic we saw at work in his philosophy of religion does give religion an institutional role to play. The "external," community-building, and visualizable aspects of religion are indeed *also* necessary after all as a "supplement" ("*Ergänzung*" or "*Ersatz*"; 76/77) to provide humans with a motivation to *do* what they know *without* these things they *should* do. Religion might not be essentially (i.e., in its material) different from the moral laws, but it is "formally" since it *takes on a form* that is necessary to influence us to act better, i.e., to be rational. In an important sense, a circle turns back on itself: "Reason in its legislation uses the Idea of God, which is derived from morality itself, to give morality influence on man's will to fulfill all his duties" (60/61). That is, religion and faith in God emerge out of morality in order (only) to assist in the practice of morality—not to dictate what morality is. But such a "second-order" use of religion is as necessary to the practice of practical reason as is reason itself.

Thus, Kant reaches a compromise not unlike Lessing's. He can accept the Bible as "a means to the introduction [of religion] among people," even a "supernatural means" (78/79), and recognizes the role that scriptures in other religions play as well, leading us to live "as if" our morals were guaranteed from on high, and making it easier—indeed, possible—to imagine a just world. This compromise, of course, is not a lasting peace. The use of the subjunctive ("as if ") and the relationship between source and means and end—the moral law of practical reason and scripturally based religion and a world of morally responsible agents—are inherently tenuous. Orthodoxy, or *Pfaffentum,* will always attempt to give the scriptural letter a greater role than that of the aesthetic means that we rely on to imagine our moral duties. And reason or philosophy must always apply its double hermeneutic of (1) comparing religious statutes to what we can *think* is right, and (2) looking to the *effects* ("*Wirkung*") beliefs have on people's behaviors.

This is a compromise that was destined to collapse for many reasons. And yet, even as we continue to pursue its (necessary, or at least historical) demise, we should think of the benefits such a compromise can confer on us. By giving a priority to rationally grounded moral principles, making them the "beginning" and *logos,* Kant does offer a means for judging, evaluating, and comparing religious doctrines. Those running directly counter to universalizable laws can and should be questioned. On the other hand, religious practices and communities have a significant role to play in organizing and motivating individual and social life in the direction of rational morality.

 **CHAPTER 4**

Hegel

Logos *as Spirit* (Geist)

> God is dead. Negation is within Spirit itself. (Gott ist tot. Die Negation ist in Geist selbst.)
>
> —Hegel, *Vorlesungen über die Philosophie der Religion* (*Lectures on the Philosophy of Religion*)
>
> A contradiction between thought and faith, thinking and believing, is therefore the most torturous alienation [diremption] in the depths of Spirit. (Ein Widerspruch des Denkens gegen diesen Glauben ist daher die qualvollste Entzweiung in den Tiefen des Geistes.)
>
> —Hegel, *Vorlesungen über die Beweise vom Dasein Gottes* (*Lectures on the Proofs of God's Existence*)

We can get an initial sense of Hegel's position within the long development of theological thought that we have been pursuing by considering again some passages from Goethe's *Faust* that capture what Hegel would have called the "Bedürfnis seiner Zeit," the lack in and need of his age, to which he was offering a philosophical response.[1] After Faust, the weary academic, quickly rejected the translation of "Word" (*Wort*) for *logos,* he turned instead to "sense/meaning" (*Sinn*). But sense, too, seemed, in principle, too abstract, and so Faust tried "force" (*Kraft*) before finally settling on "deed" (*Tat*)—or at least that translation was enough to call forth Mephistopheles and set the play in motion. The implication is, of course, that any notion of *logos* as *merely* "spiritual" remains *opposed* to deed and tied still to the *vita contemplativa* from which Faust hopes to escape. Likewise, when Gretchen later in the play poses her famous question to Faust—"What do you think of religion?"—he responds with a fiery speech that rejects any attempt to *name* God, turning instead to *feeling:* "Feeling is all! The rest

---

1. See especially the introduction to his early essay, "Differenz des Fichteschen und Schelling-schen Systems der Philosophie" ("Difference between Fichte's and Schelling's Systems of Philosophy," 1801).

is sound and smoke" (l.3415).[2] In an interesting variation of the Pauline expression, Faust seems to be saying that *both* the letter *and* the spirit are deadly when it comes to religion since neither captures the living and experiential activity that makes for a true relation to the divine.

Faust here is expressing some of the dominant approaches to religion to which Hegel feels called to respond. On the one hand, the religion of the "deed" expresses the tendency of some (like Lessing) to consider only one's moral actions in judging the appropriateness or truth of religious conviction. As Nathan the Wise says in the parable of the ring (from Lessing's play named after that character), the genuine ring—the true faith—has the power to make one act in such a way that one earns the father's—God's—favor. Moreover, the emphasis on deed speaks to those who have learned through the seventeenth and eighteenth centuries to concentrate on the wonders of *this* world, its astonishing physical and mathematical regularity, in justifying their faith in God.[3] Finitude (Hegel's more philosophical term for the turn to the "deed") has become the sphere within which human beings must act, and it alone becomes the ground of religion. On the other hand, a subjectivist turn rejects the external symbols and practices of established religion for the experience of the divine that can be felt individually but not objectified. Philosophers like Jacobi and especially Schleiermacher, and movements like Pietism, in the late eighteenth and early nineteenth centuries, come to see the essence of religiosity neither in dogma nor in practice but in the intensity of a particular inner feeling. (We will pursue Schleiermacher's understanding of religion in greater detail in the next chapter.)[4]

Hegel responds to both the empirical and subjectivist tendencies of his time by embracing the notion of God's *logos* as spirit (*Geist*), whereby his entire philosophical enterprise rests on the demonstration that genuine comprehension (*begreifen*) of spirit reveals the breakdown of the oppositions that motivated Faust. That is, in the beginning and end was *Geist,* but that

---

2. See Smith, "*Die Gretchenfrage,*" on Goethe's relation to contemporary philosophies of religion, and Wilkinson on the theological background of this call to feeling.

3. Since Goethe composed the translation scene around 1800, he likely has Johann Gottlieb Fichte in mind, who made the ethics of deed and action (*Tathandlung*) the heart of his Idealism.

4. Consider Hegel's early reference to Schleiermacher: "A phenomenon such as the *Speeches on Religion* may not immediately concern the speculative need. Yet they and their reception—and even more so the dignity that is beginning to be accorded, more or less clearly or obscurely, to poetry and art in general in all their true scope—indicate the need for a philosophy that will recompense nature for the mishandling that it suffered in Kant and Ficht's systems" ("Differenz der Fichteschen und Schellingschen Systems der Philosophie," 13).

spirit should not be considered "mere" spirit, for it *is* or has existence only insofar as it also expresses itself (takes on shape, becomes real in deed), assuming an objective form. While that spirit must be experienced subjectively in feeling, that experience is only part of the broader act of comprehension. He states this principle and project in what might almost be considered his version of the prologue to the Gospel of John near the opening of the "Philosophy of Spirit," book three of the *Enzyklopädie der philosophischen Wissenschaften* (*Encyclopedia of Philosophical Sciences*):

> *The absolute is Spirit;* this is the highest definition of the absolute. One can say that it has been the absolute goal of all cultural development and philosophy to formulate this definition and to grasp its meaning and content. All religion and science have been driven to this point and all world history is to be understood solely on the basis of this inner drive. The mere word for and *image* of spirit was found long ago, and the Christian religion has as its core content the knowledge that God is spirit. The task of philosophy, however, is to grasp in its proper element as concept and *in itself* as essence what has until now been merely *given* as an idea or image. Hence, the task of philosophy cannot be truly and immanently solved so long as it does not take conceptual thinking and freedom as its object. (§ 384; Hegel's emphasis)

Hegel thereby develops a theology or philosophy of religion that inverts the earlier reigning model. Rather than looking for a "God of science," i.e., a God that is modeled on the kind of understanding that the natural sciences first have of the world, Hegel attempts to develop a "science of spirit" or a *Geistes-Wissenschaft*[5] of God, a systematic conceptual approach that can *grasp* the absolute spirit. By including the tactile and abstract aspects of *begreifen*—to conceive intellectually is to grasp—Hegel can avoid the oppositions between knowledge and experience that plagued Faust at the opening of the play.[6] That is, while Leibniz and others had a natural scientific understanding of God (the grand geometer), and Kant a moral one (the

---

5. This term is often translated as "humanities," but that loses the broad meaning of spirit that it contains.

6. It might seem as if Hegel's approach can be considered a "flight" from religious experience into the world of the "concept." Hegel himself says: "Indeed, religion must flee into philosophy" (taken as an epigraph to the collection of essays by Graf and Wagner, *Die Flucht in den Begriff*). But my point here is that his philosophy of spirit is also profoundly religious.

grand judge), Hegel's God is *spiritual* in a new sense defined by him, i.e., religion is defined in terms of a living *Geist,* both objective and subjective, both transcendental and concrete. He spends much time differentiating this approach from those of Enlightenment thinkers and Romantics (Schelling, Schleiermacher) that generate oppositions—knowledge vs. faith, science vs. feeling, finite vs. infinite—or more precisely, he needs to show how his approach incorporates (sublates, *aufhebt*) those other positions. In so doing, Hegel develops an insistently *historical* view of religion. If for Spinoza God was identical with substance, for Hegel God reveals himself in the historical unfolding of a spirit, which, as he says, is both substance and subject. He sees himself making the greatest attempt to save religion from the limited versions of his age; after all, he argues, any conception of God that is limited (*merely* abstract, *merely* scientific, *merely* moral, *merely* feeling) ultimately limits mankind, God, and any possible relationship between them. However, as we will see, the powerful claim that human reason can grasp the divine because both are of the same *Geist* has a radical consequence (which Feuerbach pursues most forcefully); namely, in developing theology or philosophy of religion as a science of spirit, a *Geistes-Wissenschaft* that is its own product, the human spirit is grasping *itself* as much as it is *God.* The reality of God in human history makes human history divine.

To understand Hegel's approach to religion, then, we must show first, relatively briefly, how his conception of God is defined in terms of *Geist* and then unpack the significance of that concept, how it unites the oppositions that previous theologies maintained. It does so because *Geist* exists only as process and activity. But to show that, we will have to review how Hegel arrived at this philosophical and theological concept himself through a process of intellectual development, starting with his theological manuscripts (and the central ideas of *life* and the historicity of religion), proceeding through the Jena writings (1801–5) and the *Phenomenology* (with their critiques of the oppositions of his day), to his later philosophy of religion. Hegel's return to an "ontological proof" for the existence of God, we will see, arises not out of an abstruse interest in Scholasticism but because he sees in such proofs the principle confirmed that spirit unites being and thought, the same principle that motivated the *logos* of his *Science of Logic.* Hegel offers arguably the greatest philosophical justification of religion by means of his radical identity of thinking and being, God and reality. And yet, that identity will bring serious consequences for the following century since the notion of God's union with the world can lead to a loss of the sense of God's transcendence. Here we see Hegel's contribution both to the arguments for God's existence and to the slippery slope leading to his death.

God as Unifying *Geist* and Religion as *Geistes-Wissenschaft*

In 1822, when his student Hermann Friedrich Wilhelm Hinrichs published a book on the philosophy of religion, Hegel provided the introduction in order both to give support to a young Hegelian's academic career (and thus to further his own cause) and to lay out his own position on theological thought in his day.[7] Hegel's argument summarizes, often in a sharp polemical tone, ideas that he had been developing over the previous three decades. Playing on an ambivalent formulation that echoes his earliest published writings, Hegel states that he must address the *Bedürfnis der Religion,* a phrase that means both the *lack* that characterizes theological discussions of his day and the *need* within his day for a truer conception of religion. By understanding the source of the lack and how Hegel's version of God as *Geist* would meet the need, we can get a good initial overview of his position.

The "illness/evil of his age" (*Übel der Zeit*) that Hegel sees results from a process whereby philosophical thought on religion had applied limited concepts, predicates, or determinations to God. This tendency to try to pin down God by defining Him as an X or Y Hegel associates with the faculty of the understanding (*Verstand*) or "reflection"—as opposed to Reason (*Vernunft*), which operates at a higher level by seeking unities. Although we will pursue the "dialectic of the Enlightenment" that he presents here in more detail below, it is worth quoting this version at some length. Hegel provides a summary of the dialectical unfolding of the course of theological thought over the past two hundred years:

> This is, in brief, the basic outline of the path that formal reflection has taken in relation to religion. The first sin that arose within religion itself was a system of clever metaphysical and casuistic differentiations and definitions, into which the understanding shattered the unified content of religious thought and placed as much authority as if it were eternal truth. The seed of the next sin, even though it might seem like the opposite, already lay in the first and hence is a logical development out of it; namely, it is the sin of thought rising up independently, using the very formal weapons it owes to that system empty of content, which was its first activity, and rebelling against religion, turning pure abstraction itself into the highest, indeterminate Being. It is interesting for philosophy to consider how this turning

---

7. See von der Luft for English translations of all the texts in this debate.

of its former activity into the enemy is both a surprise for reflection (*Reflexion*) and yet the very nature of reflection itself. (von der Luft, 250; translation modified)

Hegel seems to have in mind the wealth of "clever" proofs for the existence of God that emerged during the seventeenth and eighteenth centuries, the use of the advances made in specific disciplines (esp. natural science) to justify faith, and then the turn against those proofs from precisely the best minds of the Enlightenment (Hume, Lessing, Kant). What Hegel here calls "*Reflexion*" we can consider the scientific *logos* that was applied to theology— only to collapse under its own logic.

According to Hegel, such a failure or lack in theological thought has led to a "critical" situation in both the common and Kantian senses of the term. That is, theology is in crisis and Kant's "Critical Philosophy" has responded by establishing principled arguments for why (theoretical) reason must be kept within its limits and not venture into the realm of metaphysical truths. Hegel associates this limiting of reason with the victory of the "understanding," i.e., the faculty capable of dealing with the finite conditions of the world (what Kant calls the "phenomenal" world of "appearances"). The triumph of this principle has disastrous consequences for religion in Hegel's view: "The evil into which the Enlightenment has brought *religion* and *theology* may be defined as a privation *of known truth, of an objective content, and of a doctrine of religious belief*" (von der Luft, 251; Hegel's emphasis).[8] Precisely the power of the mind to understand all the causes and laws of the natural universe, this power that so moved the thinkers of the seventeenth and eighteenth centuries, has led them to think only in terms of such causes and laws. What cannot be understood this way takes on the opposite status of *mere* faith, mystery, feeling, superstition. (Recall Kant's claim in the preface to the *Critique of Pure Reason* that he wanted to put reason within its limits in order to make room for faith.)

While Hegel as a post-Enlightenment, post-Kantian philosopher sees the benefit of the critique of the faulty "proofs" and of the misuse of reason, he rejects in principle any self-limitation of reason. It has resulted in a radically split approach to religion: on the one hand, philosophy withdraws from the

---

8. This formulation echoes Jacobi's critique of Spinoza and all rational attempts to ground religion since they end up necessarily in "Nihilismus" (a term he coined) or "Fatalismus." See his *Über die Lehre des Spinoza* (122). We also have here an early formulation of a principle of nihilism within Christian theology/philosophy that will emerge again in the chapters on Nietzsche and Heidegger.

sphere of religion altogether, focusing on the realm of science (what Habermas comes to call "positivism") and "finitude"; on the other, the sphere of religion then takes on the character of a "beyond" all reason, accessible only to faith or feeling. This alienated state of contemporary thought, its inherent lack (*Bedürfnis*) generates the need (*Bedürfnis*) for a new understanding of religion. By definition, that new conception must be one that responds to the divisions by unifying them—it cannot avoid them lest they merely become hardened and ingrained. That is, the fundamental principle of the divine must be such that it is accessible to rational thought but not modeled on the rational discourses of the natural sciences. Kant, of course, did make a step in that direction insofar as he, too, said that "scientific" knowledge of God is impossible; but he limited access to theological truths to a subjectivist and formalist morality. Hegel's response will be to develop a concept that can unite finitude with the infinite, reason with feeling, form with content. That concept is *Geist*.[9]

At this stage, we at least can have a sense of what Hegel feels he needs to save religion/God *from* and what therefore his solution must accomplish. He rejects first of all the absolute division between a finite world "here" and a transcendent, infinite world "beyond." Moreover, in order not to collapse the two (a move that would be either Spinozism or atheism), he must also account for the differentiation we make between them. And second, he rejects the view that there are "truths" (divine, religious, absolute) that are inaccessible to our faculty of reason. Here too, however, he must also find a way to differentiate between modes of knowing so that, for example, scientific and historical and religious truths are not made identical. Hegel accomplishes his solution by means of his developmental conception of spirit. Religion, God, and spirit are basically identified as one and the same: "Spirit finds in religion its liberation and the feeling of its divine freedom; only a free spirit has, indeed can have, religion; it is the natural feeling of the heart, particular subjectivity, which is bound or limited in religion; what is set free in religion, and thus what can truly come into being, is precisely spirit" (*Enzyklopädie*, § 552). But note how the conceptions of religion and spirit are defined in terms of processes of becoming (and becoming free).

What is spirit and how is it in essence in a state of becoming? One aspect of spirit is consciousness. Considering how human consciousness unfolds

---

9. "God is Spirit, only for Spirit, and only for the pure Spirit, i.e. for thought [*logos?*]" (Gott ist Geist, nur für den Geist, und nur für den reinen Geist, d.1. für den Gedanken) (*Vorlesungen über die Beweise vom Dasein Gottes*, 17:356).

over time (the aim of the *Phenomenology*), Hegel focuses on the way it is the nature of human beings' experience of the world to encounter limitations and to overcome them. Indeed, it is the very nature of "the experience of consciousness" (the original subtitle of the *Phenomenology*) to proceed by adopting a position ("Now I've got the answer"), only to recognize that it was wrong ("I guess I was mistaken, but now I have learned from my experience," or, as one reads in many a Platonic dialogue, "I guess I didn't know what I was talking about, did I, Socrates?"), and hence to be pushed beyond oneself to a new position.[10] This movement is, as he implied above, a "liberating" one, and hence spirit and freedom, both viewed as *processes,* are inseparable. This basic process, which is so clear in consciousness, is not limited to consciousness, however. As we shall see, it is inherent in life, social institutions, and indeed being itself. The process itself *is,* according to Hegel, *Geist.* Spirit *is* this unfolding through negation, this process, to use the Nietzschean term, of "self-overcoming," this movement of the finite beyond itself. Spirit is not some "thing" independent of its becoming.[11] A religion of spirit is, then, modeled on a new concept that unifies the opposites—thinking and feeling, self and other, reason and faith—by grasping the process underlying them. That systematic "grasping" is what Hegel calls *Wissenschaft.* He worked it out in the *Phenomenology of Spirit* in such a way that it leads to a startling conclusion about religion: the experience of consciousness is that every object, as foreign and Other as it might at first appear, is grasped in an act through which consciousness in fact re-cognizes itself. (The notion of something "wholly Other" literally makes no sense for Hegel. Insofar as something is knowable, it shares its being with us. Hence he, and the tradition he gives rise to, stands in opposition to the "crisis" theology of Karl Barth et al., explored below in chapter 8.) This notion of cognition as re-cognition involves a change of the self and the object. When I have an experience, some aspect of the world is opened up to me, and I, too, am influenced by it. The new object that emerges needs in turn to be mediated through yet more experiences. Hegel passes through a series of objects—"things" out there, perceptions/qualities of things, the essence of things, other consciousnesses, social structures that are opposed to individuals (until the two become medi-

---

10. The link to Platonic dialogue shows the origin of this dialectical approach.

11. Here we need to recall Nietzsche's wonderful critique of the false separation of the "lightning" from its "striking" in the second essay of *On the Genealogy of Morals,* § 14. And also Nietzsche's (rare) praise of Hegel for introducing the notion of being as becoming and thereby laying the foundation for Darwinism. See *Die fröhliche Wissenschaft (Gay Science),* § 357, "On the Old Problem, 'What Is German?'"

ated, i.e., enter into a free relationship), etc. One might wonder: What about the relationship of consciousness to the highest, most absolute, most transcendent, most Other "object," God? That relationship also passes through many stages until (as is the core idea of Christianity) it is recognized that God is man and man is God. That identity is captured in the idea of *Geist*. But to understand how *Geist* can carry the weight Hegel puts on it, we must show its own emergence in his thought.

The Concept of Life and the Historical Spirit of Christianity

Lessing died at the peak of his intellectual powers, only fifty-two years old, in the year that Kant published the first edition of the *Critique of Pure Reason*. Many have already speculated on what might have been if Lessing had lived to critique the *Critique,* to bring his own stylistic brilliance to bear on what was to become the notorious density of Idealist philosophical prose. But in one important sense, Lessing did live on—in Hegel. In the years before his death, Lessing grappled with the radical *historicity* of religions, the way they came to take on forms that must be shed, like a snake's skin, so that they might develop into a more mature mode of accounting for a more mature human condition. Kant, we saw, expanded this temporal development in his understanding of the necessity of "radical evil" and the endless struggle for virtue. His goal was to regulate the human faculties so that forms of unreason could be called to account before the "court" of reason or philosophy. This regulation would take place both in the abstract—his writings— and in practice—institutions like the university. Hegel's early writings on religion, his unpublished theological manuscripts, in many ways take up Lessing's historical understanding with the frame of Kantian philosophy. "The Positivity of the Christian Religion" ("Die Positivität der christlichen Religion"), "The Spirit of Christianity" ("Geist des Christentums"), and other unpublished essays on morality and love written in the 1790s make the argument that inherent within the unfolding of (the Judeo-Christian) religion[12]—and by extension in all human spiritual endeavors—there exists a tension that pulls it inevitably toward both a rigidifying "positivity" and a liberating renewal. While in many ways the young Hegel was using these writings to position himself as a writer to usher in an eventual renewal in

---

12. I will henceforth drop the parenthetical specification, but it is understood throughout. Hegel deals explicitly and exclusively with both Judaism and Christianity.

philosophy,[13] his early treatment of religion has profound implications both for the later nineteenth century and for us insofar as it allows for the study of religion as a historical entity.

The two ideas that dominate his early thinking on religion are the importance of "life" and the process by which religious institutions undergo change over time. They are closely linked and form the foundation of Hegel's mature philosophical and conceptual thought. Indeed, Bernhard Lypp argues that in these early writings, even before Hegel has developed his theoretical philosophy, "the first dialectical conceptual formations" take shape (296–97). While Lypp focuses on Hegel's engagement with Kant's ethical philosophy, I think in fact it is more accurate to see him motivated in these unpublished manuscripts by the status of *religion* (understood, of course, in its relationship to morality). Thus we see how religious issues accompanied Hegel throughout his entire career as a philosopher and influenced the formation of his conceptual apparatus.

The guiding notion of "life" underlying his writings was given a more formalized philosophical description in the fragments Hegel wrote while working as a house tutor in Frankfurt in the latter half of the 1790s. He was in contact again with his friend from his years as a student of theology in Tübingen, Friedrich Hölderlin, who exerted considerable influence on these early formulations.[14] Hegel characterizes life in terms that will reappear in both the *Phenomenology* and the *Logic*,[15] namely, a cyclical (or better, a spiral-like) process of undeveloped unity through opposition to a higher unification of opposites (here called "love"):

> Life finds itself in it [love] as a doubling and unity of itself; in *Bildung* (cultivation, formation, development) life has passed through the circle from undeveloped to complete unity; the world and the possibility of separation stood opposed to the undeveloped unity; during development, reflection produced more and more oppositions, which are united in the satisfied drive, until it [reflection] opposes the entire human being to itself and then love sublates reflection in a state of total objectlessness, robes the opposed object of its character of foreignness, and finally life finds itself without further lack. (*Frühe Schriften*, 246)

---

13. See Smith, *Spirit and Its Letter*, esp. chapter 2.

14. See Dilthey's volume on *Die Jugendgeschichte Hegels*, as well as Lukács, *Young Hegel*, for studies of this period.

15. Discussion of life in *Phenomenology*, esp. the opening to the chapter on self-consciousness (which culminates in the master-slave dialectic); in the *Logic*, one of the culminating sections deals with "the life-process" ("*der Lebensprozess*").

Hegel gives here an abstract and general formulation of the process common to all forms of life—from single-cell organisms to human beings. It is a process through which each living entity, although contained within itself (as "undeveloped unity"), must also engage with the (opposing) environment in order to form higher unities (by taking in food, establishing symbiotic relations, mating, etc.). This pure activity of life can neither be reduced to any of its moments nor exist without all of the moments—i.e., death results both if life does not emerge out of its initial (false) unity into opposition and also if life gets caught in a state of separation without the possibility of fulfilled unification. It forms the conceptual model for Hegel's entire philosophy of spirit. From his first published essays in Jena (for example, the *Differenz des Fichteschen und Schellingschen Systems der Philosophie*) through the *Logic,* this movement of life drives nature, historical development, and thought itself.[16]

Hegel extends this understanding of life as process to explain the driving force of *all* unfolding development, also in the realm of historical and spiritual matters, by way of his reflections on the history of religion.[17] In a vein akin to Lessing and Kant, he poses a rhetorical question in an early fragment, "Die Positivität der christlichen Religion" ("The Positivity of the Christian Religion," 1795/96) about the ironic way that Christianity has become an ossified set of formal ("positive") laws that are "given" to believers without any of the original inner feeling:

> How could one have anticipated that such a teacher [Christ], who spoke out not against the established religion itself but against the moral superstition that one fulfills the demands of the laws of morality by observing religious customs; who strove for a concept of virtue grounded not on authority but on inner free virtuousness—who could have anticipated that such a teacher would himself have given rise to a positivistic religion, i.e., one based on authority and which posits human value either not at all or at least not solely in morality? (*Frühe Schriften,* 108)

For Hegel, even institutions have a "life." They unfold by means of a complex though regular and systematic process from unity through opposition

---

16. Seeing this process as "life" helps us avoid that overly simplified schematic of "thesis-antithesis-synthesis."

17. For an excellent summary, see *Religion in Geschichte und Gegenwart* (3rd ed.), s.v. "Hegel": "Of central significance for the young Hegel are the concepts of *life* and *love*. . . . Life is the most originary unity and the fundamental characteristic of all reality. But it can become opposed to itself and dissolve its unity in *Reflexion*. The task of love is to mediate this opposition anew."

to higher-level unity. To the extent that an institution (like a formal religion) can be defined as such, it possesses some kind of fundamental unity. Like an organism, it is held together by a common functioning principle. But it can also force things together in an artificial and deadening way that maintains or highlights the oppositions rather than overcoming them. In another fragment he gives this process a more philosophical formulation as the imposition of the "objective" on the "subjective":

> A belief is called "positivistic" in which the practical is present in a theoretical form and [in which] the originally subjective is present only as something objective; a [positive] religion holds up ideas of something objective that can never become subjective *as the principle of life and actions*. . . . Practical unity [by contrast] is established by sublating the opposing object fully. (*Frühe Schriften*, 239; my emphasis)

This description of the way religions become "positivistic" over time (which, we will see, has remarkable parallels already to later formulations by Feuerbach on the essence of religion) shows that what lies at the heart of *true* religion is a "principle of life and actions" that allows for a renewal through a genuine sublation of the now unbearable oppositions. The historicity that leads to positivity and ossification does have the benefit of also opening up a new possibility. Indeed, opposition creates the need for unity. This is how life—and the life of the institution of religion—unfolds. Religion and philosophy are connected in their essence, according to Hegel, because they both respond to the need for/lack of existing oppositions by introducing a new unity. They do not merely posit identity (see below on *Enzyklopädie*), nor do they celebrate difference for its own sake but, rather, work through a tension that brings elements back together. Religion and philosophy are in this sense life and spirit.[18]

Religion and the Dialectic of Enlightenment (Understanding vs. Feeling)

But in this historical schema, where does Hegel find himself? What is the precise historical context of his own age? What are the false identities and imposing oppositions that need to be addressed? This is the place to turn to

---

18. In his lectures on proofs of the existence of God from 1827 he makes this connection explicit: "We see here again that the definition:'God is the universal activity of life, the soul that creates, posits, and organizes the cosmos,' this concept is not yet sufficient for the concept of God. The concept of God contains furthermore the idea that God is *spirit*" (17:521–22).

his analysis of his own culture, what he calls "the world of *Bildung*" and its paired opposites, pure insight and faith.[19]

In the last chapter we saw how Kant began to develop a dialectic between "true" (rational, moral) religion and its repetitive representations. The powerful insight that Kant introduced there is the notion of "radical evil," that is, the inevitability of the constant resurgence of the "pathological" in the world (or, institutionally, the impossibility of a final peace in the "conflict of the faculties"). And we saw how Hegel's theological manuscripts pushed this insight even further by historicizing it as a process of the life of the (human) spirit. In "Glauben und Wissen" ("Faith and Knowledge," 1802) Hegel takes the Kantian dialectic and holds it up as the core principle of the dominant philosophies of the day, what Hegel calls "philosophies of reflection." It becomes the source of Hegel's fundamental critique of both Kant and his age because Hegel sees the project of Critical Philosophy as leaving a mere opposition, especially between the unity and purity of human freedom (the realm of practical reason) and the heteronomy and dependency of the natural world (the realm of theoretical reason). According to Hegel, it takes on the general form/shape (*Gestalt*) "that a manifold/plurality stands absolutely opposed to its formal identity/unity" ("Glauben und Wissen," 329). Given the absolute nature of this opposition, Kant's world breaks down into a binarism of the knowable here and now and an ineffable beyond (the "in-itself"), a binarism that Hegel sees characterizing post-Kantian thought thus far:

> This character of Kantian philosophy is the general character of all the philosophies of reflection that we will be dealing with here, namely that knowledge is merely formal, and reason, which is defined as a purely negative force, gets located in an absolute "beyond," whereby it is the nature of all "beyond" and negativity to be determined by a "here" and a positivity. That is, the basic characteristic sees infinity and finitude as equally absolute in their pure opposition to each other. (332)

We can hear in this formulation an echo of Hegel's earlier views on the positivity and history of religions, here applied to philosophical systems—but with consequences for religion because the mistaken absolute separation of

---

19. I would also propose that "we," too, are in a state of heightened critical *Bildung* that is leaving the social fabric torn between those who are too enlightened for religion and those who see faith as antireason—even as we are "of one cloth." The fact that our world could be seen in terms of Hegel's analysis of the "world of *Bildung*" with its torn consciousness, raises interesting questions of repetition: Are we reliving his narrative? With what difference? Hegel, more than almost any other thinker, puts us into this paranoid frame of mind.

man from the "beyond" of the Absolute leads man to reestablish a relationship to the Absolute in the one sphere left open to him, namely, the inner realm of subjective feeling. In the case of Jacobi, only the inner world of the subjective becomes capable of "the beauty of feeling/sensation" (333). That is, the core of religion becomes feeling. "The common sphere of both philosophies [i.e., Kant's and Jacobi's] is the absoluteness of the opposition between finitude, nature, knowledge (thus defined implicitly as merely formal) on the one hand, and the supranatural, supersensual and the infinite; for both philosophies the true absolute lies in an absolute 'beyond' in faith or feeling and hence has the status of 'nothing' for the conceptual faculty of reason" (388). Especially Jacobi represents the emergence of the true, i.e., most extreme, form of "Protestant subjectivity" (387).

The *Phenomenology* paints the various vicissitudes, and the disastrous consequences, of the hardening of these oppositions (self vs. other, subjectivity vs. objectivity, feeling vs. reason, faith vs. knowledge, imagination vs. conceptual thinking), in greater detail and against the larger background of culture in general (not just philosophical systems). It captures the different theological conceptions of a historical period (the eighteenth century); but at the same time it lays out a conflict between religion and enlightenment in the general terms of a movement through ever-intensifying oppositions and the longing for their overcoming, terms that can be applied to our age as well.

The world of *Bildung* is one of alienation and "tornness" (*Zerrissenheit*). Culture has matured but become fragmented and alienated. Consciousness, at the level of the individual and the society at large, has reached the stage where critique is literally all the rage and the sign of being "cultured" (*gebildet*) is the ability to dig out the inner contradictions of any position:

> [The cultured consciousness] knows how to play one position against another, indeed knows that each position is nothing but the inversion of another; it knows what each position is better than it knows itself, regardless of what it is. By recognizing in any substantive position its moment of *disunity* and *contradiction,* it knows how to *judge/critique* any substantive position very well; but it has lost the ability to *grasp* it. (*Phänomenologie,* 390; Hegel's emphasis)

This mastery of the tools of rhetorical critique prides itself on the ability to tear everything apart. (On rhetoric specifically, see 386, 387, and 390). The effect on the self is equally disturbing since he concludes by defining this "pure consciousness as an alienated one" ("Dies *reine Bewußtsein* des absoluten Wesens ist ein *entfremdetes*"; 392).

The culture of alienation splits into two main modes of consciousness, the basic opposition of faith and insight (391): "insight" corresponds to the tendency of the cultured consciousness to celebrate pure form because it has the skill to empty out any content of its substantiality; "faith," on the other hand, insists on holding onto an inner core to which it assigns the "significance of an objective *being*" (394) untouched by the force of critical insight. This projection of a beyond—ironically projected *by* consciousness to be beyond the reach of consciousness—characterizes the religion of the day (392). Not that this is religion "in and of itself" (392), but given the *historical* mode that Hegel has introduced into the study of religion, he can account for the particular shape that religious consciousness has taken in modernity. Because these two opposites have the same origin as responses to modernity—"because faith and pure insight both belong to the element of pure consciousness, they are also both at the same time a return out of the real world of *Bildung*" (394)—they are tied together even in their opposition. They play off each other in an ever-escalating dance. Even as faith withdraws further inward to a realm of absolute peace, insight takes its task of enlightenment to the extreme, creating in itself the painful feeling of experiencing "the dissolution of everything fixed and firm, as if all moments of its existence were tortured on a rack and all bones crushed" (399). Since this passage occurs under the heading "Die Aufklärung" (The Enlightenment), and since Hegel had just offered as the dictum of this consciousness a version of Kant's famous definition—"*be (self-consciously) for yourselves* what you *are in fact already (in and of yourselves—namely, rational*" (398)[20]—we can think of Kant himself, whom Johann Georg Hamann called "the all-crushing" ("*der All-Zermalmer*"), as the model for this fundamental split.[21]

Of course, as we saw earlier, where life experiences division, it is also drawn by this internal lack/need (*Bedürfnis*) to find unity. So, too, at this stage, each side responds to its painful opposition by striving to impose itself on the other. Faith insists on its unchanging and inaccessible *beyond,* and Enlightenment falsely strives for a universal by merely making its insight "to the insight

20. Echoing the line from Kant's "Was ist Aufklärung?" ("What Is Enlightenment?"): "*sapere aude—habe Mut, dich deines Verstandes zu bedienen*" ("*sapere aude*—have the courage to make use of your understanding"; in Schmidt, 58).

21. Hegel offers a beautifully clear summary of this development in the first lecture on the proofs of the existence of God: thought, which must push itself to the point of extreme freedom from all faith/belief, leaves then the latter on its own, which now has adopted for itself the posture of absolute truth. Hegel calls this present state of things one of contradiction, collision, and diremption (*Vorlesungen über die Beweise vom Dasein Gottes,* 348–49).

of everyone" (399).[22] The result is a standoff: "That two equal rights/laws of the spirit stand opposed to each other and neither can offer satisfaction to the other" (417).[23] But precisely in this formulation we can get an inkling of the solution. Because both sides are in fact of the same "spirit," i.e., because each has produced the other and lives in misrecognition of its own origin, insight and faith need to recognize their status of mutual interdependence. Unity emerges not by the imposition of a (universal) solution as in a court case (one can think of Kant's conflict of the faculties) but by the collapse of the particular positions in their recognition of internal interrelationship. "True" insight into religion occurs on the ground of a higher unity of faith and knowledge that has emerged out of a process that changes the nature of both. Only having passed through this state of alienation can we experience a higher level of unity that would characterize religious consciousness. Or as he says in the *Lectures on the Philosophy of Religion:* "God is Spirit through the return from alienation to itself" (*Vorlesungen über die Philosophie der Religion,* 17:295) How might one conceive of such a movement?

Geist and the Unity of Thought and Being

The need of his time (*Bedürfnis der Zeit*) to rethink religion and philosophy in terms of a deeper conception of unity is why Hegel turns to a defense of ontological proofs. The issue for Hegel is neither a strictly speaking logical one (à la Anselm), nor a mathematical/scientific one (Descartes, Leibniz), nor a moral one (Kant), but a profoundly philosophical one. Philosophy, for Hegel, involves the identity of Being and Thought. Hence, the opposition between Being and Thought is the starting point in philosophy, the position that must be overcome or thought through. In the *Phenomenology of Spirit,* Hegel undertook the task of taking consciousness from the crassest point of opposition ("Here *I* am as consciousness, *that thing there* is Being") to the point where consciousness must realize that Being is infused with the categories of consciousness (as Kant has shown) and consciousness *is* only to the extent that it makes itself real (e.g., in social formations of "objective spirit"). In the *Science of Logic,* the endpoint of the *Phenomenology* is the starting condition, and Hegel shows how Being itself (i.e., not from the perspective of consciousness) unfolds dialectically (beginning with the identity of Being

---

22. This critical analysis of the Enlightenment is crucial and powerful and shows that Hegel cannot be so easily dismissed for imposing the universal.

23. At the height of this conflict comes the Enlightenment reduction of faith to mere superstition and then the Terror.

and Nothing in Becoming). Religion, therefore, is for Hegel nothing but a version of this absolute principle of philosophy. After all, religion declares that the Absolute is Real, in the various forms of spirits and deities that make up the world. Some remain on the level of "mere representation" (*blosse Vorstellung*) and do not capture this thought very well (e.g., by limiting the reality of the absolute to particular places or fetish objects); others come closer to grasping conceptually (*begreifen, in Begriffen*) the universality of this truth. But all reflection has in common the effort to attain a unity of finitude with the infinite, the world (of mankind) with God.

Ontological proofs for the existence of God are examples of a later and more sophisticated attempt—in Hegel's developmental and hierarchical scheme—to give expression to the truth of religion.[24] He writes: "The proofs of the existence of God have arisen from the *need within thought itself, to satisfy [the demands] of* reason" (17:348). That is, these proofs, as part of theological thinking, are already, so to speak, well on their way to being philosophy or bringing out the philosophical truth that is at the origin (*arche*, "in the beginning") and only needs to be brought out clearly. Thus, from Hegel's perspective, the thrust of all ontological proofs is legitimate insofar as they would demonstrate the reality of the thought of God; i.e., the reality of God is inseparable from the thought of God. That idea—expanded even beyond the application to God—is *the* philosophical enterprise. In this regard he must go against Kant and resuscitate the tradition, showing (1) that Kant's critique falsely "limited" the unity of thought and being to objects of experience, hence removing God from the realm of knowledge,[25] and (2) that the earlier proofs were on the right track, even if they did not (yet) know how to formulate their truth.

The problem of ontological proofs is that they start with the assumption that the thought of God, the concept of a supreme or highest or most perfect being, is just that—*only* a thought. To this extent they belong broadly speaking to the modern age (although Anselm is quite early) because they begin with a subjective principle (our *thought* of God). They pose the question:

---

24. He deals with them in his *Science of Logic* (*Wissenschaft der Logik*, 1812), both in the opening chapter and in the section on the doctrine of Essence. He turns to these proofs again five years later in § 139 of the *Encyclopedia of the Philosophical Sciences*. In the second and third editions he adds discussions of the proofs in §§ 2, 36, 50, and 68. Of course, he also addressed the proofs in the lectures on religion (1821 and 1824). However, they also have a special status given that he held lectures devoted exclusively to them in the last years of his life, in 1829 and 1831.

25. Recall that according to Kant the activity of philosophical "critique" has to do with setting limits and drawing boundaries around aspects of reason so that it does not apply itself inappropriately to objects outside its proper domain. Hegel rejects precisely this limitation of rationality.

How can this idea be shown to be real? But this very question shows that the ontological proofs assume something beyond their initially problematic formulation, namely, if they think this question can be answered, then they must think—despite their initial formulation—that God must be more than *mere* idea, i.e., that *ideas exist* (or in Hegel's terminology, thought and being are the same). The problem that they can never really get over (and why they are just the beginnings of philosophizing and not the end point) is that they have that initial assumption of separation that must (and can) be overcome. It makes sense, from this perspective, that Descartes, with his dualism and subjective starting point (*cogito*), would have been the one to bring back the ontological proof as a task for modern philosophy.

Hegel's main criticisms are addressed to Kant, for whereas Anselm, Leibniz, and Descartes might have been mistaken in beginning with a dualism (a *mere* thought of God that must be shown to exist), they at least attempted to do so from the point of the thought itself. Unfortunately, they were limited to a mathematico-scientific understanding of both thought and reality. But Kant, in attacking their proofs, ends up making the case that such an absolute identity of thought and being is impossible (it exists, for Kant, either in experience—but only for objects of experience—or in morality, for God and the soul).[26] Thus, Hegel writes that all sorts of people in his age have taken up the Kantian critique, but they miss the fact that the only problem with the proofs Kant had critiqued was that they did not see the identity they were actually assuming all along. That is, the core idea of the ontological proof—namely, "that the concept of God as most perfect presumes His existence" (17:210–11); but it is lacking the appropriate understanding of the way the "concept" unfolds and objectifies itself. In critiquing the proof, Kant does not fulfill this lack. It is thus not by chance that Hegel turns to Kant's discussion in the opening chapter of the *Science of Logic* on being (see *Wissenschaft der Logik*, 88–90).

The core of Hegel's new ontological "proof" and what makes it possible is the fact that the "object" being proven by a movement of thought is itself a thinking being: difficulties in proving the existence of external objects disappear in this case "since [the object under investigation here] is not a resting object but itself a subjective movement—the raising of spirit to

---

26. Of course, early in his life (in the 1790s), Hegel, like so many others of his day, thought that Kant's moral proof offered the best and only legitimation for God's existence. But Kant's rejection of any other cognitive argument soon became the clearest sign for Hegel of the *failure* of Kant's critical project.

God—an activity, unfolding, process" (*Vorlesungen über die Beweise vom Dasein Gottes,* 357). This makes sense only because Hegel has shown the reality of the identity of thought and being throughout his entire philosophy. After all, the basic notion of *logos* for Hegel, as we know from his *Science of Logic,* is the same as *Wissenschaft,* not just (natural) science but the very notion that thinking presents reality and reality is that which can be thought: "Thus, pure science presupposes liberation from the opposition of consciousness. It contains *thought insofar as this is just as much the object in its own self, or the object in its own self insofar as it is equally pure thought"* (*Wissenschaft,* 49). Thinking is not an *imposition* of categories onto being; thinking, in its truth, is the thinking of being (a genitive that could be taken both ways, to mean both the being is itself a thought and the being is being thought about by someone else). Such a *logos* is a theology: "It can therefore be said that this content [i.e., of the *Science of Logic*] is the exposition of God as he is in his eternal essence before the creation of nature and a finite mind" (50). Hegel does not in fact offer here his own extended version of an ontological proof. His *Phenomenology,* which leads consciousness to the point of seeing why it cannot reasonably oppose thought and being, and his *Logic,* which works through their identity, *are,* so to speak, his onto-logical proofs, bringing together *ens* and *logos* = God.

However, in the summer semester of 1829, two years before his death, Hegel did decide to offer a separate lecture course on Proofs of the Existence of God (*Vorlesungen über die Beweise vom Dasein Gottes*). He opens it by pointing out that it stands in close relation to the other course on logic that he was presenting, indeed is a "supplement to it, not in terms of content but in terms of form, since this content [proofs of God's existence] is just a particular form of the basic determinations/concepts [*Bestimmungen*] from the *Logic*" (17:347). That is, since logic offers the categories to think through all of being, they must also offer the way to conceive of the being of God. In fact, if religion/God is the "content" and logic the "form," Hegel's principle of unity demands that he even show "that the logical [*das Logische*] makes up not only the formal side but at the same time is located at the center of the content" (17:347). God's existence turns out to be just a special case of the *logos* as spirit, which in turn is very much "with God."

The first eight lectures offer a long introduction. In some of Hegel's most accessible prose, they summarize his key positions on the tensions and contradictions of his age (faith and knowledge, feeling and cognition, understanding and reason, etc.). In the ninth lecture he turns to the key issue, which can be summed up in the problematic yet simple proposition that needs to be "proven," namely: "*Gott ist.*" In Hegel's analysis, it unites a concept (God) and being. The point of all proofs is thus to show that the concept has being or that being includes that concept. Hence he divides the traditional proofs into two that go from being to the concept. These are the cosmological and teleological proofs, which take the existence of the world as a given—either as a caused entity or as a system of ends—and conclude the necessity of the concept of God (as *prima causa* or as ultimate purpose). In the actual lectures (10 through 16) he only deals with versions of the cosmological proof. In general, he argues that neither of these is solid because they both presume a "given" (the world). Hence, only the ontological proof is the true one since it proceeds from the concept or thought to its being.

In notes that we have on further lectures on the philosophy of religion that Hegel held in the year of his death, 1831, we have a brief indication of how his version of the ontological proof differs from past ones. The key for him lies indeed in the basic moves from the *Logic.* The problem with the "movement" from God to being, from concept to reality, lies in the fact that we (using our understanding) think of these as occupying separate spheres: the concept seems subjective and we want to know if it has objective reality.[27] However, Hegel locates the "movement" within the concept itself, for insofar as it is assumed to be "subjective," it is limited or finite; but anything finite contains by definition its own end or negation. Hence, it is the very nature of the concept "God" to open itself up to reality. For this reason, Hegel believes, the (Judeo-Christian) notion of revelation—in German, literally "opening up" (*Offenbarung*)—captures the essence of God's relation to the world. In this sense, God is pure movement into being, and it is not even quite correct to say that God is simply identical with being. For this we need a rich conception of life, spirit, and *logos:* "The world is a harmonic totality, an organic life that is teleologically determined; the ancients called this *nous* or 'world soul' understood as *logos.* But they only posited vitality and not yet the idea that *the world soul is differentiated from this vitality as spirit. . . .* When we comprehend vitality in its truth, then it is as *one* principle [*arche!*], *one* organic life of the universe" (*Vorlesungen über die Beweise,* 17:514). And we see in this formulation how Hegel connects his later, logical approach to God with his earlier one that began with the concept of "life." God, life, being, the concept—all are identified as parts of the same spiritual process.

---

27. We recall that this was the nature of Kant's objection: One "adds" nothing to the concept when one attaches the predicate "exists" to it.

So what has Hegel accomplished by turning back to these proofs, even if it meant rejecting Kant's critique of them? The point was not to reintroduce a precritical Scholasticism. Rather, Hegel hoped to bring out the philosophical truth that underlay these proofs. What he says about Anselm's proof applies to all: Its content, the unity of Being and thought, that is, the possibility of deriving the existence from the concept of God, is fundamentally true even if the form in which it is expressed was faulty. (See 17:210 and 17:526–27). We have seen in the previous chapters a systematic narrowing of the field of theological *logos*—once it had been introduced as a mode of reason by Humanism—to science and mathematics in the seventeenth and early eighteenth centuries and then to morality by Kant. In the one case, God exists (or can be shown to exist) *the way scientific and mathematical truths* can be said to exist; in the other, God exists *the way moral principles* can be said to be absolute. But for Hegel, both those *ways* can be shown to be too limited (indeed, that is what Kant did vis-à-vis the former). The core issue for Hegel is that philosophy studies all the different ways that thought and being are revealed to be the same (despite not initially recognizing that identity), leading us to a general insight of a unity *under which* scientific, moral, and religious ones can be subsumed.

It is thus significant that the closing section of his "system," the *Enzyklopädie,* turns to a discussion of religion and philosophy. At this crowning point, the last paragraph (§ 573) of his "scientific" philosophical system, Hegel says, "This could appear to be the place to debate *the relationship between philosophy and religion*" (379). What unites them is their common element as Spirit. Where religion emerges from the sense ("image," "belief" and "witness") of the force of spirit in human beings,[28] philosophy is its conceptual grasping in "scientific" form (*Wissenschaft*): "Everything depends on the difference between the forms of speculative thought [philosophy] and the forms of imagination and reflective understanding [religion and theology]" (379). Both are concerned with the relationship between the Absolute and the world. This relationship, as life and spirit, unfolds over time. Hegel presents a number of stages: (1) religion provides images, feelings, phantasms ("Vorstellungsweisen und Systeme des Gemüts, der Phantasie und der Spekulation"); (2) the "reflective understanding" (i.e., Enlightenment) rejects such images for the sake of ideational "purity"; (3) as a result, the idea of God

---

28. "But religion is truth *for all human beings,* while faith rests on the *witness of the Spirit* that, productively witnessing, exists as the Spirit in human beings" ("Aber die Religion ist die Wahrheit *für alle Menschen,* der Glaube beruht auf dem *Zeugnis des Geises,* der als zeugend der Geist im Menschen ist" (*Enzyklopädie,* 379).

gets emptied out and separated from the world, projected into a realm *beyond;* (4) but that separation or opposition cannot suppress the *need* for a relationship, indeed, it heightens that need even as it makes it incomprehensible (*unbegreiflich*); (5) only a genuine *philosophy of religion,* in grasping precisely this historical development or the life of the spirit, can reintroduce a unity. This unity—despite what detractors might say (one can think here of Hegel addressing Adorno's analysis of the "dialectic of the enlightenment" *avant la lettre*)—is not an abstract identity (à la Schelling) but itself a concrete result of a historical development. Hegel writes:

> Since, however, the grasping of scientific knowledge itself and all the criticisms of it come with the grasping of this relationship [between the finite and the infinite], we should recall that philosophy has to do in principle with *unity,* not with the abstract unity, or with mere identity, or with empty abstraction but with *concrete* unity (with the concept)— indeed, over the course of its development philosophy has had to do with nothing else but such unity. Hence, each stage in the progress of philosophy has dealt with a *particular, proper form* of this concrete *unity*— and the most profound and final of these forms is the unity of absolute Spirit. (389–90)[29]

That is, Hegel's powerful response to the failure of former versions of religious thought—be they traditional "positivistic" belief systems, faith based on pure feeling, proofs relying on scientific rationality, Kantian moral theology, etc.—is to incorporate them all into a historical-conceptual philosophy of religion.[30] He can do so because he understands the Absolute as Spirit that

---

29. Hegel uses the term "concrete" in close to its etymological meaning of "grown together." By "concrete unity" he means one that does not place two sides artificially together but demonstrates their inner connection. Compare his statement in the first lecture on the proofs of God's existence: "All spirit (*alles Geistige*) is concrete; here we have . . . Spirit as the concrete (*das Konkrete*) of faith and thought (*des Glaubens und des Denkens*); both are not only mixed together in some manifold way, in some kind of a back and forth, but are so internally bound together that there is no faith/belief, which is not reflection, reasoning, or thinking in general, just as there is no thinking, which does not contain faith/belief, even if only as one of its passing moments" (*Vorlesungen über die Beweise vom Dasein Gottes,* 352).

30. Hegel's notion of Spirit as the process of unifying opposites (whereby both the drive toward unification and the tension of difference are maintained) allows for a normative approach not only toward philosophical versions of religion but toward different religions themselves. Although Hegel's dismissal of and condescension toward non-Christian religions is unacceptable, and although he not surprisingly finds his own Christianity the highest form, it does not seem to me that a normative approach even to religion should be rejected in principle. It even leads Hegel to some unexpected conclusions, like his strong praise of Islam at the end of the *Enzyklopädie.* See also Leuze on Hegel's views toward non-Christian religions.

unfolds in the world over time and history, taking on different forms and passing through necessary stages of alienation and renewing unification.

The concluding paragraph of Hegel's earlier essay, "Faith and Knowledge," captures this overcoming, canceling, and preserving—*Aufhebung*—of traditional religion by and in philosophy in a combination of religious and philosophical language. He refers to the "infinite pain" ("unendlichen Schmerz") that characterizes the feeling of religion in modernity ("die Religion der neuen Zeit") and arises from the sense that "God Himself is dead" ("Gott selbst ist tot"; "Glauben und Wissen," 432).[31] The experience of the Enlightenment, the wrenching apart of earlier unities and the destabilization of traditional authorities, must be lived through in all its infinite diremption. But with a kind of paradoxical mathematics that will become formalized only in the nineteenth century, Hegel hopes to fold this infinity into a larger one, the infinity ("Unendlichkeit") associated with "the pure concept" ("der reine Begriff"). The infinite pain would thus become a moment, and nothing more than a moment, in a longer temporality that defies time. The feeling of loss must be transformed into a "philosophische Existenz." The death of God and sense of godlessness ("Gottlosigkeit") would thus have to be confronted in all its severity and seriousness as a "speculative Good Friday" ("spekulativen Karfreitag").[32] However, this reintroduction of the Christian image into the conceptualization of the end of religion demonstrates that the loss of God is an act of self-removal for the sake of a higher return. We must accept God's death/suicide in religion so that "the highest totality can and must rise up [be resurrected] again in its full earnestness and out of its most profound depths, both all-encompassing and taking the form of the most serene freedom" ("die höchste Totalität in ihrem ganzen Ernst und aus ihrem tiefsten Grunde, zugleich allumfassend und in die heitereste Freiheit ihrer Gestalt auferstehen kann und muß"; "Glauben und Wissen," 432–33).

Hegel restates this moment of double negation explicitly in the *Lectures on the Philosophy of Religion* as the moment when God's death actually overcomes death because this conception of the divine recognizes and gives form to the basic principle of process and a course of history:

---

31. He quotes Pascal, who voiced this in "empirical" language: "La nature est telle qu'elle *marque* partout un *Dieu perdu* et dans l'homme et hors de l'homme" (*Pensées*, 441).

32. This death is thus not to be taken lightly, "for the more serene, less well founded, and more individual of the dogmatic philosophies, as well as the natural religions, must disappear" ("weil das Heitere, Ungründlichere und Einzelnere der dogmatischen Philosophien sowie der Naturreligionen verschwinden muß"; "Glauben und Wissen," 432). The internalization of the negative moment must indeed be felt in its pain.

God has died, God is dead—this is the most terrible thought, that all eternity and all truth are nothing, that *negation itself is in God;* the greatest suffering, the feeling of total abandonment, the loss of all higher hopes—these are all associated with this thought. But the course [of history] does not end here; rather, at this point the *reversal* takes place; God, namely, *preserves* Himself in this process, and this becomes nothing more than *the death of death itself.*

> Gott ist gestorben, Gott ist tot—dieses ist der fürchterlichste Gedanke, daß alles Ewige, alles Wahre nicht ist, die *Negation selbst in Gott* ist; der höchste Schmerz, das Gefühl der vollkommenen Rettungslosigkeit, das Aufgeben alles Höheren ist damit verbunden.—Der Verlauf bleibt aber nicht hier stehen, sondern es tritt nun die *Umkehrung* ein; Gott nämlich *erhält* sich in diesem Prozeß, und dieser ist nur der *Tod des Todes.* (*Vorlesungen über die Philosophie der Religion,* 17:291)

For Hegel, this means that God is *Geist,* as he writes in a notebook accompanying his lectures on this point: "Spirit is only Spirit as this negation of negation that preserves the negative within itself. If, therefore, of the Son of Man is depicted as sitting at the right hand of the Father, we see before our spiritual eye the honoring of human nature which has been raised to the highest of heights and been united with the divine" (ibid., 291n). In short: the God of religion is *absconditus;* He has in fact staged his own disappearance so that, with our help, He can return again in the guise of the philosophical spirit. "The God of religion is dead! Long live the God of philosophy!" And it is the ambiguity of that final genitive—God is *in* philosophy, but philosophy also becomes God—that Hegel leaves as his lasting impact.

So what emerges from this view of religion in terms of a process of spiritual development? First, Hegel has indeed offered a brilliant solution to the "need of religion," that is to the lack of and in religion which he found in his age. Whereas Kant swept aside the false proofs, leaving only moral theology, Hegel both shifts the ground and incorporates the earlier approaches by turning to a developmental view. Nature and man are thus not opposed to God; God is not just a separate creator of the world. Nor are the world and God merely the same in the sense that one could simply do without one of them and still think to get at the truth. (Again, this was the danger seen in Spinoza's philosophy, namely, that the powerful identity of God with "all there is" might make it possible to no longer worry about God *as* God and merely stay with "all there is.") Similarly, there are no special and limited means of access to the divine (intuitive knowledge, feeling, moral law, or conscience). Rather, by seeing the world in all its components engaged in a process of becoming, and by defining that becoming as Spirit or God, then Hegel can say that the world is always in the process of becoming God, and God's becoming is the world. The human spirit comes into its own essence insofar as it comes to know, grasp, *begreifen,* that nature of spirit itself.

This powerful answer to the split between faith and knowledge as well as to the inadequate attempts to "understand" God through the limited means of particular disciplinary knowledge contains, however, the seeds of its own overcoming. Hegel argues that human reason, as finite spirit, can, over the course of time and history, systematically grasp what is encountered as Other, thereby step-by-step transcending its own finitude (the limitation originally imposed by the Other as Other) and increasing its freedom, until in religion and philosophy even the Absolute is no longer encountered as Other but as "of the same spirit." But if, with Hegel's philosophy, we are at this last stage, then can we not say that in grasping the Absolute as "of the same spirit" we are, in fact, really grasping ourselves? Have we not in essence transformed the religious experience—the encounter with the Absolute/Other—into an act of self-recognition? Might we not then formulate the ultimate insight of the philosophy of religion as follows: mankind's grasping of the transcendent God is nothing but mankind's grasping of its own spirit of transcendence defined as the process of overcoming Otherness? It was Hegel's student, Ludwig Feuerbach, who at one point came to see Hegel in Berlin as a second father, who drew this consequence for the understanding of religion. In so doing, he was not concerned per se with rejecting or destroying religion but with bringing it to a self-understanding of its own "essence." Hegel leaves us with the following insight: the core of all religion (including the ontological proofs) is the *philosophical* insight of the identity of thought and being; only religions (like other forms of objective spirit, as well as the ontological proofs) do not yet *present* this truth as such but they "dress" it up with all kinds of representations and arguments. The conclusion is therefore obvious: if in the beginning is (philosophical) *logos,* then the point should not be to use *logos* (in any of its myriad forms) to get at religious truths but, rather, to see beyond the forms of religion to the true *logos* underneath. This is what Feuerbach undertakes in his "critique" of religion, namely, an exploration into the philosophical essence of Christianity, the *logos* that it, as a religion, masks.

✎ CHAPTER 5

Logos and Its Others

Feeling, the Abyss, Willing, and Kritik *(Schleiermacher, Schelling, Schopenhauer, Feuerbach)*

The starting point for the philosophical discourse about reason and revelation is a recurrent idea: namely, that when reason reflects on its deepest foundations, it discovers that it owes its origin to something else.

—Habermas, *The Dialectics of Secularization*

Let it be remembered that atheism—at least in the sense of this work—is the secret of religion itself.

—Feuerbach, *The Essence of Christianity*

When Marx holds the critique of religion to be the premise of all ideology-critique, when he holds religion to be the ideology par excellence, even for the matrix of all ideology and of the very movement of fetishization, does his position not fall, whether he would have wanted it or not, within the parergonal *framework* of this kind of rational criticism?

—Derrida, "Faith and Knowledge" (in *Religion*)

It should be clear from the last chapter that Hegel's philosophy is one of the greatest modern attempts to save (Christian) religion by grounding the identity of *logos* and God in a notion of absolute spirit (*Geist*). It would seem, then, that to attack it would be to destroy the foundations of Christian faith. However, we will see in this chapter that four major responses and alternatives to Hegel argue that *only* by attacking the dominance and apparent self-sufficiency of rationality can the truly religious be understood and, perhaps, salvaged. Not that these four figures were somehow "outside" the Idealist tradition that culminated with Hegel; rather, they worked through the *ratio* that would embrace God, world, and man in a totalizing system and saw the need to open up *logos* toward a radical conception of Otherness that would be in fact more closely aligned with a genuine Christianity. And by the end of the chapter we will see how, ironically, those who *continued* the Hegelian tradition ended up critiquing religion. That is, if Hegel represents the apotheosis of a tradition that identifies God with *logos* as *ratio,* one strand of thought will look beyond that identity to salvage religion from rationality and another will draw the consequence that there is no God beyond the bounds of human reason. In either case, Hegel's crowning achievement calls for radical challenges.

Much of nineteenth-century philosophy and theology feeds off the carcass of the Hegelian system. The internal dynamic of Hegel's thought, which isolates each concept in order to push it to the limit of its significance and force us to recognize its necessary dependence on other, opposing concepts, cannot help but turn onto Hegel's own philosophical construct.[1] Thus, the four post- or anti-Hegelians we explore in this chapter looked to the Other of spirit, extending Idealist thought to its own anti-Hegelian conclusion by attending to its conditions in some Other. In terms of conceptions of God and religion, Hegel even prepared for a radical transformation when he posited God as *Geist* and brought out the inherent moment of negativity that moves spirit and keeps it alive. The question is, does this process mean the *end* of Hegelian *logos* and, because it strove to capture the totality of natural, logical, and historical formations, the end of systematic thinking about God—indeed, the end of God? Or does this in turn open up the possibility of renewal? That is, Hegel's argument that philosophy is the *Aufhebung* of religion can mean that it legitimates and justifies religion, gives it its highest significance; or it can mean that philosophy replaces and cancels religion; or, finally, it can mean that philosophy cancels itself and opens itself up to its Other.

Schleiermacher: Religious Consciousness and Feeling vs. *Logos*

Friedrich Schleiermacher (1768–1834) was a dominant figure of nineteenth-century Protestant theology.[2] He lived in Berlin for the first time as a pastor at the Charité Hospital parish from 1796–1802. Then he spent a number of years in Stolp, a provincial city in Pomerania, where he again had a pastoral position. He received his first academic position as a professor in Halle and then returned to Berlin in 1811 with the founding of the university there.

---

1. See Löwith, *Von Hegel zu Nietzsche,* for a summary of this process.
2. See Nowak for an extensive overview (on his impact in evangelical theology, 467–81). Although eclipsed in midcentury by David Strauss's *Life of Jesus,* Schleiermacher became central again and remained that way well into the early twentieth, in part thanks to Dilthey's famous biography.

His first major period of production took place among the circle of German Romantics (including Schelling, Friedrich Schlegel, Friedrich von Hardenberg [Novalis], Ludwig Tieck, et al.) and was crowned with his *Über die Religion: Reden an die Gebildeten unter ihren Verächtern* (*On Religion: Speeches to the Educated among Its Despisers,* 1799). Although he encouraged a return to religion in an age that, as he says in the introduction, had come to reject it, in Halle he was looked at with suspicion by the old Enlightenment theologians (like Johann August Eberhard), who saw in him and Schelling pantheistic and atheistic tendencies.[3] In addition to his extensive philosophical and theological writings, which he constantly worked over in his university lectures, he both gave hundreds of sermons as part of his continuing pastoral service and was a major figure in classical philology and philosophy, who translated the works of Plato.[4]

One way of introducing Schleiermacher is to understand his theory of religion as parallel to Kant's approach to art in the third *Critique.* Although it seems that Schleiermacher did not engage directly with the *Critique of Judgment* (1790), he was actively dialoguing with the circle around Schlegel in the late 1790s, where the force of Kant's philosophy was being expanded beyond Kant's own limits. According to Kant, aesthetic judgments are different from theoretical or practical ones in that they do not provide us with either knowledge (definite concepts) or moral precepts. Although a statement like "that picture is beautiful" might *seem* to be about a quality of the picture that, once known, demands universal acceptance, it in fact says something about our *experience* of the picture. For example, the judgment of "beauty" says something about the "attunement" of our faculties and the generation of "aesthetic ideas" in and by the imagination that cannot be reduced to stable concepts. However, it is also not a merely subjective judgment about our feelings, since it is accompanied by a legitimacy claim that it is universally valid. Hence, the aesthetic marks off not a particular set of objects and does not presume to lead to any actions. Rather, in the words of the early twentieth-century philosopher of religion Rudolf Otto (see below, chapter 8), like art, religion for Schleiermacher "was a new, unique, and independent area of human existence and the spiritual life, and . . . it possessed its own special worth with respect to knowledge and action" (introduction

---

3. Recall from my introduction above that it was Edelmann who delighted in the thought of translating the prologue to John's Gospel as with the word "reason" for *logos.*

4. His administrative work for the university and his activities with the newly founded Akademie der Wissenschaften made him a major player in educational politics and the public sphere as well. Gadamer, Hans Frei, and Manfred Frank deal with Schleiermacher's contribution to hermeneutics.

to Schleiermacher, *On Religion,* xviii). Thus, just as for Kant (and Romantic poets after him) the study of the aesthetic means a study of a unique area of human experience, so, too, for Schleiermacher religion signifies, and must be studied in terms of, a unique set of human capacities.[5]

I will approach Schleiermacher's alternative to Hegel, and place it in dialogue with him, by presenting two modes of reading Schleiermacher reductively, modes that have radically different motivations even if they are equally problematic in their one-sidedness.[6] The first mode is the one we saw introduced by Hegel himself. By associating Schleiermacher with Kant, Jacobi, Jakob Friedrich Fries, and others in what he calls *"Reflexionsphilosophie,"* Hegel dismisses his philosophy of religion for not accomplishing what both religion and philosophy must do, namely, overcome oppositions and unite them into higher, indeed absolute, identities. Instead, Hegel considers Schleiermacher's definition of religion as "feeling of absolute dependency" ("Gefühl der schlechthinningen Abhängigkeit"), a fixation on the subjective to the exclusion of the objective, a fixation that can never attain the unity of *Geist.*[7] The other mode of approaching Schleiermacher is reductive in a similar way, but with a different evaluation. Postmodernist approaches to religion (see below, chapter 10, on Pope Benedict XVI's critique) can see in Schleiermacher a forerunner of their own turn to a sphere *beyond* rationality, a turn made necessary by the recognition of the failures and limitations of reason and the "project of the Enlightenment." Hence, in both these readings, Schleiermacher, with his insistence on religion and feeling, is set up in opposition to rationality.

In order to save him from these limited interpretations, it is necessary to show that (1) Schleiermacher has a richer concept of "feeling" than is granted by either of these readings, i.e., a concept that is not merely *opposed* to reason; and (2) one needs to have a richer understanding of Schleiermacher's

---

5. Consider Schleiermacher's aim in the speeches *On Religion* to get his audience "to understand what I mean by this unity and difference of religion, science and art" (41).

6. See Michael Eckert, "Gefühl und Rationalität: Schleiermachers Religionsbegriff" ("Feeling and Rationality: Schleiermacher's Concept of Religion") in Breuninger and Welsen, *Religion und Rationalität,* 51–67.

7. This famous definition of piety occurs in § 4 of *Christlicher Glaube* (*Christian Faith*): "That which all the variations of piety have in common, and through which they are distinguished from all other feelings, [or] in other words, the self-same essence of piety, is this, that we are conscious of ourselves as absolutely dependent, or, which amounts to the same thing, [that we are conscious of ourselves] as in relation to God." Hegel offered a mocking response in the introduction to Hinrichs's book on religion that sealed the enmity between the two Berlin philosophers. Hegel wrote: "If religion were based in a person's feeling, and this feeling had no other determination than the *feeling of his/her dependency,* then a dog would be the best Christian since a dog carries this feeling most strongly in itself and lives most exclusively in this feeling. A dog even has feelings of salvation, as when its hunger is stilled by a bone" (von der Luft 260; translation modified).

conception of subjectivity and its inherently dialogical relation to otherness if one is going to save him from the charge of pursuing a limited "philosophy of reflection."[8] These are not easy tasks, and I am not sure that one can succeed in "saving" Schleiermacher because he *is* opposed to Hegelian *Geist/logos*. But it is worth pursuing these moves for a moment because they lead us to the key issues.

The first way to address the charge that Schleiermacher reduces religion to mere subjectivity would see in his concept of feeling not something opposed to human knowledge but, rather, a condition of knowledge (and hence subjecthood) that we arrive at precisely by means of the exercise of reason. It is the crisis of any philosophy of reflection that leads Schleiermacher to this position. That is, a subject that claims to know itself by means of reflection ("I know myself by means of reflecting self-consciously on myself") already presumes the very possibility of recognition (that the object I am looking at *is* "myself"), otherwise it enters into an infinite regress since it would need some other "I" or subject to deliver that knowledge, and another to guarantee *that* knowledge, ad infinitum. The sense of self-acquaintance that I have with myself that allows all self-knowledge (via reflection) to be even possible Schleiermacher calls a "living unity" ("*Lebenseinheit*"), an originary identity that is split in the process of reflection but continues to underlie it and allows that reflection to come to an end in self-knowledge.[9] The other term for the "*Lebenseinheit*" is "feeling" (*Gefühl*). It is a necessary *given,* prior, in fact, to the very notion of subjectivity defined by means of (Cartesian or Spinozan) self-reflection.[10]

The second way to save Schleiermacher's philosophy of religion based on the "feeling of dependence" is to highlight the fact that the subject's basic sense of self is never just a *cogito* but also a *sentio,* and what I feel always already about myself is my connectedness ("dependence") on Otherness. He says in *On Religion:* "The sum total of religion is to feel that, in its highest unity, all that moves us in feeling is one; to feel that aught single and particular is

---

8. In both his general argumentation and his motivation, Eckert follows the direction of Manfred Frank's efforts to resuscitate Schleiermacher's hermeneutical theory (see esp. the latter's *Das individuelle Allgemeine*).

9. He engages in an early form of "phenomenological" self-analysis: "We shall endeavour to descend into the inmost sanctuary of life. . . . There alone you discover the original relation of intuition and feeling from which alone this identity and difference is to be understood. But I must direct you to your own selves. You must apprehend a living movement. You must know how to listen to yourselves before your own consciousness" (*On Religion,* 41).

10. Again it was Friedrich Jacobi's critiques of Spinoza (and later Fichte) that forcefully raised these arguments against the absoluteness of self-reflexivity and rational grounding.

only possible by means of this unity; to feel, that is to say, that our being and living is a being and living in and through God" (49–50). It is as impossible for us via Cartesian meditation to "think away" the fact of otherness as it is to "think away" the fact of my own thinking—if for no other reason than the dialectical one that the process of "thinking it away" still thinks *it*. The self, insofar as it is a thinking, feeling, and willing entity, is tied to (dependent on) Otherness.

Combining these two points, then, we see that the subject of reflection and self-knowledge comes to the conclusion that it is dependent on or contained within a larger "unity" that cannot be known *as* an object of reflection but can only be *sensed* in some way. Schleiermacher relates the one pole of "the feeling of dependency" to God and religion, the other pole of the self's autonomy to philosophical reflection. Once it attains this conclusion, the self does not abandon all reflection but must maintain a dialectic that moves between the poles of autonomy and dependence, philosophical reason and religious faith, a focused understanding and an awareness of a broader context that can never be fully illuminated. If we recall Erasmus's approach to the understanding of the Bible within a larger interpretive community, we can see, as Manfred Frank especially emphasized, that Schleiermacher introduces here a basic hermeneutics not just for texts but for human existence as well. Each individual not only reflects on him- or herself (as if looking at oneself in a mirror) but is also embedded in a "living unity" that provides the condition for self-recognition and opens up an endless process of interpretation.

Schleiermacher himself unfolds his argument as follows: religion is identified with the process or experience of intuition (*Anschauen*).[11] This process is not so much separate from the other possible acts of thought and will but, rather, underlies and unites them precognitively. That is, he believed in the immediate sense that human beings have of the presence of the divine. All intuition, however, depends on an object. In the terminology of a later phenomenology, one could say that all intuition is intentional, i.e., intuition *of something*. Such a reliance on the object creates a *feeling* in the one doing the intuiting, which is experienced with a unique immediacy, "a feeling of being one with nature" (*On Religion*, 71).[12] Hence, the core of religion

---

11. In the 1806 version of *On Religion* "*Anschauung*" (intuition) is often replaced by "*Gefühl*" (feeling). See Robert Merrihew Adams, "Faith and Religious Knowledge" (in Mariña, *Cambridge Companion to Friedrich Schleiermacher*, 36–37). In general Adams offers a reading parallel to mine, but focuses on the tension in Schleiermacher's notion of religious "self-consciousness" between its intentional and immediate character.

12. Given this identification of feeling for God and Nature, one can appreciate Schleiermacher's praise of Spinoza (e.g., *On Religion*, 40–41, 104–5).

must be an understanding of the nature of this feeling. It is not entirely "subjective," of course, because it is, by definition, linked to the intuited object that is the source of the feeling.

In the *Weihnachtsfeier* (*Christmas Celebration,* 1806) Schleiermacher addresses such theological issues in the course of a dialogue on the nature and meaning of the Christmas event. Although this peculiar work—written quickly in the last months of 1805 in part as a kind of "gift" to his friends—received mostly negative reviews, it offers some valuable insights into the development of Schleiermacher's thought. Its mode of presentation, the atmosphere, sociability, and conversational tone are all as much a part of the significance of the work as the actual discussion because, for Schleiermacher, religious meaning can be approached only through its meaning *for us* as individuals and members of a community (in this case represented by a family with friends).[13] In particular, in a passage where one of the characters discusses the significance of the prologue to John's Gospel we should note how Schleiermacher emphasizes not the *logos* but the becoming flesh: "Flesh is, as we know, nothing else but finite, limited, sensual nature; the Word, by contrast, is thought, cognition; and the becoming flesh of the Word is the stepping forth of this originary and divine entity into a form and shape. *What we thus celebrate is nothing else but ourselves, as we are in our totality, or human nature*" (*Werke,* 4:528; my emphasis). Here we see that although Schleiermacher separates eternal being from the world of becoming, he nonetheless does see the former entering fully into the latter. God and Spirit become part of the historical process; man gains access to revelation by attaining self-consciousness of his own humanity. In the words of Karl Barth, who analyzed this text in 1926: "This is the substance of Schleiermacher's Christmas message—'the highest triumph of human nature.' Dilthey is right: the final word for Schleiermacher's ultimate pronouncement upon Christmas is the phrase 'living feeling' (*Lebensgefühl*)" (*Theology and Church,* 158). The gift giving, singing, and focus on children and family that make up the Christmas celebration are, therefore, not so much the witnesses to an unheard-of event but in a literal sense the very spirit incarnate, the finite existence of the infinite.

For Schleiermacher the term that captures the individual's relation to both God and the church is piety (*Frömmigkeit*). It is piety that produces in the individual a feeling (*Gefühl*), which is defined in relation to consciousness. Here, again, the core of religion is distinguished from actions or thoughts

---

13. See Karl Barth, "Schleiermacher's 'Celebration of Christmas,'" in *Theology and Church,* 136–58.

(*logos*). In a more radical sense than Kant, he sweeps away *all* systematic and strictly conceptual approaches to religion: "Nothing is of less importance to religion, for it knows nothing of deducing and connecting. There is no single fact that can be called original and chief. Its facts are one and all immediate" (*On Religion*, 53). No "proofs" for the existence of God are necessary because to be *certain* of that feeling of oneness with and dependence on the Other is to have *faith*.[14] The propagation of this consciousness within a community is precisely the nature of piety and the function of the church. He comes full circle, then, to define this consciousness as piety. Hence, in his later work on *Christian Faith* (1821 and 1830) he does develop a theology, but it is not the *logos* of *theos* but the study of the varieties of formations of piety, the modalities of human feelings and interactions with each other and nature.

What might be the "Hegelian" response? First, Hegel would argue that the notion of the crisis of reflection is exactly correct. Descartes' attempt to ground all knowledge in the *cogito* that knows itself must indeed be brought into relation with an otherness. And, of course, he would agree that the "bringing into relation" is best understood as a "dialectic." However, rather than seeing a permanent and absolute condition of "dependence" on some "wholly Other," he strives to show how the nature of human consciousness depends on a process of *experience* that moves, step by step, to a continual illumination of the conditions in which we find ourselves. This is why "feeling" would not be the appropriate word, according to Hegel, for that *Lebenseinheit*. Rather, it is *Geist* understood as the activity of encountering otherness and then recognizing that, in each encounter, that otherness is already overcome. Hermeneutically, this means that each moment of "misunderstanding" (= encounter with otherness) already contains within itself the seeds of reaching an understanding (since otherwise it could not even have been registered as a misunderstanding).

The difference between these two approaches is crucial when we return to the specific context in which they developed, namely, religion. Undoubtedly Schleiermacher emphasizes an essential aspect of self-experience when he points to our "Gefühl der schlechthinnigen Abhängigkeit," our recognition that we are not autonomous but find ourselves in a state of being "always-in-relation-to" (God). However, by metaphysically absolutizing that state and calling that on which we are dependent "God," he turns the dia-

---

14. "Faith in God is nothing but certainty about the feeling of absolute dependence as such—that is, as conditioned by a being posited outside us, and as expressing our relationship to that being" (*Christian Faith*, 1830 edition, § 14.1; cited in Adams, above, n. 11).

lectical *process* of moving toward freedom and understanding by step-by-step experiences into a dangerous flip-flopping. (We might see this as the difference between the imaginary posited by a Lacanian mirror stage as capturing Schleiermacher's tension between dependency and autonomy, and Lacan's symbolic mediation as closer to Hegel's dialectic.)[15] That Other, on which we are dependent, *will get filled with content,* whether that content is "adequate" or not (and, of course, by definition it cannot be). In his essay on rationality and Schleiermacher, Eckert seems to point to this problem but without recognizing it as a problem. Referring to the "religious certainty" that is, ironically, a *docta ignorantia* or sense of our inability to know the absolute Other (God), he adds in passing, "however its historical content happens to be determined or defined" (66). That is, the idea of "holding open" the space of Otherness, rather than approaching it through a (Hegelian or other) process of mediation, sounds fine. But it will not be held open, and hence we should try to understand how we relate to that Other after all. "Feeling" and "dependence" capture one important aspect of that relationship, but are, in the end, inadequate.[16]

To anticipate a later critique of Schleiermacher by Karl Barth in the twentieth century (see chapter 8), we must recognize that we have here a completion in religion/theology of the "Copernican revolution" in philosophy introduced by Kant. What Kant meant was the need to shift emphasis from metaphysical talk about "things in themselves" to epistemological analysis of the categories of human understanding through which all such things appear to us. For Schleiermacher, too, the starting point of theo-logos must be the nature of "religious consciousness." As says in his *On Christian Faith:* "All attributes which we ascribe to God are to be taken as denoting not something special in God (in God there is no multiplicity of functions, no contradiction, no differentiation), but only something special in the manner in which the feeling of absolute dependence (in which in itself there exists no real differentiation) is to be related to God" (§ 50; cited in Barth, "Schleiermacher," in *Theology and Church,* 164).

---

15. Although he mostly deals with Schelling and not Schleiermacher, Žižek also sees parallels between these early nineteenth-century theological debates and Lacan.

16. We will see in chapter 8 how twentieth-century "dialectical theology" critiques a tradition that has come down from Schleiermacher in Protestantism by targeting the notion that the object of theology is to be found in the pious consciousness of the believer. That is, according to this critique, by stressing the *feeling* of dependency, Schleiermacher detracts from the state of being in which such dependency or feeling occurs and opens the door to a psychologizing kind of theology.

Schelling: The Abyss vs. the Ground of *Logos*

Rationality is all about "grounding," i.e., tracing phenomena back to their "ground" or offering reasons that provide the ground or explanation for their appearance. We saw this in its most rigorous form in Leibniz, who used the principle of sufficient reason—in German, the "Satz vom *Grund*"—to trace back everything to the necessity of a final reason or ground. The autonomy of reason means that it stands on its own two feet and can ground itself. Just as Schleiermacher recognized that a precognitive feeling of unity underlies our conscious reflections, Friedrich Wilhelm Joseph Schelling (1775–1854) pursues the rational search for an absolute grounding of reason to the point of its own "self-sublation," where it must recognize its own abysmal groundlessness. (In German, the pun is graphic in the word for abyss, *Abgrund,* which means literally "off or from ground," i.e., "non-ground.") We can follow the development of Schelling's radical alternative to a divine beginning in *logos* by considering three stages in his work: the first (still) embraces the notion that reason can conceive of the absolute as the identity of the ideal and the real, and thus give expression to the truth of religion in philosophical terms. When he turns to the concepts of freedom and the will in 1809, however, he recognizes a fundamental gap (or "indivisible remainder") not only in the human spirit but in God's very essence, a gap that explains evil and demands a different version of creation and revelation. Although he promises at the end of the treatise on human freedom to follow it up with "a series of others in which that part of philosophy which deals with the ideal will gradually be disclosed as a whole" (*Philosophical Inquiries into the Nature of Human Freedom,* 98; *Werke,* 4:418), he does not publish another major work for the next forty-five years of his life, although we can see how he grappled with the consequences of his insight into the ground-lessness of *logos* in his multiple drafts of *The Ages of the World.*

Schelling's earlier efforts—for example, the 1804 *Philosophie und Religion*—pursue the general Idealist effort of grasping (*begreifen*) the absolute, which includes the religious, and defining it in philosophical concepts. One hears in these texts the many conversations with Hegel, with whom he had been coediting the *Kritisches Journal der Philosophie* in Jena from 1801–4. One can also hear the fundamental idea of Hegel's philosophy of religion from the last sections of the *Phenomenology* (which was being conceived in these years), namely, that the *content* of religion and philosophy are the same, only their form is different (intuitive, imaginative in the former, conceptual in the latter). For example, Schelling rejects the oppositions between philosophy and religion, reason and faith (*Glaube*) because the essence of a completed/

perfected (*vollendete*) philosophy consists in "possessing in clear knowledge and intuitive (immediately perspicuous) cognition what non-philosophy would mean to grasp in belief/faith" (*Werke*, 4:8). While Schelling never had the absolute hierarchy that placed the one conceptual kind of knowledge always above the other intuitive kind—here he was closer to Goethe than Hegel—this early work on religion is nonetheless fully in the Idealist mold.

However, in attempting to find a rational grounding, Schelling—precisely at the time when Hegel is formulating the major works of his philosophy, the *Phenomenology* and the *Logic*—discovers what we can call the unbridgeable gap or abyss between what exists for the understanding and Being as its groundless ground. He formulates these oppositions first in his essay on the freedom of human will, *Philosophische Untersuchungen über das Wesen der menschlichen Freiheit* (*Philosophical Inquiries into the Nature of Human Freedom*, 1809). Earlier in his career, in formulating his philosophy of identity, Schelling had been accused of Spinozism, a charge that means all of being is fundamentally one substance and thoroughly permeated with logical reason. Here, however, he attempts to guarantee human freedom by introducing the notion of "life." "The error of his [Spinoza's] system," Schelling writes, "is by no means due to the fact that he posits all *things in God*, but to the fact that they are *things*" (*Philosophical Inquiries*, 22; *Werke*, 4:349). This view of Spinoza results, "quite consistently, [in] his mechanistic view of nature" (22; 4:349). The task, then, is that it "must at least first be vitalized and severed from abstractness before it can become the principle of a system of reason" (ibid.). Even Leibniz saw the danger posed to human freedom if everything had its reason/ground, with God being the ultimate and necessary one. For Schelling the turn comes in considering the status of the will in relation to being, and evil in relation to good. Betraying his Fichtean roots, even as he radicalizes him, he sees in the will the originary activity of the (human) spirit, the restless drive behind reason itself to find its resting place (to be by itself) on its ground. But, unlike Fichte, this drive of the will cannot posit itself—for then it would have to ask how the one positing is itself being posited. Being itself becomes alive: "If the doctrine that all things are conceived in God is the basis of the entire system, it must at least first be vitalized" (ibid.). However, as a result, the "vitalization" of Spinoza will in fact open up a challenge to the very "principle of a system of reason" to which Schelling strives.

Schelling argues that Spinoza, "spiritualized by the principle of idealism," leads to the development of a "Philosophy of Nature" (which he himself had been working on in this first decade of the nineteenth century). However, it can "permit of being raised into a genuine system of reason only by first being completed by an ideal part wherein freedom is sovereign" (23–24;

4:350). (This seems to hint at the kind of system of the ideal to which he refers in the final paragraph of the treatise.) But this freedom is also "the final intensifying act" that is to be found, "ultimately, in will" (24; 4:350). Thus, he sees all philosophy up to his time leading to the task of giving "highest expression" to the notion of the will, not defined subjectively, however, but as a paradoxical nonfoundational being: "In the final and highest instance there is no other Being than Will. Will is primordial Being, and all predicates apply to it alone—groundlessness, eternity, independence of time, self-affirmation" (ibid.). The philosophical grasping of such an idea transcends all anthropology, psychology, or ethics, the typical domains where willing might be studied. Schelling is aware that the analysis of freedom and the will opens up ontological and theological dimensions since a "real and vital conception of freedom" must address the "profoundest difficulty" of the "possibility of good and evil" (26; 4:352). What kind of God must there be if we are to recognize the absolute nature of this free "primal Will" (*Urwille*) and/as "primordial Being" (*Ursein*)? What does it even mean to say that "God *is*" in this case? Can the beginning be the grounding of *logos* when the primal predicate is "groundlessness"? While Schelling offers a first attempt to answer these questions using the tools of his Idealism and natural philosophy, they ultimately open up a gap that he is unable to close; indeed, he will come to understand God as such a radical gap or abyss.

The problems associated with any effort of rationality to ground itself, and the implications of a basic groundlessness for our notions of freedom and God, take on broader consequences for theology in Schelling's fragmentary work, *The Ages of the World* (*Die Weltalter*). Schelling worked on this project from 1809 to 1827, a period during which he published no major philosophical texts. *The Ages of the World* underwent three significantly different revisions, none of which was completed. In it he seeks to give expression to the three modes of temporal existence—past, present, future—because the true nature of philosophy, he says, is not to present thoughts and concepts but, rather, to capture the unfolding of a living being/essence. Indeed, "in the highest science what is living can be only what is primordially alive (*das Urlebendige*) the essence preceded by no other, which is thus the first and oldest of essences" (*Ages*, 3; *Werke*, 4:575). Like Hegel, from whom he has bitterly parted paths by this time, he also recognizes that "life" can be captured only dialectically. That is, he explores the fact that any statement (A = B) contains within it movement and contradiction. Such statements assume that any thing (A) is not just itself but also something that it not itself. But he knows he cannot fly in the face of the law of noncontradiction. Hence, the notion of A = B implies that there is some third point of comparison

(= X) on the basis of which we can judge what of A can differentiate itself from itself and become other. He writes:

> The true meaning of every judgment, for instance, A is B, can only be this: *that which* is A is *that which* is B, or *that which* is A and *that which* is B are one and the same. Therefore, a doubling already lies at the bottom of the simple concept: A in this judgment is not A but "something = x, that A is." Likewise, B is not B, but "something = x, that B is," and not this (not A and B for themselves) but the "x that is A" and "the x that is B" is one and the same, i.e., the same x. (*Ages,* 8; *Weltalter,* in *Werke,* 4:589–90)

The one judgment in fact contains three. The possibility of making any judgment—and he clearly has judgments of the form "God is . . ." in mind—rests on an inherent plurality of "forces" ("*Kräfte*") or "principles" ("*Prinzipien*") within all entities. This leads him to the crucial distinction on the one hand between what is, i.e., what exists, appears, and can be grasped conceptually, and, on the other, being itself, or, in his terms, the distinction between two modalities of Being itself, *Seyendes* and *Seyn*.[17] *Seyn* comes to be *Seyendes* by a process of self-negation and wanting/willing (*Ages,* 14–16; *Weltalter,* 4:598–600). This is the very nature of any genuine beginning—the emergence out of a "hidden" state of being into appearance. It is not the act of an individual will but the self-withdrawal of Being (*Seyn*) that allows for the emergence of existing beings.

Theologically, Schelling now has a new way of conceiving the primary acts of both creation and revelation: God is not "the beginning" in the sense of a *Seyendes,* an object that initiates a process, a prime mover, but is "beginning" as such, the very process of *Seyn* becoming *Seyendes,* a primal "longing" (*Ages,* 17; *Weltalter,* 4:601). In a way, we can see Schelling's argument as a kind of ontological "proof" for the existence of God. He unfolds the very concepts, or what is in any conceptual relationship or judgment (A is B), to come up with these necessary distinctions within (divine) Being itself.

What Schelling has introduced here is conception of God and Being that contains within itself a more radicalized movement. We encounter a basic dialectical argument: ontologically, the duality within Being makes possible a self-negation, allowing each being to become something else, and thereby attain a new and higher unity; theologically, God as "beginning" is always

---

17. Recall that Heidegger lectured on Schelling in 1936 at a pivotal point of the "turn," or *Kehre,* to his ontology of *Seyn.*

already coming out of Himself into creation, which is constantly moving toward the "end"/return to God. But this very "circulation" and "inexorable progression" is the goal: "There is nothing higher to be produced in this course" (*Ages,* 19; *Weltalter,* 4:604). That is, there is no "sublimation" (*Aufhebung; Ages,* 19; *Weltalter,* 4:604). Nature, creation, God, life are all driven by "an unremitting striving, an eternally insatiable obsession (ein unablässiges Suchen, eine ewige nie gestillte Sucht)" (*Ages,* 21; *Weltalter,* 4:609), such that "we can say that it is *without* (veritable) beginning and *without* (veritable) end (es sey *ohne* [wahrhaften] Anfang und *ohne* [wahrhaftes] Ende" (*Ages,* 20; *Weltalter,* 4:606). Schelling radically reinterprets the *logos* that the evangelist posited as the *arche:* it does not provide a stable ground but contains an infinite abyss that initiates an "unremitting movement that goes back into itself and recommences," like the "wheel of birth as the interior of all nature that was already revealed to one of the apostles . . . as well as to those who later wrote from feeling and vision" (*Ages,* 21; *Weltalter* 4:607–8).[18]

It is in Schelling's later lectures, however, that some have come to see the true completion and overcoming of Idealism in a way that points to possibilities of new beginnings (taken by Schopenhauer, Kierkegaard, and Marx).[19] Walter Schulz summarizes the problem facing the late Schelling as follows: once reason has thought through all of Being and been able to formulate it in terms of appropriate logical categories (as Hegel had claimed to have done), at this point the question of the "self-constitution" of reason opens up, i.e., "Why is there reason at all?" ("Warum ist denn überhaupt Vernunft?") Reason fails in its effort to posit and conceive of itself: "It recognizes its own ungraspability (*Unbegreiflichkeit*), for its thinking is always already preceded by the *factum brutum* of its pure 'that-ness' (*ihres reinen Daβ*)" (Schulz, 5). That is, for Hegel there is also always a moment of pre-sumption (*Voraus-setzung*) to my being and thinking, but that moment is also always being overcome by the power of my reason to "get behind" it critically. For Schelling, however, the critical movement of reason stays the same (he is not an "irrationalist," "he thinks idealistically" [Schulz, 31]); and yet, this movement of reflection leads reason to the experience of the impossibility of its own completion.[20] It rests, as Manfred Frank points out, on an "infinite lack of being" (*unendlicher Mangel am Sein*).

---

18. The biblical reference here is to James 3:6.

19. See Schulz, *Die Vollendung,* and Frank, *Der unendliche Mangel.*

20. Schelling describes this movement in terms of complex and often obscure "potentialities." See Beach.

In his 1833–34 Munich lectures on the history of modern philosophy, *Zur Geschichte der neueren Philosophie,* Schelling devotes considerable effort to Hegel. He formulates four fundamental critiques:[21]

- In the opening pages, Schelling indicates clearly that his major motivation for critiquing Hegel has theological roots. Insofar as Hegel defines the "movement of the concept (*Begriff*)" as the absolute activity of spirit, he "has nothing left over for God to be besides the movement of the concept, i.e., to be Himself nothing but the concept" (543). Of course, he knows that Hegel has a more complicated notion of the "concept" than just a subjective idea, but nonetheless, like Spinoza's "substance," Hegel's *Begriff/Geist* subsumes the divine.

- Second, related to the first critique, Schelling claims that Hegel's philosophy from the start cannot think of "real events/happening/history" (572). The reason is that Hegel's God, as *Geist,* is caught up in an eternal dialectical movement that annihilates all difference and history: "God didn't project Himself into nature, but constantly does so over and over again, only to then withdraw from it again and again; this occurrence is eternal, but continuous, and thus, again, not an actual event properly speaking" (576).[22]

- Thus, in a critique that might have appealed to the likes of Marx or Engels, Schelling says the Hegelian system as continuous process, as a technoscientific machine of cyclical alienation and overcoming, produces a religion that attracts precisely the class of bourgeois upstarts: "Thus it is easy to see that this new religion that emerges out of Hegelian philosophy would find its main adherents in the so-called *grand* public (*im sogenannten* großen *Publikum*), among industrialists, businessmen and other members of this in other respects of course respectable social class" (577).

- And finally, Hegel's radical teleology—according to which meaning and justification is contained in what emerges out of a situation— does not recognize the nature of the "grounding" or reason of being. Yes, it is true, Schelling writes, that the consequence or effect does reveal the meaning or reason of what preceded. But more important,

---

21. His close reading of the opening of the *Logic* need not concern us here.
22. We have here a return of debates about continuous creation. See Saine.

each particular being attempts to ground itself and at the same time points outside itself. Each act of grounding is therefore a failure. Here Schelling uses the pun that Heidegger will pick up later: "Es begründet sich *durch* sein zu-Grunde-Gehen"—"It grounds itself *by* running aground."

Hegel's philosophy, Schelling admits, in a crucial sense thus does represent a kind of culmination of all modern thought—but has turned out "in good measure more monstrous" (544).

The theological consequences are both clear and disturbing. Schelling denies the possibility of any direct or unmediated experience of God. He rejects, therefore, all forms of mysticism (and, we could say, theologies based on feeling and inner "intuition"). The relation to God must be mediated through the action of reason. However, through its self-reflection reason strives for its originary being, its grounding, which it can never attain. It can only achieve what he calls a "negative" concept: "For reason, and this is of greatest significance and our main consequence, reason has nothing else but a *negative* conception of what being itself is. Reason, even if its final goal and intention is to grasp being, cannot give any precise determination for what *is*, it has not concept for it as the one stating that it is not non-being and not something passing over into something else, that is, only a negative concept" (*Philosophie der Offenbarung, 13:70;* cited in Schulz, 49). Where Hegel concluded his philosophical career with lectures on the proofs for the existence of God, Schelling here emerges with God as primal Being ("*das Seyn selbst*" or "*Urseyn*") that is "provable" only in our failure to determine it. God is in fact derived from the very movement of reason and in this regard Schelling continues the tradition of philosophy that led to Idealism. However, unlike Hegel's *Geist*, God is not the result of reason or its crowning achievement but the fact (*Faktum*) of its essential groundlessness. God does not exist as a "thing" in some sphere above us, but as the core moment of self-negation within reason itself.[23] Reason pushes to its limits in a more radical sense than Kant ever dreamed of, and there where reason fails is God.

---

23. One might envision how someone might combine Schelling's notion that reason derives out of itself its own basic dependence on "being itself" or God, with a Spinozist notion that God or Being are all of Nature, and end up with the Marxist dictum that consciousness doesn't determine being, being determines consciousness.

Schopenhauer: Willing vs. *Logos*

Arthur Schopenhauer (1788–1860) came to Berlin to study philosophy in 1811 and took courses for two years with Fichte and Schleiermacher. After some years of writing and traveling, he returned to Berlin about the same time as Hegel arrived there. Although his main philosophical work, *Die Welt als Wille und Vorstellung* (*The World as Will and Representation*), appeared in 1819, it was a failure on the market and sold hardly a hundred copies in its first years. He tried to make his way in Berlin as a *Privatdozent*, a kind of adjunct professor who was paid small amounts to teach courses and whose salary depended on the number of students in his courses. He self-consciously set himself up in opposition to Hegel, even scheduling his lectures at the same time, but lost the popularity battle with the reigning king of philosophy in a big way. He left Berlin and lived in a number of cities, one of which was Munich, where he attended Schelling's lectures. He ended up back in Berlin in 1825, only to flee again in 1831 in order to escape the cholera epidemic that ended up taking the life of his philosophical opponent, Hegel. He lived a long life, the last decades in Frankfurt am Main, enjoying basic comforts thanks to his inheritance from his father's business, and yet alone and bitter as he completely revised his monumental work. Only near the end did he attain some considerable fame, largely owing to his short collection of aphorisms that offered his key ideas in more accessible form.

Schopenhauer responded to the dominant Hegelianism he encountered in Berlin of the 1820s by issuing a severe critique of the kind of meta-physical consolation associated with both philosophies of reason (*Geist*) and religions promising any kind of upbeat redemption. His turn to the "will" as the underlying force moving both mankind and Nature and the pessimism resulting from the relentless brutality and frustration of this universal principle of unfulfillable willing turn against the traditions of both Western philosophy and Christianity. However, in the twentieth century from some quarters a renewed interest emerged in Schopenhauer that might correspond to a kind of return to religion. This resuscitation of Schopenhauer, the critic of religion (and just about everything else!), as a potential contributor to a conception of religion after the death of Hegel's beneficent and rational *Geist,* involves two steps. First, it is necessary to find evidence in Schopenhauer to support a deeper recognition on his part of the core values of Christianity (as well as Eastern philosophies), namely, empathy, pity, and a faithful resignation. And second, one must share if not his irrationalism then at least, as we saw in the discussion of Schleiermacher, his critique of rationality as the foundational and absolute principle of philosophy and the world itself.

That is, to say that "in the beginning was *willing*" certainly displaces the God of *logos,* but, for some, makes room for a different kind of faith.[24] In recent times, the most forceful (and in some ways most surprising) promoter of this reading is the neo-Marxist Frankfurt School theorist, Max Horkheimer.[25] His reading therefore guides my own focus on Schopenhauer as a "critic of and apologist for" religion.[26]

We must first briefly reconstruct Schopenhauer's alternative to Hegel's panlogism. Although he ends the first volume of the *World as Will and Representation* with a long excursus, a "Critique of Kantian Philosophy," Schopenhauer always considered himself fundamentally Kantian (and Kant, in turn, fundamentally Platonic). The basic starting point for Kant was the distinction between two kinds of knowledge or two kinds of world, each of which must be known differently: the world of phenomena, whereby I know things only as they appear to me, as they show up as objects of knowledge mediated necessarily through my categories of understanding; and the world of noumena, things in themselves, what can be "known" only through some other act and which forms the core of his practical philosophy (free will, God, the soul).[27] The former is secured, but limited; the latter is absolute, but may never be put in terms of theoretical knowledge (e.g., the soul cannot have number, location, etc., and the will is independent of causality).

Schopenhauer begins with the same basic distinction. The world as it appears to me is the world as it "presents itself to me," and this "presenting itself" is therefore a representation. Hence, the opening line of the book reads: "The world is my representation." In Kantian terms: I know (or experience) nothing else but that which is present to me through my faculties of

---

24. This metaphysical appeal to the will is different from Kierkegaard's turn to the individual's decision and will. To say that we "must believe" as a rational conclusion and in order to save rationality is not, in fact, actually to believe. That last step is an act of will. As Kierkegaard states: "Even if one were able to render the whole of the content of faith into conceptual form, it would not follow that one had grasped faith, grasped how one came to it, or how it came to one" (*Fear and Trembling,* 43). Kierkegaard looks at the individual human being who has been led up to this point and sees him or her acknowledging the *need* to believe and yet painfully separated infinitely from actual belief. It is precisely the radicality of this decision or act of will that would lead the individual from *having to believe* (because of a rational argument) to *actually believing,* from objective reasons for belief to the subjective certainty of belief, i.e., the radicality of this "leap of faith," that Kierkegaard addresses.

25. "Die Aktualität Schopenhauers" (in *Zur Kritik der instrumentellen Vernunft*); also Habermas on Horkheimer in *Religion and Rationality.*

26. See Peter Welsen, "Schopenhauer als Kritiker und Apologet der Religion," in Breuninger and Welsen, *Religion und Rationalität,* 85–102. Surprisingly, Welsen does not address Horkheimer at all.

27. Whether Kant's distinction is ontological or epistemological has been a focus of attention in recent years thanks largely to Allison's (1983) interpretation.

cognition. "To me" means in this case first of all my body. However, I know myself not just as a body, i.e., as an object among others presenting itself "to me"; I also "know" myself in a different way—we should say I sense myself as knowing—insofar as this "I" is the internal mover of the body. In this way Schopenhauer avoids the problem of the infinite regress that confronts all philosophies of reflection (namely, if I know myself, then there must be some prior "I" knowing the "I" that knows myself, etc., ad infinitum). That core force that moves the body and yet which never appears as such but only presents itself through the body is my will.[28] The will, as a "thing in itself," escapes all categories of understanding. In Schopenhauer's terms, it lies behind the *principium individuationis,* the principle of individuation, that presents the world of objects as a discrete array of phenomena. Borrowing from Hindu philosophy, he also refers to this (re)presented world as the "Veil of Maja." To live in the world as it is represented to us is to be driven by the will from one object to the other. The model for such a life is the pain and frustration of a life of desire.[29] Once we recognize, with a deeper kind of knowledge, the true nature of the "world as will," the question arises: Is there any way to live a different life, one that would overcome the pain and suffering that comes from pursuing the dictates of the will in the world of objects?

The last six books of the *World as Will and Representation* address this question and lead to Schopenhauer's reflections of morality and religion. The first step toward the "denial of the will," i.e., to turning it against itself in order to escape the relentless drive from one unfulfilling object to another, comes from the insight into the suffering of *others* since one thereby experiences an identification that challenges the principle of individuation:

> When, namely, that Veil of Maja, the *principium individuationis,* is raised enough so that an individual human being no longer differentiates egoistically between him- or herself and a stranger but, rather, takes as much part in the suffering of other individuals as in his or her own and thereby is not only to a high degree cooperative but even prepared for self-sacrifice in order to save another—at this point it follows that such a human being, who recognizes in all others his or

---

28. Schopenhauer's move here is not unlike the one we saw in Schleiermacher. In both cases there is a primal kind of self-acquaintance that underlies forms of self-consciousness and consciousness of objects. But whereas Schleiermacher considers this intuition a "feeling of absolute dependence," Schopenhauer identifies it with pure willing.

29. Here one could think of the "aesthetic" stage explored by Kierkegaard in *Either/Or,* whose principle exemplar would be Don Juan.

her own inner and true self, must identify with the endless suffering of all living beings and take it upon him/herself. (*Welt als Wille und Vorstellung,* 488)

At this point, the will of the empathetic individual "turns against itself, no longer affirms its own being as it shows up as an appearance in the world, but, instead, denies itself" through a deeply rooted asceticism (489). Such an act of self-denial is the mark of all genuine sacredness and saintliness and is thus at the heart of all true religion.

With a variation of the ethical arguments we saw from Erasmus through Lessing to Kant, Schopenhauer uses the fundamental principle of empathy with the suffering of others and the consequent self-denial of the will to evaluate "positive" (i.e., existing) religions. He has, that is, an ethical measure for comparison. The value of the Christian scriptures (497) and especially the Sanskrit writings of Hinduism and Buddhism (498–99) is that they teach us in essence this philosophical message. Conversely, he can raise his philosophy of the will to the level of religion by occupying fundamental theological categories. He writes: "True sacredness/holiness/salvation (*Heil*) and redemption (*Erlösung*) from life would not be conceivable without total denial of the will" (511). Much of the next-to-last section (§ 70) thus offers an existential redescription of basic religious experiences, focusing on the Lutheran doctrine of grace overcoming the human will.

One might get a sense of his "Lutheranism" by considering the summary that the theologian Friedrich Gogarten gives of Luther's key doctrine in his afterword to the 1924 edition of *Vom unfreien Willen*.[30] The decisive difference between Luther and Erasmus, between Protestantism and the "modern spirit," he writes, is "if one lives in reality or in a fantasy of reality. That is, if one knows that one's life is grounded in the encounter with an Other (You, *Du*) and finds one's life in that encounter, or in the constantly renewed and repetitious effort to objectify one's own ego" (Luther, *Vom unfreien Willen,* 366–67). He traces back to Luther the key insight of Schopenhauer: to see the truth of the world is to break through our false image that puts us at the center, with the world as our representation; instead we need to recognize the depressing yet saving dependence of our ego (soul) on the force of some Other (divine Will).

Christian pity and empathy, therefore, break through the movement of willing. They function not just as "feelings" (since feeling is just a mode of willing) but in a strong sense as a return to a basic "*Lebenseinheit*" à la

---

30. See below, chapter 8.

Schleiermacher; they destroy the *principium individuationis* that had domi-nated our lives, allowing us to become one with the world in its essence. Like Kant, he rejects all attempts to "prove" the existence of God through rational arguments (specifically the ontological, cosmological, and physico-teleological proofs). But unlike Kant, his version of a "practical" turn to God/religion rests not on practical reason but on a necessary response of the will in the face of conscious or unconscious recognition of a pessimistic real-ity. Despite his negativism, he nonetheless overlaps here with Schleiermacher: "It comes down to an experience in which a human being, confronted with the pressures of reality, becomes seized by a 'feeling of neediness, powerless-ness, and dependency,' a feeling that he can overcome by personifying the forces to which he is delivered up in order to thereby influence them through religious acts" (Welsen, in Breuninger and Welsen, 92).

Of course, Schopenhauer rejects any possibility of a "theodicy," since this is by no means the best of all possible worlds. The outcome of this insight is not happiness or goodness in any traditional sense. Rather, the all-pervasiveness of suffering characterizes existence. It has no rational explana-tion. The best we can do in the face of the unknowable and negative force of the will is to find "consolation" in "metaphysics," which has the goals of explaining the world, guiding people to actions, and offering consolation (Breuninger and Welsen, 94–95; also *Welt als Wille und Vorstellung,* 2:188, 195; *Parerga und Paralipomena,* 2:371–72). The consolation comes not from an optimistic interpretation or even the assumption that some might be "saved"; such traditional religious conceptions are rejected as illegitimate. They are at best the "truth clothed in lie" and provide, in the form of allegory and myth, the "insight" into reality that philosophy offers through other means. But no such traditional conceptions can offer true hope. Rather, the religious element emerges from the deep commonality of all beings in the face of the metaphysical principle of absolute will.

It is precisely at this point where we can see a connection to Søren Kierke-gaard (1813–55), who begins his "Speech in Praise of Abraham" that opens *Fear and Trembling* with a similar recognition of the move from despairing in the face of the will to a new communal feeling:

> If there were no eternal consciousness in a man, if at the bottom of everything there were only a wild ferment, a power that twisting in dark passions produced everything great or inconsequential; if an unfathomable, insatiable emptiness lay hid beneath everything, what would life be but despair? If it were thus, if there were no sacred bond

uniting mankind, if one generation rose up after another like the leaves of the forest, . . . how empty and devoid of comfort would life be! But for that reason it is not so, and as God created man and woman, so too he shaped the hero and the poet or speech-maker. (49)

The despair of the world as will creates the possibility for a different faith born of the inexplicable "sacred bond uniting mankind."

Although the twentieth-century new-Marxist Critical Theorist Max Horkheimer sees a danger in this quietist version of Christianity that emerges from Schopenhauer's thought, he does recognize the "transcendental" nature of its claim on us. In a world of commerce and action, in short, a world dominated by "instrumental reason," only a demand of a wholly different sort can provide the possibility of truly seeing all things differently.

Feuerbach—The Anthropological Turn

Ludwig Feuerbach (1805–72) completed his dissertation in Erlangen after his studies in Berlin with Schleiermacher and Hegel, studies that led him to abandon theology for philosophy. Its title shows that he was focused on the absolute status of *logos*—"De ratione una, universali, infinita" ("On the Unity, Universality, and Infinity of Reason," 1828)—for although he was beginning to distance himself from his teacher, the insistence on *ratio* and *unity* indicates his commitment to the Hegelian project. His first published work, *Gedanken über Tod und Unsterblichkeit (Thoughts on Death and Immortality;* anonymous, 1830), engaged in a sharply critical investigation of Christian doctrine under the motto of overcoming opposition in a more radical way than Hegel did. That is, he, too, considered the driving concern or need of his age as the overcoming of contradiction, but this mission was leading him toward a unity focused on *one side* of the opposition. He called that side, in opposition to the spiritualism of Hegel's philosophy of *Geist,* an emphasis on "sensuality" (*Sinnlichkeit*)—whereby he meant (1) what can be experienced by the senses, (2) materialism in general (in order to avoid the repetition of Idealism),[31] and (3) the otherness of other human beings (their character as *Du*-Thou). The divisions between mankind and God had to be resolved for the sake of mankind, which was the source of both the divisions and the sought-after unity.

---

31. That is, if we know only what appears to us through the senses, then we might start down the road of Kantian Idealism all over again. Feuerbach emphasized the sensual as the radical Other of spirit.

He argued that the time had come for overcoming (*aufzuheben*) the division between the here and the beyond not to attain a "higher unity" but so that humanity might concentrate with its whole soul, its whole heart on *itself*. Like Hegel, he sees mankind suffering from a split consciousness, torn between his finitude and the idea of the infinite. The only way to overcome this suffering is to destroy the idea of the infinite as separate, which means "infinitizing the finite" and seeing in the infinite just the projection of the (infinite capabilities within the) finite. He formulated these critical ideas in his *Das Wesen des Christentums* (*The Essence of Christianity*, 1841), which was first to have the title "Kritik der reinen Unvernunft" ("Critique of Pure Unreason") as an echo of the "*Alles-Zermalmer*" Kant. The task of this text is to overcome (in the Hegelian sense of *aufzuheben*) the fundamentally destructive opposition of the human and the divine by demonstrating "that this antithesis, this differencing of God and man, with which religion begins, is a differencing of man with his own nature" (*Essence of Christianity*, 33). The way he fulfilled this task of uniting the human and the divine can be approached from four directions, which we could characterize as philosophical-historical, logical, phenomenological, and anthropological-critical.

In a first approach to Feuerbach's contribution to the history of theological thought, we can pursue the way he envisioned himself growing out of the developments of modern philosophy in such a way that he solved the fundamental problem of dualism. In solving this problem inherited in the present from the past, he saw himself as offering a philosophy of the future. In his own preface to his 1846 collected works (published in the 1904 edition, 403–11) he summarized his basic position. Writing in the second person (he's addressing himself), he discusses his own development. He saw in the past a major internal split or contradiction: "One is able to recognize the truth of sensuousness in the sphere of the natural sciences, but must deny it at the same time in the spheres of philosophy and religion. . . . Bacon, Descartes, Leibniz, Bayle, more recent philosophers and even the most up-to-date philosophers of our day—all are glowing examples of this division" (408). He overcame this contradiction by his study of those who were plagued by it. When he finally got to Luther (409) he could see that not only is the heterogeneous object of religion (God) a projection but all philosophical abstractions have that character. Hence he can conclude: "This is what holds your [i.e., his, Feuerbach's] writings together: they contain nothing but the history, the involuntary origin and development, and hence the justification of your contemporary standpoint" (410). And since the history of his own writing recapitulates the history of (modern) philosophy, he is implying that the very history of modern philosophy leads to his critique of religion. The debates of the seventeenth and eighteenth centuries about the existence of God have led to Feuerbach's denial of Him:

> The question of whether or not God exists, the opposition between theism and atheism, belongs to the eighteenth and seventeenth centuries, but no longer to the nineteenth. I negate/deny God. For me this means: I negate the negation of humanity, I replace the illusory, phantasmatic, and heavenly position of humanity, which in real life leads to humanity's negation, with the sensual, real, consequently necessarily also political and social position of humanity. The question of the existence or nonexistence of God is thus for me in fact the question of the existence or nonexistence of humanity. (411)

In a second approach to Feuerbach's project, we can consider how he continues the discussions that we have been pursuing from Leibniz through Hegel concerning the nature of God as understood from the perspective of logical predicates. We recall that Leibniz drew radical and at first fully counterintuitive conclusions from the assumption that each subject contains an entire universe of predicates. That view made each being a monad, a unique "perspective" on the world, from which all other beings could be deduced by following the law of sufficient reason. (Start with Caesar and inquire into his mother, his teacher, his murderer, etc.) God emerged as the "harmonizer" of all these monads/perspectives, the being ensuring with his divine necessity that their contingent perspectives match, making this the "best of all possible worlds." Feuerbach, too, reflects on the nature of predicates, asking what it means to apply predicates to the divine being. We examine statements like: "God is X, Y, Z." We notice that all such predicates are derived from human experience (omniscient, benevolent, wise, etc.). This leads to three possibilities:

1. God cannot have human attributes, therefore all such statements and predicates of God are empty. But if that is the case, then God cannot exist, for what would it mean to say that God exists but is not anything (no predicate could be attached to Him?). Or, what is the same, what would it mean to say that God *is* but is devoid of predicates? "Where man deprives God of all qualities, God is no longer anything more to him than a negative being" (*Essence of Christianity*, 14).
2. God *in Himself* cannot have those attributes, only God *as we experience* Him, i.e., as He is for us. But this distinction between a God of experience and God as a thing-in-itself makes no more sense than Kant's (as Hegel and the other Idealists had shown), since it, by the logic

we just saw, reduces (God as) the thing-in-itself into an empty "pure Being" that might as well be Nothing.[32] That is, a "pure" but empty "God in Himself" without attributes associated with our experience of Him would not be the God of any kind of religion. Religions have at their center gods that can in some way be *experienced* (and hence they fall prey to the dialectic of experience). "To the truly religious man, God is not a being without qualities, because to him he is a positive, real being" (*Essence of Christianity,* 14).

3. This leaves the third possibility, namely, that God cannot be separated from the human understanding of Him/Her/It (even the gender attribute demonstrates this, since we *have* to attribute something like gender as a predicate). In short, all conceptions of God are necessarily anthropomorphic. We might say (falsely): there are some human predicates, but God is more, which we can't appreciate in this world. But God is *nothing but the totality of diverse human predicates.* "The mystery of the inexhaustible fullness of the divine predicates is therefore nothing else than the mystery of human nature considered as an infinitely varied, infinitely modifiable, but, consequently, phenomenal being" (*Essence of Christianity*, 23). The "is" that connects any proposition of the form "God is X," where X is a predicate derived from human experience, performs the "unity of the human and divine" in the most concrete fashion. And in so doing, "reduces" the divine from its status as radically Other to a being with human, all too human, attributes.

The third way that Feuerbach accomplishes his "task" of uniting the human and the divine is through a kind of phenomenological exploration of human experience in a quasi-Hegelian vein. Where Hegel offered a general "science of the experience of consciousness," i.e., a systematic study of the way consciousness experiences the world and itself, Feuerbach focuses on the particular phenomenon of *religious consciousness,* whereby consciousness needs to be thought of in terms of the broader ways in which mind interacts with the world, including "thinking, feeling, wanting" (intentional acts). The point of Hegel's project was to show that each time consciousness has an "experience," it goes through three steps: (1) what it experiences is held up as completely Other, as "in itself"; (2) but insofar as it experiences that Other, consciousness recognizes that the Other is actually there "for" con-

---

32. Feuerbach could be said to think through the concept of God the way Hegel did "pure Being" at the opening of his *Logic.*

sciousness (and hence consciousness is, in an important sense, experiencing *itself* for itself and not the other *in itself*); (3) but consciousness also knows that it could not have that experience of itself if it were not for that other,[33] that is, the experience actually consists of a simultaneity of the other and the self, whereby both are now changed since they cannot be understood independent of each other. Feuerbach works this argument out in relatively straightforward terms in analyzing love or desire.[34] Consider the scenario of the lover and the beloved: I love you. I say that I love you "for what you really are." But if "what you really are" did not "speak to me," then would I really love you? Hence, what I really love is the fact that something in me is being spoken to. But it would be pure egotism if I did not maintain the important "fiction"—or, as a phenomenologist might say, the intentional object of consciousness—that you are really different and that is what I love. (Note how relationships break up when the egotism takes over: "It was never really about me, was it? This relationship was really only ever about you. . . .") Real love is the maintenance of both the self-reflective aspect of the ego and the positing of a genuine Other outside that ego. It might seem as if, by recognizing that in loving another person I really only love some feeling/thing inside myself, I might be destroying love itself. But I am not—because that special feeling can take place only in relation to another person. So even though the other person and the feelings are not really separate and "in themselves" (*an sich*), they are nonetheless key components of the feeling. Transferred onto the religious consciousness, Feuerbach concludes: I know that when I love God I am loving something about my own consciousness, but it is nonetheless a special mode of loving myself to love through "God." In Feuerbach's words: "The divine nature which is discerned by feeling is in truth nothing else than feeling enraptured, in ecstasy with itself " (*Essence of*

---

33. As Kant says in schematic and nonprocessural terms, experience consists of two poles, the manifold of the senses and the addition of the categories.

34. One could play this out for aesthetic consciousness as well: first, consider the idea that "beauty is in the eyes of the beholder." There is some sense in which we want to ascribe beauty to the object. (And the fact is, we do need an object. It must exist. But as such, it is empty, nothing, has no inspiring qualities, etc., until *we* start to ascribe predicates to it.) We want to say that the "harmony of structure," or the "intensity of color," etc., are beautiful. *Really*, what we are saying is that "I like a certain interplay of color and so *I* find this object beautiful." As we reflect more on this interaction between object and ourselves, we realize that we can learn more about *ourselves* by thinking about beautiful objects than about the objects themselves. It would be a very "objectifying" and ultimately self-effacing approach to deny the role we play in the assessment of aesthetic qualities. Moreover, let's say that as our own sense of inadequacy grows, the stature of the object grows, and vice versa. The more I attribute beauty to the object, the less I see myself as capable of making or being something like that. So we need to turn this around and say that *we* are the ones who determine beauty from the start so we are not passive, having the things (or others, like priests) dictate values to us.

Christianity, 9). Likewise, I know that God is "only" my creation, but He's my creation as something different from myself.

The fourth approach that Feuerbach takes is to ask what people "really do" when they are religious as opposed to what they often think they do and what philosophers say they do. "I, on the contrary, let religion itself speak; I constitute myself only its listener and interpreter, not its prompter" (*Essence of Christianity,* xvi). This anthropological-critical perspective begins with the assumption that the goal of religious practice is to make real the unity of the divine and the human, i.e., to connect with "God" (in whatever form) and to have "God" connect with us. All forms of prayer and sacrifice make sense only under this assumption of a fundamental identity. After all, counterfactually, it is not likely that much of a religion could develop out of the notion that God is so abstract, so different, that no form of exchange or communication is possible. Similarly, as he implies, all the wars of religion are not fought over an abstract and unknowable being but over different representations and senses of a God who responds to the warring parties (after all, each thinks it has reason to believe that God is "on their side"). And yet religion—and especially the discipline reflecting on religion (theology)—time and again turns that identity into an opposition, thereby turning against its own essence. The usual response of a religious person to the notion that the basis of religious belief is an assumed *commonality* between them and God is to resist and claim: "But God is (radically, absolutely) *different.*" In so doing, religion goes against itself. "Religion is the relation of man to his own nature . . .; but to his nature not recognised as his own, but regarded as another nature, separate, nay, contradistinguished from his own; herein lies its untruth, its limitation, its contradiction to reason and morality; herein lies the noxious source of religious fanaticism, the chief metaphysical principle of human sacrifices" (*Essence of Christianity,* 197). In pointing out this essence of religion, Feuerbach is engaged in a deeply ambivalent enterprise: on the one hand he is attacking religion as such for being "noxious" and necessarily blind to its diversion of human ambitions from human goals; on the other, he can be seen to be "saving" religious consciousness, now redefined in terms as a "relation of man to his own nature," insofar as its self-transcending perspective is held up as an essential part of human nature.

One consequence of Feuerbach's view is a critique of the entire tradition of theology. For example, the entire enterprise of "proving" God's existence becomes absurd and based on a fundamental and dangerous mistake (*Essence of Christianity,* 20). If God and man are essentially the same, if all religion actually assumes in each of its real manifestations the connection between God and man, then it makes about as much sense to "prove" God's existence as it would to "prove" my feelings for God. The need for such proofs emerges only after philosophical thought has abstracted "God" as a separate being that then our connection to would have to be demonstrated. Feuerbach's goal is not to demonstrate God but to make clear the "mystery of religion," which he formulates as a kind of inverse dialectic, isolating that which is/ought to be united: "Man—this is the mystery of religion— projects his being into objectivity, and then again makes himself an object to this projected image of himself thus converted into a subject; he thinks of himself as an object to himself, but as the object of an object, of another being than himself" (*Essence of Christianity*, 29–30). Moreover, like Hegel, he offers a historical perspective because he has a normative proposition— the degree of mankind's self-alienation—against which to measure cultural/ religious developments; only in Feuerbach's case, history seems to cause the dialectic to get worse rather than better. Feuerbach sees the early stages of religion as *less* problematic than the later ones, since in more "primitive" reli- gions man makes a separation but then "just as immediately again identifies them" (197)—that is, gods are very much a part of the human world. Over time, with "theology" and an increased attention of the "understanding" to the problem of religion, the separation between man and God becomes so strong that the latter gets banished to an untouchable, ineffable, and inef- fective realm. This process reaches its height in deism. But just as we saw that Kant justified the "proofs" because they sharpened the mind, here, too, we might say that the God of the deists, or Kant's divine lawgiver, might be horribly wrong, abstracted, and objectified, but at least philosophy has also given us the tools to see through this development. Hope will emerge once philosophy turns the tools of its reasoning back onto the human realm (and becomes, in essence, anthropology).

How does philosophy lead to the separation of man and God? Or, to echo Pascal, how does the "God of the philosophers" prove to be inadequate to the "essence of religion"? We saw earlier in the chapter on Kant that the deist arguments for the existence of God, as rational as they might have seemed, were not only logically unsound but, almost more important, do not have any impact on the way we conduct our lives. A divine "watchmaker," Kant criticized, might be postulated to account for the regularity of Newtonian physical laws in the universe, but this sort of entity does not offer me a reason to be a good person. Kierkegaard and Feuerbach overlap on an essential point vis-à-vis Kant insofar as they turned this same Kantian argument against the master: the moral God, as Kant justified Him, might be "necessary" for rea- son to guarantee itself, but this argument neither guarantees my actual faith (which, for Kierkegaard, is grounded in a nonrational decision of my individuality) nor gives me any emotive or other access to that God who stands over me as judge. Hence, according to Feuerbach, the moral argument for the existence of God might be philosophical but it is profoundly unreligious because it fails to do what religion strives for: create a mutual relationship between man and God. In fact, one could say that the rational faith Kant develops in a moral God does away with religion as worship, since what such a God demands (or what we need that God to demand) is worthiness based on moral behavior and not worship. Feuerbach goes through these different proofs in the opening chapters of *Essence of Christianity,* not to "prove" or "disprove" them but to show how they in fact lead to "atheism," or more precisely, to irreligiosity, insofar as they posit a "God in heaven" (the "God of the philosophers") with ideal characteristics and hence deny the longing in humanity for the *identification* with the divine.

In the two halves of the book, then, he generally argues these two sides of the phenomenon: in the first (positively) he shows how religion functions as a product of the human spirit and in the second (negatively) he criticizes the misrecognition of the essence of religion. It is that misrecognition that is the root of man's denial of his own divinity: in a kind of Hegelian move, he is ultimately affirmative by means of a double negation, i.e., a critique of religion's mis-understanding of its real essence. Hence, it can be argued that in a crucial sense, despite the vehemence of his *Religionskritik,* he is less out to debunk religion as such than to reveal the powerful human endeavor that religion is as a mode of self-transcendence and then to reject the tendency of religion, and certainly of theology, to deny the humanity of religion because they are focused on the otherness of God. As he progresses through a wide variety of practices, sacraments, or core beliefs of (the Christian) religion, such as baptism, or original sin, or salvation, he reinterprets them in terms of their origins in the human condition. For example, baptism can be understood as an expression of the close associations humans have with water as a cleansing and life-granting element, an expression, however, that denies that origin by placing the significance in a divine commandment (*Essence of Christianity,* 275–77). Likewise, the belief in salvation emerges from the human self-recognition of incompleteness, suffering, and lack *combined with* the desire for completeness, happiness, and fulfillment: "God is the realised salvation of the soul, or the unlimited power of effecting the salvation, the bliss of man" (185).

Taken to its logical conclusion, this view of religion, the insistence on unity of *Diesseits und Jenseits*, immanence and transcendence, in a self-recognizing and self-transcending humanity, leads to two additional consequences. At the level of *philosophy,* Feuerbach comes to embrace a materialism (or, in his terms, *Sinnlichkeit*), since the emergence of "spiritual" ideas out of projections from bodily experiences reduces the former to the latter. Further, Feuerbach does not hesitate to become involved with the *political* movements of his day that are likewise addressing precisely the material conditions of a suffering humanity. He expresses support for the revolutions of 1830 and 1848 and, though never fully espousing communism, joins the Social Democrats in their efforts on behalf of the workers. And he was to suffer at the hands of the very state apparatus that Hegel had supported and even aligned with a state religion because Feuerbach rejected the way that religion blinded mankind to the lacking material conditions to which the religion was offering "spiritual" compensation. His critique of religion through philosophy came to be a critique *of* philosophy and politics.

Coda: The Continued Life of Religion in Capitalism

Feuerbach's critique of religion has an important afterlife because religion itself does. It is, of course, Marx who provides a more radically reductive account of religion than Feuerbach, making his focus not the nature of "religious consciousness" but the material conditions that produce that consciousness. In doing so he also embeds religion within the sphere of life forces in a new and productive way. The most famous passage by Marx on religion, from the introduction to "Zur Kritik der Hegelschen *Rechtsphilosophie*" ("Contribution to a Critique of Hegel's *Philosophy of Right*"), was published in the *Deutsch-Französische Jahrbücher* in 1844. It was written after Marx had spent some time in Berlin in the decade after the death of Hegel. He had been involved with the more radical "left Hegelians" and submitted a dissertation to Feuerbach on classical Greek thought. It is clear from that early work that he already had adopted a largely atheist position even before he developed his associations with and ideas on communism.[35] This relationship is important since it means that the critique of religion gets carried into his analysis of the economy, and thus even after his acceptance of an atheist position he will encounter forms of "religion." Marx writes:

> For Germany, the criticism of religion has been essentially completed, and the criticism of religion is the prerequisite of all criticism.
>
> The profane existence of error is compromised as soon as its heavenly *oratio pro aris et focis* [speech for the altars and hearths] has been

---

35. Hans Küng: "Marx was an atheist long before he was a communist! His anti-capitalist position was not the precondition but the confirmation of his atheism" (257).

refuted. Man, who has found only the reflection of himself in the fantastic reality of heaven, where he sought a superman, will no longer feel disposed to find the mere appearance of himself, the non-man [*Unmensch*], where he seeks and must seek his true reality.

The foundation of irreligious criticism is: Man makes religion, religion does not make man.

Religion is, indeed, the self-consciousness and self-esteem of man who has either not yet won through to himself, or has already lost himself again. But, *man* is no abstract being squatting outside the world. Man is *the world of man*—state, society. This state and this society produce religion, which is an inverted consciousness of the world, because they are an inverted world. Religion is the general theory of this world, its encyclopaedic compendium, its logic in popular form, its spiritual point d'honneur, it enthusiasm, its moral sanction, its solemn complement, and its universal basis of consolation and justification. It is the fantastic realization of the human essence since the human essence has not acquired any true reality. The struggle against religion is, therefore, indirectly the struggle against that world whose spiritual aroma is religion.

Religious suffering is, at one and the same time, the expression of real suffering and a protest against real suffering. Religion is the sigh of the oppressed creature, the heart of a heartless world, and the soul of soulless conditions. It is the opium of the people.

The abolition of religion as the *illusory* happiness of the people is the demand for their *real* happiness. To call on them to give up their illusions about their condition is to call on them to give up a condition that requires illusions. The criticism of religion is, therefore, in embryo, the criticism of that vale of tears of which religion is the halo. (16–17)

By declaring the "criticism of religion" to be "essentially completed," Marx is not calling for an end to the project of enlightenment or the period of Enlightenment. Rather, he is making two claims about his own status as critic, indeed the status of criticism itself, within a specific historical development. First, the "essence" of religion has been revealed (here he is obviously playing off Feuerbach's title), and so that mode of criticism, i.e., the criticism that has the phenomenon of religion as its object, would be at this point pointless. Once the "foundation" has been exposed—"Man makes religion, religion does not make man"—there is nothing left to be said about religion itself as a separate sphere of human activity. But, second, this is not to say that "all criticism" has come to an end. In fact, we still need to understand something about the "criticism of religion" if criticism in principle is going to continue. We need to understand its *form* and we need to understand the consequence of the completion of religious criticism, namely, that all such systems of belief are *products of human activity.*

Implicit in this statement is the conclusion that another product of human activity—in particular the mode of production of capitalism—itself is structured by the underlying form of religion and thus in need of the same form of critique adopted from the study of religion.[36]

---

36. Projects undertaken by Max Weber in *The Protestant Work Ethic and the Spirit of Capitalism* (1904–5) and hinted at in Walter Benjamin's intriguing fragment "Capitalism as Religion."

❧ CHAPTER 6

Nietzsche

Logos *against Itself and the Death of God*

Historia in nuce. The most serious parody that I have ever heard: "In the beginning was nonsense, and nonsense was, by God! and the nonsense was God (divine)." (*Historia in nuce.* Die ernsthafteste Parodie, die ich je hörte, ist diese: "im Anfang war der Unsinn, und der Unsinn war, bei Gott!, und Gott (göttlich) war der Unsinn.")

—Nietzsche, *Menschliches, Allzumenschliches (Human, All Too Human)*

Rationality ex post facto. Whatever lives long is gradually so saturated with reason that its irrational origins become improbable. Does not almost every accurate history of the origin of something sound paradoxical and sacrilegious to our feelings? Doesn't the good historian *contradict* all the time?

—Nietzsche, *Morgenröte (Dawn)*

What is the whole of modern philosophy doing at bottom? Since Descartes—actually more despite him than because of his precedent—all the philosophers seek to assassinate the old soul concept, under the guise of a critique of the subject-and-predicate concept—which means an attempt on the life of the basic presupposition of the Christian doctrine. Modern philosophy, being an epistemological skepticism, is, covertly or overtly, *anti-Christian*—although, to say this for the benefit of more refined ears, by no means anti-religious.

—Nietzsche, *Jenseits von Gut und Böse (Beyond Good and Evil)*

This is how Nietzsche sees himself: his thought has grown out of Christianity through Christian motivations. His struggle against Christianity in no way intends to simply abandon Christianity or remove it from history or return to a time prior to it; rather, he wants to overcome it, surpass it, with forces that Christianity and only Christianity has developed.

—Karl Jaspers, *Nietzsche und das Christentum (Nietzsche and Christianity)*

Near the opening of his essay on religion, Derrida offers an initial definition of, or approach to, the singularity of religion: "Before even envisaging the semantic history of testimony, of oaths, of the given word (a *genealogy* and interpretation that are indispensable to whomever hopes to think religion under its proper or secularized forms), before even recalling that some sort of 'I promise the truth' is always at work, and some sort of 'I make this commitment before the other from the moment I address him,' . . . we must formally take note of the fact that we are already speaking Latin" (*Religion,* 26–27; my emphasis). While Derrida will go on to make a major point of the concept of *mondialatinisation* ("this strange alliance of Christianity, as the experience of the death of God, and tele-technoscientific capitalism" [*Religion,* 13]), the unspoken reference that I wish to point out here is to Nietzsche, for whom the ultimate critique of religion comes from a *genealogy of morals,* at the beginning of which is nature's "primary task" for mankind, namely, "to cultivate a creature with the right to make promises" (*Genealogy of Morals,* 2, § 1).[1] Indeed, Derrida did mention Nietzsche explicitly in his introductory comments, where he raised the provocative question of whether Kant's thesis was, "at the core of its content, Nietzsche's thesis at the same time that he is conducting an inexpiable war against Kant" (*Religion,* 11). What connects the two is that they both discover and think through "a certain internalizing movement within Christianity" (ibid.). While, according to Derrida, for Nietzsche this movement "was his primary enemy and that bore for him the gravest responsibility" (ibid.), the key point for us is the way Nietzsche lays bare an inherent logic or *logos* ("internalizing movement") within the history of Christianity. Nietzsche, Derrida continues, thereby "tells us something about the history of the world." I present the argument that Nietzsche's genealogical argument about the history of Western thought returns to the "beginnings" in order to show how the *logos* of Christianity turns against itself.

The trajectory has been mapped out in the previous chapters. We recall that according to Kant there were three major proofs for the existence of God: the ontological, the cosmological, and the physicotheological. Having dismissed them, he avoids atheism by introducing one more, the only firm one, namely, moral theology. As in a game of musical chairs, all the places for God to sit firmly have been removed one by one until Kant left but a single remaining seat: ethics, the moral law we as rational and autonomous beings give to ourselves. The anthropological turn of the critiques of religion in the

---

1. References to the *Genealogy of Morals* give essay number and aphorism number.

nineteenth century laid the groundwork for the obvious next move. After all, if there is but *one* solid proof, and that proof rests on the status of *morality*, would that not leave but *one* target for the ultimate critique of the concept of God, namely, *morality*? Nietzsche undertakes this attack and pulls the seat out from under God. That is what Derrida means by the simultaneity of Nietzsche's Kantianism—the identification of God/Christianity and morality—and his radical anti-Kantianism—the anthropo-psycho-genea-logical assault on the very foundation and origin of morals.

The reason for Nietzsche's complicated assault is that, as we have seen in the last chapters, the "death of God" is not a one-time affair. The death of God can in fact lead to multiple resurrections—either in the form of Hegelian *Geist* after the *Aufhebung* of religion into philosophy, or in the form of different Others of reason, or in the spirits of capitalism. God and religion return again and again in different guises. Thus, Nietzsche is not out to make yet another argument against the existence of God. Rather, he, as we have been doing, must work through the very history of theological thinking in order to get to the very roots of the idea of God in the tradition of Christianity. Karl Jaspers summarizes: "[Nietzsche] asks: *Why* has God died? Only one of his answers is fully thought through and developed: the cause of the death of God is Christianity" (*Nietzsche und das Christentum* [Nietzsche and Christianity], 15). The reason for this bold and ironic assertion lies in Nietzsche's continuation of the kind of arguments we have seen before. Kant said: the earlier proofs (ontological, cosmological, physicoteleological) are all weak; if we depend on them *and* their weakness is revealed, then we lose faith. Hence, we need to abandon them, risk atheism . . . only to find another, stronger argument (the moral proof). Nietzsche says: the entire history of Christianity is a "weak" form of believing in God, including or especially its morality; since it has dominated as a fiction in the West for two thousand years, and since it is now revealed in all its weakness (and danger), we are left with atheism . . . not until we find another *argument* for the belief in God, but another belief entirely, indeed, another god.

Nietzsche and the Tradition

It is ironic that Nietzsche, the son of a Protestant pastor, came to hold the German tradition of Protestantism guilty for the continued life of the Christian God. Late in his life he characterized this German responsibility in a bitter formulation: "If one is unable to be done with Christianity, it will be the Germans' fault" (*Antichrist,* § 61). Nietzsche has in mind a unique and somewhat quirky argument about the Renaissance (an argument that he undoubtedly developed out of his knowledge of Jacob Burckhardt's studies), namely, that the Italian Renaissance was leading to a kind of self-cancellation of Christianity since the Catholic Church had internalized the "will to power" of rediscovered Roman antiquity, and that it was Luther's critique of the papacy that allowed for a resurgence of religious sentiment and faith. Nietzsche's often scathing characterizations of the "peasant" Luther, "a monk with all the vengeful instincts of a frustrated priest in his body," arose from his historical argument that Luther prevented the victory of the Renaissance's perfect, strong, pagan image of man, that he brought the dying church back to life.[2] But for our purposes, we can take the general point that Nietzsche makes as our guide: "Ah, these Germans, what they have cost us!" (*Antichrist*, § 61).

Three brief aphorisms from his early text *Morgenröte* (*Dawn*) show that Nietzsche was fully aware of the tradition of arguments we have been pursuing. Although it is well known that he did not enjoy—in all senses—a strict training and background in the history of philosophy, he saw the broad outlines of a development embedded in discussions about the existence of God. Nietzsche, too, had originally been destined to study theology and was aware of general theological debates. He had two insights into the nature of this development. The first was to sense that the "end of God" would not result from a particular argument, that proofs or disproofs were not the point. But rather, the very *history* of those arguments contains the seeds of God's end. Hence he writes:

> *Historical refutation as the definitive refutation.* In former times, one sought to prove that there is no God—today one indicates how the belief that there is a God could *arise* and how this belief acquired its weight and importance: a counterproof that there is no God thereby becomes superfluous. When in former times one had refuted the 'proofs of the existence of God' put forward, there always remained the doubt whether better proofs might not be adduced than those just refuted: in those days atheists did not know how to make a clean sweep. (*Morgenröte,* book 1, § 95)

This historical insight, which in a sense is not unlike the one we saw Hegel introduce, will have profound consequences because it opens the way to an entirely new interpretation of the direction of that history. That is, where Hegel, building off of Kant's analysis of "radical evil" and institutional pro-

---

2. See Ernst Benz, chapter 1.

cesses, described a historical dialectic between the "spirit" and "letter" (positivity) of religion that results in its eventual *Aufhebung,* Nietzsche considers its history as a movement toward self-destruction. Where Hegel saw both the inevitability of stultified or ossified theological forms *and* the possibility for overcoming them through a double negation that could open up a renewal of the inner spirit of faith, Nietzsche sees the history of theological debate, or the unfolding of belief together with *logos,* as itself a downward spiral. The reason is—and this is his second insight—that the motivations of those participating in this history (the philosophers and, he will later show, the "priests" and believers in general) must be taken into account. Indeed, in a reductive twist on Feuerbach, Nietzsche argues that the history of arguments about God is driven not by the desire for (false) "transcendence" in human beings but by the attempt to establish the optimal conditions for survival. Hence, in the first book of *Dawn* § 90, *Egoism against egoism* we see how Nietzsche very consciously plays off and reinterprets the very status of the moral "proofs" for the existence of God: "How many there are who still conclude: 'Life could not be endured if there were not God!' (or, as it is put among the idealists: 'Life could not be endured if its foundation lacked an ethical significance!')—therefore there *must* be a God (or existence *must* have ethical significance)!" Nietzsche then wonders whether such claims are not really statements of what the speakers need for their own preservation and whether others might actually find these conditions intolerable and dangerous for their own preservation. Thus, in an argument echoing though not following Marx, he states that if people put together a God for their own self-preservation, the "middle classes" need their own. But this is the gradual end of God Himself. The aphorism *On the deathbed of Christianity* (*Am Sterbebette des Christentums; Morgenröte,* § 92) argues that the turn to a moral understanding of Christianity is already part of its "euthanasia" because it simplifies religion to make it fit ("*zurechtgemachtes*"), so that it creates a God who would be nice (moral) enough to make the world fit our own reason, even if not our well-being. In fact, "the truly active men are already in their thoughts without Christianity," and it is only "the milder and more contemplative men of the spiritual middle class" ("die mäßigeren und betrachtsameren Menschen des geistigen Mittelstandes") who have worked out this weaker version.[3] We will explore the consequences of these two

---

3. Recall the conclusion of the previous chapter. The reference here to "*Mittelstand*" is not by chance since Nietzsche is presenting his own version of the impact and origin of the "Protestant work ethic." That is, for Nietzsche the same "religious" sentiments are at work in the (literal and intellectual) economy of his day.

insights—the historical and the naturalistic-motivational—in Nietzsche's thought. They combine to form the ultimate conclusion that the "euthanasia" of God is not so much a "moment" in the infinite unfolding of *Geist* but the inevitable consequence of the human, all too human, history of needs and wills.[4] This history—as he says in the aphorism that serves as an epigraph to this chapter—is thus not carried along by the unfolding of God as *logos* but by the human need to create meaning out of meaninglessness/nonsense (*Unsinn*). The God that emerges out of this need cannot last long once new sources of meaning are created.

The contradiction inherent in Christianity lies in the very nature of its *logos* and conception of the world as divine creation. The Greeks (esp. the Stoics) saw the cosmos as regulated by an inherent order that could be penetrated by reason. But beyond that was mere matter, unknowable and thus unworthy of investigation. For Christianity, however, the drive to know is without end and thus opens itself up to the unknowable. Jaspers writes:

> In the *logos* itself the drive awakens to push oneself time and again to the point of breaking (*zum Scheitern zu bringen*), but not to give up, but to gain a new and more fulfilled form of oneself and to continue this process without end or ultimate fulfillment. Such is the science that arises out of the *logos* that *never contains itself* but which instead *opens itself up to the alogon* (*der sich nicht in sich schließt, sondern dem Alogon aufgeschlossen*), penetrating it and submitting to it. . . . [It is a universal process] sparked by the tension between *logos* and *alogon*. (*Nietzsche und das Christentum*, 59)

Nietzsche pushes this tension to the point of contradiction. That is, he argues that the very logic of the Christian-scientific *logos* confronts it with the infinity and hence groundlessness of its world. What might still be conceived by Hegel as a dialectical unfolding of *Geist* contained within a system becomes for Nietzsche a drive that leaves humanity without firm ground under its feet. For some, this state becomes unbearable, and so they turn to metaphysical consolations or the distractions of modern life to grant them a hold. (This is likely how Nietzsche would have regarded the way Schleiermacher, Schelling, Schopenhauer, and Kierkegaard reacted to the crisis or groundlessness of reason.) For others, the Nietzschean "free spirits," the world is embraced not in its absolute totality but in its infinite perspectives, none of which can aspire to a "god's-eye view."

---

4. In the next chapter we will see how Heidegger raises this story of human motivations and interactions again to the unfolding of the "history of Being itself" (*Seinsgeschichte*).

The Insane Call of the Death of God

Of course, Nietzsche knows that to call explicitly for the death of that being that had been believed, from the beginning, to be the source of all *logos,* you'd have to be crazy. At least, at first, that is, until the very nature of *logos* has been rethought. Perhaps this is why his most famous and infamous aphorism on the death of God is entitled: *"Der tolle Mensch"* ("The Madman" or "The insane man"; *Die fröhliche Wissenschaft [The Gay Science]*, § 125). Like Heidegger, whose general interpretative line I will be following here,[5] I quote the text in full (here from the Kaufmann translation) because of its notoriety and ironic richness:

§ 125. Have you not heard of that madman who lit a lantern in the bright morning hours, ran to the market place and cried incessantly: "I seek God! I seek God!"—As many of those who did not believe in God were standing around just then, he provoked much laughter. Has he got lost? asked one. Did he lose his way like a child? asked another. Or is he hiding? Is he afraid of us? Has he gone on a voyage? emigrated?—Thus they yelled and laughed.

The madman jumped into their midst and pierced them with his eyes. "Whither is God?" he cried. "I will tell you. We have killed him— you and I. All of us are his murderers. But how did we do this? How could we drink up the sea? Who gave us the sponge to wipe away the entire horizon? What were we doing when we unchained this earth from its sun? Whither is it moving now? Whither are we moving? Away from all suns? Are we not plunging continually? Backward, sideward, forward, in all directions? Is there still any up or down? Are we not straying as through an infinite nothing? Do we not feel the breath of empty space? Has it not become colder? Is not night continually closing in on us? Do we not need to light lanterns in the morning? Do we not hear nothing as yet of the noise of the gravediggers who are burying God? Do we smell nothing as yet of the divine decomposition? Gods, too, decompose. God is dead. God remains dead. And we have killed him.

---

5. The next chapter will examine Heidegger's interpretation of Nietzsche more closely, and there I will distance myself from some of Heidegger's larger claims and gestures. However, some of his specific readings of passages from this aphorism are insightful. See "Nietzsches Wort 'Gott ist tot'" in *Holzwege.* Eugen Biser offers a closer reading of this passage and the very idea of the death of God in Nietzsche. Rather than locate this passage within the context of the history of Western thought in general (or as the end stage of modern nihilism), as do Heidegger and Buber (*Gottesfinsternis*), Biser locates this idea within the context of Nietzsche's own thought and intellectual history.

"How shall we comfort ourselves, the murderers of all murderers? What was holiest and mightiest of all that the world has yet owned has bled to death under our knives: who will wipe this blood off us? What water is there for us to clean ourselves? What festivals of atonement, what sacred games shall we have to invent? Is not the greatness of this deed too great for us? Must we ourselves not become gods simply to appear worthy of it? There has never been a greater deed; and whoever is born after us—for the sake of this deed he will belong to a higher history than all history hitherto."

Here the madman fell silent and looked again at his listeners; and they, too, were silent and stared at him in astonishment. At last he threw his lantern to the ground, and it broke into pieces and went out. "I have come too early," he said then; "my time is not yet. This tremendous event is still on its way, still wandering; it has not yet reached the ears of men. Lightning and thunder require time; the light of the stars requires time; deeds, though done, still require time to be seen and heard. This deed is still more distant from them than the most distant stars—and yet they have done it themselves."

It has been related further that on the same day the madman forced his way into several churches and there struck up his requiem aeternam deo. Led out and called to account, he is said always to have replied nothing but: "What after all are these churches now if they are not the tombs and sepulchers of God?"

We should first take note of the fact that this aphorism, unlike most others, directly addresses the readers. The "narrator" ("Nietzsche") asks the readers whether they have not heard of the insane man, thereby both placing us outside of and with a critical distance to the process he is describing (if we haven't yet heard of him, then we are not one of the ones being described in the aphorism) and implicating us into its logic since the aphorism itself deals with the issue of those who have not yet really *heard* the message of God's death. Hence, we are expected to take a stance vis-à-vis this message.

Nietzsche distinguishes between the insane man and the others who mock him on the basis of the nature of their (dis)belief. More precisely, for the insane man, it is not just a question of no longer believing in God. Such a state of mind seems to be a mere *absence* of faith. Nietzsche describes it in great detail in § 58 of *Beyond Good and Evil,* where he discusses those around him who, out of their earnestness and attachment to "this modern blaring, time-consuming industriousness, so proud of itself, stupidly proud," have developed a kind of "indifference" ("*Gleichgültigkeit*") and disinclination toward the religious classes. Indeed, modern life seems to be creating the conditions for a lack of interest in religion, to which German Protestants are particularly drawn: "Those indifferent in this way include today the great majority of German middle-class Protestants, especially in the great industrious centers of trade and traffic; also the great majority of industrious scholars and the other accessories of the universities (excepting the theologians, whose presence and possibility there pose ever increasing and ever subtler riddles for a psychologist)."[6] While the possibility of loss of faith may be a fact for or may plague many an individual (one could think of Kierkegaard here), and while there are social conditions that might encourage such indifference, Nietzsche implies that this state is nothing compared to the insight that the insane man bears with him. (To this extent, Nietzsche is not interested in the process of "secularization.") As we saw above, the failure of the different proofs for the existence of God might make one doubt His reality and could lead to nonbelief. But much more frightful is the thought that the entire history of mankind's reasoning has in fact "killed" God. That act is not the same as any one individual's (also Nietzsche's) lack of faith but a historical development that demands a radical change in thinking. One can no longer merely "stand around" (in belief or disbelief) but becomes shaken out of one's ordered world. (In this sense, as Heidegger points out, the man is crazy—*verrückt, ver-rückt*, out of joint.)

Moreover, it is important that he stresses the fact that *we* killed God. Not only does this emphasize the broad historical process but it also shifts the argument away from the Hegelian version of God's death. According to Hegel, God is responsible for His own death. Christ on the cross on Good Friday fulfills God's own mission, which turns that death into a "moment" in a universal history, the end of which is a spiritual second coming (the resurrection in and of philosophy). According to Nietzsche's insane man, however, God did not plan His own death. Rather, the death is characterized as *murder,* removing it from any teleologically oriented mission, indeed destroying the very possibility of teleology.

The result of this murder, then, is a terrifying open-endedness, indeed an openness as has never existed before. The insane man tries to capture this dizzying state in his three rhetorical questions couched in the metaphors of the sea, the horizon, and the planet. In each case he wonders whether man can exist in a realm beyond measure, where there is "neither

---

6. Translation by Walter Kaufmann.

up or down," where all limits can be erased. Again unlike Hegel's infinite God, who contains the infinite loss within Himself, the infinite opened up before the insane man threatens him with such a radical disorientation that he can only live out the contradiction of seeking a God he knows is dead. He has not reached the state of acceptance Nietzsche describes later. (However, I will return to his seeking with a more complex interpretation below.)

Hence, the aphorism on the insane man needs to be read in conjunction with the opening aphorism, § 343, of book 5, "We Fearless Ones" ("Wir Furchtlosen"), the book that Nietzsche added to the second edition of the *Gay Science* in 1887, published five years after the first, and called the most important: *"The meaning of our cheerfulness"* (*Was es mit unserer Heiterkeit auf sich hat*). He speaks of "the greatest recent event—that 'God is dead,' that the belief in the Christian God has become unbelievable" ("Das größte Ereignis—daß 'Gott tot ist,' daß der Glaube an den christlichen Gott unglaubwürdig geworden ist"). It opens up an entire new historical dimension. It "is already beginning to cast its first shadows over Europe," and hence for those with the right eyes, they have a sense of a tendency toward "evening" and a kind of "aging." It brings with it "this monstrous logic of terror, . . . a gloom and an eclipse of the sun whose like has probably never yet occurred on earth." But this "news" has not yet "arrived" and therefore creates a kind of suspended history. The "long plenitude and sequence of breakdown, destruction, ruin, and cataclysm" that this message brings has not yet been spread through the world (no prophet). He—"even we"— stands in this point of transition, "posted between today and tomorrow, stretched in the contradictions between today and tomorrow, we firstlings and premature births of the coming century" and look *forward* to this transition. Why? Because "we" are already "under the impression of the *initial consequences* of this event," namely, "a new and scarcely describable kind of light, relief, exhilaration, encouragement, dawn. . . . At long last the horizon appears free to us again, even if it should not be bright; at long last our ships may venture out to face any danger; all the daring of the lover of knowledge is permitted again; the sea, *our* sea, lies open again; perhaps there has never yet been such an 'open sea.'" The "horizon [is] once again free" and the "sea open."[7] What horizon has actually been opened? How can such a new chapter begin?

---

7. See also the aphorism that precedes the "madman," § 124, "In the horizon of the infinite"; and § 382, "The great health," for further development of this thematic of horizon and sea. See also Biser, 43.

Genealogy: The Birth of God from the Sphere of Morality

Given his historical understanding of God, i.e., the function of God and His shadow in our culture, one would have to go back to the *origins,* the roots, if one were to radically (from Latin *radix,* root) expunge Him from our thinking. If Nietzsche calls for a "new history" and an opening of horizons, one would need to know what actually forms the horizons of our present history. More precisely, given the notion of God as a "living" being, one would need to look at His birth to understand how the seeds of His death were always already present. The site of God's birth for Nietzsche is the sphere of morality. This sphere is not just one among others. Rather, it needs to be considered "phenomenologically," that is, analyzed as the very condition or background against which other phenomena (God Himself) appear. In the following aphorism from *The Gay Science,* Nietzsche in fact offers us a rudimentary phenomenology of moral perception: "*How far the moral sphere extends*" (*Umfang des Moralischen*).—As soon as we see a new image, we immediately construct it with the aid of all our previous experiences, *depending on the degree* of our honesty and justice. All experiences are moral experiences, even in the realm of sense perception" (§ 114). The absolute *priority* of the "sphere [or circumference, or even horizon] of morality" ("*Umfang des Moralischen*"; or, in philosophical terms, the way it functions as a historical a priori for all of human experiences of the world) means that Nietzsche must eventually find a way to explore this field itself. Because he lacks the tools of the later phenomenological movement,[8] he will interpret morals "psychologically." This means that his analysis will have a problematic ambivalence because it will be on the one hand "reductively" psychologistic, and on the other venturing forth into a more general phenomenological or even "transcendental" analysis of the a priori conditions of human experience of the divine. That is, on the one hand God becomes "nothing more" than a human projection for "psychological" reasons and his death is connected to the liberation from those motivations; on the other, given the fact that we live within the circumference or horizon of a moral interpretation of the world, an interpretation that imbues every experience with the very possibility of meaning, the premise of the death of God means that *even* the originary source of meaning needs to be "gotten behind" or "bracketed out" so that we can see what *its* source is in human experience. As Nietzsche indicates in the first aphorism from *Dawn* (cited above as an epigraph), this could mean getting behind or bracketing out rationality (*logos*) itself to consider

---

8. As discussed in the next chapter, this becomes for Heidegger the facticity of *Lebenserfahrung.*

its origins. Hence, in § 345 of *Beyond Good and Evil,* he calls for a "history of the origin" (*Entstehungsgeschichte*) of moral feelings and values, "which is something different from their critique and also something different from the history of ethical systems." From within the great circle of the history of (Christian) morality itself, one would have to explore its limits and beginnings. He undertakes this exploration in the *Genealogy of Morals.*

Although Nietzsche lays out the basic ideas of his psychological critique of the moral origins of Christianity in a number of places (esp. in "The Essence of Religion" in *Beyond Good and Evil*), the *Genealogy of Morals* provides the most sustained argument (indeed of all his works). It is divided into three essays that approach different aspects of the basic question of the motivation behind the morality that carries the Judeo-Christian tradition. Each essay needs to be understood less as an argument that supplies "proof" of a point than as an "experiment" (*Versuch*), in the sense of "thought experiment," that offers the readers a chance to *imagine* a different way of conceiving the world in which they live—that is, each essay attempts to indicate that the moral sphere, to use the phrase we just saw, has an limited circumference (*Umfang*) and is not a necessity of nature but a product of human history. In this, Nietzsche offers a strict contrast to Kant, who argued that the categorical imperative could be formulated in a way that would incorporate natural law (and hence naturalize it): "Act as if the maxims of your behavior could be made a law of nature." For Nietzsche, this is exactly what has happened: Christian morality has come to attain the status of a law of nature and it is his goal to denaturalize it or, more precisely, indicate alternate versions of nature. Perhaps one of Nietzsche's own motivations for this effort was his attachment to the classical world, an attachment so profound that he could "feel" the force of an alternative belief system—and once another "paradigm" is recognized, it relegates the full-blown "world" in which one lives to "nothing but" a paradigm (or in Nietzsche's words, a perspective).[9] Nietzsche's way of formulating this "relativization" of what has come to be the absolute standard or system of interpretation is his phrase from the preface: he says he raises the question of "the value of (our) values," where one could mark the repetition of the same word differently, i.e.,

---

9. Schiller (e.g., in his mournful poem "Die Götter Griechenlands") and Hölderlin (throughout his oeuvre) are examples of "moderns" who truly experienced their *difference* from the Greeks. By an effort to "inhabit" imaginatively the world of the Greeks, they gained an alienated perspective on the contemporary world. We could compare these "worlds" to the "paradigms" that, Thomas Kuhn argues, provide a deep order to stages of scientific thought. Furthermore, Nietzsche's "perspectivism" involves not random subjectivism but an awareness of our historical groundedness in a "world" (e.g., "Greek" vs. "modern").

as "the value1 of (our) values2," since the first literally *dis-places* the second, puts "our values2" within a different context of a wider/different/more primary sphere of values1. For Nietzsche, the standard given by value1 is the one we had seen already in Hegel, *life* (*Leben*). Three points need to be mentioned concerning this enterprise: (1) there is, of course, no reason to assume the absoluteness of value1; it is enough that it raise the possibility of relativizing values2; (2) the fact that both are characterized as values means that the positing of values as such (*Wertsetzung*) is an activity that cannot be circumvented; and (3) if values2 (Judeo-Christian values) are to be evaluated within or measured against the sphere of value1, then there must be some common element making the comparison work, i.e., even Judeo-Christian values must, in some sense, be offering something to human beings for the sake of their "lives" (an issue that will be explored below in the discussion of the third essay).

The first essay tells a story that expects the reader to make an imaginative leap outside the present sphere of values. It first provides a contrast between two different modes and then offers an explanation of how the one that exists at present might have arisen out of the other. As an imaginative—or more precisely, rhetorical—exercise, this story relies on historical references so that it can make sense to the reader, but its success must be measured by its persuasive impact not a historical accuracy.[10] Hence, although Nietzsche presents a developmental story of one system of morality yielding to another, we might approach it differently at first, beginning with the present to understand the nature of the contrast he intended to highlight. The dominant morality consists of the basically Christian[11] values laid out in the New Testament. Nietzsche has in mind the priority given to such values as humility, meekness, asceticism (submission of the body to the spirit), self-control, and restraint (not for the sake of balance or future heightening of experience, but for their own sake).[12] All these are marked "good," in contrast to the "evils" of power, strength, physical force and pleasures, domination,

---

10. Here, too, it is useful to think of Kuhn's notion of the need for "rhetoric," and not just factual argument, in order to accomplish a leap into another paradigm. If what counts as "fact" to some extent depends on the sphere of morality, then the reader must first be made to consider the world from the perspective of another paradigm before a new set of "facts" would even be considered as such.

11. There is a tendency, also on Nietzsche's part, to think of this system as "Judeo-Christian." But the actual target is Christian.

12. To understand different forms of asceticism, one could compare Ovid (in his *Art of Love*) and Augustine (in his *Confessions*) on drinking, for example. The former says that one should show some restraint so that one will have a better chance of landing a lover. The latter criticizes drinking as such.

etc. Nietzsche's insight, however, is that such "good" values cannot arise on their own because they are fundamentally inimical to the propagation of life itself. Hence, they must in fact be *responses* to another situation, be the result of a process that has made them—given the circumstances—the best possible solution that people could have come up with. That is, there must be some explanation for why these life-denying values arose; *in some sense* they must offer the creators and followers of these values *something.* The third essay will explore that issue in greater detail. But the first at least looks at what this "good/evil" morality responds to/against.

Nietzsche posits a "prior" morality that serves as the necessary precondition for the negation that yielded the present state of things. Although his presentation begins with this earlier value system, we should think of it as the stories of "states of nature" or "social contracts," namely, as historical fictions to serve as contrastive backgrounds to the present. The good/bad morality is defined in a sense "quantitatively," i.e., that is "good" which has more—power, strength, control (over self and others, in the interest of exercising strength), wealth, etc.—while that is "bad" which has less. Nietzsche claims to have support for this view in the very etymology of these terms, where good relates to possession of land, wealth, power, and where Latin *bonus* relates to war. Accordingly, the values are determined by those who possess them (the powerful, nobles, "masters"). The others (the weaker, the slaves) are "bad" not in some essential way but only "quantitatively" insofar as they *lack* what it takes to be "good."

The story of how the one morality ("good/bad") developed into the other ("good/evil"), i.e., how the fundamental negation behind Christian values took place, hinges on the phenomenon of *ressentiment.* It is crucial that this concept does not belong to either one as an explicit value. It operates on a different level, which Nietzsche calls "psychological," and hence has remained hidden from previous analyses of morals and even from psychologists, especially the British, who derived their categories of analysis from morality. (These are reasons why Nietzsche generally uses the French word to indicate both its alienness in the realm of ethical philosophy and the blindness of all but a few French psychologists to its force.) *Ressentiment* can be grasped only by taking into account two different forces, or perhaps, given their structural nature, force *fields,* that interact: the first is an inherent effect of any value system, namely, the hierarchy created that puts those who "measure up" to the values "higher" than the others; the second is Nietzsche's "discovery" of the "will to power," which, as a "striving" to be higher, balks at all relegation to a "lower" status. The development can be mapped as shown in figure 6.1.

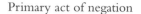

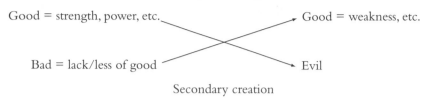

Primary act of negation

Good = strength, power, etc.   Good = weakness, etc.

Bad = lack/less of good   Evil

Secondary creation

FIGURE 6.1. Ressentiment and the inversion of values.

The driving force of the inversion of values, the reason for the primary act of negation that would say "no!" to the positive values of the good/bad morality, is *ressentiment*, which itself is driven by the desire, on the part of those defined as lacking, to exercise their own "will to power." Since, by definition, they cannot do so on the terms of the existing order, they negate it and, secondarily, create a new order in which their condition is "good." This process, which for Nietzsche has a historical and individual psychological dimension, need not, indeed *should* not, be specifically or uniquely delineated, and it would be dangerous (as in the Nazi appropriation of Nietzsche) to link it to one people or type of person (e.g., the "Jews"). Rather, Nietzsche's ultimate goal with this thought experiment is to leave us with the possibility that (1) values are "fabricated," (2) in ways that enhance or detract from life, (3) for motivations that are not expressed by those values, and (4) for motivations that can be connected to the "will to power" acting in all living beings. If he has accomplished this goal, then he has offered some insight into the formation of the *Umfang,* or sphere of morality as such that we inhabit. And if "God" is linked to morality, then he has pushed back the boundaries of discussion of God to the state of his precondition. Perhaps, then, it is less a matter of God's death than the conditions of His birth.

The second essay does not continue with the contrast or explanation of the different moral spheres in toto but instead examines key concepts/ values operating within the present system. If, as we have just seen, the present sphere is both temporally and conceptually circumscribed (has a limited *Umfang*), then its major concepts/values likewise must derive, ultimately, from outside its existence. Nietzsche tries to show how such master concepts as punishment, guilt, and conscience, and associated notions of selfhood, can be traced to sources outside their present range of application. Indeed, all interpretations that see their present application as the source of their meaning are not so much wrong as turned in the wrong direction (focused on effects or the sphere of application instead of cause, ironically like the inhabitants of Plato's cave, looking at shadows instead of the light source). In Nietzsche's terms, the meaning of a concept needs to be traced back to its origin and not its present purpose.

The core of Nietzsche's argument involves the notion of (good and bad) conscience, since ultimately it is a basic notion of conscience that provides Luther with the grounding of his faith and Kant with the grounding of his ethics, from which he derives a "moral theology." It would be absurd, of course, to challenge the "givenness" of conscience, to claim it does not exist, etc. After all, the power of Kant's appeal to it rests on the *fact* of its apparently universal "voice" (see the opening of the *Critique of Practical Reason*). Instead, Nietzsche poses the question of what has *made* this *fact* (what makes it a *factum*) or what has "given" it to us in the first place, i.e., what constitutes its "givenness." Or we might rephrase his project: How did an "inner life" (which forms the most intimate and self-aware aspect of each self) emerge in human beings?

Nietzsche's story is roundabout but has a basic delineation. Before an inner self could emerge, humans needed to form a continuity along a temporal axis. After all, if nothing about our physical body remains unchanged over time, the notion of a "core self" or conscience must be produced "inside" us as a constant feature. Nietzsche summarizes this notion of temporal constancy in the phenomenon of the promise: "To breed an animal *with the right to make promises*—is not this the paradoxical task that nature has set itself in the case of man? Is it not the real problem regarding man?" (2, § 1). But how does the arc of constancy over time get drawn into us? Through violence and punishment, an entire "mnemotechnics" (2, § 3), since if something is to stay in memory, "it must be burned in; only that which never ceases to *hurt* stays in the memory" (ibid.). Here we have the origin of both conscience and subjectivity itself.

By definition, punishment is meted out by those who have the power to do so. The basic relationship is one of creditor/debtor. Punishment does not "make good" the loss to the creditor but allows him/her to "move on," to discharge the affect experienced as a result of the breached contract. But from the perspective of the debtor, however, the experience is different. In being "re-minded" through punishment of the failure, the debtor comes to *internalize* the debt. In a peculiar dialectic, the greater the "forgetful largess" of the creditor, the more intense the memory of the debt. Debt becomes guilt and a sense of self gets "folded into" the human being. This internalized exterior gains a "life of its own" and becomes the inner world of conscience and consciousness. The "ultimate" source of morality, therefore, has itself a history/genealogy that is not "psychological" or even sociological in a limited sense, since the process must be the "condition of possibility" of any psychology or sociality.[13] Hence, the condition of morality (conscience) that is the condition for the "moral proof of the existence of God" is itself resting on a condition of the making of human being (a creature who can make promises).

The third essay is both the most "polemical" in this "polemic" and the most "understanding" because it tries to explain the "meaning of ascetic values," i.e., it tries to see different aspects of the present lifeworld as *necessary* for the preservation and intensification of the life of those living in it. Here Nietzsche does not judge from the "outside" but from the significance of the values themselves for those holding them. He is, so to speak, testing his basic hypothesis, which played a role already in the justification of the creation and adoption by the "slave" of values inimical to life, that human being (all life) is motivated by a will to power (more life) so that even in those places where we see people acting apparently *against* their interests we need to explain the conditions that make that action the best choice. Nietzsche summarizes this principle at the end with the powerful phrase: "One would rather will *nothing* than not will at all." We do not need to explore the particular classes of individuals—artists, "priests," philosophers, scientists—who adopt certain "ascetic" ideals because (despite their nihilistic influence) they create the optimal conditions for those individuals to thrive. But this principle will be crucial for us later when we explore the "return of religion." After all, the questions we will have to ask there are: How and why do people adopt values that run counter to life? What form of "life" is being propagated in them that makes this choice "logical"?

So what has Nietzsche accomplished? The phrase "the death of God" never appears in the *Genealogy of Morals,* but this work undermines the last remaining kind of argument that the philosophical tradition has left and the sphere that Nietzsche sees providing the hermeneutic context for all beliefs. Nietzsche summarizes the interconnection between the development of religious concepts and the creation of a morality in the interest ("will to power") of the "priestly class" in a note from the 1880s. In this version, the "priests" play the role of the dominant class in Marx:

> The holy lie has, therefore, 1. invented a *punishing* and *rewarding* God, who recognizes exactly the priests' book of laws and sends them out as his mouthpieces and representatives;—2. a *beyond of life,* in which the great punishing-machine is thought to operate—and for this purpose

---

13. The individual is not a given but must be "individuated"—see Habermas on Mead in *Postmetaphysical Thinking.*

the *immortality of the soul;*—3. human *conscience,* as the consciousness that good and evil are established and that God Himself speaks when it advises conformity with the priests' prescriptions;—4. *morality* as the *denial* of the natural course of things, as the reduction of all history/ occurrences to a morally conditioned history, and moral consequence (i.e., the idea of punishment and reward) as permeating the world, as the sole power, as the *creator* of all change;—5. the *truth* as given, as revealed, as coinciding with the doctrines of the priests: as the condition of all salvation and fortune in this and the future life. (*Aus dem Nachlaß,* 818)

Especially the final point, the belief of (monotheistic) religions that there is *one* truth, which is presented as a divine law, which, in turn, it is our duty to follow ("religiously"), leads to a reduction of the openness and options that provide challenges and make life worth living. In brief: "The concept 'God' represents a turning of one's back on life, a critique, indeed a despising of life" (*Aus dem Nachlaß,* 818–19). Not just the tendency of the religious spirit toward "positivity" (Kant, Hegel), but the religious spirit itself is the danger.

Life without God(s)? New Horizons and Pieties

Because of the ambivalence in Nietzsche's genealogical analysis, we can say that he attacks the psychological origins of God, but in fact he has only "bracketed" Him out. That is, the psychological critique "kills off" our notion of a kindly Christian God by undermining the psychological notion of "pity" that underlies it. However, the "phenomenological" analysis leads us to envision what kind of life we must now lead once the borders of our world have been destabilized. In fact, we cannot live without horizons. The question will be how to establish new, more open ones. If we return to the insane man, we might now reinterpret his search for God in a slightly different way. Earlier, we considered him incapable of living the life of the "fearless" on the "open sea." But perhaps the insane man, otherwise so insightful, is also telling us something about ourselves by searching for God as he is. Why carry a lamp in midday? The brightness of noon seems to have destroyed all shadow and wiped out the very possibility of horizon. But the lamp reintroduces a more limited circle of light, a moveable horizon within the newly opened-up godless world. A life that moves within a so newly de-fined sphere would have a kind of "religiosity," and seems to be characterized by Nietzsche with a reconceptualized notion of "piety" (*Frömmigkeit*).

On the one hand, of course, Nietzsche attacks all traditional forms of "piety". We can imagine him rejecting all versions of Schleiermacher's "feeling of absolute dependence." He says in an aphorism from *The Gay Science* that it is time to celebrate the end of Christian values, "for even the pious of the old faith will die out" (denn auch die Frommen des alten Glaubens sterben aus; § 122). And Zarathustra calls on his "brothers" to smash the "old and new tablets" of "the pious" (*der Frommen*) and of the "pious meta-physicians" (*der frommen Hinterweltler; Also sprach Zarathustra,* book 3, § 15) who propagate the "truths" that would reduce this world to insignificance and destroy the pleasure of creative willing.

But on the other hand, he is clear that Christianity and its piety do not make up the only form of religion. We see Nietzsche's praise of polytheism in *The Gay Science*. In *The greatest advantage of polytheism (Größter Nutzen des Polytheismus),* he attacks the belief in one god but leaves open the need for others: "Monotheism, on the other hand, this rigid consequence of the doctrine of the one normal human type—the faith in one normal god beside whom there are only pseudo-gods—was perhaps the greatest danger that has yet confronted humanity. . . . In polytheism the free-spiriting and many-spiriting of man attained its first preliminary form—the strength to create for ourselves our own new eyes—and ever again new eyes that are even more our own: hence man alone among all the animals has no eternal horizons and perspectives" (§ 143). Likewise, a short saying from *Beyond Good and Evil* implies that his "love" is too great to be limited to a single deity: "Love of *one* is a barbarism; for it is exercised at the expense of all others. The love of God, too" (§ 67). The godlessness that results from the initial critique must yield to a consideration of how to posit values, measure out a sphere in which life can unfold meaningfully.

For this reason, one must be careful not to merely substitute one "god" for another. This danger is the source of his critique of science as a mere ersatz religion. In the second aphorism in the section "We Fearless Ones" from *The Gay Science,* that is, right after he celebrates the bliss of the open horizon he wonders "to what extent we, too, are pious" (Inwiefern auch wir noch fromm sind; § 344), where "*wir*" here includes Nietzsche himself. He argues that science (*Wissenschaft*) tells us to leave all convictions (*Überzeugungen*) at the door for the sake of tentative hypotheses. Science opposes convictions. And so, he continues: "Only we still have to ask: *To make it possible for this discipline to begin,* must there not be some prior conviction—even one that is so commanding and unconditional that it sacrifices all other convictions to itself? We see that science also rests on a faith." Here he introduces the notion of the "will to truth" that is ultimately a *moral* conviction not to deceive or be deceived (*täuschen*). As he says in a short aphorism: "'Knowledge for its own sake'—that is the last snare of morality: with that one becomes completely entangled in it once more" (*Beyond Good and Evil*, § 64). This danger of getting pulled back into the sphere of morality is associated with the tendency that everyone has, including the followers of Zarathustra, to grow tired, to accept the common and comfortable path, and thus to listen to "the cowardly devil" ("der feige Teufel") speaking inside who says, "There *is* a God!" ("Es *gibt* einen Gott!") Such a turn or giving in of the apostates is marked by the religious refrain: "We have become pious once more!" ("Wir sind wieder fromm geworden!" "On the apostates" ["Von den Abtrünnigen"], *Also sprach Zarathustra*, 227).[14] But I am more interested in the paradoxical relationship to piety (*Frömmigkeit*) that he proposes. That is, the new piety *opposed* to Christianity. As he writes: "We are no longer Christians; it is our stricter and more spoiled piety itself that prohibits us today from still being Christians" (*Nachlaß*, 13:318). Here we have a clear claim that there is a "higher," ironic form of piety that surpasses Christianity and thus survives the death of God.

Section 59 of *Beyond Good and Evil* plays with a more complex notion of piety that corresponds to his complex notion of art and the artist. The opening sentence tells us to read paradoxically: "Anyone who has looked deeply into the world may guess how much wisdom lies in the superficiality of men." But then he goes on to discuss those who develop a "cult of the surface," those "philosophers and artists" who feel the need to foreground the forms and surfaces. He wonders whether all artists and *homines religiosi* might not be creating "false" images of the world out of fear of the paradoxical truth that there is no truth; that is, they flee the thought of a dangerous truth because they are not strong enough to bear it and hence flee what would lead them to pessimism: "Piety, the 'life in God,' seen in this way, would appear as the subtlest and final offspring of our *fear* of the truth, as an artist's worship and intoxication before the most consistent of all falsifications, as the will to the inversion of truth, to untruth at any price. It may be that until now there has been no more potent means for beautifying man himself than piety: it can turn man into so much art, surface, play of colors, graciousness that

---

14. He then has the old gods say: "And the gods laughed back then and almost fell off their stools and called out: 'Isn't it precisely divine, that there are gods, but no God?'" (230). Note the commentary by Hans Weichelt in *Zarathustra-Kommentar*: "Over the course of its development, strict monotheism displaces the idea of God into further and further nebulous removes. The concept of God becomes more and more abstract and contentless, until it descends into nothingness. Monotheism can take only one path—leading to atheism" (142).

his sight no longer makes one suffer.—" There are two implications to this analysis: one, the "old" piety, like the old art, did, indeed, also serve a purpose, namely, to protect human beings from the recognition of a truth "too early" (*zu früh*), before they were ready to embrace its consequences;[15] and two, this old piety and art will give way to a new one, also full of "surface, color, and goodness," but not driven by *fear* of the "truth of untruth" but by the strength to embrace it.

A way to resolve this paradox of piety—its necessity and yet its danger if not overcome—would be to consider Nietzsche's distinction between religion as means and end. The religious attitude, even the "Christian" and "Buddhist" one that would degrade the present world for the sake of an imagined "life with God" and that thereby introduces an ascetic falsification against life, might nonetheless serve life as a *means* to survive long enough to overcome this very attitude. Hence, Nietzsche can even accept and embrace religion as a "pedagogical and disciplinary means": "Perhaps nothing in Christianity or Buddhism is as venerable as their art of teaching even the lowliest how to place themselves through piety in an illusory higher order of things and thus to maintain their contentment with the real order, in which their life is hard enough—and precisely this hardness is necessary" (*Beyond Good and Evil*, § 61). The danger comes when religion raises itself and its attitude to a "sovereign" view of the world, when it becomes the end in itself, when the notion of "the need to bear life" no longer serves to live on but to make life not worth living. At the heart of piety (*Frömmigkeit*) is a deep ambivalence.

A new attitude, "godless" yet "pious" (*fromm*)? Can Nietzsche be envisioning a kind of "becoming pious" (*fromm werden*) as a return to genuine religion, which arises not out of the exhaustion and weakness of the apostates but out of the strength to see in "religion one more means for overcoming resistances, for the ability to rule—as a bond that unites rulers and subjects" (*Beyond Good and Evil*, § 61). To grasp this possibility we have to perform the kind of philological investigation that Nietzsche called for in the *Genealogy*. Looking at the Grimm's dictionary, one sees that the origin of the word *fromm* is probably the Latin *primus*. The medieval and early modern uses highlight the kind of aspects Nietzsche himself found in "*gut*" (and in Middle High German indeed it often appears in the pair "*fromm und guot*"). Luther begins to oppose it to "böse." If just believing in God is not enough

---

15. We see that the Apollonian/Dionysian dualism from the early *Birth of Tragedy* (1872) is still at work in the later Nietzsche.

to make one *fromm,* so, too, one might in fact be *gottlos* and *fromm.* This is what Nietzsche seems to be postulating: a "Frömmigkeit" beyond God and good and evil. A piety not born of pity.

In "Außer Dienst" ("Out of Service" or "Dismissed") from part 4 of *Also sprach Zarathustra,* Zarathustra meets "the last pope," who is also caught between paradigms, historical moments, world-historical transitions: "I served this old God until his last hour. Now I am unemployed, without any lord, and yet not free, and never happy except in my memories" (498). He had sought out someone who didn't know "what the entire world knows already," namely, "that the old God no longer lives, in whom the whole world once believed" (498). But the last believer is also dead. Now he seeks out Zarathustra, "the most pious of all those, who do not believe in God" (den Frömmsten aller derer, die nicht an Gott glauben) And so the last pope poses the question to Zarathustra as to how God had died: "Is it true, what one says, that he choked on pity—that he saw how *man* hung on the cross and could not bear the way his love of man became man's hell and, finally, death?" (498–99). The pope describes how God aged and became weak and tired. But Zarathustra responds that we should "let him go his way" (*laß ihn fahren!*), this God who was "ambiguous" (*vieldeutig*) and "unclear" (or contradictory, *undeutlich*), who criticized mankind for being imperfect but who made mankind imperfect. Zarathustra criticizes the old God's behavior for going "against *good taste*" (500). He thereby brings in *aesthetic criteria* rather than moral for judging this "theological issue": "There is also in matters of piety good taste" (Es gibt auch in der Frömmigkeit guten Geschmack, 500). The pope responds by calling Zarathustra himself "pious": "Oh, Zarathustra, you are more pious than you believe, with your unbelief! Some god in you must have converted you to your godlessness. Is it not your piety itself, which does not allow you to believe any more in God? And your overwhelming honesty which leads you beyond good and evil?" (500) This scene is important because it shows how Nietzsche does want to develop a kind of aesthetic and human-oriented "faith," a "piety" that is uplifting and respectful.

The constructs of the *Übermensch* and Zarathustra are intended to give some flesh and blood to this new being, this insane creature who recognizes that in the beginning was *Unsinn,* who participates (with us all) in the historical developments that kill God, and yet who nonetheless creates flexible realms and *Lebenswelten*—or perhaps we should say cocreates them, since they are always also superseding any individual's grasp and scope—within which to shape a meaningful life. The incessant psychological attack on the moral sphere that has thus far defined our parameters is necessary to dissolve the sense of naturalness and inevitability associated with it and hence to "bracket" its way of presenting things. That attack is also necessary to make sure that substitutes, which *must* come along to respond to the *horror vacui* (*Genealogy of Morals,* 3, § 11), do not simply draw from the same nihilistic motivation. (He names science, nationalism, Wagnerian music, and mass-commercial culture as the worst culprits or "ascetic ideals" of his day.) To this extent, God, the Christian God of pity, is not just dead, but murdered without the possibility of resurrection.

And yet, the radical sense of in-betweenness and transition, which Nietzsche tries to capture as the nature of his historical period, points to the need for a relationship and attitude toward the world that he characterizes with the historically rich word *fromm.* This is not a "return to religion" or a second coming after the death of God. Rather, it recognizes the need for a kind of self-overcoming that reveals itself in a simultaneous self-restraint or measure.[16] For Heidegger, as we shall see, the end of philosophical *logos* and the death of the Christian God are contained in the overcoming of "onto-theology." What comes "after" he calls the "last God" and the "piety of thought."

---

16. In a short section on "Das Extreme und das Maß" ("The Extreme and Measure"), Jaspers discusses the contradiction that runs through Nietzsche's life and work insofar as he was drawn by both of these poles. He quotes Nietzsche: "Who will prove themselves the strongest? The most moderate, those who have no need of extreme beliefs" (*Nietzsche und das Christentum,* 76).

 CHAPTER 7

Being after the Death of God

Heidegger from Theo- to Onto-logos

The question of God hovers from the very beginning over Heidegger's intellectual development.

—Rudolf Bultmann, "Reflexionen zum Denkweg Martin Heideggers"

We are standing at a methodological crossroads that will decide the life and death of philosophy as such, we are standing before an abyss: we either leap into nothingness, that is, into absolute objectification, or we achieve the leap into an *other* world, or more precisely: into the world as such.

—Heidegger, *Zur Bestimmung der Philosophie*

Philosophy cannot effect any direct change in the present state of the world. This is true not only of philosophy but of all merely human thought and action. Only a God can save us (Nur noch ein Gott kann uns retten). The sole possibility remains open to us, in our thinking and creative work, to prepare for the appearance of God or for the absence of God in the final catastrophe.

—Heidegger, *Spiegel* interview, 23 September 1966

So God is dead, the study of God and religion reduced to sociology, psychology, economics. Where do we go from here? Is there any way to "save" theology or the philosophy of religion or religion itself from being anything other than "historical" disciplines/phenomena that consider the past and since superseded beliefs? And what role could philosophy play? One option, we saw, was taken by the anti-Hegelians of the early to mid-nineteenth century: the radical withdrawal of belief into subjectivity and a critique of rationality. This represents a return to a pure Lutheranism, a rejection of both the historico-rational-critical direction started by Erasmus and the intervening institutional formalization of Protestantism. But the other option we must now explore is the possibility of passing *through* the very development that has lead to the death of God to discover, within this very insistence on finitude, a moment that transcends it, or, at least, where it becomes aware of its limitation. For Heidegger, this involves in large part a *methodological* issue, the possibility of a phenomenological analysis that tries to get at the "foundational" *lifeworld* (*Lebenswelt*) that other "reductive" and scientistic approaches cannot even *ask* about. It will involve a different approach to history itself, for to view God and other theological concepts in a "historical" context—what Heidegger will call the "history of Being" (*Seinsgeschichte*)—will mean something other than relegating them to the past in the way Nietzsche hoped to with his "genealogy" (*Entstehungsgeschichte*). For Heidegger, the entire metaphysical tradition of the West (including God) has become "*frag-würdig*," questionable in a double sense: it now lacks its former significance and has become worthy of a new questioning that has the power to reshape our relation to the world. Heidegger arrives at his rethinking of Being itself (ontology) through a long trajectory that begins with a reevaluation of the very status of theology—and that original questioning of theo-*logos* accompanies his thought throughout his life.

Stated differently: if Marx saw that the way to all general critique had to pass through *Religionskritik,* for Heidegger, the way to his own unique ontological phenomenology was to pass through the *Phänomenologie der Religion.* In fact, the young professor in his first years at the University of Marburg was preoccupied with a project, and held numerous lectures, on the phenomenology of religious life. Religion and religious experiences become the first "test cases" of his adoption and adaptation of Husserl's powerful phenomenological method. As a result, religion gets absorbed and transformed, *aufgehoben,* into his philosophy at an early stage, even if in a different way than we saw in Hegel. Moreover, his particular conception of religion will allow for a certain divine survival even after the death of God. This will become especially clear/relevant after Heidegger's later encounter with Nietzsche. In fact, I will read that encounter and the resulting "turn" (the so-called *Kehre*) in his philosophy nonetheless as a kind of "phenomenological project"—however, rather than "bracketing out" (*epoche*) religious terms from the analysis of human existence (*Dasein*), as he had done in his earlier philosophy, the late Heidegger hopes (via Nietzsche) to "bracket out" the entire *epoch* of metaphysics that he saw as responsible for a certain conception of God, *Technik,* and philosophizing that can only lead to nihilism. In this project, he attempts to "out-Nietzsche" Nietzsche: if Nietzsche had seen the need to place a limit on the "sphere" (*Umfang*) of morality, Heidegger tried to map out the horizon of "Western metaphysics" as such (with Nietzsche still on the inside). Passing through that epoch and its resulting nihilism allows

Heidegger to return to what he finds "more originary" than the sphere of religion and theology—Being itself as a kind of wholly Other before/after God.[1] For this reason this chapter will have two sections, one focusing on his earlier working through of theological thought from a new phenomenological perspective and the other looking at his later thinking about Being and God from the perspective after the death of the metaphysical "God of the philosophers."[2]

Human Being *before* God, or the Phenomenology of Religion vs. Theology

Heidegger, like so many of the other thinkers we have looked at who led us further along on the path to the death of God, began as a student of theology.[3] Raised Catholic, he attended a Jesuit high school and studied, briefly, in a seminary. After a few weeks there, in 1909, he left for health reasons. Transferring from theology to philosophy and mathematics at the University of Freiburg, he concentrated during his initial studies on both the back-

---

1. Laurence Paul Hemming, in his essay "Nihilism: Heidegger and the Grounds of Redemption" (in Milbank, Pickstock, and Ward, *Radical Orthodoxy*), takes a different route toward similar conclusions. He writes: "I want to ask what nihilism is and how it came about, and to answer this question by showing its relation to the unfolding of scholasticism's concern with *esse* as determinations of being, and to Nietzsche's understanding of the death of God. If scholasticism concludes by seeking to speak of being as a way of speaking of God, nihilism, in speaking of the death of God, is also seeking to speak of being—which means to speak of how things are. I want in particular to appeal to Martin Heidegger as one who seeks to understand what it means to speak of being, and thereby to show how his speaking of being speaks of the overcoming of nihilism. I want to raise the question of how we might speak faithfully again of God and being in consequence of Heidegger's work" (92).

2. It is certainly true that Heidegger occasionally states explicitly, as in the "Brief über den Humanismus," that "Das 'Sein'—das ist nicht Gott und nicht ein Weltgrund" (in *Wegmarken*, 331). But we will see first of all that he does address the "God question," and second, that he does often speak of Being in terms that recall a certain theological tradition (from Pascal through Schelling and Kierkegaard), according to which God is also not a "*Weltgrund*."

3. While the importance of theology for the formation of Heidegger's thought has certainly entered the field of vision of Heidegger scholars—see Pöggeler and de Vries—it is remarkable that theological discussions often play no role in studies of the formation of his early thought. For example, although César Lambert does deal with the Freiburg lectures on religion, this treatment occurs in a complete vacuum, as if no one else existed except for Heidegger and Husserl. Ironically, this in a book that explores the notion of "World" in Heidegger, a concept that emphasizes the situatedness of *Dasein*! Likewise, Charles Bambach looks at the "roots" of Heidegger's thought and begins with a chapter "situating Heidegger" that calls for a "historical" reading, but there is hardly a word about theology. Granted, Bambach is interested in Heidegger's political thinking and its relationship to National Socialism; but the "roots" are embedded in an original exchange with theology. Thus, Bambach's nice formulation concerning "The Origin of the Work of Art" (1935)—"In Heidegger's terms this narrative [of the history of Being] will be played out as the triumph of ratiocinative-technological *logos* over the Heraclitean-Sophoclean *logos* of oracular speech and poetic thought" (xxi)—needs to be fleshed out with Heidegger's earlier engagement with the *logos* of theology.

ground of classical and German philosophy and contemporary issues in the philosophy of religion. His earliest publications, for example, were reviews of books on theological topics (like *Das Gottesbedürfnis [The Need of/for God]*). After receiving his doctoral degree and writing his *Habilitationsschrift* on the medieval theology of Duns Scotus, he received an appointment as a lecturer (*Privatdozent*) in Freiburg. During this period (beginning 1916) he met and began to work with Edmund Husserl (1859–1938) and pursued his version of the phenomenological method. Early in 1919 he wrote to Father Engelbart Krebs, who had performed his wedding ceremony and whom he had assisted at the university, that he was breaking with "the dogmatic system of Catholicism." And yet, in his conversation with a Japanese philosopher in the later work *Unterwegs zur Sprache (On the Way to Language)*, Heidegger reflects back on his early engagement with the Catholic tradition (esp. Aquinas on Aristotle): "Without this theological background I would never have arrived at my way of thinking" (96; Pöggeler, *Heidegger in seiner Zeit*, 8). It is his early lectures in Freiburg as an unsalaried assistant to Husserl between 1919 and 1923 that will occupy us here first. For it was in this period that he strove to redefine theological issues by using the methods of phenomenology. In so doing, he also, we will see, redefined the task of philosophy. During the five years he spent in Marburg with his first professorship (1923–28), he both completed his magnum opus, *Sein und Zeit (Being and Time, 1927)*—which made it possible for him later to take over Husserl's chair in philosophy at Freiburg—and worked, together with the theologian Rudolf Bultmann, on pushing back the "pre-understanding" (*Vor-verständnis*) of religious concepts to the point where they would have to yield to a different kind of analysis.[4] This, we will see, is in part what he called the necessary "destruction" of such theoretical categories and concepts as are derived from the "science" of theology for the sake of a "historical" reading of such categories in terms of "factual experience of life" (*faktische Lebenserfahrung*). Pöggeler states directly the importance of Heidegger's engagement with theology for his turn to a new direction in phenomenological method: "There is no doubt that it was thanks to the application of phenomenological philosophy to the new disputes in theology that gave Heidegger's methodological procedure the character of a 'formal indicative' hermeneutics" (*Heidegger in seiner Zeit*, 267–68).

First we need to understand how Heidegger modified the phenomenological method, indeed converted it from a method to a mode of philoso-

---

4. We will deal with Bultmann separately in the following chapter since he developed an explicit theology, using existential analysis in part, that grew out of the "crisis" of post-WWI European thought.

phizing that criticized a key aspect of Husserl's aim, namely, to develop a "scientific" philosophy. According to Husserl, all previous philosophy suffered from the split between subject and object and hence fell into the two opposing and false categories of subjectivism-psychologism-idealism or empiricism (with its "naturalist" attitude toward existing objects). Previous philosophies did not take the fact of intentionality into account: all consciousness is "consciousness of an object." The simultaneity inherent in that phrase— "consciousness of an object"—means that the proper object of investigation is not consciousness alone (psychologism, etc.) or the independently existing object ("mere" empiricism or objectivism); what needs to be brought before us for study is the "object of consciousness" (i.e., phenomenon) as it exists, taking into account *both* the necessary intention of consciousness to grasp something *and* the something being seized by consciousness. As his philosophy developed, he also would consider this the object of lived experience, i.e., objects as they present themselves to us in lived experience. To make them the proper object of study, one has to "bracket out" all tendencies that we might have to interpret our experience based on assumptions, often the result of sedimented theories and philosophical positions (like empiricism's belief in "objects existing independently of us" or Fichte's in "the ego positing objects"). A "phenomenological" analysis of phenomena—as Heidegger received Husserl—thus calls for clearing away preconceived theoretical notions and understanding instead the way experiences are embedded in a "lifeworld" of the human subject.[5]

Heidegger, in part thanks to his reading of Dilthey—although also radicalizing him beyond traditional hermeneutics or historicism—emphasizes the *historical* nature of the lived experience as the only context in which objects/phenomena could ever appear. Objects appear in a context of our

---

5. Pöggeler cites Husserl's letter to Rudolf Otto in response to his *Das Heilige* (see next chapter), which states that it is the beginnings of a phenomenology of religion. He says of the present day that people need and desire nothing more than "that finally the true origins become word, in a higher sense, become *logos*" (*Heidegger in seiner Zeit*, 249). Since Husserl undoubtedly discussed this book with his assistants (who evidently gave it to him), we have here an indication of a direction that the next generation can take: a phenomenological analysis of religion that goes back to its origins, embedding its language in those origins, and thereby allowing the true *logos* to emerge. This would be an approach that must purge ("bracket out" or, in Heidegger's term, engage in a *Destruktion*) the theoretical apparatus that has developed over the centuries; i.e., to return to the pure *logos* of origins via phenomenology, the *logos* of theology must be critiqued. One can imagine how Heidegger, who was interested for his own personal and biographical reasons in stepping out of the shadow of his own theological training (without abandoning it!), saw in this call for a phenomenology of religion a new approach to the originary *logos* without theology. After all, according to Pöggeler, Heidegger writes to Karl Löwith on October 20, 1920, that he's still upset with Husserl for considering him not a philosopher but "actually still a theologian" (eigentlich noch Theolog, 252).

"understanding" (*Verstehen*). That broader context, which includes both the "viewer" (who is not just an "onlooker" since he/she is implicated in the historical process) and the "object," he calls the "factual experience of life" or *faktische Lebenserfahrung*—*faktisch* meaning that it is a given for all of our experiences, a *factum* that we can't get "behind" (it is *unhintergehbar*). He spends much of his early career trying to explain how we might gain meaningful, pretheoretical access to concrete, immediate lived experience. Heidegger characterizes the difference between the two realms of investigation as that between the "ontic," which is the realm of phenomena or "beings" (*das Seiende*) as they "show up" or appear to us thanks to a particular mode of viewing or being conscious (seeing, believing, hoping, desiring, etc.), and the "ontological," the necessarily assumed and unthematized (indeed, unthematizable) background of Being itself (*das Sein*): "Each entity or being reveals itself only on the basis of a prior, even if unknown, preconceptual understanding of what this specific entity is and how it is. All ontic interpretation proceeds on the basis of an initially and mostly hidden ontology" ("Phenomenology and Theology," 62; hereafter PT).[6]

Two important considerations about this method need to be mentioned:

1. The background that is "illuminated" together with the object is in neither a "causal" nor a "logical" relation to the foreground (hence, not the same as a reductive interpretation; this is more consistent than in Nietzsche's ambivalent approach we saw above). One cannot "derive" or deduce knowledge of things in the world on the basis of one's preconceptual understanding of Being. In this way Heidegger differentiates himself both from natural scientific and from Hegelian methods; that is, "Being" is neither the "cause" of objects in the way that Leibniz thought of the chain of sufficient reasons, nor a *Geist* that "expresses" itself (so that objects in the world do not arise "dialectically" out of Being nor can they be dialectically traced back to their "ground"). Rather, one can get a sense of the ontological background only by means of a systematic "destruction" of dominant theoretical perceptions. But this background as such can never be fully illuminated.

---

6. Or, as he says at the beginning of *Being and Time:* "Ontological questioning is more originary than the ontic questioning of the positive sciences. But it remains naive and unclear if its researches into the being of beings are not oriented by the meining of Being as such" (Ontologisches Fragen ist zwar gegenüber dem ontischen Fragen der positiven Wissenschaften ursprünglicher. Es bleibt aber selbst naiv und undurchsichtig, wenn seine Nachforschungen nach dem Sein des Seienden den Sinn von Sein überhaupt unerörtert lassen, 11).

2. The viewing "subject" is also inhabiting that background and hence one with it and itself radically historical. We do not stand "above" it or in an abstract relation to the object; the best we can do is to inquire into our own position reflexively and therefore come to understand our "situation" as a condition of embeddedness within a lifeworld.

To grasp how Heidegger came to use philosophy/phenomenology in order to "put theology" in its place, i.e., to initially limit the domain of theological (and other scientific) thinking, we can start with the work that emerged as the culmination of this earlier period, "Phenomenology and Theology."[7] Delivered as a public lecture only twice, in 1927 and 1928 (i.e., from the period of publication of *Sein und Zeit*), and not published until 1969 in the collection *Wegmarken,* it was Heidegger's way of radically shifting the ground, so that he would no longer deal with theology as such but, like the call in Nietzsche's aphorism on proofs for the existence of God, "clear the table." This lecture, which Heidegger dedicated to the theologian Rudolf Bultmann, "in memory of the years of friendship in Marburg, 1923–1928," closes off Heidegger's initial period of thinking through—and beyond—theology.[8]

Heidegger defines theology as "the science or systematic knowledge of faith or belief" (die Wissenschaft des Glaubens, PT, 55). This means that it is the science or study of "that which is revealed in faith" (ibid.). All theology presumes faith, and this faith is, for theology, its "given." But this given also illuminates or reveals a sphere of beliefs that are all associated with that fundamental faith. One might here think of Nietzsche's aphorism on the "Sphere of morality" (Umfang der Moralität)—for the believer, a certain realm of his/her life in the world is illuminated by the faith. Theology would be the "scientific" study, with the rational logic of *logos,* of all that is illuminated or revealed by that faith. Since that sphere is not so much spatial as temporal, the study of the realm opened up by faith is fundamentally a study of a particular history provided by that faith: "Therefore theology, as the science of faith and as an essentially *historical* mode of being, is in its innermost core a *historical* science; it is historical according to the historicity that is uniquely contained in faith—'the unfolding history of revelation'—

---

7. We sense the radicality of this effort to limit the domain of theology when we compare it to the opposite view (as expressed by Schulte in Scheffczyk, *Rationalität,* 359) that saw in theology the theory of the totality of reality.

8. The lecture was then incorporated into volume 9 of the collected works, with the other essays and lectures in *Wegmarken.*

and thus a unique historical science" (PT, 55–56). Faith grounds the believer in history in a manner that is particular to that faith. Theology illuminates to the fullest extent the space of that history and the place of the individual in it. (Hence, conflicts of faith are conflicts over history that as such cannot be mediated by theological debate because there is no "neutral" historical ground.)

But what about philosophy? It seems there are two roles that philosophy can play in relation to theology. First, the sphere that faith opens up for the believer, the history it illuminates for him/her, does not need philosophy. The believer (and the theologian as believer) merely inhabits that sphere. However, to the extent that theology is a "science" or *logos,* the conditions of its existence as a *science* can and must be interrogated, even though, like all sciences, it cannot pose that question about its own condition. That is the role of philosophy. Heidegger writes: "Faith does not need philosophy, but the *science* of faith as *positive* science does. But one must differentiate here: the positive science of faith does not need philosophy to ground itself or to reveal its positivity, [in this case] Christianity [as a particular faith]. Rather, theology needs philosophy only in consideration of its claims to be a science" (PT, 61). If one envisions a "positive science" as a particular light illuminating a particular field in a particular way (again, where that field has a *temporal-historical* character), allowing certain phenomena to "appear," the phenomenon of illumination itself—its scientificity as such—would have to be addressed in a different way in order to "appear." This would also include the very concept of *historicity as such,* the presumption that any understanding of faith as providing us with a (place in) history must presume.

Second, concepts that are found within the specific sciences or disciplines (for example, "faith") do not have their *origin* there, and the question of origin is not posed by the "positive" sciences (which have the function of illumination). Hence, the phenomena and concepts must instead be connected to and grounded in the world of experiences from which they "more originally" emerge (i.e., "more originally" than their appearance under the light of science). Heidegger writes: "All explication at the level of foundational concepts strives in the direction of allowing us to see the initial closed-off ontic relationships, toward which all basic concepts point, in their originary totality, and to keep that totality in view" (PT, 63). In the case of theology, this means that its basic concepts must be decoupled from all the assumptions that accompany it, first and foremost God and a human relationship to God. This "methodological atheism" is both more and less than the call for the death of God. It is more to the extent that it pushes the nature of human experience (which Heidegger will come to call "Dasein," or our being-in-the-world) back as a necessary precondition for the understanding of any divine categories. That is, human existence is given a radical priority. But it is less because the domain of the divine is left in its place. Heidegger is not saying that theology is impossible but only that we cannot take *any* concepts—even God—for granted but must first understand the situation of human existence and the place such concepts have within the totality of our being or our "factual life experience."

Heidegger gives the concrete example of the difference between phenomenology and theology in terms of the concept of sin (*Sünde*). As a *theological* concept, the notion of sin makes sense only in terms of a particular system of belief. It arises within a field of other phenomena that are likewise connected to and illuminated by that same faith. If one inhabits that space of belief, one operates with such concepts; and it would be the role of theology as the "positive science" of faith to illuminate the connections within that space. However, such a concept only has meaningful content thanks to a more basic debt and guilt (*Schuld*), in the sense that human beings sense intuitively that they "owe" their existence to others/some Other. Clearly picking up on the basic definitions that were developed by Schleiermacher, Heidegger argues that the core of faith itself is a sense of "being part of a primary closed interrelated web of being" (den primären geschlossenen Seinszusammenhang).[9] Indeed, he quotes Luther: "Luther says: 'Faith is the giving oneself over (*das Sichgefangengeben*) to the things we cannot see' " (53). Therefore, all theological concepts "contain/hide (*bergen*) within themselves necessarily *that* understanding of being which human being as such has of itself, insofar as it exists" (PT, 63). While different theologies will provide different accounts for sin, responsibility, the Other as God, etc., the function of phenomenology is to point to the underlying relations that inhere in human existence (awareness of fundamental dependence even as we strive for autonomy, recognition of mortality, etc.). Heidegger calls this pointing function the "formal indicative ontological corrective" (formal anzeigende ontologische Korrektiv; PT, 66). It reveals an ontological network of the ontological concepts of human lived experience out of (or, like a background, against) which the illuminated

---

9. From Schleiermacher he gets a deeper sense of the historical, i.e., not the facts but the ground of our "schlechthinnige Abhängigkeit." In this way he comes to a different kind of answer than Troeltsch to the question of what "faith" actually is. That is, he comes to see that it must be approached *as* history, i.e., in terms of man's position within history. Hence the importance of Dilthey, who, especially in the *Einleitung in die Geisteswissenschaften* (*Introduction into the Human Sciences*), looks at "the original vitality of early Christian religiosity" that got distorted by dogma and Scholasticism, until it was renewed by Luther (254). It was precisely this rediscovery of early Christian eschatology that was leading theology out of "liberal theology."

spheres of the positive sciences emerge. Such concepts make up the nature of the "pre-Christian content of basic theological concepts" (PT, 66), where "pre-Christian" (*vor-christlich*) has a sense not unlike Nietzsche's turn to the "good/bad" morality "before" the "good/evil" morality, namely, different modality of being in the world is being indicated, not a claim about a specific historical period.

We might illustrate Heidegger's analysis of the relationship between philosophy (phenomenology) and theology as follows. The wider sphere is that of the lifeworld, the human realm. That "background" can never be revealed or illuminated or brought out as such, because all revelation or illumination can occur only against a background. The job of making things show up for study is the role of the sciences, each with their particular methods and hence each able to illuminate a particular place within the lifeworld. (However, one must also consider that this spatial representation cannot do justice to the fact that the lifeworld and the particular sciences illuminate a *historical dimension* in which phenomena, and human being, unfold.) It would take a particular form of "science" that functions differently from others to provide a form of access to the conditions of the functioning of the science and to show how the contents of the sciences have roots in the wider lifeworld. In his early thought, the function of phenomenology that could accomplish this is an "indication" (*Anzeige*), a pointing beyond the horizon of the sciences, and Heidegger strove to show "that philosophy, which is the free questioning of human being as it exists essentially on its own, has the task of giving ontologically grounded direction to all other nontheological positive sciences" (PT, 65). And while philosophy does not *have* to perform this function for theology, it can. As a diagram we can imagine his approach as displayed in figure 7.1.

Heidegger's early philosophy involves the phenomenological circumscription of theology and the exploration of different ways to think this "ontological-ontic" difference. Hence, the "putting into its place" of theology is inseparable from the basic formation of his thought. Once he writes "Phänomenologie und Theologie" he can explicitly formulate his position: he is interested in the ontological world of life experience, the usually invisible, though very real, given world, which cannot be "gotten behind" and within which the "positive" ontic sphere of illuminated beings exists for theology. Theology never asks about that background, against which its given world appears, that is, what "gives" it to theology to begin with. On the one hand, then, he breaks with his own theological background. But on the other, the philosophical approach allows him to "embed" theology and the discussion of God with a broader "context" (in the sense of *Leb-*

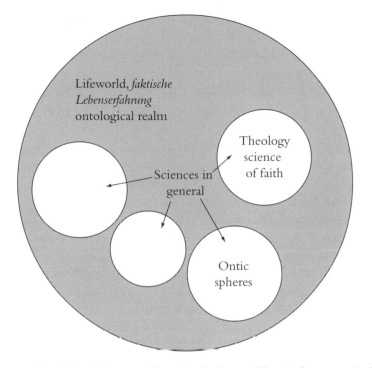

FIGURE 7.1. The relationship between lifeworld and sciences, philosophy (phenomenology) and theology.

enszusammenhang) of ontology. His "grounding" of theology in ontology is thus radically different from the projects undertaken by Leibniz, Kant, Feuerbach, Marx, and to an extent Nietzsche. Each of them sought to provide support for theology by turning to other sciences of their day (mathematics and the natural sciences, ethics, anthropology, political economy, psychology). They connected, to use my diagram, one ontic sphere with another rather than inquiring, as only human being can, into the world that provides its unthematized ground, the "there" of its "Da-sein." He spends the next years analyzing that world. This will culminate in the analysis of Dasein in *Sein und Zeit,* but we should look at a few of his earlier lectures to see how he had arrived at this philosophical position of "ontological phenomenology" by working through the study of theological categories.

Heidegger's lectures on theology and the philosophy of religion are gathered together in volume 60 of the collected works (*Gesamtausgabe,* conventionally abbreviated GA), not published until 1995. He had originally gathered together his writings from these years, 1918–21, under the title *Phänomenologie des religiösen Bewußtseins* (Phenomenology of Religious

Consciousness), but he later changed the title from *consciousness* to *life* (*Phänomenologie des religiösen Lebens*). The shift of terms is polyvalent. It retraces in some ways Hegel's development, which had begun with extensive theological manuscripts focusing on the concept of life and ended with a broader understanding of consciousness and spirit, but in reverse, since Heidegger here strives to return to a broader conception of the function and meaning of religion in terms of life. In so doing it also retraces in some ways the movement from Feuerbach's initial focus on religious consciousness to his broader anthropological conception and Marx's concentration on "conditions and processes of life" (*Lebensverhältnisse und -prozesse*). Of course, the issue for Heidegger will come to be how to differentiate his and Husserl's phenomenological approach from a (reductively) anthropological or economic-political one. His years in Marburg and most of his first lectures were focused on the project of a phenomenology of religion. In large measure, this arose out of his work together with both Husserl and Bultmann. After this period he starts to devote himself to Aristotle more intensely and leaves explicit theological issues behind until the 1930s.

The volume contains three large projects, each with a different presentational and philological status: (1) the *Nachschriften* of his students of lectures he held in the winter semester 1920/21, "Introduction to the Phenomenology of Religion" (to an extent a response to Ernst Troeltsch); (2) lectures on "Augustine and Neoplatonism" from the summer semester 1921;[10] and (3) "The Philosophical Foundations of Medieval Mysticism," which are notes for a lecture announced for 1919/20 but never held. These notes date from 1918/19 and are in part a response to a manuscript by Adolf Reinach, "Über das Absolute" (GA, 60:348).[11]

---

10. His lectures on Augustine focus on his *tentationes* (temptations) and prepare for the phenomenological analysis of "fallenness" (*Verfallenheit*) in *Being and Time*. That is, they provide an extended example of how religious/theological concepts or experiences can be traced back to or grounded in those of human being in general.

11. Among his papers from this period we also find a short sketch on what he might do in a lecture course on Hegel. It is noteworthy that he looks at Hegel at this stage from the perspective of the philosophy of religion and locates him within the tradition we have been considering. The following is his summary: "*Hegel's original and earliest position on religion—and consequences. Decisive influence of Kant*, who from the beginning barred any immediate relationship, based on an original experiential connection to the sacred. *Morality* is Kant's guiding interest, religion is then degraded to a mere means. The meaning of Jesus' mission is 'to raise religion and virtue to the sphere of morality' [Dilthey]. This basic starting point that sees religion as *means* is decisive for Hegel's entire spiritual development. I will pursue and critically present this conception. And furthermore I will explore how the problem of the historical gets placed on a specific path and can emerge in full originality—unfettered—as a philosophical problem" (GA, 60:328). This brief outline shows that Heidegger (1) was first interested in Hegel's early theological writings (which include the discussions of *Leben*),

We should first discuss the notes on his never-held lecture on mysticism because they are his earliest efforts to address the methodological problems at the heart of phenomenology, problems that came to challenge theology. As a philosopher, he cannot aim to inspire faith: "Our goal cannot be to give rise to religious life. That is possible only through faith itself (GA, 60:304)—i.e., that would be the purview of theology as a specific sphere of analysis that takes its faith for granted. Rather, the phenomenological analysis involves "attaining and understanding" the phenomena (of religious consciousness) *"from the historical"* (*aus dem Historischen;* GA, 60:303; Heidegger's emphasis). He deals with the methodological problem that "only a religious person can understand religion" by turning to the very issue of phenomenology as method. Its mode of *Verstehen* is not *"Rationalisierung"* (theoretical in a way that turns the religious life into an "object"); but neither does it leave the (religious) self "unedited" (GA, 60:304–5). That is, he will attempt "to understand the religious absolutely and in its originary state, independent of any naturalistic or theoretical approaches . . . or philosophy of religion" (GA, 60:309). In this methodological application, the phenomenological approach would "understand" religious life/consciousness against a background of human life and Being, but not "reduce" it to another scientific theory (as did Feuerbach with anthropology, etc.). Methodologically this means "the forms of experience are to be grasped always only, *only* out of their genuine possible situations and situational spheres," and not as isolated "facts" (GA, 60:307).

That situation or background ("das religiöse Apriori") cannot be considered a "System" (that is what churches do with their dogmatics and thereby destroy the subject's primal experience) but "a genuine sphere of experience and application" (GA, 60:313). Hence the need for a special kind of historical understanding, internal to religion itself and without applying "standards from outside of religion, even 'scientific' ones" (GA, 60:322–23). This methodological principle, won from phenomenology, is tied to a recognition of a radical consciousness of the historicity of all human experience: "Religion, like every other sphere/world of experience, can only take shape in historical consciousness and can attain a totality—not universality—only in relation to other spheres of value" (GA, 60:323). He is particularly interested in religion

(2) saw the problematic impact of Kant's moral arguments as divorcing religion from the world of facticity and lived experience, and (3) sees a wider trajectory for the way that "history" (as in the nineteenth-century movement of "Historicism") contains the same problematic effects that it inherited from theology. Heidegger's alternative would be to look at the notion of the unique *Seinserlebnis* (experience of being) that is opened up to someone living in a particular *Lebenswelt*. Since this follows the section on Hegel, we can say that Heidegger was working out his philosophical position through a reading of the theological tradition.

because it, as a phenomenon, draws us more to precisely this kind of questioning *beyond* religion because it is itself primordially historical, grounded in an "originariness" (*Ursprünglichkeit*) tied to revelation and tradition (ibid.). And even more specifically, the phenomenon of mysticism, although a theological concept that makes sense only within a specific historico-conceptual context, functions within that context as a challenge to it; that is, mysticism tends to be a "countermovement" to the distancing from the "immediacy of religious life" that takes place under dogmatism (GA, 60:314). Mysticism thus offers Heidegger an ideal test case to explore a method that would isolate religious concepts ("bracket them out") from dogmatic-theoretical-scientific frameworks and ground them within experience, or more precisely, tie them back to their primal connection to life itself. Just as Hegel was drawn by his reflections on positivity to think about the living *Geist* behind religion, so, too, Heidegger would use a reflection on mysticism to think about the "more originary" grounding of religion itself in human existence.[12]

The 1920/21 lecture "Introduction to the Phenomenology of Religion" demonstrates how he was able to think through key theological issues from a new perspective. It is divided into two large sections. The first involves methodological considerations on the nature of experience and its grounding in "history." This seems to be necessary so that he can then get to the grounding of specifically *religious* concepts and experiences in history. The abrupt turn to the second part, a discussion of selections from Paul's Epistles, may even have been motivated by student complaints that the first two terms in the lecture's title had threatened to eclipse the third. The discussions of the opening weeks of this seminar on the relationship between history ("*das Historische*") and religion/theology, as a propaedeutic to a reading of Paul, in fact links Heidegger directly to the debates raised by the radical new Protestant theologians Karl Barth, Friedrich Gogarten, Rudolf Bultmann, and Eduard Thurneysen. They will be dealt with in the next chapter, but it is crucial that the attack of a certain *kind* of historicizing is the common thread that links Heidegger with the new theology.[13] They differ in that he turns

---

12. Here we see why it is a mistake too quickly to identify Heidegger's approach with mysticism. Mysticism is a theological concept (like sin), and Heidegger *uses* it to go back to the basic human place in the world "prior" to the theological systems.

13. He (like the new "dialectical theology") has to differentiate himself from Troeltsch, the leading philosopher of religion of the day. He implies first (GA, 60:19–20) that Troeltsch changes his philosophical methodology too often, but says he nonetheless will try to understand him. He associates him with the descriptive sociological and psychological methods of Max Weber and William James (*Varieties of Religious Experience*). According to Troeltsch, Heidegger writes, "the religious phenomena are to be viewed naively, not yet polished" (20). Troeltsch then moves to analyzing the

this critique against theology *as such* (i.e., as *science*) so that he can legitimate his turn to philosophy, whereas they insist on the consequences of the same insights for a new theology. The parallels, however, show that his philosophy is structured along the lines of their theology, and their highly critical theology is more "philosophical" in an existential sense than they (with the exception of Bultmann) might admit.

Heidegger begins with a long discussion of the concepts in the title and the nature of philosophy. He states radically "that philosophy emerges from the factual experience of life. And then it leaps back into it again" (GA, 60:8). "Experience" (*Erfahrung*) needs to be understood here in both an active and passive sense, uniting the subject and object of experience. And "factual" (*faktisch*) is "not real in the sense of 'natural' or 'causal' or 'objective'" (60:9). Hence, *faktische Lebenserfahrung* is "the entire active and passive positioning of the human being toward the world" (60:11), whereby "*Welt*" is also not "*Objekt*" because one can *live* in a world, not in an object. The "facticity" of the "fact" of our living in the world means that it is given to us and not (as in forms of Idealism) posited by my subjectivity. "It is specific to factual experience of life that the 'how-I-relate-to-things,' the manner of my experience, is *not* experienced as well" (60:12). The "background" of my being-in-the-world must therefore be "phenomenologically abstracted," illuminated in a particular way that does not objectify it. The knowledge that will emerge from this exploration, both of myself and of the world, cannot be a pure "theoretical" knowledge (*Erkenntnis*) but is, rather, a "taking into account" of my interactions in/with the world: I only experience myself "in *that which* I achieve, suffer, encounter" (60:13). "Das faktische Erkennen" (as opposed to traditional philosophical *Erkenntnis*) plays itself out as "taking into account" or becoming aware ("*Kenntnisnahme*"), i.e., not by isolating self and object but by understanding the meaning, the "relation" or "connected order" (60:14), that exists in my world.[14] "Pure taking into account does not take preformed objects but

---

epistemological core, the "synthetic Apriori," or the "rational element" in religious phenomena (21). That is, Troeltsch, according to Heidegger, is too much the sociologist and historian in a limited sense. His turn to religious experience does not get beyond the "ontic." We get a hint of Heidegger's own position when he sets up an implicit contrast: "Faktische Lebenserfahrung hat (in diesem Zusammenhang [i.e., in Troeltsch as opposed to phenomenology] *nicht* die Funktion eines Bereichs oder Gebiets, in dem Objekte vorkommen" (21). That is, in phenomenology, which is not a pre-science to philosophy but is philosophy itself, the "faktische Lebenserfahrung" is the pre-given of phenomena; it doesn't "explain" them (since there's no causal relation), but our job is to locate them with it.

14. One can think here of the example of the meaning of a "tool" as a model for such knowledge: I only really understand what a tool is if I have an understanding of its function within a wider arrangement and my own place in it (e.g., how I might use it).

only contexts of interrelated meanings" (Die reine Kenntnisnahme nimmt keine ausgeformten Objekte, sondern nur Bedeutsamkeitszusammenhänge zur Kenntnis; 60:16). He rejects any approach—all forms of *logos,* we can say—that forgets the "lived" character of our experience of the world. Under the hands of "science" (or the scientific method), these living-experienced relations *degrade* (*abfallen*) into "objectified connections" (*Objektzusammenhänge*) and a "logic of the surrounding world or environment" (*Logik der Umwelt;* 60:16–17). All science tends toward such objectified "thing-logic" (*Sachlogik*).[15] Heidegger's phenomenology of religion would go beyond such a *logos.*

All this serves as a preparation for his actual approach to religion. He will approach this question through the "more comfortable path" (*bequemeren Weg*) of looking at the history of past and recent philosophies (of religion) to see how *they* relate to the *Lebenswelt.* This path parallels in many ways the course of my argument throughout this book. Rather than undertaking a sociological, anthropological, or political-economic study of the role of religion in society, I, like Heidegger, hope to trace different philosophies of religion, the way they engage with their discursive *Umwelt* (natural science, historical philology, institutional developments, etc.). We have seen a complicated relationship: on the one hand, they strive to tie discussion of God to the discursive conditions of the day (making Him relevant to their environment); but precisely this process brings with it an objectification, a splitting off of the theological from the *faktische Lebenserfahrung* (and hence a kind of positivistic death). That course was particularly clear in Nietzsche's view of the movement from polytheism, through monotheism, to atheism. The "return of religion" can be seen as an attempt to retie the connection of and to the *Lebenswelt,* an attempt on the part of society to reestablish its sense of cohesive, constituting history (*re-ligare*) and on the part of theory to "reread" (*re-legere*) such that it also no longer exists in a rarified, abstract realm. Heidegger's phenomenology ironically makes both moves—putting theology onto the level of the merely "ontic" and turning philosophy back toward the roots of religion in human existence—at the same time.

In introducing his interpretation of Paul, Heidegger makes clear that his new approach should change theology: "The phenomenological approach

---

15. This is also the tendency of philosophy (even when it takes a subjective turn à la Fichte). Here already is a version of the history of Being (*Seinsgeschichte*) as the tendency to objectify our *Lebenserfahrung/Welt,* leading to *Technik* and the "forgetting of Being" (*Seinsvergessenheit*). His basic question: If *faktische Lebenserfahrung* itself tends toward this degradation, is there anything we can find IN it that gives us a hope for a "turning" (*Umwendung*) in the sense of a "transformation" (*Umwandlung,* 18, also 10)?

to understanding opens up a new path for theology" (GA, 60:67). That is, he wants to read the Epistles and present a "taking into account" (*Kenntnis-nahme*) that is neither just historical nor a religious meditation, but a certain kind of *Lebenserfahrung* and *-zusammenhang* such that he can "penetrate into the basic phenomena of the life of early/original Christianity" (68). Only on the basis of that kind of "preunderstanding" could other "sciences" (like theology) develop. I will show in the following chapters how this "renewal" of theology or new approaches to religion, made necessary after the death of the God of the metaphysicians, was also the task of a variety of thinkers coming from different traditions (both Protestant and Jewish).

When Heidegger turns to his actual discussion of religion (that third concept in the title of his lectures), he claims to be finished with the methodological discussion (§ 14), but he seems not to be able to stop himself from focusing on questions of phenomenology. A real key is § 24 (60:90–93) where he analyzes the phenomenological concept of a "Situation." As a restatement of *faktische Lebenszusammenhang* in more straightforward terms, a "situation" is what we seek to understand through our phenomenological investigation. It is not static, not limited in time, not objectified as opposed to us. In this case, if we want to grasp key theological concepts like gospel, call, doctrine, warning/prophecy (*Verkündigung, Berufung, Lehre, Mahnung;* 79–80), we need to understand their emergence in a particular situation so that they make sense for us in ours. That is, to understand the "situation" of the apostle Paul is already to be connected to it through the association of life. Both the subjective, ego-oriented ("*Ichliches*") and nonsubjective ("*Nicht-Ichliches*") components of human experience are necessarily involved in a situation. He seems particularly interested in Paul and the Epistles because that "situation" (the epistolary form) unites him with his readers. Paul is not presenting dogma; his message (*Verkündigung*) is tied in with life (see § 30, 60:116–17: "It is essential that the Gospel/message always remain alive for us.")[16]

Heidegger concludes these lectures with the following summary: "Genuine philosophy of religion does not emerge out of preconceived notions of religion and philosophy. Rather, the possibility of conceiving it philosophically results from a certain religiosity—for us, Christian" (60:124). That is, rather than approach (preexisting) religious beliefs from the perspective of, say, mathematics or ethics, he says we need to understand something prior to

---

16. Thus he sounds a lot like the original Lessing and young Hegel, even if we take into account that he is offering a different notion of "life." He even goes so far as to indicate that the emergence of theoretical dogma (Hegelian positivity!) would have to be explained.

either religion or philosophy, namely, the basic categories of "life." They are offered in texts like the Epistles.

With his rejection of theo-logy for the sake of a different mode of analysis, one could say that Heidegger rejects the God that is associated with *logos*, or more precisely, indicates and points to a sphere prior to that illuminated by *logos* and hence he can circumscribe the realm of that God/*logos*. He has liberated himself from theology but allows it to have a place. One senses a kind of release in his final "definition" of the relationship between the two: "Philosophy is the possible, formally indicative ontological corrective of the ontic, indeed pre-Christian content of the basic theological concepts. But philosophy can be what it is without exercising this corrective function in fact" (PT, 66). The task of philosophy is no longer beholden to theology. It is neither derived from it nor a *mere* propaedeutic to the study of God. Rather, it has its own unique and specific function of grounding all concepts of the other sciences (including the science of faith, theology) in the facticity of human life and thereby opening up the question of Being itself, since that "facticity" can in turn not ground itself. Thanks to this insight, during the 1930s Heidegger will come to imagine something else beyond the horizon within which theo-logy has now been confined.[17] Indeed, he generalizes as follows: instead of the God that we can "see" thanks to the sphere illuminated by theology, we need to inquire into Being that is likewise blocked out, made invisible, "forgotten" because of the blinding light of the theoretical investigation of beings through the science of metaphysics (and all science in general). Hence, on the rejection of *logos* as an approach to Being, he says in the essay on Nietzsche's "God is dead," which will be discussed below, that the same blocking out of Being that is the very nature of metaphysics holds true for logic: "This is also true of every logic, granted that it is capable

---

17. Although a reading of *Being and Time* would go beyond the confines of this book, two points can be made to indicate the way theological discussions form a background for the analysis of Dasein or human existence. (In his book on Heidegger, Karl Löwith went so far—perhaps too far—to argue that *Being and Time* was a secularized Christian theology.) First, basic categories like care or fallenness were derived from his earlier lectures on the Christian tradition (esp. Augustine). Second, he holds up theology early on in the text as an example of a "positive science" that has reached the limits of its "ontic" exploration and poses "more originary" questions. In this, theology serves as a model for Heidegger and hence he himself follows the lead of Luther: "*Theology* strives for an interpretation of man's Being in relation to God that is more originary and indicated in advance by the meaning of faith itself, which is its sphere. It is slowly beginning to understand *Luther's* insight, namely, its dogmatic systematic rests on a 'foundation' that has not grown out of a primarily faith-oriented questioning and whose conceptual apparatus is not only insufficient for the theological problematic but even covers and distorts it" (*Sein und Zeit*, 10). With some modifications, this summary of the project of theology could apply to Heidegger's ontology. For traces of theology in *Being and Time*, see Pöggeler (*Heidegger in seiner Zeit*, 269) where he refers to 44, 139, 190, 249, 338, 427.

of thinking what λόγος is" (Das gilt auch von jeder Logik, gesetzt, daβ sie überhaupt noch zu denken vermag, was λόγος ist; GA, 264). In a sense, in the beginning was God and *logos*. But Heidegger hopes to go to an "earlier" or "more originary beginning" and ask a more primary question about Being itself. Theology now gets replaced not by phenomenology but by onto-*logos*. A bold and problematic undertaking.

Return to/of Being; or, "God" before/after God

In the 1930s Heidegger began to read Nietzsche intensely and held lectures on his philosophy for five semesters from 1936 to 1940. With Nietzsche, as we saw, we seem to have come to the end of a centuries-long development of Western thought. He not only declared the death of God but also challenged the entire metaphysical tradition—the "sphere" (*Umfang*) of morality—that is based on the divisions between good and evil, here and beyond, world and divine, being and essence, subject and predicate, change and timelessness. And one could say that it was not so much Nietzsche's doing, i.e., the result of an individual philosopher's particular penchant for critique, as the culmination of a cultural logic set in motion at the latest in the sixteenth century. And it might seem that after this end point, nothing is left for religion except empirical studies that explain the origins and consequences of the phenomenon ("false consciousness") of religion, be they economic histories (esp. Marxist varieties), sociologies (Weber), or psychologies (Freud).

But what if Nietzsche's very approach, the genealogical and nihilistic critique, were itself a part of the tradition that he has attacked? What if we need to include Nietzsche himself within the critique he so successfully waged? In this case, he would have both brought about the "overcoming" (*Überwindung*) and implicated himself in the culmination or completion (*Verwindung, Vollendung*) of the metaphysical tradition of God. Such a thought would imply that Nietzsche opens the possibility for a rethinking of religion that "departs from" the categories of metaphysics (being/nonbeing, cause/freedom, existence/essence), and especially that of *logos,* in a rich sense of "departs from" (i.e., uses them as a starting point even as this rethinking diverges from them). Such is Heidegger's enterprise, one that lays the foundation for other theological efforts "after the death of God."[18] I will

---

18. One might consider the parallel between his essay "Die Frage nach der Technik" ("The Question after/concerning Technology") and his thinking "die Frage nach dem Tod Gottes" ("the question after/concerning the death of God") or "die Frage nach der Theologie" ("the question after/concerning theology") —where "*nach*" is ambivalent and involves thinking about the "essence" of the thing being inquired into once it has passed. See also John Caputo's *Weakness of the God.*

approach it through a reading of his essay "Über Nietzsches Wort 'Gott is tot'" ("On Nietzsche's Phrase 'God Is Dead'") and his *Beiträge zur Philosophie (Vom Ereignis) (Contributions to Philosophy [From the Event]).*[19]

A prefatory note is in order concerning the historical background of these pieces. The essay, published in *Holzwege* (*Wood Paths,* 1950) and based on a talk held "in a small circle of friends" in 1943, is an extreme distillation of lectures Heidegger delivered on Nietzsche. He began writing the *Beiträge* around the same time he began lecturing on Nietzsche, in 1936, as an effort "simply to speak the truth of Being," finishing the manuscript in 1938. He had given explicit instructions not to publish it as a volume of the collected works until the Freiburg lectures on "Basic Problems of Philosophy" appeared, to serve as a fuller context. Given the years of composition, we cannot help but ask about the relation between these texts—including their discussions of the death of God—and the rise of National Socialism in Germany, including Heidegger's involvement. Indeed, it is not by chance that Heidegger developed these ideas in the 1930s. They carry the marks of his relationship to National Socialism. He undoubtedly first saw the movement as the possibility of a human transformation of the entire world of Being (as he expressed, for example, in his lecture as new *Rektor* of the University of Freiburg in 1934, "Die Selbstbehauptung der Universität" ["The Self-Assertion of the University"]). He saw himself as one of the leaders who could guide this process and perhaps establish himself as a kind of philosopher king. But both his disillusionment with/exclusion from the party's plans and his intense reading of Nietzsche led him to rethink the nature of the world to come. My goal here cannot be to go over ground that has been covered in much greater detail by both supporters and detractors of Heidegger.[20] But in answer to the key question of whether there is a necessary relationship between NS ideology and Heidegger's thought, or can the latter be separated (even considered a critique), I would say that Heidegger was generally "brilliantly ambivalent." Such ambivalence itself may well be grounds for moral and political critique. But the dominant feature is nonetheless ambivalence. Like a gestalt-shifting figure, sections of Heidegger's philosophy from the

---

19. The English translators, Parvis Emad and Kenneth Maly, make a case for translating *Ereignis* as "enowning" in order to capture the sense of "coming-into-its-own" that one hears because of the German root, *eigen* (proper, own). Certainly Heidegger mines a richness in the term *Ereignis* that is impossible to capture in one English word. But I think it is better to use "event" in order to express the everyday character of his language, rather than a strange word or *terminus technicus*, even at the expense of etymological echoes.

20. The discussion of Heidegger and National Socialism was (again) unleashed by Victor Farias's *Heidegger et le nazisme* (1987). For a (polemical) summary, see Wolin.

1930s on can flip back and forth (in my reading) between fascist and radically resistant.[21] That is, as we will see in the discussion that follows, there are times when one cannot help but shiver at Heidegger's use of NS rhetoric and modes of argumentation, even though in the next line one might convincingly (even if occasionally tortuously) argue that Heidegger is performing a "destruction" of that rhetoric. This ambivalence, I believe, characterizes many post-Nietzschean and post-Heideggerian "returns to God after the death of God" (as we will see in the following chapters).

Because the essay on Nietzsche compresses many years of lectures, it is extremely dense and rich. A summary of the overall argument is difficult but useful. The madman's statement that "God is dead"—with all the emphasis he gives it (namely, *we killed* Him)—means that His loss is not just a matter of indifferent atheism but rather a deep sense of nihilism. As Nietzsche wrote in 1887 (*Will to Power,* § 2): "What does nihilism mean? *That the highest values have been devalued.* There is no goal or purpose; there is no answer to the question 'Why?' " (222). This "true" nihilism demands a positing of new values (*neue Wertsetzung*), and so we need to understand the nature of *values.* To establish a value is synonymous with life understood as the process of always going outside itself to pursue its "goal" of self-preservation and, even more important, intensification (*Erhaltung und Steigerung*). That process of living by projecting a "value" and pursuing it, and thereby constantly extending one's existence beyond oneself, is what Nietzsche calls the "will to power." But at this point in his reading of Nietzsche, Heidegger reaches a startling conclusion. On the one hand, Nietzsche proposes the will to power as a chance to *overcome* nihilism; but on the other, we see that it is in fact the culmination of the *history of nihilism,* i.e., of the historical movement of thought that leads with a kind of inherent necessity of law (*Gesetzlichkeit*) to the death of God and the will to power as its fulfillment. Heidegger writes: "Nietzsche thinks of nihilism as the 'inner logic' of Western history" ("Nietzsches Wort," 223). Here we have the function of *logos.* Nietzsche and Heidegger seem to be saying that "in the beginning was *logos*" and the unfolding of that *logos* has an "inner logic" that is the logic of Western metaphysics, the logic of nihilism, and hence the self-destruction of its own values. God's death was already there "from the beginning" as an inner necessity of Western *logos.* Hence Heidegger wants a *different logos* or, more precisely, a thinking that is also there from the "beginning," indeed there even *before* the beginning—an originary, "ursprünglich, anfänglich" thinking of Being that has been cov-

---

21. This is not unrelated to Karl Löwith's powerful descriptions (and critiques) of Heidegger's combination of "violence and subtlety" (e.g., *Heidegger,* 240) as a reader of others.

ered up by the metaphysical *logos* since the beginning. This means going back to the beginning in order to undo or re-prepare the ground for the non-*logos* or "onto-logos." (Note we see here a parallel to the movement we saw in his earlier work: there he saw the methodological necessity of performing a phenomenology of human being and the facticity of lived experience "before" the positive science of theology to provide the "indicative corrective"; here he says that Being itself has the ontological priority over the *logos* of the history of metaphysics.)

The concept of the *Übermensch,* and as we will see below, the "event" (*Ereignis*) of God's death, merely mark the point where the history of the West—and specifically the *logos* of God—have played themselves out so that we must make a turn (*Kehre*) to a different kind of thinking. Only God's death seen as a historical-logical necessity can force us to consider the need for a new beginning, a beginning that is a return to an earlier origin. The appearance of the *Übermensch,* Heidegger writes, is not an "open call for the venting of willfulness" but "the law of a long chain of the most sublime self-overcomings, a law grounded in Being itself"; the emergence of the *Übermensch* prepares mankind for "the last epoch of metaphysics" ("Nietzsches Wort," 253). And here again, the closing of the "epoch" of metaphysics recalls at the level of the "history of Being" (*Seinsgeschichte*) the "bracketing out" (*epoche*) of theology that Heidegger called for in his earlier work. That is, the chain of reasoning that we have been pursuing throughout this book and that has lead to the death of God is identical with the fulfillment and end (*Vollendung*) of the age of metaphysics and its theology. By removing God from the picture and making the (human) will the essential principle of the world, this long chain of arguments has allowed metaphysics to take over completely. Heidegger uses Nietzsche, in a sense, to push Western metaphysics to its limit, to "bracket out" phenomenologically the entire history that has led to this point, to reduce it into a "mere" "epoch": "Metaphysics is an epoch of the history of Being itself. In its essence, however, metaphysics is nihilism" (265).[22] It is "in its essence" nihilism because its end is contained in its beginning (*logos*). Heidegger uses the Nietzschean term *Erdherrschaft* to mark this ultimate victory of the principle of nihilism. It is the point of his deepest ambivalence toward the occurrences around him: both a justification of the historical developments that are pushing National Socialism to its own version of global domination, and the closing off of that entire mode of thinking at a level more radical (i.e., at the roots) than ideological or political

---

22. This is exactly Gianni Vattimo's line as well.

or economic criticism. This ending/fulfillment of the regime of *logos,* for Heidegger, creates the possibility of a new beginning, a return to the primacy of Being itself, a thinking of God without and after God.

Given his skepticism toward any form of theology, we need to consider why Heidegger still seeks God and how he still hopes to save the day (and God) by dropping *logos* for "thinking." The answer lies in his view that the unfolding, and the undoing or self-overcoming of metaphysics, occurs within the history of Being itself. That history, i.e., Being itself, forms the invisible horizon within which metaphysics and all the traditional talk about God have taken place. If we can get some sense of the *essence* of nihilism (as the history of metaphysics within the history of Being), then we will see how it points (*verweist, anzeigt*) to something beyond itself because it was only our fixation on metaphysics that blocked our "view" of the horizon of Being. For this reason, the tradition of metaphysical theology constituted the "forgetting of Being" (*Seinsvergessenheit*); the nihilistic end or self-destruction of that tradition, what Nietzsche called the "greatest event" (*das größte Ereignis*) makes for the return, the "arrival" of a more originary Being. We must try to hear a different "tone" so that "perhaps we, with this other tone in our ears, one day will think of the age of the beginning of the end of nihilism differently" (266). Just as Hegel reminded us that the terrible words of our age, "God is dead," signaled hope for a divine rebirth, so, too, Heidegger would celebrate the coming of nihilism as an opening up toward Being as that which has allowed all this to come to pass (he speaks of Being in terms of its "letting things be" [*seinlassen*]). Thus he writes, echoing Schelling's sense of "ages of the world," that a revolution is occurring not within specific spheres of being (ontically) but at the limits of all such experience: "Perhaps we will recognize that neither political nor economic, neither sociological nor technical or scientific, indeed not even metaphysical or religious perspectives can go far enough to *think* what is happening in this world epoch" (266).[23] What we always "go past" (*Übergehen*) in our metaphysical thinking—and for Heidegger this means the philosophies of all the thinkers we have addressed in the previous chapters—is what is closest (*das Nächstliegende*). This is why the madman still seeks God. The others ("jene öffentlichen Herumsteher, 'welche nicht an Gott glauben'") do not seek God because they have stopped thinking (267). We have to listen to how he cries out "*de profundis*" (267), and in hearing him, we can start to think. "Thinking only begins when we have

---

23. Heidegger also held a lecture course on Schelling's essay on the essence of the free will in 1936.

learned through experience that reason [*logos*], which has dominated and been celebrated for centuries, is the most stubborn opponent to thinking" (267). And yet, for all its claims to break radically with the entire Western tradition, Heidegger's thought continues to work with precisely the oppositions and tropes that have guided the past centuries of theological dialogue between faith and reason.

In the *Beiträge der Philosophie (Vom Ereignis)*, the unpublished manuscript that is the only book-length project Heidegger undertook after *Sein und Zeit*, Heidegger rethinks these issues from a different perspective not tied explicitly to Nietzsche. (It was characteristic of Heidegger to claim that all of his philosophical efforts beginning in the 1930s consisted of "paths, not works" [Wege, nicht Werke]. Pöggeler claims, however, that the *Beiträge* in fact represents his *only* true work, since Heidegger never wrote the promised second part of *Being and Time*.)[24] It consists of 281 sections of varying length (from a half page to numerous pages), in eight chapters (the first, "Pre-View" [*Vorblick*], is a kind of introduction; the next six are the real body of the text; and the last, "Being" [*Das Seyn*], is considered a summary and offers a slightly different approach to the same material).[25] With its exploitation of the etymological connections between words and its musical rhythms, repetitions, and echoes, it is virtually untranslatable. The parenthetical subtitle captures the new guiding concept (*Leitwort*) of his later period. Rather than providing an analysis of human being in the world (*Dasein*), he hoped to think through "the essence of Being as event" (das Wesen des Seyns als Ereignis). What he could mean by this is not that all being is heading toward some cataclysmic "event" (although a sense of decline will play a role); rather, our human existence and the existence of all things (beings, *das Seiende*) need to be understood within the horizon of a history (happening, *Geschehen*, *Geschichte*) of Being itself. The happening of this history (or, to speak Heideggerese, its "eventing" and "coming into its own") of Being can be glimpsed only when we no longer fix our gaze on the mastery of things (beings) but instead allow the question of what things *are* to be posed. We will see in the next chapter the similarities between Heidegger's call for an opening up toward Being and contemporary theological discussions about revelation. Because the last two sections of the *Beiträge* address the status of "God" (in quotes, as we will see,

---

24. Pöggeler (*Heidegger in seiner Zeit*) considers the *Beiträge* Heidegger's "actual *magnum opus*" (13). See Vallega-Neu for an excellent introduction to this text.

25. The chapters are called *Fugen*, a term that can be rendered "joints" or "jointures," since they each capture "pivotal points" in the history of Being, or "fugues," since there is a musical themes-and-variation structure to the entire text.

because he tried to redefine this concept/being), we need to consider this work in some more detail.

To understand the significance of this text for a rethinking of God, let us consider two quotes. The first defines the topic of the next-to-the-last main section on "The Coming Future Ones" (*Die Zukünftigen*): "The future ones are those yet to come, on whom, in their anticipation of return and in their sacrificing restraint, the wink and the nearing and passing of the last God will fall" (Die Zu-künftigen sind jene Künftigen, auf die als die rückwegig Er-wartenden in opfernder Verhaltenheit der Wink und Anfall der Fernung und Nahung des letzten Gottes zu kommt; § 248). Like Nietzsche looking forward to the coming of the *Übermensch,* Heidegger here imagines men (it is unlikely he has women in mind, even Hannah Arendt)[26] who are yet to come and who can maintain an appropriately open disposition in order to receive and read the signs of "the last God," who in turn approaches and recedes. This last God, he says in an epigraph to the seventh chapter with that name, is "the wholly Other as opposed to those who have come before, especially the Christian God" (Der ganz Andere gegen die Gewesenen, zumal gegen den christlichen; 403).[27] That is, Heidegger envisions a return of God and a turning to God, but this God must be defined in categories that escape the ones we have pursued throughout this entire book. Notions of presence or appearance, for example, belong to a metaphysical tradition or "onto-theology," according to Heidegger, that reached its fulfilling culmination and hence completion with Nietzsche—hence "der alte Gott ist tot." Thus the way has been paved for the "new" God, or in Heidegger's terms, "der letzte Gott," neither to "appear" (we saw after all how the notion of God being one phenomenon among others led down the road to Feuerbach) nor to be absent (as in a negative theology) but to give its "gesture" (*Wink*) as an "event" for us to "read" (and in that act of interpretation we unfold our own lives). We see that Heidegger is working with an alternate conception of history, and so we need to understand his new "thinking of the history of Being" (*seynsgeschichtliches Denken*) *and* his place in history at this time. And it is in this light that he develops a view of "the last God" that is at one and the same time informed with a kind of Nazi fantasy and infused with

---

26. Consider, for example, his disparaging remark from his lectures on the "Introduction into the Phenomenology of Religion": "Interest in the philosophy of religion is on the rise these days. Even the ladies are writing philosophy of religion, and philosophers who want to be taken seriously greet them as the most important occurrences in decades" (GA, 60:19). However, he did have an extensive correspondence (and an affair) with Arendt.

27. This notion of "the wholly Other" will show up in the next chapter when we discuss theological concepts of the early twentieth century.

an alternative spirit that connects him to contemporary post-Nietzschean theology.

What is this notion of the "last (or final) God" (*der letzte Gott*)? If we translate "last" back into Greek as *eschatos,* we can locate Heidegger within a radically new theological context. It will become clearer in the next chapter that this actually is best understood in terms of the rediscovery of an eschatological perspective of or in the New Testament. Heidegger was undoubtedly aware, at least from his time in Marburg, that theologians like Barth and Bultmann (as well as others like Franz Overbeck and Albert Schweitzer) were taking seriously the strong belief expressed in the Gospels and Epistles that "the end was at hand."[28] Although there were conflicting interpretations of the meaning of eschatology, and although it is unlikely that Heidegger is reacting directly to this theological debate, it is remarkable how his formulations demonstrate the same radical rethinking of temporality in the light of a notion of a last or final (appearance of) God. In fact, the last God neither arrives nor departs. Rather, from Hölderlin's poem "Friedensfeier" Heidegger gets the idea of the "passing" (*Vorbeigang*) of God, who reaches to man in an "instant" (*Augenblick*), offers a "wink" or "gesture" (*Wink*) in departing, and leaves only a "trace" (*Spur*). (In fact, Heidegger's reflections on Hölderlin guide much of the *Beiträge.*) The "last God" does not come at the end of some long, linearly conceived period of time. Instead, He is always passing by, always touching our realm of existence but never entering into it as yet another "thing" within the sphere of beings. For this reason, this "God" as Other is both infinitely close and infinitely far. As Pöggeler says: "The final sections of the *Beiträge* connect 'the coming future ones,' who transport men into their place within Being and thus transform them into momentary sites of truth and the sacred, to the 'last God' and his passing. The last God is not the last within a series; rather, he raises the sacred and divine into the last and highest state of being, only to be there for the instant of his passing" (*Heidegger in seiner Zeit,* 260). Given this status of the "passing" of the last God, Heidegger argued in principle against the "return" of this God as a new mythology or a metaphysical theology (or "religion") or art like Wagner's, since that only masks the ultimate destruction of Western metaphysics (i.e., nihilism).

"History," therefore, is not the coming-to-appearance or coming-to-itself of *Geist,* or the realization of the proletariat/freedom, or human actions. For Heidegger, God is not a part of the human spirit or something revealed by or at the end of history. The "history of Being" (*Seinsgeschichte*) is instead the

---

28. See Torrance, 74–80, for this context. And Jacob Taubes (*Abendländische Eschatologie*) on eschatological thinking in Western thought.

nontemporal opening up of the possibility of our real, unfolding history.[29] If we think of the discussion above about phenomenology and theology, this *Seinsgeschichte* corresponds to that ontological horizon, indirectly accessible to philosophical thought, that surrounds the narrower sphere of things studied by positive sciences. Also, if in *Sein und Zeit* Heidegger considered history as the process of human being's interpretation of its place in the world, here he recognizes that that "place," the "Da-" of "Da-Sein" must be "within" a "wider" sphere of Being, a horizon (to use phenomenological language) in relation to which we stand. Our development/lives involve a constant moving toward that horizon with our projects and plans (the *Entwurf*) even as that horizon/Being "withdraws" from us and is never present. That is not to say that we do not often objectify it, imagine it as a conquerable border, a limit that we can transcend. That is the mode of science and metaphysics, and hence Nietzsche, for all his critique of those modes, actually brings them to conclusion by developing a philosophy of the *Will to Power*. Such a philosophy might be the culmination of the Enlightenment, the belief that we could illuminate the entire realm of things around us; but in fact, it is the deepest moment of the "forgetting of Being" (*Seinsvergessenheit*), a denial of the very "condition" of our being-in-the-world.

What can save us from this nihilism? According to Heidegger, it is only indirectly and ironically Nietzsche. Nietzsche thought he was saving mankind and life itself from the destructive force of Christian values by declaring the death of God and replacing Him with the Will to Power. But for Heidegger, this murder extends the logic of Western thought to its necessary conclusion and thereby prepares us for the possibility of an alternative thinking that might recall or call together what has been eclipsed all along. This means that for Heidegger, a glimpse of the "last God," his "wink," can come to us only once we have abandoned our hope in the metaphysical tradition that had falsely tried to conceive God as an existing thing. In fact, "things" must come to an end (*untergehen*) so that the condition for their being can be witnessed. He writes:

> Our hour is the age of decline or passing away (Untergangs).[30]
>
> Passing away, in its essential sense, is the passing over to a silent preparation of what is to come, namely, of the instant and the site in

---

29. If one wanted to visualize this, one might think of Homer's *Odyssey* in which the withdrawal of Poseidon (who goes off to Ethiopia) creates the "space" for Odysseus to continue his journey homeward. The connections to the Judeo-Christian God of creation and revelation will play a role in the next two chapters.

30. *Untergang* has developed overtones that cannot be imposed on Heidegger but which undoubtedly do echo in his thinking here, namely, the "collapse" of the Nazi enterprise.

which the decision about the arrival or absence of the gods is made. (*Beiträge,* 397)

Like the late Schelling or Kierkegaard, Heidegger insists that only by facing the groundlessness of our world, the abyss (*Abgrund*) over which our attempts to secure a foundation for ourselves is suspended, can we be brought to the decision (which, therefore, is both active *and* passive) of belief. But who is this "we" who can experience the "decline" in such a way? "The age of de-cline is knowable only for those who belong/hear (*die Zugehörigen*). All others fear the de-cline and thus deny and reject it. For *them* it is only weakness and the end" (ibid.). This description is rich and head spinning in its implications. It recalls undoubtedly the core Lutheran or Calvinist spirit of the "elect," those who can experience the despair of the thought of predestination and yet "know" they are saved—to whom Heidegger, given his own distancing emphasis on *"them,"* belongs. Hence he follows that last passage with what could almost be a citation from the end of Luther's *On the Bondage of the Will:* "Those who are truly passing away do not know anything of the disturbing 'resignation' . . . any more than they do blaring 'optimism'" (ibid.). And yet, written in the mid-1930s, this description of those who experience the *Untergang* refers as well explicitly to a conception of *Volk* that must send shivers up our spine after the fact. According to Heidegger, a *Volk* defines itself through its sense of "belonging" and in relation to its "God": "A people is *only* a *Volk* if it receives its history as a mission in finding its God, that God, namely, that forces it out beyond itself. . . . The essence of a *Volk* is grounded in the historicity of those who belong *together out of* their sense of belonging to their God" (398–99). The ambivalence here is captivating. On the one hand, how can one not read this as a parallel to the Nazi conception of *Volk*—albeit crucially not based on "Blut und Boden"—with its mission of pursuing its will to power, even (or especially) to the point of collapse? But on the other, does this not radically challenge the "optimism" of precisely the will to power, presenting in the future-ness of the *Volk* a profoundly Lutheran *abandonment* of (freedom of) the will? And is Heidegger, for all his latent and real anti-Semitism, not echoing conceptions of *Volk* precisely from the Judaic tradition?[31] Hence, Heidegger envisions the need for quasi prophets to guide the *Volk* to its God: "But how should it ever find its God, if not for those who do its *seeking* for it in silence and who, as seekers, must even take on the appearance of standing *against* this people that is *not yet* a *Volk?*" (398) Heidegger is here describing his own status in the mid-1930s.

---

31. See chapter 9 on Rosenzweig and Buber.

His naive effort to become directly involved in Nazi (university) politics failed. Now he stands on the outside, prophesying both the decline and the rebirth of the *Volk,* both the death and new Being of its God. He himself is on the decline and adopts the position of the eternal questioner: "Those going under are always the ones asking the questions" (Die Unter-gehenden sind die immer Fragenden; 397). Such is the direction of a new theology. "Only a God can save us now" (Nur ein Gott kann uns retten), Heidegger says in his interview with *Spiegel* many years later, a "God" that will not "appear" but will only pass by so that in that passing we might remember what we have destroyed and receive an answer to our questions. Heidegger writes of this "last God": "He has its *essence* in the gesture, the bursting in or absence of an arrival as well as the flight of the previous gods and their hidden transformation" (Seine *Wesung* hat er im Wink, dem Anfall und Ausbleib der Ankunft sowohl als auch der Flucht der gewesenden Götter und ihrer verborgenen Verwandlung; 409). God's possibility is only in the absence of God/gods.

We can now see why Heidegger felt uncomfortable with the concept of "God" even though he was clearly working with theological categories. Heidegger had an ambivalent relation to the theologians. On the one hand, we can see from a letter from Heidegger to Löwith in 1921 that he did identify with them in an important way. Pöggeler comments on the letter as follows: Heidegger differentiated himself from other post-Nietzschean philosophers in that "he called himself a 'Christian theo*logian*.' He emphasized the second part of this word because he wanted to work out the *logos* of that understanding of human existence that in Christian faith had led to new fundamental life experiences" (*Heidegger in seiner Zeit,* 265).[32] We see here that Heidegger was deeply concerned with a *logos* that originated with Christianity ("in the beginning") and that captures something about our basic relation to Being (= onto-logy). Although it had been displaced and distorted by the Western tradition, especially by a *theo*-logy that reduced God to just one more being whose existence was to be proved or disproved, he, like theologians around him, hoped to retrieve its original significance. He points out how only the "death of God," the "God of metaphysics," can open up the possibility of the new beginning of the "last God":

The last God has its most unique uniqueness and goes beyond those miscalculating determinations like "mono-theism," "pan-theism," and

---

32. See Derrida, "Faith and Knowledge" (*Religion,* 59), as well on this letter and on the way Heidegger calls for an "atheistic philosophy" and yet provides a source for a kind of faith.

"a-theism." "Monotheism" and all varieties of "theism" came about only as a result of Judeo-Christian "apologetics," which have "metaphysics" as their conceptual presupposition. With the death of this god, all theisms pass away. . . . The last God is thus not the end but the other beginning of unmeasured possibilities of our history.

[Der letzte Gott hat seine einzigste Einzigkeit und steht außerhalb jener verrechnenden Bestimmung, was die Titel "Mono-theismus," "Pan-theismus" und "A-theismus" meinen. "Monotheismus" und alle Arten des "Theismus" gibt es erst seit der jüdisch-christlichen "Apologetik," die die "Metaphysik" zur denkerischen Voraussetzung hat. Mit dem Tod dieses Gottes fallen alle Theismen dahin. . . . Der letzte Gott ist nicht das Ende, sondern der andere Anfang unermeßlicher Möglichkeiten unserer Geschichte.] (*Beiträge,* 411)

Heidegger was thus profoundly moved by the history of theological thought even as he distanced himself from the theologians.[33] In terms of his relationship to his Marburg colleague, Rudolf Bultmann, the contemporary philosopher Helmut Vetter comments: "Why did Heidegger not take the path of Christian faith? Certainly not because he wanted to hold firmly to philosophy at any price but because the concept of God had become deeply questionable for him as a result of the experiences of his age, especially through the encounter with Nietzsche's articulation of the death of God. Bultmann certainly took this experience seriously as well, even if differently than his philosophical partner" (14).

---

33. For Löwith, all those who seek "salvation via a radical about-face" (das Rettende aus dem Umschlag)—including Fichte, Kierkegaard, Marx, and Heidegger—demonstrate "how their thinking has deep roots in the theological dialectic of sin and grace" (*Heidegger,* 227 n. 34).

❧ Chapter 8

Dialectical Theology (Gogarten, Barth, Bultmann)

> I certainly do not want to debate with Bultmann, which of us is the more radical.
>
> —Karl Barth, preface to the third edition of *Römerbrief*
>
> The confrontation between Protestantism and the modern spirit, whose hour has likely come today, is not a theoretical matter.
>
> —Friedrich Gogarten, afterword to the republication of Luther's *Der unfreie Wille* (*The Unfree Will*)

Western philosophy had taken its course and reached its end in the death of God. Theology and religion would have to be reconceived out of the collapse of *logos*. Indeed, this collapse was seen, after the disaster of the First World War, as the consequence of a three-hundred-year development of "modernity." We will look at two attempts to formulate a theology in light of these developments, both decidedly post-Nietzschean and often in tandem with Heidegger. First, in this chapter, Protestant theology as it formed in the first half of the twentieth century (Gogarten, Barth, and Bultmann) and second, in the following chapter, Jewish "new thinking" (Rosenzweig and Buber).[1]

Hegel saw theology *aufgehoben* in philosophy. Nietzsche and Heidegger saw the end of philosophy as the dawn of an epochal possibility of a new relation to the world/Being. The thinkers we will address will try to reformulate this new possibility in theological terms. At some level they all address the issue of God as "wholly Other." That is, once some notion of an unthought and, with the tools of *logos* unthinkable, "wholly Other" of philosophy has been raised as a necessary consequence of philosophical thought itself, then

---

1. On historical connections between these two simultaneous and largely parallel movements, see Lazier's excellent study and Smith, "Heretical Thinking."

"God" can reemerge from the dead to stand in for this radical response to a self-limiting reason.

Excursus on "The Sacred" as "Wholly Other"

Rudolf Otto's work on the sacred (*das Heilige*) was important as background for the developments in early twentieth-century theology and philosophy of religion. While he recognized the need to apply clear and meaningful predicates and concepts to the deity, he rejected the notion that the divine was a "rational object" that could be fully grasped in this way. On the contrary, the irrational creates the larger context for such rational understanding: "But if rational predicates have usually been in the foreground, they do not exhaust the idea of the deity but rather receive their validity from and in an irrational element" (*Das Heilige*, 2). Such rational concepts can only be properly used "if they are ascribed to an object that itself is not grasped by them but must be grasped in some other manner" (ibid.). Although thinkers like Heidegger will distance themselves from Otto's use of psychology to get at this notion of the deity—Otto uses as his point of departure our feeling and experiences of dependency—Otto radicalizes the relationship between the human and divine in ways that will have a powerful impact.[2] In particular, he stresses the experience of our "feeling of creature-liness" (*Kreatur-gefühl*) that separates us completely from the realm of "the numenous" (*das Numinose*). It is experienced not as a moment of piety but as a "mysterium tremendum," a moment of fear and terror vis-à-vis the mystery of that which radically surpasses our realm of being (as creatures). Since he consistently associates this with the example of Abraham, he thereby associates his approach to Kierkegaard's. He thus circles time and again around "the *religious* mystery, the authentic *mirum*, [or] to express it perhaps most appropriately, the '*wholly Other*,' the *thateron*, the *anyad*, the *alienum*, the foreign and estranging, that which lies beyond the sphere of the known, understood, familiar and thereby 'canny,' that which opposes all sense of 'at home' and *thus* that which fills the spirit with transfixing wonder" (*Das Heilige*, 28). As he says in his essay on "The 'Wholly Other'" ("Das 'Ganz Andere'"): "And this uncanny, this 'wholly Other' that stands opposed to all that is human, is the mysterious foundation on which all rationality is built up and which shines through all 'human likeness'" (*Aufsätze*, 16).

Where Otto has an impact on Christian theological thinking is in his effort to show that the early Christian community experienced Jesus pre-

---

2. Heidegger does refer explicitly to Otto in his lectures on the phenomenology of religious experience.

cisely in this radical way, not as a mere "teacher" or "wise/good man" but as "the numenous," the shocking revelation of the divine that casts all previous meaning and experience in its shadow (*Das Heilige,* 176–82).[3] But he wonders, both in his book and in the essays that followed, what about Christians today? Could they possibly have such an experience? He answers yes because he sees in Paul the one who understood the true, numenous nature of Christianity like no other (184). He saw the "sacredness" of Jesus and gave us the terms that, if properly understood, could allow us to reestablish the appropriate relation to this "wholly Other." Those religious terms—sin, fallenness, flesh vs. spirit, need for salvation—place us in the situation of accepting simultaneously the absolute difference between us and God and the possibility of salvation precisely by the decision to accept that difference. For the idea of Pauline faith is not that we can approach God but that, in judging that we cannot, we open ourselves up to God's judgment. Moreover, it is this aspect of God "in the terrifying majesty of his divinity . . . before which all creatures [tremble] in their 'naked' creatureliness" (114) that he finds in Luther, an aspect that connects Luther to the tradition of the mystics.

All these elements—the turn to Paul, the critique of all theologies that undermine the "wholly Otherness" of the divine, the emphasis on the "fallen" creatureliness of human being, and the decision-quality of faith— will characterize the revival of theological thought in the early twentieth century.

"Dialectical Theology": Gogarten, Barth, Bultmann

The emergence of a highly influential Protestant movement in the first third of the twentieth century can be seen as a new Reformation that would make good on the true spirit of Luther's revolutionary impact. Major theologians—I will focus on Gogarten, Barth, and Bultmann—said what Luther would have said had he been able to look back on the consequences of "modernity": "You see," Luther would have stated unequivocally, "I told you so. I warned Erasmus already in 1524 of the dangers of historicizing the Bible, of giving mankind even the slightest inkling of 'freedom of the will,' of expecting a justice in the world instead of a divine justification of the world through the gift of grace. You start going down that road and you

---

3. We will see below how theologians associate this idea with eschatology and Christ as the *Eschaton,* the end of all things.

will find that the historical world of human culture will become the place of God's revelation and reality, in which case, you might as well kiss God good-bye." The important thing is, however, that they lived through the development that Luther in his own way "predicted." For the theologians of the early twentieth century, that development, as disastrous as it was, had the same sort of advantage that fevers associated with severe illness have, namely, it has led to a "crisis," a low point and a turning point, that has created the possibility—indeed necessity—for a revitalization.

What I will focus on in this chapter is not the developed theological positions, certainly not in their full systematicity (esp. Karl Barth's monumental, multivolume *Church Dogmatics*). I will also not explore in detail the differences that emerged among these positions, implicitly at first and then explicitly, leading to the breakup of their common effort later (e.g., the abandonment of their journal project). Rather, I will emphasize the explosive and exciting moment of protest and crisis that these thinkers initiated in the first quarter of the twentieth century, not only in the limited discipline of theology. How did they assess the situation of modernity (as it unfolded over some four hundred years from 1500 to 1900)? How did they register their "No!" to this situation in order to offer a new approach to religion and God? How might their assessment of a theology that grew out of a cultural crisis in the early twentieth century offer parallels to "culture" and "value" wars a century later?

Exactly four hundred years after the original debate, in other words, only now with the benefit of historical experience and understanding, the positions of Erasmus and Luther would again become central. For this reason, Friedrich Gogarten's afterword to the republication of a German translation of Luther's essay against the free will captures the spirit of the debates in early twentieth-century Protestant theology. Gogarten was one of the intellectual fathers of the movement that came to be called "crisis" or "dialectical" theology. He posed perhaps more dramatically than any of the others the radical situation in which the younger generation saw itself. From him comes the title of the journal that this group of new Protestant thinkers published for a little over a decade (1920–33), *Zwischen den Zeiten* (Between the Times), a phrase that expressed their position at a turning point, a point of decision, now that the past values have collapsed so that, from this place of absolute instability and uncertainty, a new question is posed to God, whose Word they are now open to receive as never before. Born in 1887, Gogarten worked in a series of pastoral positions in Bremen and small communities in eastern Germany until he received his first academic position at the University of Jena in 1925. From 1931–35 he taught in Breslau, and then until 1955 in Göttingen. He presented his last public lecture in the year of his death, 1967. Although largely forgotten now, he not only exerted a tremendous influence on the younger generation of students but also delivered some of the most forceful arguments against the older generation of theologians and philosophers, especially Troeltsch and Dilthey. He cast them in the role of Erasmus as opposed to the rise of the new Luthers. I will introduce this section, then, with a somewhat extended discussion of Gogarten before turning to Barth and Bultmann because he brings the issues in a particularly sharp formulation.[4]

The sentence by Gogarten that serves as one of the epigraphs to this chapter sets the stakes of the battle as he saw it. First of all, it was to be between "Protestantism" and the "modern spirit." Second, there is something about "today" that is ripe for this conflict; its hour has come. And third, the debate is not just between academic theologians but has wider consequences and is therefore of interest to a wider public as well. All three of these issues lay the foundations for the renewal of theology after the death of God.

Gogarten knew that he was making a bold claim in opposing Protestantism to the "modern spirit." For centuries the opposite claim seems to have attained the status of a truism, i.e., as Hegel stated directly, the Reformation ushered in the modern era. The culmination of this view we saw in Weber's analysis of capitalism—the rationalization of the modern world was motivated by the new "spirit" introduced by Protestantism, a spirit that thrust on the individual the responsibility to exercise freedom (of conscience) and to show through individual and collective (historical) success the will of God active in the world. Gogarten attacks all those theologians who attempt to make "peace" between Protestantism and the modern age because they do so "at the expense" of the former (afterword to *Vom unfreien Willen,* 347). His main target is Ernst Troeltsch (whom Heidegger dealt with and dismissed in his lectures on the "Phenomenology of Religious Experience"). Troeltsch and the other "liberal" theologians were willing to accept the developments we have explored in the previous chapters. For example, Troeltsch praises the rise "of a Protestantism that thinks and feels in a historico-critical mode" (346) and the fact that, as we saw emerging out of Schleiermacher's theology, "the path of personal conviction became more important than the goal of

---

4. In a letter, Bultmann says: "I found it interesting that Heidegger was familiar with modern theology and especially an admirer of Hermann [one of Bultmann's teachers]—and also knows Gogarten and Barth, particularly appreciating the former as I do" (cited by Vetter ["Heidegger und die dialogische Philosophie"] from Pöggeler, *Neue Wege,* 467).

supernatural salvation" because the former opened the door to "Commercium und Connubium" (347). By turning Protestant dogma into "universal truths of reason," German Idealism was able to make God immanent in human spiritual (*geistigen*) life (354).

It is important that Gogarten does not simply propose an alternative history for the sake of academic argument. Rather, the motivation to challenge the notion of a "continuity" between modernity and Protestantism comes "because today for the first time since its original emergence the modern spirit has been shaken to its innermost core" (348)—a fact that Troeltsch and others who are co-opted by modernity have failed to recognize. Given this historical development, he must argue that there is *another* Protestantism that goes against the modern spirit. That is, he will argue for *two* Protestantisms, both of which contributed to the formation of modernity but one of which can be separated from it, indeed must be in order to avoid going down with it in flames:

> One will not be able to escape from the bitter awareness that Protestantism certainly played a most emphatic role in the formation of the modern world. That might seem to contradict what was claimed earlier—namely, that there is no continuity between Protestantism and the modern spirit. But earlier it was a question of whether the modern spirit is a legitimate consequence and development of Protestantism. The answer to that question is: No! But it is a different question whether Protestantism did not have any part at all in this by no means homogeneous modern spirit. And the answer to this is: Yes, it did. (349)

In other words, there are in fact two Protestantisms, the one leading to and the other opposed to the spirit of modernity; and they can be named for their founders: Erasmus and Luther.

Protestantism contributed to the formation of modernity by breaking the hold or bond (*Bindung*) of the church on both individuals and society. However, whereas Erasmus accordingly celebrated this new freedom as such, the true reformers "did not intend to exchange this bond for absolute freedom; rather, they wanted to tear this false, illegitimate bond [of the Catholic Church] for the sake of a new, legitimate bond" (349).[5] Ironically, he argues, because the one "false" Reformation focused on individual freedom from

---

5. Consider also: "But it should also be noted that this liberation [from the Catholic Church through the Reformation] was not accomplished for liberation as such, as if freedom were the deepest and last word to be spoken to the world" (afterword to *Vom unfreien Willen,* 370).

all ties, it did indeed open the door to the bourgeois liberal order, which now threatens to destroy freedom in its most fundamental form.[6] Indeed, he envisions the destruction of all social and political institutions that developed since the beginning of modernity (the eighteenth century) out of the foundation of the thinking subject and its supposed freedom. On the contrary, the "true" Protestant Reformation envisioned a release of individuals from the binds of the Catholic Church, not in order that they might be "free" as such, but so that they might confront the real limits of their freedom vis-à-vis divine justification. Theological/religious concepts (creation, sin) form the wider context of human existence. As he says, the bourgeois order was made autonomous from (Catholic) church authority and "it is placed on its own foundation with its own laws, but it receives its truly by no means loose bond from the recognition of the sinfulness of all human life" (349). Or, at the level of the individual: "The ego knows itself as a creature, created by the same higher power that created the world of objects. Here it is a question of allowing for the validity of everything given in the world" (357–58). Moreover, it is precisely through the doctrine of predestination, i.e., through the *Bindung* that is stronger than freedom, that man guarantees his relation to God: "In the most exclusionary way imaginable [this doctrine] makes it impossible to ground the certainty of salvation in the subject, i.e. in man himself; rather, the ego is cast in relation to the You, through which it lives, and man in relation to God, who justifies him. . . . The doctrine of predestination, the 'central teaching of Protestantism,' is the clearest expression of the bond tying the created ego to the creating You, the responsible/responding man to the God addressing him" (369). It was Luther who introduced this anthropological—or better, to speak with Heidegger following Schelling, ontological—insight into human being as "grounded" in an unfathomable Being.[7]

---

6. It is remarkable how the "dialectic of Enlightenment" was depicted so clearly by these Protestant theologians *avant la lettre*. Also: "The modern conception [cult?] of personality is nothing but the absolutization of subjectivity and the ego . . . the violence of subjectivity prevalent in the modern spirit and its blindness towards all that is truly real" (Der moderne Persönlichkeitsgedanke ist also nichts anderes als eine Verabsolutierung des Subjektes, des Ich . . . die ganze Gewaltsamkeit der Subjektivität des modernen Geistes und seine Blindheit für alles Wirkliche; afterword to *Vom unfreien Willen*, 356).

7. Gogarten describes the core insight of Protestantism into human nature as a kind of "thrownness," "whereby man is left to reality and through this doctrine he faces himself and reality alone" (afterword, 355). This is not a vision of human "autonomy" in the sense of mastery. On the contrary: "In contrast to the modern idea of personhood, one could say of the subject or ego of the Reformation that it is only truly real when it abandons its absolutization, its pure, free, limitless and unconditioned egoism, and its reliance on its sense of self" (357).

Hence, the goal is not to revive the dead God of modernity or the Reformation itself, but to learn from the present situation in light of the missed opportunity of the past: "It cannot be a question of a replaying of the Reformers. Our task today—a lawless world calls out for laws! an irreal world hungers for reality!—has nothing to do with refreshing forgotten historical memories" (352). Rather, the aim is to use the collapse of the project of modernity as an experience of the inner truth of Luther's Protestantism: the impossibility of human self-justification (through reason or history or deeds) and the dependence on faith for salvation in a God who "stands opposed to me as a real You" (358). He formulates the basic dialectic at the heart of this theology as follows: "I and You are bound together only in the strict and irreconcilable oppositionality" (361).[8]

In *Theologische Tradition,* Gogarten makes clear the choice that Protestant theologians faced in terms of the history of ideas: Reformation or Idealism? Hellenic influences or pure Bible? "It is a question in this debate of whether Christianity is to be understood from the perspective of Reformation theology or from Idealism. . . . But mutatis mutandis it is also a point of contention in the exegesis of the New Testament whether it is to be interpreted from the perspective of Hellenism or from out of itself and its relation to the Old Testament" (1–2). In other words, it is a question of the status of *logos.*[9]

The choice here is not just an "academic" matter. It emerges from a position of severe crisis in the specific historical configuration of post-WWI Germany: "For us today this autonomy and sovereignty of man is by no means unquestioned. Through and in the [First World] War, our generation has fallen into the grip of a terrible fate that no man is capable of mastering, indeed, to attempt to master it would be frivolous" (*Politische Ethik,* 3). Thus, Gogarten's "ethics" pits Lutheranism against the Enlightenment views based on the self-positing of human reason: "Recognition of sin, justification by faith alone, the Last Judgment on the one hand and an ethics on the other hand that proposes human self-empowerment—these two sides are mutually exclusive. There is no such thing as a 'both-and' " (4). That is, one must make the choice à la Kierkegaard: either/or. Hence, he gives the title to his

---

8. Note how his formulation counters Habermas—rather than an unfinished project of modernity he sees a failed modernity because of the unfinished project of the Reformation: the issue is "that Protestantism still owes the world a new bond (*Bindung*) and has led the world into the chaos that knows no limits. Here Protestantism still has its work cut out for itself" (afterword, 370). The reference here to a relation to God as a "You" in dialogue with mankind will also connect with Buber and Rosenzweig (see chapter 9). The I-You relationship was central to Gogarten's later thinking in Göttingen after WWII.

9. This is an example of what Pope Benedict XVI will call "dehellenization" (see chapter 10).

earlier collection of writings: *Die religiöse Entscheidung* (*The Religious Decision*, 1921).

What is particularly interesting and problematic about Gogarten is that he puts this "existential" crisis also into a very specific historico-political framework: the Treaty of Versailles that ended World War I placed the blame and guilt on the German *Volk*, he argues, in the name of a bankrupt concept of "*humanitas*." This makes it possible for him, like Heidegger (recall above on § 251 of the *Beiträge*, "Das Wesen des Volkes und Da-sein"), to see in National Socialism the possible antidote to what they saw as the individualistic, technoscientific, and human-centered (autonomous) ethos of the time.[10] Thus, in the 1933 pamphlet, *Einheit von Evangelium und Volkstum?* (The Identity of Gospel and Nation), he tries to justify the formation of a *Reichskirche* under National Socialism because the "revolution of 1933" is radically different from any that has come before. It is not just an external, political event; rather, "it has touched somehow our entire existence" (7). The "claim to totality" (8) of the new state, which now lays hold of every aspect of human existence and demands an absolute choice (although it's a false one, since the state cannot recognize the *privater Mensch* as valid anyway, 9), corresponds for Gogarten to the religious conversion through crisis: "For us in Germany the National Socialist movement represents a decisive turn against the entire past history; it arises out of the depths of the self-preservation of human existence, out of the terror when faced with the abyss. Because it emerges from the middle, the center of human life, it therefore seizes our existence in its totality" (11). The new state represents "genuine hegemony" (*echte Herrschaft*, 12). The church itself must recognize the necessity of this *Herrschaft*: "If anywhere at all, then certainly in it [the church] one should know something about domination and about the fact that domination belongs to human existence" (13). Hence, a theology of human dependence on a divine Other yields to a politics of accepting human domination by the NS state. This was one route that the Lutheran Church, with the "German Christians," took in the 1930s in Germany.[11]

---

10. Barth, for reasons that will be clearer below, rejects Gogarten's position not just on political and ethical grounds (he saw the inhumane treatment of colleagues by the Nazis) but also on theological ones, since Barth saw in Gogarten's embracing of this new ideological movement a revived "anthropological" focus that turned attention away from the radicality of the divine Word.

11. Note how easily his theology spills over into a faith in authority, as in his pamphlet from the 1930s, *Wider die Ächtung der Autorität* (Against the Disrespecting of Authority), in which he argues for the need not to accept laws and orders from the "outside" but to be seized within our very being by authority. According to Gogarten, I should abandon "*sozial-liberale Ressentiments*" and give myself over to a figure of authority as lord and master (*Herr*) "with my being, so that I belong

Connecting his arguments to the long philosophical tradition we have been studying, Gogarten also (*Weltanschauung und Glaube* [Worldview and Faith]) makes clear that the "moralizing" interpretation of Christianity, which already began with Erasmus and culminated with Kant, is a disaster for Christianity and the world: "The moralizing of Christian faith caused great, indeed the greatest spiritual harm that Christianity, and with it, the world, could ever experience. Wherever such moralizing took hold, faith loses its power to overcome the world, a power grounded in the trust in Jesus Christ, the Lord, who can overcome the deepest terrors of human existence" (116). The response to such a moralizing stance to religion echoes Kierkegaard's existentialism, for example, in Gogarten's essay "Die Bekenntnis der Kirche" (The Confession of the Church), which begins by stating that faith emerges from man's confrontation with the limits of his being, i.e., with death and nothingness: "The church has its proper location on the most extreme limit of human existence. There, where time comes to an end and eternity begins and where one thus no longer has time; where earthly life becomes in death nothing, and where we face the fact that we do not give ourselves life but depend on an origin that is beyond our power, where our freedom and autonomy and self-control encounter an insurpassable limit, and where it is therefore revealed that we have a Lord over us" (5). All these views of faith as our acceptance of the complete Otherness of God, of the experience of despair and the decision to overcome it by faith (which therefore "justifies" us), emerge out of the crisis of the death of the God of the philosophers. Although I have gotten ahead of myself by tracing Gogarten's development through the 1930s, and although his relatively brief association with the "German Christians" supporting the NS regime was a cause for his break with Barth and Bultmann, we see in him the way early twentieth-century Protestant theology had to face the philosophical tradition that had led to the death of God. The theologians Karl Barth and Rudolf Bultmann joined Gogarten in the project of developing such a new/

---

to him, even more, so that I pledge him my obedience" (mit meinem Sein, sodaβ ich ihm gehöre, ja, deutlicher noch: daβ ich ihm als meinem Herrn hörig bin; 7). The terminology ("*gehöre*" and "*hörig*") echoes Heidegger's. His position is essentially the same, although cast in a different, more philosophical rhetoric, after the war. In his *Wirklichkeit des Glaubens (The Reality of Faith,* 1957), he continues the argument against the trends of the nineteenth century—i.e., against the view that faith is a matter of subjective "attitude" (à la Schleiermacher) or an objective fact to be studied historically (à la Troeltsch). He offers instead the view that faith has its own unique "object," outside the realm of human existence, which we can never "know" but are brought to only by recognition of the limits of our existence.

old Protestant theology—and had a longer and deeper influence on the future generations.[12]

Karl Barth initiated, by all accounts, a "conflagration," or perhaps more neutrally, an intellectual explosion, in the post-WWI period in Germany, and which was soon to catch hold in the United States. His monumental theological project, developed from the early 1900s through the 1960s, is often compared with Augustine's, Thomas Aquinas's, and Luther's. Barth was born in Bern, Switzerland, in 1886, and thus is of the same generation as others we have been and will be treating (Heidegger, Rosenzweig). After his studies in Berlin, Tübingen, and especially Marburg, under the liberal theologians Wilhelm Herrmann and Adolf von Harnack, he spent an extended period in Switzerland, serving as minister for ten years in the small industrial parish of Safenwil. Those were influential years for Barth, because of both his involvement in social issues and, more important, his weekly ministry, which forced him to be constantly engaged in preaching the Word of God. He faced the question: How can one understand and speak the Word of God, that which must in an essential way transcend our own understanding and speech? That engagement culminated in his yearlong study of Paul's Epistles to the Romans—where "study" does not mean the historical-critical, academic research into the philological or factual "accuracy" of the words but the intense and methodical unfolding of the *meaning* of the words' message. His five-hundred-page commentary on Romans (*Der Römerbrief*, 1919, revised 1922), published without any major philological apparatus as Barth's direct confrontation with the Bible, "fell," in the words of one contemporary, "like a bomb on the playground of the theologians" (Karl Adam, cited in Torrance, 17). And even his critics (like the liberal theological dean in Germany, Adolph von Harnack) recognized in Barth a deep religiousness that was contributing to a revival of spirit after WWI.

To his great surprise, since he had never pursued an academic career, Barth received a call to the University of Göttingen and took over the chair in Reformed or Calvinist Theology, funded in part by U.S. Presbyterians. He occupied that chair for four years before being called to Münster. As a result of his strong stance for the Confessing Church (*Bekennende Kirche*) and against the German Christians under the National Socialists, he was forced to emigrate to Switzerland in 1935. His exchanges with his former

---

12. This is not to say that Gogarten didn't have an impact on interwar German theology (and even beyond, after WWII). As we will see in the following chapter on Buber and Rosenzweig, it is remarkable how their thought echoes formulations by Gogarten; but compared to Barth and Bultmann he had less widespread influence.

friend and colleague Gogarten, in the years directly following the Nazi rise to power (1933–34), present both the political and especially theological reasons why he took the route of opposition.[13] He taught at the University of Basel and was a dominant figure in Protestant theology worldwide until his death in 1968.

Although expressing a different kind of passion than Gogarten, Barth, too, felt that both the church and theology had reached such a crisis in the early twentieth century that they were threatening to pass away. The bankruptcy of the theological tradition became clear to him during the First World War, as he wrote in the afterword to an edition of selected works by Schleiermacher (1968): "And then the First World War started and brought—for me almost worse than the breaking of Belgian neutrality—the horrific manifesto of the ninety-three German intellectuals, who identified before the whole world with the militarism of Kaiser Wilhelm II and his chancellor. And among the signatories I discovered to my horror the names of almost all my German mentors. For me, a whole world of theological exegesis, ethics, dogmatics, and homiletics, in which I had up until then placed my faith, became loosened from its moorings when I read that and the other statements of the German theologians" (*Schleiermacher-Auswahl,* 293). In short, we can say that the generation of thinkers we are dealing with *experienced* nihilism; it was not just something they learned from Nietzsche. Thus, a key to the lively theological debates after World War I—a surprise since it would not be obvious that there could be much theology after the death of God—is the response that the younger generation had precisely to the developments of the nineteenth century that we have been exploring. Certainly, there were always those who simply ignored the interactions between philosophy and theology, i.e., who rejected the different rationalizations. They were the orthodox theologians who turned "by faith alone" into a dogma that, they felt, protected them from the infiltration of *logos*. Then there were those who saw their mission as the continuation of the developments that began with Schleiermacher or Hegel. These "liberal" theologians took seriously the notions that God was revealed in history, that reason demanded the fundamental identity between man, world, and God, and that hence the path to God was through the study of the realizations (or, with Schleiermacher, experiences and feelings) of Spirit on earth. For them (Troeltsch, Harnack, et al.), the mission of theology was to understand the historical, social, anthropological, and cultural sig-

---

13. Documented in Moltmann, *Anfänge der dialektischen Theologie,* and Fürst, "Dialektische Theologie" in *Scheidung und Bewährung 1933–1936.*

nificance of religion (also, for example, the historical personage of Christ).[14] They did not undertake this task to explain religion away, but to see God at work in the world.

Karl Barth (and Friedrich Gogarten) led the charge of the younger generation against both of these directions.[15] Against the former, they insisted that theology must include *logos,* rational investigation and discourse.[16] Against the latter, they insisted that theology must make God, not human or social phenomena, its primary object. Theology, therefore, could not be permitted to be blind faith or mere anthropology. Ironically, they avoided these two positions by combining them in a peculiar way. Barth learned a similar lesson as Nietzsche from the history of thought about God in the nineteenth century, namely, that such thought had reached its limits and essentially killed the God of its thoughts by making Him an anthropological being. However, that nihilistic insight could be compared to the kind of "despair" that Luther himself experienced or that Kierkegaard described as the necessary precondition of faith, i.e., an opening up to a God who is "wholly other." It was a paradoxical or "dialectical" approach in two ways. On the one hand, there was a dialectic between faith and reason since one could not avoid reason but only pass through it fully to reach faith. On the other, the relationship between man and God could not be explained directly; man could never approach God but only help establish the conditions—the recognition of human limitation—for God to address him.[17] And that address always comes *at* man, never from him.

---

14. Harnack especially was important for uniting history as a "science" (*Geisteswissenschaft*) and theology. In this he contributed immensely to the understanding of the real origins of biblical texts and continued the critique begun with Reimarus and Lessing. He wrote in a correspondence with Barth: "The task for theology is the same as the tasks of science" (cited in Miltenberger, 145–46). We could say that he would translate John's prologue: "In the beginning was historical *Wissenschaft*." And what that historically oriented theological "science" discovers is the core message of the original Jesus without the overlays of Hellenism or 1,900 years of dogma.

15. "Barth veered away from orthodoxy as he veered away from liberal theology; that is why some want to lump him with the modernists" (von Balthasar, 19).

16. Far from avoiding the "slippery slope" that led to the death of God, Barth thought it was necessary to confront it. He often had beginning theology students read Feuerbach not only so they could "know the enemy" but also so they could understand where an entire centuries-long development of modern theology would necessarily lead. See his essay on Feuerbach in *Theology and Church.*

17. Bultmann, "Die Bedeutung der 'dialektischen Theologie' für die neutestamentliche Wissenschaft" (in *Glauben und Verstehen,* 1:114–33) summarizes: "Why do we believe now that theological knowledge must have such a dialectical character? If theology is not to speculate about God or talk only about a *conception* of God, but about the real God, then it must speak of human being at the same time as it speaks of God. Theology presumes in its assertions a certain understanding of mankind" (117). It is precisely this tension—theology is only about God but also about man—that is the source

One direct path into Barth's thought is to understand the nature of the essential "turn" that he makes from all dominant theological thinking of modernity. He writes, for example: "We can have what we lack—including materially—only if we execute a *turn*. None of us have this turn wholly behind us, for we can execute it only when we are given the freedom to do so, in the event of obedience. Each morning, then, and perhaps each hour, we must execute it as we face each new philosophical task" ("The Gift of Freedom," in *Karl-Barth Reader*, 12). What is it that he is turning away *from*? All approaches to theology, all *logoi* about God, that begin with the assumption that human beings, through an understanding of their world (history, culture, rituals, consciousness, nature), can reach an understanding of God. We have seen such approaches in Descartes' focus on the absolutely certain contents of our thought, or deism's focus on the order of the natural world, or Kant's focus on the requirements of our practical reason. Lessing provides us with one of the most graphic and bold formulations of this "thesis." In the *Education of the Human Race,* he uses the parallel between an individual's and the race's development in order to claim that "education gives man nothing which he could not also get from within himself; it gives him that which he could get from within himself, only quicker and more easily. In the same way too, revelation gives nothing to the human race which human reason could not arrive at on its own; only it has given, and still gives to it, the most important of these things sooner" (*Theological Writings,* 83). This destruction of the fundamental and absolute distinction between history and revelation, between human knowledge and the divine call, is, for Barth, the beginning of the end of all true faith since faith is not a particular state of the human condition but a gift presented by God to man. Indeed, the one absolute that theology must never forget is that "without grace reason is . . . incurably ill and incapable of any serious theological achievement" (in Fürst, 232).[18]

In many variations, Barth reiterated throughout his entire life the basic position: "We cannot close our eyes to the fact that what we have here [in the Bible], in antithesis to all religions, is not a human movement to God but a divine movement to humanity" (*Barth Reader,* 29). This means that he rejects the association of Christianity with either social movements or *Kultur,* because the core of Christian faith is the radical uncertainty vis-à-

---

of the (need for) dialectic. Other modes of theological language, like Idealism or (Schleiermacherian) Romanticism, seem to speak about God, but because they see God as identified with reason or feeling/experience, they in fact speak only about man. See also 118.

18. This is made clear in Trevor Hart's essay "Revelation," in Webster, *Cambridge Companion to Karl Barth* (37–56). He analyzes the opening part of *Church Dogmatics.*

vis God, the necessary openness to the Word of God, and the sea of paradox and dialectic on which we find ourselves. Lazier cites Barth's paradoxical formulations from his commentary on Romans and associates him with a "Gnostic revival": "The truth has encountered us from beyond a frontier we have never crossed. . . . It is as though we had been transfixed by an arrow launched at us from beyond an impassable river. . . . We speak as prisoners at liberty, as blind seeing, as dead and behold we live" (Lazier, 31). Like Kierkegaard, he brings two infinities into conflict/paradox: man's infinite longing to find God and the infinite futility of his search. Like Calvin, Barth proclaims that only when one reaches the absolute crisis in recognizing the weakness of one's own thought (reason) can one be ready to receive a revelation (faith). But the two are opposites. This is why Barth began his book on dogmatics with the claim that the liberal tradition from Schleiermacher to Harnack had been "the plain destruction of Protestant theology and the Protestant church" (cited in Dorrien). At the end of the afterword he wrote to the selection of Schleiermacher's works in 1968, Barth posed four questions to/on Schleiermacher and gave two possible, opposing answers to each. Depending on the answer, there could still remain a channel of communication between the two. The second question seems to be the more crucial, and here we see his position distilled to a central issue. Barth wonders whether Schleiermacher does point to "an Other whose difference could not be overcome" (*einem unaufhebbaren Anderen*)—i.e., whether he truly emphasizes the notion of God as the "*whence* of the feeling of absolute dependency" (*Woher des Gefühls schlechthiniger Abhängigkeit*)—or whether in fact Schleiermacher's emphasis on the *feeling* posits a oneness with that Other that denies its essential difference (*Schleiermacher-Auswahl,* 310). Only the former answer could make Schleiermacher acceptable to Barth.

Barth's initial position, therefore, had to skirt the dangers he had seen for theology as the result of a centuries-long development (the fact that he later wrote a monumental work on the history of nineteenth-century theology demonstrates that he also knew that development had to be taken into account).[19] He needed to avoid the subjectivism that would define the core

---

19. His monumental *Die protestantische Theologie im 19. Jahrhundert* (*Protestant Theology in the Nineteenth Century*) retraces the path that led to the present crisis. The basic question is: What marks the period of the nineteenth century as a specific and in a crucial sense closed chapter of church history? Some had said that it was the time of the "church" (in the way that, say, the third and fourth centuries were the time of overcoming "gnosis," or the Reformation was the time of "justification"). But for Barth, the notion of a church means that revelation unfolds "in the unfolding and changes of the times" (15). Not that he has an organic view of history. But he does need to look to the past to understand "to what extent and how we have come to be in a particular

of religious belief as individual feeling, since such a position offers no universal grounding for faith. He also needed to avoid the collapse of theology into cultural history or anthropology and religion into an expression of human needs.[20] Already in one of his first published essays, "Moderne Theologie und Reichsgottesarbeit" ("Modern Theology and the Work of the Kingdom of God"; 1909), Barth raised the central critical issue for the historically oriented liberal theology, namely, how it could escape relativism and establish an absolute standard for faith.[21] (This initial questioning has remarkable parallels, we will see, to the early work of Rosenzweig.) The answer for Barth lay in the absolute objectivity of the divine Word that, in its Otherness, nonetheless reaches the world as the radical "events" (he uses the word *Ereignis* independent of Heidegger; see Torrance, 98, and below on Rosenzweig) of creation, revelation, Christ's incarnation, and the saving grace of biblical faith. According to Ronald Goetz: "In his famous 1922 *Letter to the Romans,* [Barth] wrote of God as the 'wholly other' of whom we can have absolutely no natural knowledge. God is the unknown who is disclosed to us exclusively in the death and resurrection of Jesus Christ. Even with the incarnation, all language about God entails an unresolvable dialectic, and thus remains perpetually flawed. Faith always creates a totally disruptive crisis for all human thought, enterprise and values" (458). Goetz points out that this stance taken

---

way" (ibid.). The key is Schleiermacher: "This [the nineteenth] century has seen many deviations from Schleiermacher, many distorting images, almost to the point of unrecognizability, and many dismissals and suppressions of him. But in the area of theology, it is nonetheless *his* century" (379). Which leads Barth to the anxiety of influence: "No one can say today if we have really overcome him or if we are not—despite all loud and radical protest against him—deep down still the children of his century" (380). This is why Barth must work through the history of the nineteenth century. He must show the development of "liberal theology" from its roots so that he can bring the whole thing to its end. The eighteenth century raised many questions and gave some more or less well-formulated answers (Rousseau, Lessing, Kant, Novalis, Hegel). But it turns out that, for better or worse—according to Barth, for worse!—Schleiermacher's answers to the questions of the eighteenth century were the ones that dominated (381). Barth "praises" Schleiermacher for undertaking the hard task of theology, namely, dogmatics. But he points to the most pressing question: "Whether his dogmatics did not reinterpret theology as a form of general humanities (*Geisteswissenschaft*) and thereby fully historize it" (384). The question is rhetorical. This is precisely the aim of Barth's critique: Schleiermacher turned theology into a historical discipline and the nineteenth century continued this development of the reduction of the Word of God (theo-logos) to a cultural phenomenon. This is not to say that Barth did not have profound respect for the achievements of Schleiermacher (also for his personal commitment), as he notes in his short autobiographical statements in the afterword.

20. "How could he have a theology that took seriously the human pole in the God/man, Creator/creature dialectic without letting it pass over into an ideology, a theology of man that did not pass over into an independent anthropology or become little more than an ideological expression and justification of man's cultural background?" (Torrance, 136)

21. Published in *Zeitschrift für Theologie und Kirche,* 19. See Dannemann for a discussion of this essay, 26–29.

by Barth in the end leaves little room for human freedom: "The 'early' Barth affirmed a version of the sovereignty of God that came close to precluding human freedom from the start. God's lordship was absolute. In 1920, Barth declared that God 'must be true to himself; he must be and remain holy. He cannot be grasped, brought under management, and put to use; he cannot serve. He must rule. He must himself grasp, seize, manage, use. He can satisfy no other needs than his own' (*Word of God and the Word of Man,* Harper, 1957, p. 74). Such a doctrine of a divine management that cannot serve but can only rule effectively precludes any serious talk about human freedom" (ibid.). And in this way, the radical post-Nietzschean theologian embraces again Luther and Calvin. However, his later thought on election moved in the direction of universalism, i.e., God's grace is unlimited and hence, in a crucial sense, all—Christian and non-Christian—are saved, even if, according to Barth, only the Christians are called to testify to their salvation. The fact that human beings fall, indeed have fallen, and hence need salvation, makes Barth's God a "suffering God." In Goetz's words: "Indeed, [God] has tied his own destiny to human destiny so tightly that our suffering is his suffering, and our growth in freedom is his growth in freedom" (ibid.).

This interpretation has harsh consequences for what it might mean to be "religious." It is not a question of quiet piety and happiness. Rather: "One cannot wish religion upon someone or extol someone for it: it is a catastrophe that breaks in on certain individuals with a fatal necessity and can then be transferred from them to others. . . . To be a religious person means to be a torn, unharmonious, conflicted person. For only a person who has not posed the great question of unity with God could ever be one with himself" (*Römerbrief,* 2nd ed., 1922, 240). So much for the Hegelian notion of religious consciousness as the (re)identity of man and God (and hence of both man and God with themselves). So much for religious consciousness as fulfilling the needs of human beings, as a response from out of themselves to their inner longing. Instead, like a comet from beyond streaking across our horizon, faith disturbs our self-absorbed orbit. Barth even goes so far as to say that religion itself can no longer exist as we know it. "Religion compels us to the perception that God is not to be found in religion. Religion makes us to know that we are competent to advance no single step. . . . Religion brings us to the place where we must wait, in order that God may confront us—on the other side of the frontier of religion" (*Römerbrief;* on Romans 7:7–11).[22] Thus the comet, as we saw also in the discussions of the *Ereignis*

---

22. This radical position—a return to Christ and grace after the death of God, but a destruction of religion—is not maintained in the late Barth of *Church Dogmatics.*

of Heidegger's Being and "last God," will appear only after the sunset and decline (*Untergang*) of the old gods.[23]

Hence, one important element of Barth's theology was referred to near the end of the last chapter when we discussed Heidegger's notion of the "last God," namely, the importance of eschatology—the understanding of "last things" or the end of time—for the understanding of the New Testament. Whereas (as we have seen) the nineteenth century developed a largely teleological view of biblical temporality—i.e., a movement whereby God was revealed over time in (human) history—the early twentieth century discovered in the New Testament a wholly different view of time. For the early Christians, the "end was at hand"; it was about to break in on them as the Kingdom of God. The fact that this view permeated the Gospels and especially Paul's Epistles introduced the need for a new interpretation of the relationship between man and God. (Consider, for example, Romans 13.11–12: "Now it is high time to awake out of sleep; for now is our salvation nearer than when we believed. The night is far spent, the day is at hand.") While some (like Schweitzer) saw in the failure of God's advent the necessity to abandon such "mythological" accounts, Barth insisted on maintaining an eschatological view that meant changing *our* conception of time. The "closeness of the end" only makes sense, according to Barth, if we abandon completely the teleological (and historical, unfolding, evolutionary) perspective of revelation. The "end," i.e., "divine time," is always "at hand" because the present cannot account for its own origin but is related to an infinite or eternal Otherness, even as it is infinitely, because absolutely, qualitatively different from it. "The 'last' hour, the time of eternity, was not an hour which followed time. Rather at every moment in time we stood before the distinctive feature of the frontier of 'qualified time'" (*Church Dogmatics*, 2:635; cited in Torrance, 78). The fact that this "other time" or "end time" or "new time" might always be breaking into our time with an infinite closeness and infinite distance, and had even become a real "event" in the Incarnation of Christ and the Word of the Bible, makes up the event (*Ereignis*) of revelation that strikes our reason as a *skandalon,* or offense, even as it makes up the

---

23. Despite the striking parallels in certain of the structures of thought developed by Barth and Heidegger, Barth voiced concern (even disdain) about Heidegger, esp. over his engagement with the National Socialists. See the *Barth-Bultmann Briefwechsel.* He mocks Heidegger's turn to the NSDAP (the National Socialist German Workers' Party), which he did "with drums and trumpets" (*mit Pauken und Trompeten*; letter to Bultmann, July 10, 1934). Barth's rejection of Heidegger (letter to Bultmann, June 21, 1931): "I can only repeat to you that with your association with Heidegger (not because it's Heidegger but because he's a philosopher), you have done what an evangelical theologian should avoid."

root of all faith. In a way that will make more sense in a moment when we turn to Rosenzweig, we can represent this relationship mathematically as the relationship between a tangent and a curve. Divine time comes from "out of nowhere" and exists always on a different plane from the fall of human time. It is always "touching" our time in the constant crises of revelation, and although it is what has set us on our present path, it always stands in a dynamic tension to it. (See figure 8.1.) These various points of contact are the "occasions and possibilities and witnesses of the knowledge of His righteousness," Barth says, the main one being Jesus of Nazareth (*Römerbrief;* on Romans 3:21–22a).

Barth brings together these key features of his theology at the opening of his commentary on Romans. On the one hand, he insists on the radical Otherness of the divine order. The descent of Christ into our world comes from another plane: "Jesus as the Christ is the plane that is unknown to us, which intersects with ours vertically from above" (*Römerbrief,* 6). Christ's appearance on earth, and especially his resurrection, would be the point where the divine and the earthly touch. But they do so in a paradoxical way because they do not lose their ontologically opposite character in their point of contact: "In the resurrection the new world of the Holy Spirit touches the old world of the flesh. But it touches it as a tangent touches a circle, without touching it, and precisely by *not* touching it, it does touch it as its limit, as *new* world. Thus, the resurrection is the event before the gates

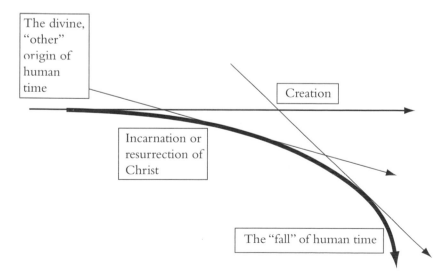

FIGURE 8.1.   Relationship of "other" time and human time.

of Jerusalem in the year 30 insofar as it 'entered' [the world]" (ibid.). With this construction, Barth argues against all previous theologies that would see any kind of "melding between God and man" (*Verschmelzung zwischen Gott und Mensch*), or the rise of the divine in man, or the pouring of the divine into the human vessel ("*Ergießung Gottes ins menschliche Wesen*"). Any theology that posits an *identity* between man and God leads to the death of God. Having experienced the nothingness of that God who is drawn down to the human level, having recognized it as in fact *Nicht-Gott,* having seen that it is better to challenge such a being rather than support him with "proofs" and absolute characteristics—in short, having reached a stage of atheism (13–14), it is now time, according to Barth, for the affirmation (*Bejahung*) of "the wholly Other" (*der ganz Andere*; 15), in all its dialectical and paradoxical, i.e., nonidentical, relationality to man. We are, he writes, "at the threshold and meeting-place of two worlds . . . [across] the abyss dividing sinners from those who are under grace. . . . Grace is the freedom of God by which men are seized. Within the sphere of psycho-physical experience, this seizure is, however, nothing but vacuum and void and blankness. . . . There is no stepping across the frontier by gradual advance or by laborious ascent, or by any human development whatsoever" (*Römerbrief*; on Romans 7:7–11).

Such is the message Barth finds in Paul. It is the core of the matter (the *Sache*) that guides his entire hermeneutics. It allows him to put the historico-critical method of reading the Bible in its place (*Römerbrief*; preface to first edition, v) as an aid to reconstructing the actual text, because the key for him is to measure all philology and interpretation against the absoluteness of this fundamental message (preface to second edition, xii). In this he is a follower of the Reformers: "I consider true understanding and explanation that activity which Luther pursued in his interpretations with intuitive certainty and which Calvin set himself as the goal of his exegesis" (preface to second edition, xi). And like Luther attacking Erasmus, Barth wages a virulent campaign against the historicist and culturally oriented "liberal theologians" who see the need to distill out of the philological confusion of the Bible a *human* message, instead of thinking with the New Testament in a Reformation spirit "until the wall between the 1st and the 16th [or 20th] century becomes *transparent,* until Paul *speaks* and the reader in the 16th century *hears,* until the conversation between original and reader concentrates on the *matter*" (ibid.). Only such a hermeneutics and new theology can address the crisis of his age.[24]

---

24. Reading Badiou's interpretation of Paul against the background of Barth's brings out the eschatological aspects of this postmodern interpretation.

I conclude this discussion with two critiques that do not go so much to the heart of Barth's theology itself but that raise questions about its consequences and address issues of relevance for present debates about approaches to religion. The first was raised originally by Harnack, the imposing academic liberal theologian in Marburg who engaged in an open exchange of letters with Barth in the journal *Christliche Welt* throughout the year 1923 (reprinted as an appendix in Moltmann, *Anfänge*). Harnack expresses concern that if Barth's antihistorical, anticritical, antiphilological approach to the Bible wins widespread support, then "[the Gospel] will no longer be taught but will fall exclusively into the hands of revivalist preachers who freely invent their understanding of the Bible and thus set up their own biblical hegemony" (333).[25] One wonders whether this concern is not particularly relevant today, when the Bible is indeed widely read, interpreted, and preached without a critical apparatus. One hears as well here the echo, over some four hundred years, of the Humanist Erasmus warning Luther of the dangers of dismissing philological authority in biblical hermeneutics.

The second critique deals with the political consequences of Barth's position; given the politics in Germany in the decades after the birth of dialectical theology, and given the different reactions of its members, and, finally, given the politics of religion in our own time, this point must be raised. Barth himself admits that his view of faith cannot completely avoid "the necessity of a more or less 'radical' protest against *this* world" (response to Harnack, in *Anfänge,* 326; his emphasis). The question remains, however, what the extent of "*this*" world is. At some level Barth always remained true to his socialist-leaning roots (going back to his time with the workers in the

---

25. It is interesting that Rosenzweig voices a similar concern when, as translator of the Bible, he compares methods. See "Die Einheit der Bibel: Eine Auseinandersetzung mit Orthodoxie und Liberalismus" (The Unity of the Bible: A Dispute with Orthodoxy and Liberalism, in *Zweistromland*). This is a letter to Jacob Rosenheim written in Frankfurt and dated April 4, 1927, in which Rosenzweig distances himself and Buber from the historical-critical method insofar as facts about the composition of the Bible do not affect its inherent message. He refers, for example, to the difference between the two creation stories in Genesis 1 and 2. It is not important whether they were in fact written by two authors. The key is to learn "from the harmonizing of their apparent contradictions, from which the critical distinction is made between the 'cosmological' creation leading to man (in the first chapter of Genesis) and the second's 'anthropological' creation that emanates from man (in the second)" (832). As much as this does connect him to the Barthian project, he also distances himself from it in a short postscript to the letter. There he warns the reader not to assume that he (and Buber) dismisses the importance of science. "What is expressed in the letter does *not* mean a distinction between 'science' and 'religion.' This divorce, the latest fashion from Protestant theology, seems to be the dernier cri in our [Jewish] 'irrationalists' as well. . . . It stems from Kant—all the worse for Kant! And it is in tune with the melody of Barth and Gogarten—all the worse for Barth and Gogarten!" (Er stammt von Kant—um so schlimmer für Kant! Er stimmt sich auf die Barth- und Gogartenweis—um so schlimmer für Barth und Gogarten! 834).

small parish of Safenwil) and he supported those in Germany who, in 1933, protested the Nazi influences on the church, including the policies regarding the Jews. For example, in his "Departure from 'Between the Times,'" he rejects the theological doctrine, or theologumenon, that the Nazis expected the church to adopt, namely, "that the law of God should be identified with the *nomos* [human law] of the German *Volk*" (in Moltmann, *Anfänge,* 316).[26] And yet, as Barth also admits, the radical opposition between "life in God" and "life in this world" means that no morality bridges the two. That is, he would accept neither option that Kant discussed: neither "theological morality" (which would imply that God speaks of the things of our world) nor "moral theology" (which, we saw, opens the door to judging God by *our* standards). Given this radical opposition, he can offer no theological *reasons* for moral positions and hence could be seen as adopting at best a problematic neutrality. Hence, his strong rejection of the Nazi identification of "revelation" with *Volkstum,* a rejection that led to the explicit break with Gogarten and the end of the journal, *Zwischen den Zeiten.* He does so to protect the "purity" of the divine message and hence closes off the church from historical reality.[27] This critique in general terms (i.e., not related directly to Barth's response to National Socialism) is unfolded in the essay by Ronald Goetz in *The Christian Century,* where he points to the limited extent to which Barth's theology can support the promotion of human liberty (no surprise, given its Lutheran and Calvinist roots!). Eduard Thurneysen, one of Barth's oldest and most loyal friends, and a collaborator on the project of the "dialectical theology," wrote his own "Departure from 'Zwischen den Zeiten'" in 1933 (in Moltmann, *Anfänge,* 213–328). In rejecting the stance that Gogarten and the German Christians were taking toward the Nazis, he puts the issue in stark terms. In general he stresses the "two realms" approach: "Let [the church] give to the state its own, completely and without holding anything back—but then also to *God* what is *God's!*" (326). He thus rejects also the political movements of his day, along with the earlier effects of the French Revolution, which supplant faith in the divine Word with worldly categories, or which at least try to "harmonize" the two through the kinds of natural theologies we saw emerge in the seventeenth century (not to mention the more brutal Nazi "*Gleichschaltung*"): "As if historical events as such could

---

26. Barth's role in these intense debates beginning before Hitler's rise to power through his forced exile in Switzerland is documented thoroughly in Hans Prolingheuer, *Der Fall Karl Barth.*

27. See Moltmann, *Anfänge,* 2:313–37, for the exchanges between Barth, Thurneysen, and Gogarten. As we saw above, Gogarten insists on the need for another "decision," namely, for the necessary task of the church to participate in "the historical life of our *Volk*" (333).

be a source of the revelation of the divine will and kingdom alongside the one source of revelation, the source of the Word" (324). The *logos* has made its reentry as a Word from a wholly Other place—independent of *this* world, even though in some dialectical relation to it. This sentiment, of course, points out tensions in Protestantism—on the one hand antipolitical, on the other hand missionary (i.e., the belief that a particular political direction is in keeping with "God's will")—that are prominent in, among other places, the United States today.

In the decisive years of the 1920s, when Barth's *Römerbrief* and Gogarten's attacks on modernity were being formulated, another young academic, Rudolf Bultmann (1885–1976), was engaged in exploring these issues as well at the University of Marburg. Not only did he work with the others on *Zwischen den Zeiten,* and not only did he publish reviews and defenses of this new direction in Protestant theology, but he also from 1923–28 was the colleague and friend of another young Marburg professor, Martin Heidegger. Hence we can now have a better appreciation than was possible in the previous chapter of the significance of Heidegger's attendance in Bultmann's own seminar on Paul and their discussions of the relationship between theology and philosophy. As the friendship and collaboration between Barth and Bultmann became increasingly strained during the 1920s (although they did work together in taking a stance against the "Aryan Paragraph" in the early 1930s), Barth came to dismiss Bultmann increasingly as an "existential" theologian under the influence of Heidegger. However, the relationship between Bultmann and Heidegger, especially in Marburg, is more complex.

Pöggeler offers one of the most extensive and cogent discussions of the link between Heidegger and Bultmann (via Kierkegaard). Heidegger's *"formal anzeigende Hermeneutik,"* he writes, tries to accommodate both a (Greek) analysis of human being in the world and the "leap into faith or morality that cannot be made on philosophical grounds" (*Heidegger in seiner Zeit,* 277). Bultmann pursued the connections between such a separation of (traditional) philosophy and (traditional, now untenable) theology and a *new* kind of theology: "This hermeneutics of the formal indication, viewed as an existential analysis of human being and its absolute, nondeducible decision, was brought together by Bultmann with the new 'dialectical' theology of 'crisis'" (ibid.). Although this relationship is often taken to indicate Bultmann's theological application of Heidegger's existential philosophy, in fact Bultmann saw the theological impulse within Heidegger himself, writing to the dean of the theological faculty in Marburg, Hans von Soden, on December 23, 1923, that Heidegger understands Luther better than the theologians (ibid., 256).[28] Hence, it was Heidegger who benefited undoubtedly from a common reading of John while Bultmann was writing a commentary in his first years in Marburg. Indeed, on taking up his position in Marburg, Heidegger writes to his friend Julius Ebbinghaus in Freiburg that Bultmann is "the only one" (*der Einzige*) from whom he could learn anything (Pöggeler, *Heidegger in seiner Zeit,* 9). During winter semester 1923 he attended Bultmann's seminar on Paul and conducted two guest sessions in February 1924.[29] On July 24, 1925, Heidegger describes in a letter to Arendt the intensity of his work with Bultmann (which he misses in the students): "They [the students] have no sense of adventure and forget that for Bultmann and me—given the differences in the foundations of our intellectual developments—we can inspire each other on our uncharted journeys and can derive an intensity of collaboration that is otherwise missing today" (*Briefe,* 42). On August 23, 1925, Heidegger tells Arendt that she might want to prepare for the seminar with Bultmann—winter semester 1925/26, "Neutestamentliches Seminar (Anthropologie des Paulus)"—"so that you get something out of it," and recommends some books as historical background on discussions about early Christianity. Heidegger himself attended this seminar periodically. He describes the friendship with Bultmann as "lively" (51) and "moving" (52). Thus, the relationship was by no means one-way, with the philosopher dictating to the theologian. In fact, Pöggeler (*Heidegger in seiner Zeit*) points out that a number of formulations from "Phänomenologie und Theologie" appear almost verbatim in Bultmann's lectures, *Theologische Enzyklopädie,* so that one does not always know who influenced whom at this point (e.g., 29).[30]

Bultmann summarized his point of departure as a response to traditional theology in the opening contribution to his collected essays, *Glauben und Verstehen (Faith and Understanding),* the first volume of which, as a sign of his great debt, he dedicated to "Martin Heidegger, in grateful friendship" (*Martin Heidegger in dankbarer Freundschaft*). This essay, on "Liberal Theology and the Newest Theological Movement," takes a stance on the challenge that

---

28. See also Pöggeler's summary of Heidegger's work with Bultmann (e.g., on Luther on Paul) in *Heidegger in seiner Zeit.* Josef Bleicher (*Contemporary Hermeneutics,* 104–8) summarizes Bultmann's approach but only in light of Heidegger.

29. On, among other things, interpretation of Genesis: when Adam and Eve discuss God with the snake, they enter into a new relation with God and from then on lose sight of His face; God exists, through His mercy, only as a "call" and "trace" (*Ruf* and *Spur*).

30. Heidegger was going to dedicate this essay to Bultmann, but decided against it because he thought it would make him look too much like a theologian. Instead, Heidegger did dedicate the published edition of his lectures on religion to him much later.

the new "dialectical theology" has posed to liberals. He characterizes it as follows by defining theology as such: "The object of theology is God, and the critique made against the liberal theology is that it deals with man and not God. God means the radical negation and cancellation of man; theology, whose object is God, can therefore have nothing but the λόγος τού σταυρού [*logos tou staurou* or *logos* of the Cross] as its content; this *logos,* however, is a *skandalon* for mankind" (*Glauben und Verstehen,* 1:2). Bultmann rejects the developments that have led to the identification of God and man, and hence to the death of God, in order to define a new *logos,* arising out of this death (cross), which does not deify man's reason but is an affront to it. This *logos* is an "offense" or even discredit (*skandalon*) to the traditional religion (or at least to the theology that has emerged out of the nineteenth century) that would too readily and optimistically strive for an identity of God with the world of man. The method of his new theo logy proceeds from the understanding and recognition (*Verstehen*) of man's finitude and limitation, or more forcefully, his death and nothingness, to a state of openness to faith (*Glaube*) in God as radically other. While Heidegger was engaged in writing his analysis of *Dasein,* which he came to see as the philosophical precondition for any possible theology, Bultmann strove to see in the Gospels and Paul's Epistles precisely the same nature of human existence. And it is the nature of this existence that it must come to recognize its radical and paradoxical separateness from and nearness to God.[31]

Like Barth, Bultmann is thus threading his way between or around the competing positions that have played themselves out, namely, those of a rational (natural) theology and a faith-based irrationality. Thus, on the one hand, he writes: "*God is not what is given up or nongiven (nicht das Aufgegebene oder*

---

31. For this reason, Bultmann's project stands in an uneasy tension with Barth's. Although they grew out of the same crisis situation and were searching for ways to "save" theology after the death of God at the hands of philosophical anthropology and science, Bultmann remained truer to the roots that went back through him (and Barth's teacher, Herrmann) to Dilthey. Hence, he tried to develop what we can call a "*verstehende Theologie,*" an effort to grasp the relationship between man and God through a nonreductive hermeneutics. The early Heidegger and the *Daseinsanalyse* of *Sein und Zeit* always remained important for Bultmann because he saw the need to understand Christianity by working out of the "*faktischen Leben*" of the isolated, *geworfen,* individual. Leo Scheffczyk, in his contribution to *Rationalität,* summarizes two major twentieth-century theological positions on the relationship between faith and reason: the one (Barth) separates them, while the other incorporates faith into rationality: "The dualistic or the separatistic view was embodied by K. Barth and dialectical theology, which can be summarized in the principle that the Word of God breaks into the world of mankind like a meteor, bringing its understanding or comprehensibility with it. The monistic conception, however, which posits in understanding a unity of faith and thought, comes to light especially in the work of R. Bultmann, who expunges every *notitia* from faith and views it as an act of understanding one's own existence. Faith and understanding are therefore the same" (393).

Ungegebene) in the sense of Idealist philosophy, for which God becomes real in the process of revelation in mankind, or real in the sense of the *logos* underlying the rational life of man" (*Glauben und Verstehen,* 1:18). He rejects the nineteenth-century identification of God and history, since that means that we look for God *in* history; that makes history divine and places the emphasis on both our searching and our history. This means a fundamental rejection of the identification God = *logos* = reason. (God is therefore also not revealed in the nature that is accessible to reason, as he was in the seventeenth century.) However, on the other hand, the new movement is not a return to orthodoxy or a *"sacrificium intellectus"* (8). "For a meaning of history can be found in the relationship of visible history to an invisible origin, not in the positing of a foreign history parallel to other histories" (8–9). The goal is not to establish an alternative to the history of Western rationality or to make some "leap" into blind faith, but to explore the very conditions of human existence to the point of their limit so that a new questioning of the meaning of that existence can emerge. In short, all theology must proceed from the point of nihilism.

Hence, any relation to God, i.e., any faith, must first proceed from the *"total cancellation/sublation of man, his negation, a judgment for man that places him in question"* (*totale Aufhebung des Menschen, seine Verneinung, seine Infragestellung, das Gericht für den Menschen*; 18, his emphasis). Here is where he connects to Heidegger and the debates on eschatology.[32] We must view our lives and history from their "end," i.e., eschatologically, i.e., from our death.[33] That places us completely "in question," makes our very being "questionable," so

---

32. He refers to Barth's commentary on Romans and summarizes his critique of modern theological thinking: "Everywhere Christianity has lost its *skandalon,* i.e., it is not seen that the otherness of God, God's transcendence (*Gottes Anderssein, Gottes Jenseitigkeit*), means the crossing out (*die Durchstreichung*) of man and his entire history. People try to give faith a grounding, which would annihilate its very essence" (*Glauben und Verstehen,* 1:13). It is noteworthy that he employs the notion of "crossing out" or "placing under erasure" here well before Heidegger in his famous essay on Humanism.

33. Dialectical theology doesn't offer a special method of interpreting the Bible. Rather, it aims to take seriously the Bible's presumption—namely, the historical nature of human being—and must first understand what both experiences and concepts could possibly mean under the assumption of historicity. Like Heidegger's *Daseinsanalyse,* dialectical theology must first understand that all human existence unfolds within the horizon of its end/death, a fact that, if taken seriously, would give new meaning to everything in human history (including the Bible). This is why the early Christian movement was so important for this theological movement: it (esp. under the guidance of Paul) lived and interpreted the world in the light of its imminent "end." It is not important that they were in one sense "wrong," because in an essential sense they were right. See "Die Bedeutung der 'dialektischen Theologie' für die neutestamentliche Wissenschaft" (in *Glauben und Verstehen,* 1:114–33).

that we can then be open to the answer that would come from God. "Man as such, in his totality, is placed in question by God" (19). This questioning is not a matter of mere "skepticism" or irrationality. Rather, reason must be pushed to its limits, since "precisely if [reason] goes to the end of its path can it reach the point of crisis and lead man to the fundamental question of his meaning" (19). In somewhat Lutheran terms, he says that the "basic sin" (*Grundsünde*) of man is "*that he wants to assert himself as man*" (19), i.e., exercise free will and become godlike. This "sin" must be confronted with the (last) judgment (*Gericht*) or justification of God: "Thus the whole world is brought out of joint, thus man places himself under God's judgment. The whole world—for it had been *His* world—is thereby annihilated" (19). That is, Nietzsche's nihilism, the thought of the death of God, is actually the culmination of a tradition that has made man into God; radicality of nihilism arises because it leads to the recognition that, *if it is true that man is everything,* then there is no meaning outside of man; but then the radical questioning of man's being would involve the opening up in a new, more meaningful way, to the question of God, and hence to the answer, which is "the origin" (*das Ursprüngliche*). Bultmann has redefined the relationship between reason/knowledge and faith on the basis of the insight into the course of the Western tradition: "To know *that* [namely, the end of man], *is* faith" (19). That is, faith is the knowledge that arises at the end of knowledge, a new Word/*logos* of revelation that is spoken to us when we have exhausted our old *logos*. What he says elsewhere about Barth applies, therefore, to his own view: faith must be derived "from the invisible and un- and suprahistorical *logos*" (*vom unanschaulichen, un- und überhistorischen Logos*; an essay in *Christliche Welt* in 1922 [in Moltmann, *Anfänge* 119–42] as a review of the second edition of the *Römerbrief*, 133).

We can get a sense of his theological position by looking at his 1926 book, *Jesus and the Word*. In writing of the "paradox" of the "remote and the near" ("the paradox of belief in the remote God who is also near"), Bultmann stresses that it is crucial to Christian faith that God not be understood as "immanent" in history. For this reason he is against Stoicism and Schleiermacher and all forms of natural law/theology. This leads him to argue against the "Greek" influence on Judaic influences (a position that will have significant consequences in the 1930s since it offers him and others *theological* reasons to oppose the Nazi efforts to imagine a non-Judaic Christianity).[34] That is, although he does not say so explicitly, he is against the notion of God as *logos* in the form

---

34. For an excellent and extensive review of the different positions, see Smid.

that Philo and the Stoics introduced it into the New Testament—namely, that God is the all-pervasive and organizing force of the cosmos. He writes:

This view [namely, his own] does not rest on the conception of *a law of life permeating nature*. It is characteristically different from any pantheistic view of nature, such as Schleiermacher for example represents, which assumes that the modern world has progressed beyond Jesus' childish view of nature, that we have succeeded in penetrating deeper into the understanding of nature than Jesus could have done. This "deeper insight" consists in seeing in the spectacle of change which nature presents, the supremacy of life, which draws even apparent death into the process of change to generate new life; so that not only in all changing phenomena but in existence itself the work of the spirit, of deity, is revealed. Such a conception is in no sense, as compared with the viewpoint of these sayings of Jesus, further developed or more profound; rather it results from a wholly different premise, a wholly different conception of God and man; it is based on the concept of law, aesthetically applied, which is entirely alien to Judaism and to Jesus. In fact a similar point of view is found in the Stoic philosophy. (163)

In his many exegetical works on the New Testament, Bultmann is concerned to show the significance of this status of God as both wholly other and yet in contact, through the divine Word, with the world of man: "The essential element in the Jewish conception is the peculiar conjunction of the supramundane character and transcendence of God with the dependence of the world on God or with God's direction of the world; more simply expressed, the union of the remoteness and the nearness of God. The thought that God is remote, far above the world and man, is just as necessary an element of the idea of God as the other, that He is nevertheless constantly near" (137). We will see how this view connects him conceptually to the contemporaneous work of Jewish thinkers such as Rosenzweig and Buber.

To get a sense of how Bultmann used Heidegger and how both were linked to the interpretation of Paul's Epistles, note the passage in Bultmann's essay on Barth and "dialectical theology" ("Die Bedeutung der 'dialektischen Theologie' für die neutestamentliche Wissenschaft," in *Glauben und Verstehen*, 1:114–33). A biblical passage is to be understood "out of its relation to human existence (*Existenz*)" (129). To achieve that understanding, we must adopt a critical perspective on—or, in phenomenological terms, we must "bracket out"—our traditional conceptual apparatus (*Begrifflichkeit*) that is determined "through the modern development . . . , namely, through Rationalism, Classicism, and Romanticism, through natural science and psychology, and through the Greek understanding of being and existence (*Sein und Dasein*) that functions as a motivation within all these movements" (ibid.). If we can take this approach, we will see, for example, that the notion of "cosmos" or "world" in Paul has a different meaning than the earlier Greek use, one which sounds remarkably like Heidegger's: "For example, *kosmos* is [traditionally] understood as the world within which man finds himself as a being among others, as the world of nature, as a *what*, whereas for Paul *kosmos* is meant in an existential sense as the *wherein*, in which human existence can unfold its life (*lebt*) as such; Paul's *kosmos* is to be considered not as a *what* but as a *how* of human being" (ibid.). Indeed, after the word *lebt* comes a footnote to *Sein und Zeit* 1:65. Here we have a full circle. Heidegger had sat in on Bultmann's seminars on Paul in Marburg and learned a new way of reading the Bible "anthropologically" but not like Feuerbach. Now Bultmann, via Barth, returns to this biblical understanding with new philosophical ammunition from Heidegger's existentialism.

In his later work, Bultmann contributes broadly to the Heideggerian program of separating out philosophy and theology, but he seeks a kind of middle ground that also unites the two. He, too, has as his starting point the fact that *logos* kills *mythos,* that the long history of Western reasoning has killed God. He cannot go against that process and by no means would introduce a "remythification" against reason. Instead, in his later thought, he calls for a "demythologization" (*Entmythologisierung*) of basic doctrines of Christianity (original sin, Incarnation, physical resurrection of Jesus, etc.). However, he does not see this demythification as a mere continuation of the Enlightenment rejection and debunking of faith as superstition. Because he has seen the way reason/*logos* has turned against itself, he would rather place these doctrines into an *onto-logical* context and reinterpret them within a new and broader horizon of understanding. In the words of Thomas Altizer, the U.S. proponent of so-called death-of-God theology in the 1970s: "Bultmann believes that demythologizing began with the Gospel of John, but the advent of the scientific consciousness and of our modern history demands a more radical transformation of the language of faith than that which was effected by the Fourth Gospel. All theological language deriving from the prescientific and mythical age of humanity must now be negated; or, rather, it must be translated into the contemporary language of the existing man of faith" (*Toward a New Christianity,* 6).[35]

---

35. "Bultmann is convinced (1) that a past mythical worldview left traces in the Bible, and (2) that this worldview must be reinterpreted in the frame or horizon of understanding of the present day, i.e., Heidegger's existential analysis. He did not simply want to eliminate the mythic" (Waldenfels in Scheffczyk, 270).

This effort to "demythologize" the Bible led to a sharp exchange between Karl Jaspers and Bultmann.[36] Jaspers argues that Bultmann's call for demythologization rests on two basic theses (which he finds questionable). First, modern science (broadly conceived) has made belief in many aspects of Christian faith untenable; and second, the true contents of faith must be attained by means of an existential analysis grounded in philosophy (i.e., Heidegger's early position vis-à-vis theology) (*Die Frage der Entmythologisierung*, 9). That is, science has killed faith, but faith can return if we reach an understanding (in the weighty way that word functions in Heidegger's *hermeneutic* phenomenology) of our human being in the world. For that understanding, reached through a free confrontation with our temporal, dependent, indeed absurd situation, leads us to the fundamental *decision* of faith à la Kierkegaard, namely, the decision to accept God's grace and faith. Bultmann follows Heidegger back to Luther (and, behind him, Augustine), rejecting the modern humanist's faith in "works" (we could reach God through our own rational efforts) and then working through the "despair" (or *Angst, Sorge, Leben/Krankheit zum Tode*) to a renewed faith-as-gift.

For Bultmann, the motivation for "demythologization" comes neither from the specific effect of modern science nor from a particular philosophy (Heidegger) but from the task that theology has set itself since the late nineteenth century (Troeltsch), namely, "the problem of history that has become acute for theology through the historical understanding of the Bible" (das für die Theologie durch das geschichtliche Verständnis der Bibel akut gewordene Problem der Geschichte; *Die Frage der Entmythologisierung*, 60). The solution of Lessing and Kant and liberal theology no longer works, namely, a strict division between the "historical" and the "rational," or the "temporal" and "eternal" truths, because man, God, and faith are all now considered to be, in their essence, historical.[37] Somehow, theology must come to grips with this radically historical dimension of human being, not by avoiding it and not by using it to "reduce" faith to naught. This is why, as we saw, Heidegger began his lectures on the phenomenology of religious experience with a discussion of "the historical" and why he proposes his hermeneutical phenomenol-

---

36. Even Hannah Arendt wrote to Heidegger that she felt the response of her former teacher, Jaspers, to Bultmann was overly harsh. See Arendt and Jaspers, *Briefwechsel*.

37. The idea here is that Lessing and Enlightenment historical biblical criticism did not go far enough. They saw that a historical view of the Bible rendered direct access to faith impossible. But the hope was that some other way would remain open. Kant claimed to have found that way in his morality based on practical reason. Here, however, the task is to push both the historical reinterpretation of the Bible to its limits (demythologization) and to interpret human existence also as radically historical—and in both cases one can attain a renewed faith.

ogy as the only approach that radically asks this question of our historical/ temporal being. All that Bultmann does is show that from that historical-hermeneutic-phenomenological analysis, we are led again to the issue of faith, or, more precisely, to the *skandalon* of the question/decision of faith (61). He calls this task the only valid one for a theologian in his age, "the making visible of that which is Christian faith, the making visible of the question of decision" (ibid.).

❧ CHAPTER 9

"Atheistic" and Dialogical
Jewish Theologies of the Other
(Rosenzweig and Buber)

> The psyche we are talking about is not even Judeo-
> Christian in general; it is strictly Judeo-Protestant—
> that is to say, thanks to Luther, Judeo-German.
>
> —Derrida, "Interpretations at War: Kant, the Jew, the
> German"

At the same time as Heidegger was formulating his existential ontology out of a revision of Husserl's phenomenology and Protestant theology was renewing itself through a critique of liberalism and historicism, Jewish thinkers were reconceptualizing the place of their tradition in relation to modern (esp. German) life. In fact, just as we have seen that the first two developments were mutually influential—e.g., the overlap between Heidegger and Bultmann, the prominence of the turn to Saint Paul after WWI, the focus on "decisionism"—so, too, the German-Christian-Jewish dialogue between philosophy and religion created a network of intersecting personages and interests in the first quarter of the twentieth century.[1]

---

1. Derrida's essay "Interpretations at War: Kant, the Jew, the German" focuses on Hermann Cohen and Franz Rosenzweig. Interestingly, in discussing Cohen, Derrida sees the second-century Alexandrian Jew and Platonist Philo as a crucial mediator, whose notion of *logos* will connect up with the modern philosophical tradition as well: "In order to *render an account* . . . of the Jewish-German phenomenon . . . in its often delirious forms, is it possible not to involve logic, the *logos* in this delirium?" (49–51, here 51). What Derrida does not address at all in this essay is the fact that while Cohen might have appealed to the Greek *logos* as a mediator between Germans/Christians and Jews, in the same decades others were trying to purge the Gospels of Hellenic influence and return to a more originary "Palestinian" message of Christ (e.g., Bultmann's *Jesus and the Word*).

I will be able to delineate only a few of these most important linkages by looking at the work of Franz Rosenzweig and Martin Buber.

Rosenzweig was born on December 25, 1886. This places him in the same generation as Jaspers (1883), Heidegger (1889), Barth (1886), and the slightly younger Bultmann (1905). He began studying medicine in Göttingen in 1905, went to Munich, and finally moved to Freiburg in 1906. (It is interesting that Heidegger and Jaspers also began as students of natural science.) His interest in science became increasingly philosophical (e.g., the epistemological foundations laid by Kant in the first *Critique*), and he ended up switching to history in order to study with the preeminent historian of the day, Friedrich Meinecke, for whom he wrote his dissertation, which is still to this day the major work on Hegel's political philosophy, *Hegel und der Staat (Hegel and the State)*. However, already by the time he completed his dissertation in 1913, he had profound questions concerning the basis of historicism. In a famous letter to Meinecke he wrote that he suffered a collapse because, although he recognized that a historian's "talent" allowed for a variety of stories to be told about significant figures and their times, he could not see what held them together on a deeper level. He was searching, in short, for the *meaning* of history. This questioning of the relativism of historicism parallels, of course, the critique of historicist and subjectivist theology that we saw Barth engaged in during precisely the same years. Later, he was to characterize this period as his transformation from a historian into a philosopher. But at the same time, he was deeply engaged with questions of religion and theology. Most important were conversations he had in the summer of 1913, culminating on July 7, when Rosenzweig spent the night discussing theological questions with his cousin Rudolf Ehrenberg and close friend Eugen Rosenstock. They presented him with a strong Protestantism that moved him immensely. Further discussions with them and with Rudolf's brother, Hans Ehrenberg, were the ground in which the seeds of his future thought germinated. He thought about converting, but first wanted to work through Judaism, and hence turned to Hermann Cohen in Berlin.

In 1917, while serving in Macedonia during the First World War, in the midst of his existential anxieties and his detailed analyses of the progress of the battles, Rosenzweig wrote a long letter to Rudolf Ehrenberg that contains the so-called *Urzelle*, or primal core, of his major work, *Der Stern der Erlösung (The Star of Redemption)*. Rosenzweig claimed that he had finally found his much-sought "Archimedean point" (*Zweistromland*, 4:125). The book came out in 1921 but was not well received at the time. And although it appeared seven years before *Being and Time*, Heidegger never seriously engaged with it.[2] After completing this major work, he did not pursue an academic career but instead dedicated himself to teaching as a public act. To pursue this goal, he founded the Freies Jüdisches Lehrhaus (Free Jewish School) in Frankfurt. He worked there until a debilitating disease, amyotrophic lateral sclerosis (Lou Gehrig's disease), led to a gradual paralysis that made even speaking impossible. Eventually he was able to move only one finger, with which he tapped out letters that his wife transcribed into words and sentences. In that way he continued a monumental correspondence and published numerous essays. In his later years, he dedicated himself mostly to translating and interpreting the Hebrew Bible with Martin Buber, one of the most brilliant efforts to grapple not only with the scripture but with the problem of translation as such. He died in 1929.

We can see how Rosenzweig, despite considerable differences in the details of his biography and despite the lack of direct influences, was passing through many of the same developments as others of his generation, not just Heidegger, but also, as we saw, Barth and Bultmann and the "dialectical theologians." All faced a similar crisis and saw limited options for a solution. The crisis emerged from the failure of both the historical turn in the cultural sciences and the subjective turn in religion to answer fundamental questions concerning faith. In the former case, the absorption of God into history as the site of his revelation and being in the world led either to an abandonment of God for the sake of history or a kind of relativism, since whatever happens is justified just because it happens. In the latter case, subjectivism, which, we saw, grew out of a Protestantism of the late eighteenth and early nineteenth centuries and located faith in *feelings* of piety, could not withstand the demands for objective argument. Unfortunately, thanks to the long nineteenth-century critique of Idealism, culminating in Nietzsche's radical skepticism, philosophy could not offer the kind of absolute knowledge that Hegel had promised. A new kind of faith, connected to a new kind of thinking, was necessary after the death of the old values. Heidegger's task of thinking in the wake of a phenomenological method cleared the path for an analysis of (human) existence in the light of a withdrawn Being.[3]

---

2. In the essay "Neues Denken" ("New Thinking") that he published in 1925 to address responses to his book, Rosenzweig points out first that, despite the marketing, it only creates confusion and disappointment to consider this a *"jüdisches Buch"* (*Zweistromland,* 4:139–40), and second that this is not a book about religion or theology but "merely a system of philosophy" (*bloß ein System der Philosophie,* 140). He also agrees self-ironically with one critique that it is "not for the daily use of every member of every family" (ibid.).

3. Torsten Meyer sees a direct parallel between Heidegger's differentiation between theology and philosophy and Rosenzweig's between a traditional and a new mode of rationality. Heidegger

Barth, Bultmann, and the "dialectical theologians" found their way out of this crisis by turning to the Reformation and the faith in the revealed Word of the Bible that would justify existence. As Emil Brunner wrote later: "We do not inquire into revelation from the perspective of reason but, rather, as a church of faith, we inquire into reason from the perspective of revelation. . . . This stance of the Reformation has been lost in much of post-Reformation theology" (*Offenbarung und Vernunft,* vii). For Rosenzweig and Buber, the "new thinking" (*neues Denken*) would emerge out of a faith in the revelation of the Hebrew Bible.

Later in his life Rosenzweig stressed the impulse he received for the "new thinking" from theological concerns of his day. He explained that he did not feel he had written a "theological" book; rather, it is a book of systematic philosophy that employs theological concepts in order to show their significance for thinking. He summarizes the influence of theology as follows:

> Theological interests helped . . . .the new thinking to its breakthrough.
> At the same time, it is not actually theological thinking. At least not
> at all what one has understood up until now as theological thought.
> Neither in its means nor its end. Neither does it address the so-called
> 'religious problems' as such—since it treats them instead under or
> indeed in the midst of logical, ethical, and aesthetic issues—nor does
> it take that approach, so characteristic of theology, that is a mixture of
> polemic and defensiveness and thus never calmly deals with the matter
> at hand. If this new thinking is theology, then it is both new and also a
> form of philosophy. . . . The true relation between these two renewed
> disciplines . . . is fraternal, indeed those who pursue them must unite
> them in their person. For theological problems must be translated into
> human ones and human ones pushed to the theological. (*Zweistrom-
> land,* 4:152–53)

---

sees theology as the "*positivum*" that needs to be connected to a more original totality of prescientific experience and multidimensional relatedness (*Seinszusammenhang*) in which human existence unfolds. The understanding of that broader sphere by means of phenomenological-hermeneutical analysis provides the "corrective" and "formal indication" for theological concepts so that they can be grounded in the facticity of life. For Rosenzweig, the logical cognition of philosophy needs to be supplanted or put in its place by a new mode of thinking through language and reality: "There is 'in' (or, better, 'with') reason something nonrational, something grasped by the concept of truth (because truth always [means] 'correspondence of a representation with an object')" (Meyer, 83, citing "Urzelle" in *Zweistromland,* 4:128). For this reason, Meyer summarizes, the new mode of thinking proposed by Rosenzweig must "translate" conceptual content into "experience-able realizations" (*erfahrbare Verwirklichung*; 86).

What we see here is the way he also understands his enterprise as a new theology after the impact of philosophy and a new philosophy after the impact
of contemporary "theological interest." This connection puts him in the
same sphere as Heidegger, Barth, and Bultmann.

Rosenzweig's first effort to work through these ideas was an essay he
wrote with the significant title "Atheistische Theologie" ("Atheistic Theology"). It was written in spring, 1914, on Buber's invitation, for the second
yearbook *Vom Judentum* (On Judaism). It wasn't accepted, perhaps because
of its critical discussion of Buber's "Reden über das Judentum" ("Lectures
on Judaism"). The key to the argument, and the link to other "returns" in
early twentieth-century Protestant theology, is that he draws strict parallels
between developments in Christian theology from the Enlightenment to the
point of "decision" in the present (on the one hand) and Jewish thought and
movements (on the other). Phrases like "it is the same" (*es ist das Gleiche*)
and "thus one could demonstrate point for point" (*so ließe es sich . . . Punkt
für Punkt aufzeigen*) connect the arguments. It is clear already in Protestantism the way the nineteenth-century, for good reasons, historicized Christ
and turned him into an "ideal human being" and "teacher," thereby stressing the identity between man and God but also paving the way for atheism.
Rosenzweig uses this common knowledge to structure his interpretation of
Jewish thought over the last century or so, which did the same to its central
concept of revelation, the Jewish people as the "chosen *Volk.*" If the parallels work, then Jewish thought is also culminating in an "atheistic theology."
However, if Protestantism is on the verge of renewal through the radicality of
the Divine Word and through God as "wholly Other" (à la Otto, Gogarten,
Barth, Bultmann, Heidegger), then there might also be hopes for Judaism to
come to its senses and rediscover the full force of revelation.

He begins with a reference to the "peculiar spectacle" (*merkwürdiges
Schauspiel*) that is unfolding in Protestant theology, namely, the collapse
of "life-of-Jesus theology" (*Leben-Jesu-Theologie*), a part of liberal theology
(*Zweistromland,* 4:687). This approach goes back to Lessing and Kant and
the attempt to present the historical Jesus as a teacher and true Christianity
as his (ethical) teaching. It allowed for a peace between the Enlightenment
and Christianity, since it argued that they basically taught the same thing.
For example, David Strauss, following in Hegel's footsteps, tried to show the
origin of Christianity as a necessary historical development. Generally, the
effort was to paint a picture of the "person" of Christ in its totality such
that it could be "familiar" to the contemporary audience.

Rosenzweig characterizes the status of Protestant theology with remarkable precision. After focusing so long on the historical, human side of Jesus,

was it now time for the opposite? he asks. Or could the true paradox of Christ be maintained? "Must philosophical theology take the place of historical, must the idea of Christ take the place of the life-of-Jesus approach? Or is it rather a question of having the courage to adopt the full paradox? And will it be possible to place the concept of historical-suprahistorical revelation at the center of disciplinary knowledge? The theological consciousness of Protestantism stands in the present moment before this choice, from here future struggles will emerge" (689). It is remarkable that he penned these words in 1914 and that, although they were not published until much later, the years following the First World War bore out his prediction with the development of the "theology of crisis," which saw itself as a theology of "decision," an alternative to both liberalism and orthodoxy.

Although Judaism clearly has no parallel to the emphasis on personality, he does see a consistently similar trend in the history of Jewish and Christian thought, where the central issue is not Christ but the center of Jewish revelation, "the chosen people." The nineteenth century brought with it a "flight into narrow historical research" such that both the idea of Christ in Christian philosophy of religion and the idea of Judaic revelation were robbed of their radicality, namely, "the striking mark of the divine that enters as reality into history even as it is of a wholly different order of reality" (690). The echoes here of what is found in Otto, Gogarten, and Barth are clear. Of course, the problems for the development of a Jewish theology were more complicated in terms of nineteenth-century thought. Whereas the Christian ideal of Christ could be universalized to the ideal of the "human as such" (each individual shares in the divine), the notion of a "chosen people," "the pure existence of a people" as "a continuous entity" (691), could not fit into the historical conceptions of a Fichte or Hegel who saw nations as part of a process of development. Recently, he argues, an idea of a *Volk* has emerged that "without concern or consciousness lives [its life] like a product of nature" (691). It no longer exists for the higher purposes set for it by philosophers but is anchored in a concrete naturalness. This naturalistic, racial idea of the "essence of a *Volk*" comes to serve the same function for Jewish thought that the "personality" of Christ could serve for Christian. And just as the latter paved the way (we have seen) over the course of a century for an "inevitable" atheism, so, too, "on the Jewish side it could now come to an atheistic theology" (692) because the idea of the "Jewish people" became a historical entity. The object of faith is made comprehensible as a mythic projection from a historical reality (the person of Jesus or the actual people). The idea of a revelation is lost in both cases, i.e., the idea of a "wholly Other" that breaks into history from another level of being is no longer part of these theological movements. "That is the final significance of the entire movement. The differentiation between God and man, this terrible affront to new and ancient paganism, seems pushed aside; the offensive thought of revelation, the crashing in of a higher content into an unworthy vessel, has been silenced" (693). Of course, something of this idea of revelation remains, even in its attempted "philosophical" resignification. Hence, it must be reinterpreted not as a call from the outside of man but as a result of the mediation of internal contradictions (*Polarität*) within humanity (e.g., Feuerbach). The unity of the Jewish people is not grounded in the revealed unity of God but in its own internal will or longing for unity.[4] It is interesting that he claims that "atheistic theology" emerged out of both Christian and Jewish traditions out of an inner logic (695). Future developments therefore cannot avoid confronting this reality (ibid.). And the last line of the essay shows where they must lead: "Theology cannot avoid or circumvent the idea of revelation" (697). That such developments might indeed be on the horizon he signaled early on when he referred to Cohen's work on a "religion of reason," a sign of the "reawakening of philosophy" (*Wiedererwachens der Philosophie*; 690). Although he would return over the years to Cohen, it is his own monumental work, *The Star of Redemption,* that supplies the philosophical/theological "thought of revelation."

Rosenzweig retraces the philosophical motivation behind the *Star* by recalling the movement that Nietzsche traced in the Western tradition by which *logos* undermined itself. For Rosenzweig as well, the drive behind Western thought from the Greeks to Hegel ("Iona to Jena," as he wrote— *Stern,* 18) was a will to total knowledge, the principle of *logos* that creates the underlying unity of all being and thought: "The unity of *logos* grounds

---

4. Hence, Rosenzweig (and Buber) tries to think through the simultaneity of unity and difference between man and God. He differs from the dialectical theologians to the extent that they emphasize exclusively difference. In "Der Ewige: Mendelssohn und der Gottesname" (*Zweistromland*), Rosenzweig characterizes the key feature of biblical monotheism. It is not just a divine unity, since even "pagan" or "polytheistic" religions have some unifying principle behind their gods. The biblical God presumes such a pagan unity "but also recognizes this God in his oneness as the God of Abraham, who is experienced absolutely personally and immediately (*persönlichst und unmittelbarst*; 810). The biblical God is thus the paradoxical "identification (*Ineinssetzung*) of the distant and the near, the 'total' and the 'particular' God" (ibid.). This contradictory "positing-as-one" makes up, he continues, the essence of both Judaism and Christianity, although the latter often runs the danger of falling into a pre- or non-Judaic split. He adds parenthetically: "The seriousness and the relevance of this danger is revealed today again by Barth and Gogarten" (ibid.). We see that he has a critique of the project of the new Protestant theologians to the extent that their overemphasis of the "complete otherness" of God might lose the paradoxical *Ineinssetzung* of the Judeo-Christian tradition. Ratzinger/Benedict XVI will echo this critique (see below, chapter 10).

the unity of the world as a totality. And that unity in turn proves its truth value in the grounding of this totality" (Casper, 81; *Stern,* 18). In terms of the history of philosophy, this will to total and presuppositionless knowledge (presuppositionless because self-grounding) has found its logical end, as Nietzsche argued, in nihilism. And in terms of individual experience, this self-grounding reason finds its end in the recognition of the sheer "facticity" of human existence. As he says in the "Urzelle": "After [reason] has thus absorbed everything into itself and proclaimed itself as existing on its own, suddenly the individual discovers that he, having been philosophically digested, is nonetheless still there. . . . [This is the] triumph of the ineffable individual" (*Zweistromland,* 127). But—and this he gets from the late Schelling (despite differences here too)—this end of the *logos,* the fact that it has reached its end, this fundamental crisis, does not mean that we abandon it but, rather, must recognize its fundamental relation to some Other. In asking the question "What *is?*" reason is led to the question of its own being, a being that it cannot ground in itself. Through this radical self-questioning, our understanding of God as a "beyond" raises the possibility for a new "meta-physics," our understanding of the world as non-self-grounded opens up to a "meta-logic," and our understanding of man as dependent on others points to a "meta-ethics." *Stern* is therefore a complex and above all *systematic* investigation of the opening of *logos* to a relation to its Other, and the nature of that relationship.[5] We can explore four central ideas of this theology "beyond" the death of a divine *logos,* ideas that will allow us to see both connections with and transformations of the long philosophico-theological tradition we have been examining.

God

The starting point of this more involved "atheistic theology" is thus a negation that yields an affirmation. The first line of *Stern,* after the introduction,

---

5. In a different sense than Hegel's dialectical logic, the book is constantly working with sets of triads. Thus, these three modalities—"God and His Being or Metaphysics," "The World and Its Meaning or Metalogic," and "Man and His Self or Metaethics"—form the three chapters of the first part of the book. It serves as a kind of phenomenological ground clearing or "bracketing" of all previous knowledge. The second part, which Rosenzweig considered the true heart of his argument, is organized around the three main theological categories of "Creation," "Revelation," and "Redemption." Part 3 discusses the forms of religious community and experience in terms of their relationship to the temporality, or "end," or eternity of revelation, whereby Judaism exists in a direct relation under the sign of "eternal life" (and is "with the Father") and Christianity is always "on the path" to realization; only their unity (or, better, their dialectical supplementarity) could contain the possibility of a truly holy community.

reads: "Von Gott wissen wir nichts" (About God we know nothing; 25). However, the very acceptance of the consequences of philosophical nihilism, the clearing the ground of all prior conceptions, marks a radical new beginning. The text continues: "But this 'knowing nothing' is a 'knowing nothing' about God. As such, it is the beginning of our knowledge of Him" (Aber dieses Nichtwissen ist Nichtwissen von Gott. Also solches ist es der Anfang unseres Wissens von ihm). We can begin to think about God only from the end of the long tradition that has thought everything about Him and come up empty. This is not a call for a flight from thinking, as if thinking itself has failed and so we should turn to blind faith or orthodoxy. But also, we cannot avoid the tradition that got us here and return to naive judgments of the form "God is X" that we attempt to "prove" (since to do so would be just to repeat the tradition and end in nihilism). Rather, in a Socratic manner I embrace this lack of knowledge so that it becomes the ironic or paradoxical starting point. For to know nothing about God is already to know that God is "not nothing" and to affirm this "not-nothing" (Bejahung des Nichtnichts). The question is, how can we understand this jump from the nothing to something? This question replaces the older metaphysical "proof" of the existence of God. To understand Rosenzweig's answer, we need to consider the concept of the "correlation."

Korrelation and the Infinitesimal

How can I define the relationship I could possibly have with such a God? Philosophically, Rosenzweig developed the notion of *Korrelation* (or *Beziehungsdenken*) from his mentor Hermann Cohen to insist on thinking through paradoxes, i.e., holding on to the *and* when other forces tried to collapse the two sides (God *and* man, chosen people *and* universal humanity, etc.).[6] Löwith characterizes it as follows: "Cohen's basic concept of the 'correlation' between God and man not only binds the two sides mutually but also preserves in this bond their unbridgeable distance" (*Aufsätze,* 140). Or more paradoxically still: "There is a distance and a closeness to God, but also in the greatest proximity God he remains infinitely distant" (Es gibt eine Ferne und eine Nähe zu Gott, aber auch in der größten Nähe bleibt Gott ewig fern; *Aufsätze,* 141). Behind these descriptions is Cohen's underlying model of differential calculus and the infinitesimal. This apparent "paradox" (if one thinks of Kierkegaard) is a statement

---

6. Consider especially Cohen's *Religion der Vernunft.*

of the nature of any continuous function that approaches a value as it grows toward infinity. One can think of an asymptotic line: even as it becomes infinitely close, it remains infinitely far from its value. This basic equation (*Fundamentalgleichung*) that characterizes the correlation between God and man not as identity but as infinitesimal and infinite difference forms the foundation of the ethical correlation between man and man: "If the correlation between God and man is the fundamental equation of religion, then man must first of all think this through in terms of his relation to his fellow man" (*Aufsätze*, 142; Cohen, *Religion der Vernunft* [1966], 132–33/167). That is, the ethical dictate of a God to approach Him with infinitesimal proximity while never denying unbridgeable distance becomes the model or ideal for man's relation to his neighbor. For this reason, Cohen rejects the introduction of Greek *logos* into Judaic thought that occurred with Philo and is captured in the prologue to the Gospel according to John. Löwith cites Cohen: "The Greek spirit, which is the model for all scientific approaches to the world, seeks the mediation . . . between God and man. The Jew, Philo, fell victim to this Greek magic with his concept of *logos*. . . . If Philo had never come up with *logos*, no Jew would have ever lost faith" (*Aufsätze*, 140). The implication here is as clear as it is radical. With the introduction of *logos*, interpreted either as Holy Spirit or Christ the God-Man, Christianity establishes a mediating function between man and God, indeed the becoming human of God (and vice versa), but also introduces a mode of "scientific" thinking that, as we have seen, eventually leads to the greatest of doubts in the difference between man and God.

Only the *ratio* of the infinitesimal calculus can capture the fundamental paradox of this relation that is not one, of this mediation that never collapses into sameness, of this absolute proximity that cannot be bridged. Here Rosenzweig based his thinking on Cohen's "Logik des Ursprungs" (Logic of Origin) from *Das Prinzip der Infinitesimalmethode und seine Geschichte* (*The Principle of the Infinitesimal Method and Its History*, 1883). However, rather than merely "apply" a mathematic reasoning to the sphere of theology or merely see in the realm of numbers the "essential" and timeless truths as models, he recognized in the infinitesimal a logical tool for thinking through the problem of nothingness and the leap from nothing to something in a new way "because it [this method] generates its elements not out of the empty nothing of the one, universal zero but out of the nothing of the differential that is assigned specifically to the sought element" (*Stern*, 23). Bernhard Casper summarizes the mathematical argument, which is the formal version of the images I offered above (figure 8.1) in the discussion of Barth:

For the nothing, with which the infinitesimal calculus works, is the nothing of something; for this reason it can emerge for thinking as a pure phenomenon. The nothing of the differential quotient dy/dx for lim dx → 0 allows the tangent of the curve (tg τ) at a specific point, that is, the original reality of the movement, to be seen. The nothing at this point is not "the" nothing defined as the denial or covering of the essence of being, as it is for "the great inheritor of two thousand years of philosophy" (Hegel); rather it is "the particular nothing," the nothing of "this something." According to Rosenzweig, thanks to his discovery of the place of nothing in infinitesimal calculus, Cohen "against his own self-conception and against the appearance of his own works," in fact completed the turn away from Idealism and found a new method of thinking, which in turn became the method of the new thinking. (96–97)

We have here, therefore, not a mathematically based "proof" for the existence of God but a discovery in the everyday reality of the world that can describe by such equations the very mystery of the paradoxical relationship between the earthly and the divine, between nothing and "not-nothing." In the spark that crosses this infinitely great and infinitesimally small gap, the world and humanity are opened up, all being is revealed.

Offenbarung—Revelation

The central concept ("Urzelle," *Zweistromland,* 125) that expresses this relationship is revelation (*Offenbarung*). As the "gift" to man, revelation is "what takes place between the absolute and the relative 'before' him" ("Urzelle," 129). By casting this relationship between God and man into theological terms, we see the proximity of Rosenzweig and dialectical theology. In focusing on revelation, this theology must be "dialectical" because revelation unites opposites (God/man, eternity/temporality). God must be unknowable but then known (as unknowable). This notion of the "unknown God" responds to Hermann Cohen's late philosophy of religion, which had influenced Rosenzweig. But it is also not unrelated to Otto's 1919 *The Sacred* (*Das Heilige*) that makes God "the wholly Other," "*das ganz Andere*" (but more psychologically as theologically), which, we saw, was widely received by, among others, Heidegger and Gogarten. While liberal theology had a generally optimistic God in view, this God as Other rendered in His judgment (*Gericht*) our existence a crisis or nothing. Hence, Barth on Romans: "The true God is, as origin without objectivity, the source of the crisis of all objectivity, the judge, the nothingness of the world" (Der wahre Gott ist aber der aller Gegenständlichkeit entbehrende Ursprung der Krisis aller Gegenständlichkeit, der Richter, das Nichtsein der Welt; *Römerbrief,* 57). Rosenzweig's entire system is a similar attempt to capture these paradoxes of the absolute Otherness of the revealed word, which nonetheless seizes us.[7]

The mistake of natural theology (esp. the physico-cosmological proofs), of Hegel's philosophy of history, and of liberal theology (from the perspective of the dialectical theologians) was that these movements attempted to find God expressed in creation. In doing so, these movements tended toward a logical conclusion that did away with any God outside of creation. (We saw Spinozism as the figure for this doctrine.)[8] Of course, even for opponents to this approach, God as creator must have some relation to his creation. But in order to maintain the absolute difference between the two orders, God must remain unknown and hidden. It is only in revelation that God and mankind "appear" in some relation toward each other.[9] The act of revelation, for Rosenzweig, is a unique event; he refers to it as an "event erupting out of the instant, an evented event" (*augenblicksentsprungenes Geschehen, als ein ereignetes Ereignis; Stern,* 178) that allows both God and man to face each other in their separate being and freedom.[10] Like the Lutheran doctrine of grace, this revelation cannot be sought after or brought about by man's actions but at best be prepared for by our adoption of a pure humility (187–88).

Dialogue

It is crucial for the "new thinking" of Rosenzweig that the revealed relationship between both man and God and man and man unfolds within the modality of language, specifically in the dialogical form of I-You. The condition for all relationship can be established only by breaking out of alienating structures. He states this with great clarity in the "Urzelle":

> That individual does this [namely, enters into a true relation with God] who has not lost himself in the objectifying thicket of relations, the individual outside of the theoretical-practical system, the individual as

---

7. On Rosenzweig's (and Leo Strauss's) "qualified defense" of miracles, see Lazier, 101–5.

8. On the continued significance of Spinoza for this period, see Lazier, esp. part 2.

9. According to Rosenzweig, Islam cannot capture this act as "*ein lebendiges Ereignis zwischen Gott und Mensch*" (*Stern,* 185–86).

10. Casper (145 n. 67) claims that this formulation is the closest etymological source for Heidegger's use of these terms.

I. He can and must demand that God return his love. Indeed, he must demand even that God love him first. For his I is dumb and speechless and awaits the redeeming word from the mouth of God, "Adam, where are *you*?" in order to respond to that first spoken you, which asks about him, with his own muted and tentative and shameful I. The relationship moves within the [space opened between] I and You and again I.

(Zweistromland, 131)

As this core idea is unfolded in the *Stern,* Rosenzweig makes clear that this dialogue is a genuine two-way street. Just as the individual human being first appears as inwardly turned and silent (on the origin of the self, see *Stern,* 71–90) until addressed by an other as a You, forcing him to speak out as "I," so, too, the God of creation, who speaks only to Himself ("Let us . . ."), is "not yet an open/revealed (*offenbares*) I" (on the dialogical relationship, see 191–209). For *both* God and man, the dialogical principle holds true: "Only insofar as the I recognizes the You as something outside of its own existence, and thus makes the transition from monologue to genuine dialogue, does it become an I [that can express itself]" (erst indem das Ich das Du als etwas außer sich anerkennt, also erst indem es vom Selbstgespräch zum echten Dialog übergeht, wird es zu jenem Ich [das laut werden kann]; 195). God's question to Adam, then, "Where are *You*?" serves to bring forth humanity but also to give God the possibility of revealing Himself. In a significant way, then, Rosenzweig reinterprets the anthropomorphic tradition that culminated in Feuerbach: God is both the radically Other "before" man, but in their relation "before" each other, in the face-to-face of their dialogue, man and God are also mutually dependent. Moreover, this primary relationship between man and God that seizes each individual in his individuality as a particularly addressed *You* is called, simply, "love," and creates the possibility as well of an ethics of the "love of the neighbor."[11] And it is in this possibility that we also see a difference between Rosenzweig (and Buber) and Barth. Especially for the early Barth, God's Word always comes to man in the form of a shattering "No!" to his existence; and any belief in the power of the human word to reach God leads to the negation of God. Thus, Rosenzweig is interested in the paradox of a *dialogue* across these levels of otherness, whereas Barth keeps the paradox at a more abstract level of the "meteor-like" entrance of the Word into our world.

---

11. "Urzelle," in *Zweistromland,* 132. See also the volume by Žižek, Santner, and Reinhard.

Although it is impossible to do justice to the immense structural complexity and linguistic richness of Rosenzweig's magnum opus, we can see the way he responds to the same conceptual and existential crises as the major Protestant philosophers and theologians (Heidegger, Gogarten, Barth, Bultmann, et al.) with a similar turn (*Kehre*) of thought. The nihilistic collapse of the tradition that produced the God of metaphysics opened up for all of them a new possibility that demands the embracing and understanding of the paradox of a "relation to the absolute Other."

In a short essay written in the form of a letter to Martin Buber on a collection of his essays in 1923, Rosenzweig opens with a testimony to "the degree that you have really been the announcer and speaker (*Vor- und Fürsprecher*) of our generations, mine and the following" ("Die Bauleute: Über das Gesetz," *Zweistromland*, 699). What we will see is the way that Buber was in fact a partner in dialogue (we could say a *Mitsprecher*) with those who came of age in the early twentieth century. His emphasis on language as the medium for the unfolding of the two parallel dialogical relationships between man and man and between man and God itself arose in a lively exchange with both Jewish and Christian thinkers, both philosophers and theologians.

Buber was raised in Vienna in the tradition of Midrash studies and Jewish Enlightenment. He discovered in the Hasidic tradition of Galicia, however, a living form of Judaism that allowed him to develop a deep and profound sense of the reality of faith. From 1923–33, he taught the philosophy and history of religion at the University of Frankfurt. He left Germany for Palestine in 1938 and was a professor until 1951 at the Hebrew University of Jerusalem. Like Rosenzweig, he also founded a separate school for adult education, at which he taught. His version of Zionism was more culturally and spiritually rooted than the political Zionism of Theodor Herzl. Thus, although he insisted on the importance of Israel as a site of the completion of the formation of a true Jewish community, he felt that Jews and Arabs should coexist in a shared state. He also always continued to encourage Jewish–Christian dialogue because although he did not believe in the "Incarnation," he nonetheless saw in Christology a mode of revelation between man and God that captured a sense of the mystery of that relationship. He died in Jerusalem in 1965.

Buber's early encounter with the world and writings of Hasidic Jewry was the decisive moment in his intellectual development. A movement within Judaism that started in the southern provinces of Poland (Podolien and Wolhynien) among the population that was suppressed by the Cossacks, Hasidism was influenced by the Kabbalah of Isaak Luria Aschkenasi and Sabbatai Zewi. It took hold as well in parts of Lithuania and Belarus.

The actual founder of the movement was R. Israel ben Eliezer (called Ba'al Shem Tov or Bescht) from Miedzyboz (approx. 1700–60). The basic idea of Hasidism is that there is nothing in which God does not exist. In an important sense it is not pantheistic, however, because God remains an addressable partner. God is also not "at home" in the world but in exile and suffering. Since everything, including human acts, contains the divine spark, it is possible to gain access to the divine through an act of revealing the inhering divine intention. Hasidic life is characterized by a joyful spirit and affirmation. Nothing is actually "profane," and everything that spreads joy (dance, alcohol, even properly practiced ascesis as means not end) can have religious value. Rather than the intellectual tendencies of rabbinism, this movement celebrates feeling and intuition. It is possible to work toward an ecstasy (*hitlahawut*) that is a release of the body and union with God. According to Buber, the zaddik, as community leader, has the task of making it easier for others to experience an encounter with God ("*anderen den unmittelbaren Umgang mit Gott zu erleichtern, nicht zu ersetzen*"). In his many works on this tradition, Buber tries to capture the liveliness and reality of the relationship between the Hasidim and their simultaneously present and absent God.[12] Hasidism can be considered a lens through which he read the history of the Judeo-Christian theological and philosophical tradition, a norm or standard against which he could measure the possibility of living up to the ideals (like the role the "Greeks" played for Classicism—the fact of the existence of this group testifies to the possibility and reality of the ideas).[13]

---

12. *Der große Maggid und seine Nachfolger* (*The Great Maggid and His Followers*, 1922)—"Maggid" (= wandering preacher) was one of the early followers of Israel ben Eliezer; *Die Legende des Baalschem* (*The Legend of the Baaschem*, 1922); *Die Erzählungen der Chassidim* (*Tales of the Chassidim*, 1949); *Gog und Magog* (1949); Die *chassidistische Botschaft* (*The Chassidistic Message*, 1952); all in *Werke*, vol. 3.

13. This is how he responds to a comment by Barth. In his afterword to the collection of some of his major works, Die Schriften über das *dialogische Prinzip* (*The Dialogical Principle*), Buber provides a brief intellectual autobiography and paints a picture of some of the important exchanges between Protestant theologians and Jewish thinkers in the first third of the twentieth century. He stresses the importance of Gogarten. Although Buber credits Gogarten with raising the I/You relation anew in the twentieth century, taking it beyond the anthropological atheism of Feuerbach, we see how Buber claims that Gogarten fails to extend this relationship beyond that between human beings to a relationship between man and God. Buber also offers a response to a comment by Barth in his *Church Dogmatics.* With a certain air of condescension, Barth points out that he is pleased to find a view not unsimilar to his "even from completely different positions" (e.g., from the pagan Confucius, from the atheist Feuerbach, and the Jewish Buber) (cited in *Dialogical Principle,* 318), although he fears that they lack "that freedom of the heart between man and man" that can emerge only under a Christian perspective. To this Buber opposes the Hasidic world of faith (*die chassidische Glaubenswelt*) that *lives* the "heart's freedom [as] the innermost presupposition, the ground of all ground" (*Herzensfreiheit [als] die innerste Voraussetzung, Grund des Grundes,* 319).

In keeping with the movement we have been pursuing from the death to the return of God, we can begin with Buber's *Gottesfinsternis* (*Eclipse of God*) so that we can see how he also is writing out of a postnihilist position. This collection of essays spanning over twenty years (from 1929 to 1952) deals with the "relationship between religion and philosophy" (as the subtitle states). Its point of departure is the late phase (*Spätphase*) of the Western tradition that has led to the "de-realization of God and all absolutes" (*Irrealisierung Gottes und aller Absolutheit*; 145) or the process, "whose last stage is the intellectual abandonment of God" (146). We arrived at this state from two directions. Philosophy began by turning God into an object of thought (*Denkobjekt*; ibid.), like the *logos*, i.e., an object that can be adequately penetrated and grasped through thought. The logical consequence of this move is the melding of the absolute with the power of the human spirit (146) to the extent that everything that could stand opposite us in the freedom of its being (*alles Gegenüber*; 147) is lost. This culminates in the annihilation of the independence of the human itself—in short, nihilism.[14] From the direction of religion, the process unfolds to the same end. God begins as a "countenance" (*Angesicht*; 148) standing vis-à-vis mankind, as in a genuine prayer in which one opens oneself up to sense the presence of the divine Other. However, religions strive to develop the power to call up and demand the revelation of the gods. Even the attempt to reverse this hubris, to "save" religion, fails: the effort (as we saw in the late eighteenth century, for example) to focus on the subjectivity of faith, the *feeling* in the religious individual, might shift the emphasis away from the power relation but nonetheless continues to put the "I" in the foreground and objectivizes the Other.

The result of these processes is the condition of *Gottesfinsternis*, the "eclipsing" of God. The open relation to God is blocked, no longer allowing either man or God to appear in their essential relatedness to each other. In Buber's terms, the I-You relation has become replaced evermore by I-It. In his version of Heidegger's "forgetting of Being" (*Seinsvergessenheit*),[15] this situation is described as follows:

---

14. The failure or self-cancellation of nihilism is the failure of the attempt to ground religion and God ethically (*Gottesfinsternis*, 137).

15. Buber says about Heidegger: "For me the concept of a Being that means something else than the fact inhering in all things . . . remains empty, unless I take flight into religion and see in it—as some Christian scholastics and mystics have done—the philosophical term for the divine, insofar as it is considered (or believed to be considered) in itself and before all creation" (*Gottesfinsternis*, 88–89).

> In our age the I–It relation has expanded to gigantic proportions, domi-
> nates almost without resistance, and determines the regime. The I of
> this relation gets along with everything by trying to take possession
> and control of everything; it is incapable of saying "You," incapable of
> encountering a being as it essentially is. This I is right now the one in
> charge. This all-powerful Ego, surrounded with all its Its, can recognize
> neither God nor any other absolute that manifests itself to man as com-
> ing from a nonhuman source. The Ego steps in the way and blocks all
> heavenly light. (152–53)

Or, as he defines it simply, atheism is not so much a denial of God as speaking of God in/as the third person (57). However, unlike Heidegger's call for
a reversal of an entire historical development that began with the Greeks,
Buber's sense of the inherent duality of human nature, i.e., the constant and
essential possibility for both I–You and I–It relations, gives him cause for
optimism. Human history is not a "fate" but "embodied possibility" (153)
that at any time can—indeed does—open up to renewal.

Such inherent possibility is not a cause for mere quietism, however. Buber
responds to the situation of twentieth-century nihilism by developing the
fundamental teachings he has learned from the Judaic tradition. He uses
rational means to increase the understanding and experience of dialogue
(faith). He thus turns to the tradition not as "dogma" but as a mode of being
in the world. Consider the following passage by Buber from his lecture (to
Christian missionaries!), given in Stuttgart, in March 1930 (published by
Buber in *Der Jude und sein Judentum* [*The Jew and His Judaism*], 1963; here
cited from *Geis and Kraus, Versuche des Verstehens* [*Trials of Understanding*]). In
his effort to characterize the "Jewish soul," he uses the figure of the ellipse
formed by two points, hence also a metaphor taken from mathematics, to
capture the nature of the human-divine paradoxical relation:

> The one is the primal experience that God is absolutely removed from
> man, incomprehensible; and [the other] that He is after all present and
> facing man in an immediate relation to this absolutely incommensu-
> rable human being. To know both at the same time that the one is not
> isolated from the other, this characterizes life at the heart of each faith-
> ful Jewish soul. Both—"God in heaven," i.e., wrapped in the absolute
> mystery, and man "on earth," i.e., wrapped in the refraction of his
> understanding and senses; both—God in the perfection and incom-
> prehensibility of His essence and man in the abysmal contradiction of
> his miraculous existence between birth and death. Both—and between
> them, unmediated relationality! (148)

Not to collapse them into the same, but we must nonetheless be ourselves amazed at the similarity of both the vocabulary and the conception that is at work here and in "dialectical theology." If we add that the interaction between these two points unfolds in language as a dialogue between an I and a You, we then arrive at the heart of Buber's thought.

Buber's interest in the Hasidic community, in the *reality* of the Jewish "soul" and *Volk,* and in the unfolding of human existence in the linguistic interactions *between* individuals—all these provide his thought a kind of sociological and anthropological point of departure. However, what makes his approach different from the turn in the nineteenth century that led gradually to the death of God is that he finds *within* these very aspects of human existence the opening up of or toward the divine. Like Rosenzweig, he has a conception of Jewish "history" that is nonteleological. God is not at the end of the line, or in the process of slowly revealing himself through ever more significant actions. Rather, the very analysis of human community, in a different way from Heidegger's *Daseinsanalyse* but with similar results, demonstrates[16] that Being is not "located" in any of the individual beings of the world (even in the self of mankind) but emerges out of the relating to-otherness of their I-You correspondence. For this reason Buber can say that Feuerbach was one of the first to concentrate on the relations between human beings as the foundation of an understanding of the divine. He quotes Feuerbach, who was on a "wave of genial inspiration," when he discovered the "secret of the necessity of the you for the I" (*Das dialogische Prinzip,* 302). Unfortunately, Feuerbach goes on to claim, "the unity of I and You is God" (ibid.), thereby not so much *denying* God as substituting man for Him ("not claiming to deny radically the concept of God itself but, rather, substituting an anthropological ersatz God"; ibid.). Buber's goal is to follow others—Kierkegaard, Gogarten, Cohen, Rosenzweig—in continuing Feuerbach's grasp of human reality while avoiding the "mystic construction" of man-become-God. Instead, the analysis of human existence reveals its inability to ground itself without reference to Otherness and transcendence—not as projection or hidden essence but as its reality. It is as simple as the inability to explain the nature of a genuine conversation.

Buber's analysis of the human world escapes the dangers of reductivism therefore in two ways. Methodologically, his "anthropology" proceeds along the lines of a kind of phenomenological description that seeks the "facticity"—he uses the word *faktisch*—of the dialogical nature of being

---

16. Shows/displays, or *zeigt,* as Wittgenstein says in the *Tractatus,* 2.172.

itself. Thus, so much of his highly poetic writing takes the form of concrete "descriptions" (see part 1 of the long essay "Zwiesprache," called, simply, "Beschreibung"), extended examples of how dialogues unfold. But second, at the level of content, the nature of dialogue itself is nonreductive. The essence of the communicative act is not "locatable" in a thing, or even in either of the partners, but in the process of exchange that performs an act of transcendence. He says: "But in its most sublime moments dialogue transcends these limits. It reaches its true conclusion beyond any communicated or communicable content, even the most personal. And yet it does not unfold in a 'mystical' process but in a precise way within the facticity and temporality of the shared human world" (*Das dialogische Prinzip*, 144). To insist on the dialogical relationship between man and man is to insist on the radical temporality of our existence, since by definition the dialogue unfolds in time, specifically in a present tense, and cannot be reduced to an essence (a *Wesen,* or something that was, *gewesen*).

The key to Buber's "theology" derives directly from this reality of human existence. He states his core idea, "my most essential issue" (*mein wesentlichstes Anliegen*) in the afterword to *I and Thou:* "The close bond between the relation to God and the relation to our fellow men" (*Das dialogische Prinzip,* 122). By analyzing and describing the way dialogical human relations exist "factually" in a paradox of "primal distance and relationality" ("Urdistanz und Beziehung"—the title of a late collection of his "contributions to a philosophical anthropology"), he can both give concrete form to the "encounter" that is (religious) "revelation"—namely, the event (*Ereignis*) of genuine exchange that allows each partner to be and to grow in freedom—and also, conversely, inject a theological dimension into the most "mundane" of interactions. Both the religious and the ethical spheres have one simple starting point, namely, "that I am spoken to and addressed so that I might have the responsibility to respond; I know who speaks and calls for an answer" ("Zwiesprache," *Das dialogische Prinzip,* 159). His goal is not to speak of God "as He really is" or even to prove *whether* He really is (see 133), but rather to discuss what the nature of the relationship must be between man and some Other so that being as such (our human being and the existence of things) makes any sense. Meaning does not emerge out of our subjectivity alone. Here he goes beyond post-Cartesian modern philosophy and its culmination in Idealism.[17] Rather, as we see in the actual practice of language, meaning arises only in the

---

17. This is also the basis of his critique of Kierkegaard, who, despite his deep recognition of the dependence of human existence on the Other, focuses on "the individual." Buber, "Die Frage an den Einzelnen" (The Question to the Individual) in *Das dialogische Prinzip.*

exchange between an I and a You about an It. Indeed, the "It" appears to us only as a phenomenon insofar as we can have such an exchange. Therefore, if either the I or You is reduced to an "It" (through either thoroughgoing subjectivism or objectivism), then the world becomes meaningless and being itself is fundamentally threatened. Redemption comes, again and again, through the reawakening of dialogue. Such is the "life rhythm of the pure relation," Buber's version of Hegel's "positivity" of religion or Heidegger's *Seinsgeschichte:* "And yet we turn the eternal You time and again into an It, into a something, turn God into a thing—this is our essence, not our caprice or willfulness. The reified history of God, the course of this God-thing through religion and its epiphenomena, through its illuminations and eclipses, its living intensity and its destructions, the movement away from the living God and back to Him, the transitions from presence to representations to objectifications to conceptualizations, to dissolutions, and to renewal—this is a path, indeed, it is the path" (*Ich und Du,* in *Das dialogische Prinzip,* 114). Thus, it is less a matter of avoiding than of living through the "false" options: "'Here world, there God'—that's It-talk; and 'God in the world'—that's also It-talk; but to exclude nothing, to leave nothing behind, to grasp everything, the whole world within the You, to grant the world its right and truth, to have nothing alongside of God, who can embrace everything—*that* is perfect relationality" (ibid., 80).[18]

Another theological consequence of Buber's approach becomes clear in his definition of faith (*Glaube*). Like his contemporaries in evangelical theology, he resists the reduction to subjective feeling or piety. Instead, he writes, faith is man's "entry into reality, *total* reality, without cuts or abbreviations" (*Gottesfinsternis,* 7). This definition offers almost a parody of Kant: rather than praising Enlightenment as mankind's stepping into autonomy, he upholds faith as the stepping into relationality. However, unlike Hegel's dialectical opposites—faith and insight—Buber's contrast here does not imply either a "terroristic" imposition of reason or an irrational flight into otherworldliness. The relationality of faith is the relationality of a dialogue (I-You) in which both partners gain their autonomy—or true reality—only insofar as they can interact freely with each other. He neither sacrifices individuality nor defies it, neither abandons rationality nor absolutizes it. Instead, faith

---

18. With what can only be understood as a critical gesture to the contemporaneous theologies, he follows this passage with his take on the notion of God as "wholly Other": "Certainly God is 'the wholly Other'; but he is also the wholly same: the wholly present. Certainly he is the mysterium tremendum that appears to and floors us; but he is also the mystery of the self-evident" (*Ich und Du,* in *Das dialogische Prinzip,* 80).

as dia-logue is possible only thanks to a *logos* that stretches in between and across the partners.

Of course, the conditions of such a dialogue get pushed to their limits when the partners belong to different religions. Here they enter into a sphere beyond mere opinions ("ein Reich, in dem das Gesetz der Ansicht nicht mehr gilt"; "Zwiesprache" in *Das dialogische Prinzip,* 147). As representatives of the Word of God and the divine will, they promote their truth and are even willing to die for it. But for Buber the key truth must always be the fact that the relation to God can unfold only within the relation to others, even in their difference. *Logos* breaks forth into the unfolding dia-*logos*. This view creates the demand and hope for such exchanges, as difficult as they are.[19] For us, he says in words that seem to echo Lessing's Nathan the Wise and the parable of the ring, "there is no unambiguously understandable or representable word of God, because the words as they are handed down to us are interpreted through our changing human face-to-face (*in unserem menschlichen Einanderzugewandtsein*)" (149). Only within the space opened by genuine religious dialogues—"not those so-called pseudodialogues in which no one really looks at or speaks to the other, but authentic exchanges, from one position of certainty to another, but also from one open person to another" (ibid.)—could the word of God be revealed to us.[20]

Given the significance of the Word for both Buber and Rosenzweig as the element that connects the two parallel relationships of man-man and God-man, it was only logical that they take seriously the reality of the Word by attempting a new translation of the Hebrew Bible into German. This monumental task, which Buber was able to complete only after Rosenzweig's death, attempted to grasp the nature of both dialogues—man-man and God-man—by addressing the problem of interlanguage communication as well as the interpretation of the divine message. Their aim was to capture the "bodiliness" (*Leiblichkeit*) of the original language of the Bible, treating it like a song whose "content" cannot be isolated from its rhythm.[21] In striving to render the "living unity" (*lebendige Einheit; Werke,* 2:1113) of the Word, they want to translate into German the sound effect of the original. The translator, they say, "must experience the writtenness of scripture largely

---

19. Buber made constant attempts at dialogue with Christians and Muslims.

20. Because for Buber the I-You or I-It relationships also get played out with the world of nature, he develops an ecological and anticapitalist stance (see *Ich und Du,* in *Das dialogische Prinzip,* 109).

21. See, for example, Buber's essay "Über die Wortwahl in einer Verdeutschung der Schrift" ("On Word Choice in a German Translation of the Scripture"), dedicated to the memory of Rosenzweig, in Buber's *Werke,* vol. 2 (e.g., 1112–13: "Actual revelation is always the human body and human voice and that means *this* body and *this* voice in the mystery of their uniqueness").

as the recording of its spokenness (*als die Schallplatte ihrer Gesprochenheit*)" (1114).

Out of this concrete experience of the Bible, both Buber and Rosenzweig hoped to develop a "pedagogical" program that would lead to a Renaissance of Jewish thought, what Buber called "*biblischer Humanismus*" (see the essay of that title in his *Werke*, vol. 2). The important thing, however, is to teach a version of the scriptural Word that is true to the dialogical spirit of Judaism. Buber writes:

> And as the nature of the Word is fundamentally different here and there, so too is the Word understood here and there in fundamentally different ways, something fundamentally different is taught or reported of it. The logos of the Greeks *is;* its being is eternal (Heraclitus); and when the prologue of the Hellenizing Gospel according to John, like the Hebrew Bible, begins with "In the beginning," it follows this with a completely non-Hebraic formulation, namely, "*was* the Word." At the beginning of the biblical story of creation the Word *is* not, but is, rather, *happening,* it is *spoken*. Here there is no "Word" that is not spoken; the only being of the Word is its spokenness; but all being of existing things comes from the being spoken of the primal word: "He himself spoke, and it came to pass." The Greeks teach the Word, the Jews report it. (1091)

In this theory and practice of translation we might say that we have come full circle and yet with richer results: the dialogical theology of Buber and Rosenzweig makes it possible to grapple with the philosophical and philological issues of an Erasmus (we recall that Erasmus translated *logos* in John 1 as *sermo* in order to stress the spokenness of the Word) even as they strive for the mystery of revelation in the spirit of Luther. Ultimately, their version of *logos* is neither *ratio* nor *verbum* nor *Geist* but *dia-logos*.[22]

---

22. Even *Geist* has to maintain its "physicality" as wind, breath, related to *Gischt,* spray. ("Über die Wortwahl," 1112).

❦ CHAPTER 10

Fides et Ratio

"Right Reason" and Europe in Contemporary Catholic Thought (Benedict XVI)

> I would speak of a necessary relatedness between reason and faith and between reason and religion, which are called to purify and help one another. They need each other, and they must acknowledge this mutual need.
>
> —Joseph Cardinal Ratzinger, "What Keeps the World Together," in *Values in a Time of Upheaval*
>
> After all, as St. Peter reminds us, we are obliged to give reasons for the faith.
>
> —Joseph Cardinal Ratzinger, cited in Neuhaus, *Biblical Interpretation in Crisis*

Beginning in the 1990s, both Pope John Paul II and Joseph Cardinal Ratzinger, now Pope Benedict XVI, published a series of encyclical letters, major writings, and highly publicized lectures in which they addressed what they considered the crisis of the contemporary period. Given the strong philosophical interests of these two religious leaders and scholars, it should come as no surprise that they offer a powerful version of the historical developments we have pursued up to this point. As we will see, however, their somewhat less "ironic" or "dialogical/dialectical" conception of the unfolding relationship between faith and reason than the one I have offered, or that we have seen in the previous chapter, leads Ratzinger (on whom I will focus) to think of the contemporary situation, particularly the political identity of the West (even more specifically, Europe) in oppositional terms. His stories about *fides et ratio,* therefore, clearly overlap in places with mine, and I have deep affinities with his efforts to stress the complementary relationship of faith and reason; but where I tend to see an inherent tension within the Western tradition—with *logos* implicated in both the birth and the death of the Christian God, and with faith offering both lifesaving and problematic responses—he sees a tradition imbued with rationality and threatened by "outside" forces.

I will organize my argument around three concerns:

1. Benedict XVI's thesis on the importance of the "Hellenization" of Judaism as the founding condition, or "event," of Christianity (including his motivation, namely, a response to his understanding of our present "crisis").

2. How this "event" brings with it a version of the history of Christianity and Europe as a history of *logos,* a history that has had to confront the process of devolution that is characterized as "de-hellenization" and the reduction of reason/*logos* to a purely secular concept, divorced from its theological connection to faith.

3. Political conclusions that Benedict XVI has drawn for contemporary Europe. Because he considers the identity of Europe as bound up with the founding entry of Greek *logos* into early Christianity, he defines the present "crisis" of European culture as the consequence of the loss of that logocentric identity. Hence, the solution to the present crisis lies in a return to a broader, unified concept of *logos.*

Despite the extensive range of publications by Joseph Cardinal Ratzinger/ Benedict XVI in which he has presented clear yet nuanced versions of these arguments, it is unfortunate that what is known of his position emerged largely from his earlier function as head of the Congregation of the Doctrine of the Faith—where he defended the church's orthodoxy and gained the reputation of Pope John Paul II's "Rottweiler"—and from the controversy over his remarks on Islam during his Regensburg address in September 2006 (more about that below). Thus, it is valuable to review his main premises because of the way they contribute to the ongoing academic and public dialogue on our "postsecular" world (or, we might say, on a world with religion after the death of God). But I also intend to propose a series of challenges to Ratzinger/Benedict XVI's position, challenges not in the sense of undermining attacks but as ways in which his position needs to be extended. In large measure, the challenges come from the alternative perspectives that I have been presenting throughout this book. That is, if we view the history of (modern) Western thought on Christian theology as an insistent and tension-filled dialogue between faith and reason, then we would see not an identity (*logos,* hellenization) that has been lost (through dehellenization) and must be regained but, rather, an inherently oppositional and pluralistic tradition. Such a perspective replaces the metaphysical positions (faith or reason) with a non- or postmetaphysical emphasis on the (rhetorical) exchanges between them and also shifts the focus from the singular identity of Europe to a more internally dialectical and dynamic conception.

My thesis is that the present pope is deeply committed to a broad conception of *logos* that is necessary for us to move forward politically in our global age, that his conception overlaps in remarkable ways with such disparate thinkers as Adorno and Horkheimer, Heidegger, and Habermas, but that, finally, the metaphysical and nonlinguistic grounding of the pope's logocentrism makes it untenable and even undermines his own dialogical mission.

Ratzinger/Benedict XVI on the "Event" of "Hellenization"

As Benedict makes clear in the Regensburg lecture, the prologue to the Gospel according to John—"In the beginning was the *logos,* and the *logos* was with God, and God was the *logos*"—captures the defining moment, or as he calls it, "event," of the West, indeed, of human history. "The encounter between the Biblical message and Greek thought did not happen by chance," he writes. It arises out of "the intrinsic necessity of a rapprochement between Biblical faith and Greek inquiry" (*Lecture,* 135). A few years earlier, in his book on "truth and tolerance," the then cardinal Ratzinger stressed that the convergence of Israelite and Greek thought was by no means a contingent occurrence. Rather, he looks for "the inner basis—and the inner necessity—of the historical encounter of Hellas and the Bible. . . . What unites the two is precisely the question of truth, and of good as such, which they put to religion, the Mosaic-Socratic distinction, as we may now call it" (*Truth and Tolerance,* 223). This "inner basis" was already present in the Hebrew Bible, according to Ratzinger, and so it was really a matter of the Greeks "bringing out" the universal principle contained there. This "intercultural encounter" had "the widest possible implications" (ibid.). He argues that "the seeds of the Logos, of divine rationality" were present "not in the religions [plural], but in the movement toward [monotheistic, monological] rationality that destroyed these religions" (228). What we see here is a largely Hegelian model of the history of religion (perhaps with some Heideggerian overtones of *Seinsgeschichte*—this is why I stress Benedict XVI's use of the word "event," *Ereignis*—as he says in the lecture: "This inner rapprochement between Biblical faith and Greek philosophical inquiry was an *event* of decisive importance not only from the standpoint of the history of religions, but also from that of world history—it is an event which concerns us even today" [my emphasis, *Regensburg Lecture,* 138]). While Ratzinger elsewhere critiques Hegel's dialectic for a problematic eschatology, here he takes over the overall structure of an "inner necessity" driving the "movement" of history to draw out the kernel of truth within older forms ("religions" in the plural). He does not see an "overlaying" of Greek thought on Judaism (a negative version of the "hellenization" thesis, as he describes it in a short chapter in *Truth and Tolerance* [90–94]). Rather, this encounter's "intrinsic necessity" lay already within the Judaic tradition. Its power—the "widest possible implications," as he says in *Truth and Tolerance*—was the breakthrough to a true and absolute universalism. "Christianity," he writes in *Truth and Tolerance,* "first brought about a breakthrough here, having 'broken down the dividing wall' (Eph. 2:14)," i.e., Christianity made "full universalism" possible because full membership was open to all (155). Ratzinger sees this universalism as the result of "the Logos, the Wisdom, about which the Greeks spoke, on the one hand, and the Israelites, on the other" (157).

Elsewhere, the "Hegelianism" of Ratzinger's position is stated even more strongly. The original "encounter" of the early Christian message with both Greek and Judaic thought "was made possible because within the Greek world a similar process of self-transcendence had started to get underway" (*Truth and Tolerance,* 200). The motor that drives a particular culture beyond its own borders, i.e., the "self-criticism of that world's own culture and its own thought" (ibid.), is defined as, on the one hand, philosophy—or, we could say, the movement of reason to challenge any limit or finitude— and, on the other, faith ("From that starting point, faith drew these peoples [non-Europeans who encountered Christianity] into the process of self-transcendence"). For this reason, Christians who did reach out into other cultures "sought points of contact, not with the religions, but with philosophy [because] they were not canonizing a culture but did find it possible to enter into it at those points where it had itself begun to move out of its own framework, had started to take the path toward the wide spaces of truth that is common to all, and had left behind its comfortable place in what belonged to it" (201). Thus, the thesis of "hellenization" contains an entire philosophy of history according to which each culture and religion has within itself the seeds of its own self-overcoming; that seed is the Word underlying the particularity of words (see *Truth and Tolerance,* 184–93, where he addresses Pope John Paul II's encyclical *Fides et Ratio*); because Christianity is defined from its "beginning" in John 1:1 as *the logos,* it is, as *religio vera* (184), the *alpha* and *omega* of the life of all cultures, that which gives them the dynamism of their lives and their teleological end point.

From a Habermasian perspective we can see what is powerful and yet problematic about this position. The self-transcendent drive inherent in language (words) derives not from an underlying and eschatologically emerging "Word" but from that aspect of the *use* of words in communication that guarantees its success, namely, the necessary presupposition that any particular speech act surpasses its own instantiation (for a variety of reasons; e.g., in order to be recognized as a sign, a word must be repeatable and hence not radically particular; also, the function of words presumes a stability of the external, referential world of objects and of the disposition of the subject). A notion of communicative reason has, therefore, the benefits of accounting for universalizing features of human interaction and culture, without the metaphysical grounding of *the logos* that would provide them with an absolute *telos*. Such a dialogical perspective will reemerge at the end of this chapter when we address the geopolitical formation of Europe.

Modernity and Dehellenization

Pope Benedict XVI has taken a strong position against the war conducted by the United States against Iraq. One prominent reason is the long-standing position of the Catholic Church on just war and nonaggression. But there is a more subtle argument that differentiates the pope from common arguments that the Bush administration and numerous (neo)conservatives—and even liberals—have used to justify the enterprise of "bringing democracy to the Middle East." A typical line claims that the crisis experienced within many Islamic societies has emerged as the result of a first step toward modernity. What we see, the argument runs, is not just (or not so much) a "clash of civilizations" as a clash of premodern, nonsecular societies with modernity. The mission of the neoconservatives would be to make possible the completion of the "project of modernity" in the Middle East. It could be summarized in the statement, heard in many variations: "What Islam needs is a Reformation!"—i.e., the kind of challenge that leads to such key aspects of secularism as tolerance, the separation of church and state, or the relative relegation of religion to the private sphere.

Against this argument, the pope adopts a position that is most closely allied to the "dialectic of Enlightenment" presented by the Frankfurt School as well as to the critique of technology presented by (that enemy of the Frankfurt School) Martin Heidegger, namely, the idea that a dynamic within Western modernity itself is the *problem*. That is, we can say that Benedict's statements about Islam in the Regensburg lecture, i.e., the quotations from the Byzantine emperor Manuel II calling Islam "evil and inhuman," are indeed not to be taken as direct disparagements. Interestingly, he does not have the perspective of the neoconservatives, for whom the problem is that Muslim societies must be drawn *into* the process of modernization. On the contrary, Benedict would see both Islamic (indeed, Protestant) antirationalist "transcendentalism" and modernity's limited technoscientific rationality as betrayals of the "idea of Europe," namely, a unifying *logos*. (The question of why he makes no mention of the strong rationalistic tradition in Islam, I have to leave open.)

We need to be clear that Benedict by no means rejects modernity itself. Rather, the dynamic that Benedict criticizes involves, on the one hand, the reduction of reason to the purely instrumental, technological, and efficiency-oriented, and, on the other, the disparaging of *logos* in the realm of religion. He states explicitly: "We Christians are summoned today, not to limit reason and oppose it, but to resist its reduction to the rationality of production" (*Values,* 111). What he refers to as "a sick reason" and "a misused religion" (or, at times, the "pathologies" of reason and religion) are what need to be addressed. Both are flip sides of the one historical coin: "dehellenization."

Concerning the limitation of reason, Ratzinger characterizes the "present-day crisis" in various ways as a crisis of reason brought on by its self-limitation and self-opposition. Much of his description sounds like the young Hegel or milder versions of the Frankfurt School. As one example among many, consider the following description of a kind of "dialectic of Enlightenment" where a limited concept of reason opens up the floodgates of the irrational:

> The present-day crisis is due to the fact that the connecting link between the subjective and objective realms has disappeared, that reason and feeling are drifting apart, and that both are ailing because of it. Reason that operates in specialized areas in fact gains enormously in strength and capability, but because it is standardized according to a single type of certainty and rationality, it no longer offers any perspective on the fundamental questions of mankind. The result is an unhealthy overdevelopment in the realm of technical and pragmatic knowledge, as against a shrinking in that of basic fundamentals, and thus the balance between them is disturbed in a way that may be fatal for man's humanity. On the other hand, religion today has by no means been made redundant. In many ways there is indeed a real boom in religion, but religion that collapses into particularism, not infrequently parting company with its sublime spiritual context. . . . People look for what is irrational, superstitious, and magical; there is a danger of their falling back into an *anarchic* and destructive form of relationship with hidden powers and forces. (*Truth and Tolerance,* 143; my emphasis)

The notion of an "anarchic" position could be understood in terms of its etymological roots in *archein,* "to begin" and "to rule." What is needed, according to Ratzinger here, is a return to the unifying *beginning and reinstatement of the lost ruling principle*. And what constitutes them? We know from John's Gospel: *logos*. That is, to overcome the crisis (an-archy) of a self-limiting reason we must return to the proper rule of the pure beginning—*logos*, the "working together on the basis of a single rationality" that he mentions in his lecture as characteristic of an idealized (might I say medieval?) *universitas*.[1]

Benedict XVI's argument, which echoes the core of Critical Theory, has enabled him to engage in productive dialogue with Jürgen Habermas. The exchange that took place between these two major public intellectuals at the Catholic Academy of Bavaria in January 2004, shortly before Joseph Cardinal Ratzinger was elected pope, explores both a historical dynamic of secularization and the role of religion in modern liberal democracies. The point, as Habermas says, is not a sociological one (the persistence of belief in a supposedly secular world) but a philosophical and "cognitive challenge" (Habermas and Ratzinger, *Dialectics,* 38). Post-Enlightenment philosophy, as we have seen in our discussions of Hegel and his critics (chapters 4 and 5), has long been caught in a dialectic that moves between the radical expansion of reason to its self-limitation and recognition of some (theological) Other. The failure of the technoscientific rationality that has guided economic globalization seems now to be leading to a similar turn to the opposite, namely, a total devaluation of reason itself by both (postmodern) philosophers and religious fundamentalists of many creeds. The response to this dangerous spiral of "pathologies," Ratzinger claims, can only be a broader conception of reason that recognizes "that religious convictions have an epistemological status that is not purely and simply irrational" (*Dialectics,* 50–51). Indeed, in terms of social organization, religious modes of interaction provide a "pre-political moral foundation" (Ratzinger), i.e., forms of legitimation and cohesion building, which have not (yet) been replaced by other discursive means (where "yet" in parentheses would likely be supplied by Habermas, who does not in principle think that liberal democracies could develop alternatives to religious approaches).

Given his critique of the West's own loss of its hellenized, logocentric roots, Ratzinger/Benedict XVI can take aim at any other approach to religion that does not embrace this same conception. He can use it to critique not just feeling-based religiosity of the Schleiermacherian variety, but also

---

1. It is not the "factory-like" institution, with its "conflict of the faculties," described by Kant. Instead Ratzinger addresses the "Magnificent Rector . . . [about] the experience . . . of the fact that despite our specializations which at times make it difficult to communicate with each other, we made up a whole, working in everything on the basis of a single rationality with its various aspects and sharing responsibility for the right use of reason" (*Lecture,* 131).

pre- or nonmonotheistic religions, including Asian forms, or, as we see controversially in the Regensburg lecture, Islam—which is interpreted as non-*logos*-based. While there is no reason to assume that Benedict was out to insult or devalue Islam, he was using a general criterion—the significance of *logos*—in order to make a comparison. As James Schall has argued in his essay on the lecture, the pope offered a legitimate (even if, I might say, problematically and self-defeatingly and perhaps even disingenuously formulated) challenge to Islamic theologians to engage in debate over the status of rational discourse in their respective religious traditions.

Two Alternative Dialogical Histories

We have seen that Ratzinger tells a powerful story of a primal hellenization that gives way over time to a dehellenization that would rob Christianity of its "right reason" (*orthos logos*). But I want to summarize versions of history that we have pursued in the previous chapters that indicate ways in which these two forces have been always already at work dialectically. Indeed, we occasionally see them at work in precisely the opposite way than that presented by Benedict: at times it is *logos* itself that is the problem leading to its flipping into its irrational Other.

As we can see from passages in the Regensburg address as well as in his other writings, Ratzinger/Benedict argues for the logocentric interpretation of Christian (indeed, Catholic) universalism, by appealing to both Paul and John the Evangelist. Time and again we see a basic Hegelian conception of true religion as granting unity (between subject and object, reason and feeling, etc.). I would at least like to indicate that these two poles can be seen to represent a tension *within* Christian thought as much as a synthesis (as he proposes early in the lecture where John and Paul are used to gloss each other [135]). Benedict refers to the "dehellenizing" move of the Reformation and points to the problematic conception of *sola scriptura* (a hermeneutic principle he and others challenged in the 1988 Erasmus lecture and conference, published in *Biblical Interpretation in Crisis*).[2] I will return to biblical exegesis. But for now it is enough to point out that it is not by chance that the "event" of Christianity for Luther took place not in John's turn to *logos*—that "whore Reason," as he so often says—but in *Paul*'s appeal to faith. Hence, the true adversary for Benedict would be not so much Harnack, or even Bultmann (who is his constant point of critique), but the

---

2. Edited by Richard John Neuhaus.

twentieth-century giant of Protestant theology, Karl Barth. After all, what Barth learned from Paul (and Luther's Paul) was that the history of modern theology, culminating in Hegel's divinization of *Vernunft* and rationalization of the divine, both grew out of an overemphasis of *logos* and led to the end of true religion as faith in the "wholly Other." Recall the following passage from Barth's commentary on Romans, which sent shock waves through German theology when first published in 1919: "One cannot wish religion upon someone or extol someone for it: it is a catastrophe that breaks in on certain individuals with a fatal necessity and can then be transferred from them to others. . . . To be a religious person means to be a torn, unharmonious, conflicted person. For only a person who has not posed the great question of unity with God could ever be one with himself" (*Römerbrief*, 2nd ed., 1922, 240; in Moltmann, *Anfänge,* Part 1:XVI). Barth's Gnosticism, his radical divorcing of man's position in this world from the perspective of divine grace, his rejection of any possible rapprochement of man to God and the Lutheran "healthy despair" it produces even in the faithful, his denial of reason's ability to recognize God in the world—these stances provide the foil for Benedict's embracing of *fides et ratio.* My point here is not to espouse Barth per se or to pit Protestantism against Catholicism, but to propose the presence of a dialectic within the biblical tradition. From this perspective, John and Paul represent two *conflicting* moments in the originary logic of Christianity; the conflict between reason and faith, or Catholicism and Protestantism, might have been there "in the beginning"—*en arche.* There is no pure unity or Hellenic fusion to which we can appeal.

A brief discussion of another powerful counterposition, namely, the interpretation of Paul provided by the contemporary phenomenologist, hermeneut, and poststructuralist Alain Badiou, allows us to see the tension *within* the Christian tradition. Consider the passage from 1 Corinthians 2:1–5 (cited in Badiou, *Paul*): "When I came to you, brethren, I did not come proclaiming to you the testimony of God in lofty words or wisdom. For I decided to know nothing among you except Jesus Christ and him crucified. And I was with you in weakness, and in much fear and trembling; and my speech and my message were not in persuasive words of wisdom, but in demonstration of the Spirit and power, that your faith might not rest in the wisdom of men, but in the power of God" (27). Badiou glosses this as follows:

> The problem lies in knowing how, armed only with the conviction that declares the Christ-event, one is to tackle the Greek intellectual milieu, whose essential category is that of wisdom (*sophia*), and whose instrument is that of rhetorical superiority (*huperokhē logou*). . . . Paul opposes

a show of spirit (*pneuma,* breath) and power (*dunamis*) to the armed wisdom of rhetoric. The wisdom of men is opposed to the power of God. It is thus a question of intervening *ouk en sophiai logou,* "without the wisdom of language." This maxim envelops a radical antiphilosophy; it is not a proposition capable of being supported by a *philosophia.* . . . There is a failure before the "Greeks." The Jews raise the question of the Law; the Greeks, that of Wisdom, of philosophy. Such are the two historical referents for Paul's enterprise. One, i.e. Paul, must find the path for a thought that avoids both these referents. (27–28)

According to Badiou, far from the synthesizer of the two traditions, Paul initiates a radical universalism—on this he and Ratzinger do agree—which, however, *opposes* the two traditions Ratzinger insists are one.

The one place where Ratzinger does point to this tension within the biblical tradition itself, indeed within Paul, is in the matter of the law. On receiving an honorary doctorate from the Faculty of Jurisprudence at the Libera Università Maria SS. Assunta, then Cardinal Ratzinger gave a short address entitled "Crises of Law." He connected the search for a universally valid law with the concept of *logos* via the concept of "*recta ratio,*" "right reason," a central concept for then Pope John Paul II's encyclical, *Fides et Ratio.* Most of the address criticizes the consensus theories of postmetaphysical philosophy and the utopian Marxism of liberation theology. But at one point he says in passing that "a mistaken Pauline idea has rapidly given way to radical and even anarchic interpretations of Christianity" (*Essential,* 379) and again that "the concept of 'law' (Torah) appears in Pauline writing with problematic accents and later, in Luther, is thought to be diametrically opposed to the gospel. The development of law in modern times has been profoundly characterized by these contradictory positions" (*Essential,* 377). What I am interested in emphasizing is precisely the "contradictory positions" that are inherent within the *logos* of the Christian tradition. Thus, although I have doubts myself about what is a renewed interest among contemporary thinkers for St. Paul, we at least see that the primal event is less a fusion than an inherent conflict of interpretations that gets played out, more or less peacefully or violently, over the history of Christianity.

Finally, I would stress that the entire argument of my book has made the case that the history of Christianity, especially in the modern period from the Reformation to the present, is much more ironic than a process of "dehellenization"—i.e., a gradual loss of the unity of faith and reason—that must be countered by a return to a unifying *logos.* It must be considered, rather, a constantly revisited, failed and failing dialogue between Paul and

John, faith and reason. It is ironic because the very "Hellenic" moment, *logos,* does indeed initiate a historical unfolding, but this unfolding leads to its own "undoing"—even as it seems to get driven again and again to new formulations. Here I am proposing a history of the Christian West that consists not of a universal reason countered by "exceptions" (like Duns Scotus or Pascal or Harnack) but of a tradition that is more inherently dialogical and radically self-questioning (even undermining). In Benedict's terms, we must wonder whether "hellenization" and "dehellenization" are not even more intimately linked. Hence, recall the question that Hans Küng, the then cardinal Ratzinger's adversarial colleague from Tübingen, asks: "Looking back over the dramatic history of reason and faith in modernity, which has led to the elimination of God from politics and science, the observer cannot avoid a conflicted impression: To what extent was this history 'necessary,' to what extent not? Is this historical process toward de facto godlessness irreversible, has it run its course once and for all? Or does belief in God have a future after all, indeed, under the condition of and acknowledging the modern process of secularization and emancipation, a new future?" (*Existiert Gott?* 119).

In its briefest form, the "dramatic history" that Küng refers to (and which one finds hints of in Gianni Vattimo's writings) has been presented as follows: the injection of *logos* into the *beginning* of Christian faith and religion places a demand, as Ratzinger powerfully emphasizes, to "give reasons," to "inquir[e] into the reasonableness of faith" (*Lecture,* 131). Hence, one of the lines he cites from the Byzantine emperor Manuel II Paleologus—with its implicit and explicit critique of Islam—states that the true believer (Christian) "needs the ability to speak well and to reason properly, without violence and threats" (*Lecture,* 134). He writes in *Truth and Tolerance:* "In a free society truth can find no other way to prevail, and should seek no other way, than simply by power of persuasion" (144). (I shall return to this rhetorical component presently, but for now recall Badiou above on Paul's rejection of rhetorical wisdom.) That is, beginning with the Scholastics and then Renaissance Neoplatonism, different versions of *logos* are brought to bear on faith and God, the point being not to argue Him *away* but to discover Him and justify faith. This process of applying *logos,* indeed generating varieties of *logoi,* to matters of faith turns out to be much more problematic. Despite the efforts of the encyclical by Pope John Paul II (written undoubtedly together with Ratzinger) to unite *fides et ratio* (the encyclical's title), that very unification could be said to lead to the death of God. Erasmus can be a starting point insofar as he applies his love of *logos,* i.e., the means of his powerful *philo-logos,* his linguistic-rhetorical-historical exegetical method, to biblical exegesis. The "linguistic turn" and the "philological method" that

Ratzinger critiques as being focused on "mere words" (*Truth and Tolerance,* 187–89) arose from the very love of *logos.* Of course, in developing this approach, Erasmus also comes to recognize the immense *complexity* of the Bible. Luther, understandably, responds against Erasmus with a vehement diatribe ("On the Bondage of the Will") because he knows that to start down the road of giving philological reasons for faith will only make the philologists more enamored of their own words until man displaces God. The conflict between these positions, we know, became ugly. In response to the violence unleashed by conflicting faiths and interpretations of scriptures in the Thirty Years' War, it is only logical that Descartes, Spinoza, and Leibniz, in their different ways, would bring the newly discovered *logos* of scientific calculability—another meaning of *logos* besides "reason" and "word"—to bear on issues of faith. Three proofs—the ontological, the cosmological, and the physico-teleological—offered a kind of mathematical certainty that supplanted both the Bible and faith. For a while it seemed as if the *logos* of theoretical reason had provided the firm ground or "sufficient reason" for faith. At least until Kant, the "*Alles-Zermalmer*" (literally, the one who could grind any argument to bits) near the end of the eighteenth century, recognized the philosophical weaknesses in these "speculative" or "metaphysical" proofs. In the first and third *Critiques,* and in his lectures on philosophical theology, Kant demolished the former *logos.* He teetered on the abyss of atheism until he pulled a different *logos* out of his sleeve. He wrote, for example: "Thus all speculation depends, in substance, on the transcendental concept. But if we posit that it is not correct, would we not then have to give up the knowledge of God? Not at all, . . . a great field would still remain to us, and this would be the belief or faith that God exists. This faith we will derive a priori from *moral principles*" (*Lectures on Philosophical Theology* [1783–84], 39). He turned, that is, to a different grounding: practical reason or what we might call "ethical *logos.*" The untenability of Kant's own dualisms led, we saw, to Hegel's identification of *logos* and history, which he interpreted as the true salvation of religion, only to lead to Feuerbach and Marx, and conclude with Nietzsche. For if Kant knocked the three logical legs, the theoretical proofs, out from under theology, only to leave it (he thought) standing firmly on the last one, morality, Nietzsche—yet another son of a Protestant minister— kicked the final one away with his *Genealogy of Morals.* The point of this version of history—which Heidegger called the history of metaphysics or ontotheology within the wider unfolding of the *Ereignis* of Being—is that the danger to Christianity lies not so much in the irrationality of the outside as in the very "inner necessity" of its logic. The *logos* Benedict sees as the saving grace can be, when applied in its different forms, the very source of doubt. This is why Nietzsche's madman claims that the real issue is not that "God is dead" but that "we have killed Him." It has been a question of killing Him softly with *logos*. Precisely the demand to give an account of, to give reasons for, faith, which Ratzinger has seen from the start as the defining "Hellenic" feature of Christianity, has indeed set "us" on a historical mission. But the results have been much more ambivalent than Ratzinger claims. He seems to see only two options for *logos,* the positively universal ("the basis of a single rationality" and "the coherence within the universe of reason," *Lecture,* 131) and the negatively instrumental. The history of the West, as we have seen, is riddled with others. Each has had its shot to do what John the Evangelist calls us to do. And time and again one can hear Paul (or Luther, or Barth) issuing a warning that you can't have your *religio* and *logos,* too. In other words, Benedict's call for a "critique of modern reason from within" implicates him in alternative histories that get off to a dialectical start at the "beginning" (*en arche*) and continue through the unfolding of the very *logos* to which he turns to avert crisis.

Note that I am *not* calling for an end to this dialogue. In that regard I fully agree with Ratzinger/Benedict XVI. But I am saying that the dialogue is more radically open-ended and tension filled. The pope calls for the "essential complementarity" of faith and reason: "I would speak of a necessary relatedness between reason and faith and between reason and religion, which are called to purify and help one another. They need each other, and they must acknowledge this mutual need" (*Dialectics of Secularization,* 78–79). And I would agree, but this view generates a more complex dialogue defined, to use Habermas's term, "post-metaphysically."

Logo-centric vs. Dialogical Europe

I would like to conclude with a gesture in the direction of the geopolitical.[3] The stakes are high for Ratzinger not just in terms of human salvation but concretely for Europe. He is very clear that the decisive event—the fusion of Judaism and Hellas, or more precisely, the Greek "fulfillment" of the truth of the Judaic tradition—literally *defines Europe.* This leads to a number of direct consequences: the loss of this unifying *logos,* be it at the hands of technological rationality, irrational Romanticism, or a dialectics of the Enlightenment, has led to a "turning point for Europe" (to cite one of his books from 1991,

---

3. Here I will also have to skip over the polemic with liberation theology, which left a strong stamp on Ratzinger's thought from the late 1960s on.

although I should mention that the actual title is formulated as a question). As he says there, "The idea of Europe has fallen into a strange twilight today" (*Turning Point,* 113). While his concern is with real phenomena, from drug abuse, to AIDS, to technoscience, to terrorism, his stress is really on the *idea* of Europe. These phenomena, he believes, have their deeper roots in the decline of this *idea,* the collapse or twilight of Judaic-Hellenic *logos.* Their solution can be envisaged, therefore, only by the resuscitation of this idea. I can only gesture in the direction of the remarkable similarity of his program here to the conservative tract, "Die Christenheit oder Europa" ("Christianity or Europe"), written by the young Romantic, Friedrich von Hardenberg, known as Novalis, in 1799 (not published until 1826). What is at stake is "Europe's Identity," or its "Common Identity and Common Will" (talks he gave in 2004 and 2001 respectively; published in *Values in a Time of Upheaval*). Although the pope recognizes that "Europe has always been a continent of contrasts" ("Common Identity," 151), his effort remains consistently to discover the "historical and cultural concept" that forms *the* (singular) "inner" or "internal identity" of Europe (*Values,* 129, 136, 146).

However, if it is true that the real history of that *logos* is more fraught than he implies, that the dialogue has proceeded through a wandering path of dead ends and restarts, or slippery slopes, then the "idea of Europe" would also have to be enriched. Habermas and Derrida overlapped briefly on this project after 9/11, even if the basis and the reasoning for some new "idea of Europe" in fact must be radically different for the two thinkers. But I turn to Étienne Balibar, who has been, in my mind, one of the more interesting intellectuals to contribute an analysis of the status of Europe. I would like to discuss briefly, in conclusion, his talk and essay from 2003, "Europe: Vanishing Mediator" (published in *We, the People of Europe?*). He has raised the question of what we need to think about in our present situation as intellectuals addressing the political, namely, "the difficulty of giving a geographical, cultural, or institutional definition of the 'place' or 'position' where intellectuals are working, where they could 'meet,' where they write and talk from. This place has become, more than ever, *intermediary, transitory,* and *dialogic.* And it has to take into account the irreversible effects of the globalization of culture" (205). He does believe that universalist claims need to be raised, but European intellectuals cannot *presume* to adopt such a universalist position. Rather, "the universality that we associate with the very idea of politics and the vocation of the intellectual has to be constructed practically and empirically; it has to be approached through confrontation and conflict. One of the ways to contribute to this process, for us European intellectuals, is to critically listen to objections and calls that we receive from other parts of the world: East, West and South, including America" (206). The idea here is that

Europe itself needs to be understood much more dialogically, transnationally, and conflictually, rather than monolithically (or, should I say, monotheistically). He warns, moreover, of "substitut[ing] an imaginary Europe for the real one" (214).

Indeed, Balibar asserts that in a crucial sense "Europe does not exist, it is not a political 'subject'" (216–17). But this does not mean that Europe should be resigned to a lack of agency. Rather, the point would be "to completely reexamine the relationships between 'strategy,' 'power,' 'agency,' and 'subjectivity' (or 'identity')" and to "draw all the consequences from the fact that *Europe is a borderland* rather than an entity that 'has' borders" (220). And while, as Balibar states, history has shown that political entities need some kind of an "idea" to "unify their material and human resources" (218), he warns us that we should not think of such a collective identity as "a given, a metaphysical prerequisite of agency, and it is certainly not a mythical image that could be forcefully imposed upon reality by inventing this or that historical criterion (for example, '*Christian Europe*')" (221, my emphasis; his footnote refers to Novalis and the then pope John Paul II).[4]

The issue now becomes: What would a dialogical *logos* look like that can continue to speak, even rationally, about faith, even given this genuinely pluralistic possibility of an identity—and not just of Europe? Let me briefly indicate four characteristics. First, in thinking of *logos,* we must keep in mind its *linguistic,* indeed *rhetorical* nature. "Right reason" always unfolds within argumentative and persuasive contexts that must take into account the methods and effects of speech on particular audiences. Failure to think in these terms could account for the way the pope (if we want to give him the benefit of the doubt that his intentions were positive) failed to see that his choice of quotes in his Regensburg address would lead to misunderstanding at the least—if not vehement, indeed violent, reaction. For all of the rapprochement between the pope and Habermas, and for all of the latter's own limitations, Habermas recognizes more than Benedict the pragmatic and rhetorical breadth of "communicative reason," which, he says in his *Philosophical Discourse of Modernity,* "recalls older ideas of *logos,* inasmuch as it brings along with it the connotations of a noncoercively unifying, consensus-building force of a discourse in which the

---

4. While I couldn't explore the historical experiences that Balibar turns to for support for a new "idea of Europe"—like "hybridization and multiculturalism," or the process of "institutionalizing conflicts" (221–24)—I will merely point out that his proposal for rethinking Europe is radically different from Ratzinger's—and inherently dialogical: "As Umberto Eco has proposed, the only genuine 'idiom of Europe' (and as we know that any political entity needs an idiom or a linguistic institution) *is the practice of translation*" (234).

participants overcome their at first subjectively biased views in favor of a rationally motivated agreement" (315).[5] Second, it cannot be one-sidedly "secularist." Interestingly, Balibar would concur with not only Ratzinger but also Talal Asad, Charles Taylor, Jürgen Habermas, and others, that "secularism" in some strong form is also a problem that cannot be assumed as a given of European identity. Not unlike Benedict, Balibar warns us, for example, that "the dominant form of European 'secularism' (this is particularly the case with French *laïcité*) is also a form of resistance to real multiculturalism, since many cultures are deemed to be too 'religious' to become acceptable in the picture. This is not far from transforming Western culture into a secular form of religion indeed" (336). But nonetheless, Ratzinger's appeal to an idealized "Christian Europe" that fused the Judaic and Hellenic traditions by translating the former into the latter will not form the appropriate basis for the kinds of difficult dialogues that are necessary—and that Benedict himself calls for so movingly.[6] Third, to return to an issue that emerged earlier in this book, a dialogical *logos* that could move us toward rethinking European identity and "the West" will engage in a "universalizing" discourse, but must do so carefully. A broad array of contemporary thinkers has addressed the need not to abandon universalism to an embrace of particularism or—one of Ratzinger's most oft-mentioned harbingers of catastrophe—"relativism." Any form of *logos* (here I agree with Hegel and Habermas) is rooted in a particular historical, social context that it simultaneously transcends. What has too often happened—here with truly catastrophic results—is that a Western, even European *logos* has set itself up monologically in opposition to others, allowing only a "hellenized," Christian, Orientalist, or scientific modality the right to speak. I share the goal of Immanuel Wallerstein: "The issue before us today is how we may move beyond European universalism—this last perverse justification of the existing world order—to something much more difficult to achieve: a universal universalism, which refuses essential-

---

5. The pope's understanding and deployment of rhetoric may be more complex than indicated here. He does refer to *logos* and "persuasion" in the Regensburg lecture. And a case could be made that far from making a naive mistake concerning the rhetorical context of that lecture, he cannily exploited it. That is, on the one hand it seems that he did not take into account the public, indeed global nature of his university lecture (James Schall's point); on the other, perhaps he used the incendiary quote precisely to *create* global interest in his speech.

6. "In this sense theology rightly belongs in the university and within the wide-ranging dialogue of sciences, not merely as a historical discipline and one of the human sciences, but precisely as theology, as inquiry into the rationality of faith. Only thus do we become capable of that genuine dialogue of cultures and religions so urgently needed today" (*Lecture,* 145).

ist characterization of social reality, historicizes both the universal and the particular, [and] unifies the so-called scientific and humanistic into a single epistemology" (*European Universalism,* 79). And finally, this *logos* must be self-reflexively critical. I end therefore by agreeing with Tariq Ramadan's statement from his response to the Regensburg lecture published in *Time* magazine (November 27, 2006): "What the West needs most today is not so much a dialogue with other civilizations but an honest dialogue with itself—one that acknowledges those traditions within Western civilization that are almost never recognized."

🍂 BIBLIOGRAPHY

Agamben, Giorgio. *The Time That Remains: A Commentary on the Letter to the Romans.* Palo Alto: Stanford University Press, 2005.

Allison, Henry E. *Kant's Transcendental Idealism: An Interpretation and Defense.* 1983. Revised edition, New Haven, CT: Yale University Press, 2004.

Altizer, Thomas. *The Gospel of Christian Atheism.* Philadelphia: Westminster, 1966.

———. "Overt Language about the Death of God—In Retrospect." *Christian Century,* June 7–14, 1978, 624–27. http://www.religion-online.

———, ed. *Toward a New Christianity: Readings in the Death of God Theology.* New York: Harcourt, Brace and World, 1967.

Altizer, Thomas, and William Hamilton. *Radical Theology and the Death of God.* New York: Bobbs-Merrill, 1966.

Arendt, Hannah, and Karl Jaspers. *Briefwechsel 1926–1969.* Edited by Lotte Köhler and Hans Saner. Munich: Piper Verlag, 1985.

Asad, Talal. *Formations of the Secular: Christianity, Islam, Modernity.* Stanford: Stanford University Press, 2003.

———. *Genealogies of Religion: Discipline and Reason in Christianity and Islam.* Baltimore: Johns Hopkins University Press, 1993.

Badiou, Alain. *Being and Event.* 1988. Translated by Oliver Feltham. New York: Continuum, 2005.

———. *Saint Paul: La fondation de l'universalisme.* Paris: Presses universitaires de France, 1977.

Balibar, Étienne. *We, the People of Europe? Reflections on Transnational Citizenship.* Translated by James Swenson. Princeton, NJ: Princeton University Press, 2003.

Balthasar, Hans Urs von. *The Theology of Karl Barth.* 1962. Translated by John Drury. New York: Holt, Rinehart and Winston, 1971.

Bambach, Charles. *Heidegger's Roots: Nietzsche, National Socialism, and the Greeks.* Ithaca, NY: Cornell University Press, 2003.

Barth, Hans-Martin. *Atheismus und Orthodoxie: Analysen und Modelle christlicher Apologetik im 17. Jahrhundert.* Göttingen: Vandenhoeck und Ruprecht, 1971.

Barth, Karl. *Der Römerbrief.* 1919, 1922. Zurich: Theologischer Verlag, 1984.

———. *Die kirchliche Dogmatik.* Vol. 1, *Die Lehre vom Wort Gottes.* 1932. Zollikon-Zurich: Evangelischer Verlag, 1955.

———. *Die protestantische Theologie im 19. Jahrhundert: Ihre Vorgeschichte und Geschichte.* 1946. Zurich: Theologischer Verlag, 1981.

———. *The Epistle to the Romans.* Translated by Edwyn C. Hoskyns. New York: Oxford University Press, 1933.

———. *A Karl-Barth Reader.* Edited by Rolf Joachim Erler and Reiner Marquard. Translated by Geoffrey W. Bromiley. Grand Rapids, MI: William B. Eerdmans, 1986.

——. *Theology and Church: Shorter Writings 1920–1928.* Translated by Louise Pettibone Smith. New York: Harper and Row, 1962.

——. *Witness to the Word: A Commentary on John I; Lectures at Münster in 1925 and Bonn in 1933.* Edited by Walther Fürst. Translated by Geoffrey W. Bromiley. Grand Rapids, MI: William B. Eerdmans, 1986.

Barth, Karl, and Rudolf Bultmann. *Briefwechsel 1911–1966.* 2nd ed. Edited by Bernd Jaspert. Zurich: Theologischer Verlag, 1994.

Baur, Ferdinand Christian. *Historisch-kritische Untersuchungen zum Neuen Testament.* In *Ausgewählte Werke in Einzelausgaben,* edited by Klaus Scholder. Stuttgart-Bad Cannstatt: Friedrich Frommann Verlag (Günther Holzboog), 1963.

Beach, Edward Allen. *The Potencies of God(s): Schelling's Philosophy of Mythology.* Albany: State University of New York, 1994.

Beets, M.G.J. *The Wordless Voice: A Philosopher's Approach to St. John's Gospel.* Baarn, Netherlands: Duna, 2003.

Beiser, Frederick. *The Fate of Reason: German Philosophy from Kant to Fichte.* Cambridge, MA: Harvard University Press, 1987.

Bencivenga, Ermanno. *Logic and Other Nonsense: The Case of Anselm and His God.* Princeton, NJ: Princeton University Press, 1993.

Benedict XVI. *See* Ratzinger, Joseph Cardinal (Pope Benedict XVI).

Benjamin, Walter. "Kapitalismus als Religion." In *Gesammelte Schriften,* vol. 6, *Fragmente vermischten Inhalts, autobiographische Schriften,* edited by Rolf Tiedemann and Hermann Schweppenhäuser. Frankfurt am Main: Suhrkamp, 1986.

Benz, Ernst. *Nietzsches Ideen zur Geschichte des Christentums.* Stuttgart: W. Kohlhammer, 1938.

Berger, Peter L. *The Sacred Canopy: Elements of a Sociological Theory of Religion.* New York: Doubleday, 1967.

Biser, Eugen. *"Gott ist tot": Nietzsches Destruktion des christlichen Bewußtseins.* Munich: Kösel Verlag, 1962.

Bleicher, Josef. *Contemporary Hermeneutics: Hermeneutics as Method, Philosophy and Critique.* London: Routledge and Kegan Paul, 1980.

Blond, Phillip, ed. *Post-Secular Philosophy: Between Philosophy and Theology.* London: Routledge, 1998.

Blumenberg, Hans. *Die Legitmität der Neuzeit.* Frankfurt am Main: Suhrkamp, 1966.

——. *The Legitimacy of the Modern Age.* Translated by Robert Wallace. Cambridge, MA: MIT Press, 1983.

Bowie, Andrew. *Schelling and Modern European Philosophy: An Introduction.* London: Routledge, 1993.

Breuninger, Renate, and Peter Welsen, eds. *Religion und Rationalität.* Würzburg: Köningshausen und Newmann, 2000.

Browning, Don S., and Francis Schlüssler Firenza, eds. *Habermas, Modernity, and Public Theology.* New York: Crossroad, 1992.

Brunner, Emil. *Offenbarung und Vernunft: Die Lehre von der christlichen Glaubenserkenntnis.* Zurich: Zwingli-Verlag, 1941.

Buber, Martin. *Das Problem des Menschen.* Heidelberg: Verlag Lambert Schneider, 1948.

——. *Die Schriften über das dialogische Prinzip (Ich und Du, Zwiesprache, Die Frage nach dem Einzelnen, Elemente des Zwischenmenschlichen, mit einem Nachwort).* 1954. Heidelberg: Verlag Lambert Schneider, 1984.

——. *Gottesfinsternis: Betrachtungen zur Beziehung zwischen Religion und Philosophie.* Zurich: Manesse Verlag, 1953.

——. *Werke.* Vol. 2, *Schriften zur Bibel.* Munich: Kosel-Verlag, 1962.

——. *Werke.* Vol. 3, *Schriften zum Chassidismus.* Munich: Kosel-Verlag, 1962.

Buckley, Michael J. *At the Origins of Modern Atheism.* New Haven, CT: Yale University Press, 1987.

Bultmann, Rudolf. *Glauben und Verstehen: Gesammelte Aufsätze.* 4 vols. Tübingen: J.C.B. Mohr (Paul Siebeck), 1933, 1961, 1962, 1965.

——. *The Gospel of John.* Translated by G.R. Beasley-Murray. Philadelphia: Westminster, 1971.

——. *Jesus and the Word.* 1926. Translated by Louise Pettibone-Smith and Erminie Huntress. New York: Charles Scribner's Sons, 1958.

——. "Reflexionen zum Denkweg Martin Heideggers nach der Darstellung von Otto Pöggeler." In *Briefwechsel 1925–1975.* Edited by Andreas Grossmann. Frankfurt: Klostermann, 2009.

Caputo, John D. *The Prayers and Tears of Jacques Derrida.* Bloomington: Indiana University Press, 1997.

——. *The Weakness of the God: A Theology of the Event.* Bloomington: Indiana University Press, 2006.

Casper, Bernhard. *Das dialogische Denken: Eine Untersuchung der religionsphilosophischen Bedeutung Franz Rosenzweigs, Ferdinand Ebners und Martin Bubers.* Freiburg: Herder Verlag, 1967.

Cassirer, Ernst. *Kants Leben und Lehre. Kants Werke,* Vol. 11. Berlin: Bruno Cassirer, 1918.

Cobb, John B., Jr. *Christian Faith after the Death of God.* Philadelphia: Westminster, 1970.

Cobb, John B., and D.R. Griffin. *Process Theology: An Introductory Exposition.* Philadelphia: Westminster, 1976.

Cohen, Hermann. *Das Prinzip der Infinitesimalmethode und seine Geschichte: Ein Kapitel zur Grundlegung der Erkenntniskritik.* 1883. Frankfurt am Main: Suhrkamp, 1968.

——. *Logik der reinen Erkenntnis.* Berlin: B. Cassirer, 1914.

——. *Religion der Vernunft aus den Quellen des Judentums.* 1919. Cologne: J. Metzler, 1959.

Connolly, William E. *Political Theory and Modernity.* Oxford: Basil Blackwell, 1988.

——. *Why I Am Not a Secularist.* Minneapolis: University of Minnesota Press, 1999.

Cooper, John Charles. *The Roots of the Radical Theology.* Philadelphia: Westminster Press, 1967.

Cox, Harvey. *The Secular City: Secularization and Urbanization in Theological Perspective.* New York: Macmillan, 1965.

Crowe, Benjamin D. "Dilthey's Philosophy of Religion in the 'Critique of Historical Reason': 1880–1910." *Journal of the History of Ideas* 66, no. 2 (2005): 265–83.

Culpepper, R. Alan. *The Gospel and Letters of John.* Nashville: Abingdon, 1998.

Cunningham, Conor. *Genealogy of Nihilism: Philosophies of Nothing and the Difference of Theology.* New York: Routledge, 2002.

Damrosch, Leopold, Jr. "Hobbes as Reformation Theologian: Implications of the Free-Will Controversy." *Journal of the History of Ideas* 40, no. 3 (July–September, 1979): 339–52.

Dannemann, Ulrich. *Theologie und Politik im Denken Karl Barths.* Munich: Kaiser Verlag, 1977.

Dawkins, Richard. *The God Delusion.* Boston: Houghton Mifflin, 2006.

Dennett, Daniel. *Breaking the Spell: Religion as a Natural Phenomenon.* New York: Viking, 2006.

Derrida, Jacques. "Interpretations at War: Kant, the Jew, the German." *New Literary History* 22, no. 1 (Winter 1991): 39–95.

Derrida, Jacques, and Gianni Vattimo. *Religion.* Stanford: Stanford University Press, 1996.

Descartes, René. *Discourse on Method and the Meditations.* Translated by John Veitch. New York: Cosimo, 2008.

———. *Regulae ad directionem ingenii: Rules for the Direction of the Natural Intelligence; A Bilingual Edition of the Cartesian Treatise on Method.* Edited and translated by George Heffernan. Amsterdam: Rodopi, 1998.

Dethloff, Klaus, Ludwig Nagl, and Friedrich Wolfram, eds. *Religion, Moderne, Postmoderne: Philosophisch-theologische Erkundungen.* Schriften der Österreichischen Gesellschaft für Religionsphilosophie. Berlin: Parerga Verlag, 2002.

Dietzgen, Joseph. "The Religion of Social Democracy: Six Sermons." 1870–75. In *Philosophical Essays,* 90–154. Chicago: Charles H. Kerr, 1906.

Dilthey, Wilhelm. *Das Leben Schleiermachers.* Berlin: W. de Gruÿter, 1922.

———. *Die Jugendgeschichte Hegels.* In *Abhandlungen der Preußischen Akademie der Wissenschaften.* Berlin, 1905.

———. *Einleitung in die Geisteswissenschaften: Versuch einer Grundlegung für das Studium der Gesellschaft und der Geschichte.* 3 vols. 1883. Stuttgart: B.G. Teubner Verlagsgesellschaft, 1966.

Dorrien, Gary. "The Origins of Postliberalism." *Christian Century,* July 4–11, 2001, 16–21.

Eckert, Michael. "Gefühl und Rationalität: Schleiermachers Religionsbegriff." In Breuninger and Welsen, *Religion und Rationalität,* 51–67.

Ehrenberg, Hans. *Disputation: Drei Bücher vom deutschen Idealismus: Fichte, Schelling, Hegel.* Munich: Drei Masken Verlag, 1923.

Encyclopedia of Religion and Ethics. New York: C. Scribner's Sons, 1951.

Engels, Friedrich. *Ludwig Feuerbach and the Outcome of Classical German Philosophy.* 1888. New York: AMS Press, 1981.

Erasmus, Desiderius. *Ausgewählte Schriften.* Edited by Werner Welzig. Translated by Winfried Lesowsky. Vol. 4, *De libero arbitrio diatribe sive collatio (Gespräch oder Unterredung über den freien Willen)* and *Hyperaspistes diatribae adversus servum arbitrium Martini Lutheri. Liber Primus (Erstes Buch der Unterredung "Hyperaspistes" gegen den "unfreien Willen" Martin Luthers).* Darmstadt: Wissenschaftliche Buchgesellschaft, 1969.

——. *Vom freien Willen.* Translated by Otto Schumacher. Göttingen: Vandenhoeck & Ruprecht, 1998.

Erasmus, Desiderius, and Martin Luther. *Discourse on Free Will.* Edited and translated by Ernst F. Winter. New York: Continuum (Frederick Ungar), 1999.

——. *Free Will and Salvation.* Edited by E. Gordon Rupp and Philip S. Watson. Louisville: Westminster John Knox, 2006.

Faber, Richard, Eveline Goodman-Thau, and Thomas Macho, eds. *Abendländische Eschatologie: Ad Jacob Taubes.* Würzburg: Königshausen & Neumann, 2001.

Farias, Victor. *Heidegger and Nazism.* Translated by Joseph Margolis and Tom Rockmore. Philadelphia: Temple University Press, 1989.

Feuerbach, Ludwig. *The Essence of Christianity.* Translated by George Eliot. New York: Harper & Row, 1957.

——. *Sämmtliche Werke.* 7 vols. Edited by Wilhelm Bolin and Friedrich Jodl. Stuttgart: Fr. Frommanns Verlag (E. Hauff), 1904.

Frank, Manfred. *Das individuelle Allgemeine: Textstrukturierung und -interpretation nach Schleiermacher.* Frankfurt am Main: Suhrkamp, 1977.

——. *Der unendliche Mangel am Sein: Schellings Hegelkritik und die Anfänge der Marxischen Dialektik.* Frankfurt am Main: Suhrkamp, 1975.

Frei, Hans W. *The Eclipse of Biblical Narrative: A Study in Eighteenth and Nineteenth Century Hermeneutics.* New Haven, CT: Yale University Press, 1974.

Fuchs, Ernst. *Marburger Hermeneutik.* Tübingen: J.C.B. Mohr (Paul Siebeck), 1968.

Fürst, Walter, ed. "Dialektische Theologie." In *Scheidung und Bewährung 1933–1936: Aufsätze, Gutachten und Erklärungen.* Munich: Chr. Kaiser Verlag, 1966.

Gadamer, Hans-Georg. "Mythos und Vernunft." In *Kleine Schriften,* 4:48–53. Tübingen: Mohr, 1977.

——. *Truth and Method.* Translated by Joel Weinsheimer and Donald G. Marshall. New York: Crossroad, 1989.

——. *Wahrheit und Methode: Grundzüge einer philosophischen Hermeneutik.* Tübingen: Mohr, 1960.

Garaudy, Roger. *Dieu est mort.* Paris: Presses Universitaires de France, 1962.

Garrett, Aaron V. *Meaning in Spinoza's Ethics.* Cambridge: Cambridge University Press, 2003.

Geis, Robert Raphael, and Hans-Joachim Kraus, eds. *Versuche des Verstehens: Dokumente jüdisch-christlicher Begegnung aus den Jahren 1918–1933.* Munich: Chr. Kaiser Verlag, 1966.

Gestrich, Christof. *Neuzeitliches Denken und die Spaltung der dialektischen Theologie: Zur Frage der natürlichen Theologie.* Tübingen: J.C.B Mohr (Paul Siebeck), 1977.

Göckeritz, Hermann Götz. "Friedrich Gogarten." In *Profile des Luthertums: Biographien zum 20. Jahrhundert,* edited by Wolf-Dieter Hauschild, 215–58. Gütersloh, 1998.

Goethe, Johann Wolfgang von. *Faust: Der Tragödie erster Teil.* Edited by Erich Trunz. Munich: C.H. Beck, 1972.

Goetz, Ronald. "The Karl Barth Centennial: An Appreciative Critique." *Christian Century,* May 7, 1986, 458.

Gogarten, Friedrich. Afterword to *Vom unfreien Willen,* by Martin Luther. Edited by Justus Jonas. Munich: Chr. Kaiser Verlag, 1924.

——. *Die Bekenntnis der Kirche.* Jena: Eugen Diederich, 1934.

——. *Die religiöse Entscheidung.* 1921. Jena: Eugen Diederich, 1924.

——. *Die Wirklichkeit des Glaubens: Zum Problem des Subjektivismus in der Theologie.* Stuttgart: Friedrich Vorwerk, 1957.

——. *Einheit von Evangelium und Volkstum?* Hamburg: Hanseatische Verlagsanstalt, 1933.

——. *Ich glaube an den dreieinigen Gott: Eine Untersuchung über Glauben und Geschichte.* Jena, 1926.

——. *Politische Ethik: Versuch einer Grundlegung.* Jena: Eugen Diederich, 1932.

——. *Theologische Tradition und theologische Arbeit: Geistesgeschichte oder Theologie?* Leipzig: J.C. Hinrich'sche Buchhandlung, 1927.

——. *Verhängnis und Hoffnung der Neuzeit: Die Säkularisierung als theologisches Problem.* Stuttgart: Vorwerk, 1953.

——. *Weltanschauung und Glaube.* Berlin: Furche-Verlag, 1937.

——. *Wider die Ächtung der Autorität.* Jena: Eugen Diederich, n.d.

Gollwitzer, Helmut. *The Existence of God as Confessed by Faith.* Translated by James W. Leitch. London: SCM Press, 1965.

González, Justo L. *The Story of Christianity.* 2 vols. New York: HarperCollins, 1984.

Graf, Friedrich Wilhelm, and Falk Wagner, eds. *Die Flucht in die Begriff: Materialien zu Hegels Religionsphilosophie.* Stuttgart: Klett-Cotta, 1982.

Habermas, Jürgen. *Das Absolute und die Geschichte: Die Zwiespältigkeit der Philosophie Schellings.* Bonn: H. Bouvier, 1954.

——. *The Philosophical Discourse of Modernity: Twelve Lectures.* Translated by Frederick Lawrence. Cambridge: Polity, 1987.

——. *Postmetaphysical Thinking.* Cambridge, MA: MIT Press, 1992.

——. *Religion and Rationality: Essays on Reason, God, and Modernity.* Edited and with an introduction by Eduardo Mendieta. Cambridge, MA: MIT Press, 2002.

Habermas, Jürgen, and Joseph Ratzinger. *The Dialectics of Secularization: On Reason and Religion.* Translated by Brian McNeil. San Francisco: Ignatius Press, 2006.

Handbuch der Dogmengeschichte. Freiburg, 1982.

Harnack, Adolf von. *Das Wesen des Christentums.* 1900. Introduction by Rudolf Bultmann. Stuttgart: Ehrenfried Klotz Verlag, 1950.

Harris, Sam. *The End of Faith: Religion, Terror, and the Future of Reason.* New York: W.W. Norton, 2004.

Hegel, Georg Wilhelm Friedrich. "Differenz des Fichteschen und Schellingschen Systems der Philosophie." In *Jenaer Schriften 1801–1807,* vol. 2 of *Theorie Werkausgabe.* Frankfurt am Main: Suhrkamp, 1970.

——. *Enzyklopädie der philosophischen Wissenschaften.* Vols. 8, 9, 10 of *Theorie Werkausgabe.* Frankfurt am Main: Suhrkamp, 1970.

——. *Frühe Schriften.* Vol. 1 of *Theorie Werkausgabe.* Frankfurt am Main: Suhrkamp, 1970.

——. "Glauben und Wissen oder Reflexionsphilosophie der Subjektivität in der Vollständigkeit ihrer Formen als Kantische, Jacobische und Fichtesche Philosophie." In *Jenaer Schriften 1801–1807,* vol. 2 of *Theorie Werkausgabe.* Frankfurt am Main: Suhrkamp, 1970.

——. *Phänomenologie des Geistes.* Vol. 3 of *Theorie Werkausgabe.* Frankfurt am Main: Suhrkamp, 1970.

——. *Vorlesungen über die Beweise vom Dasein Gottes.* Vol. 17 of *Theorie Werkausgabe.* Frankfurt am Main: Suhrkamp, 1970.

——. *Vorlesungen über die Geschichte der Philosophie II.* Vol. 19 of *Theorie Werkausgabe.* Frankfurt am Main: Suhrkamp, 1970.

——. *Vorlesungen über die Philosophie der Religion.* Vols. 16, 17 of *Theorie Werkausgabe.* Frankfurt am Main: Suhrkamp, 1970.

——. "Vorrede zu Hinrichs' Religionsphilosophie." Orig. in H. Fr. W. Hinrichs, *Die Religion im inneren Verhältnisse zur Wissenschaft,* Heidelberg, 1822. In vol. 17 of *Theorie Werkausgabe.* Frankfurt am Main: Suhrkamp, 1970.

——. *Wissenschaft der Logik.* Vols. 5, 6 of *Theorie Werkausgabe.* Frankfurt am Main: Suhrkamp, 1970.

Hegel-Jahrbuch. Glauben und Wissen. 2 vols. Edited by Andreas Arndt, Karol Bal, and Henning Ottmann. Berlin: Academie Verlag, 2003, 2004.

Heidegger, Martin. *Beiträge zur Philosophie (Vom Ereignis).* Frankfurt am Main: Vittorio Klostermann, 1989.

——. *Contributions to Philosophy (from Enowning).* Translated by Parvis Emad and Kenneth Maly. Bloomington: Indiana University Press, 1999.

——. "Einleitung in die Phänomenologie der Religion" (1920/21) and "Die philosophischen Grundlagen der mittelalterlichen Mystik" (1918/19). In *Phänomenologie des religiösen Lebens,* vol. 60 of *Gesamtausgabe.* Frankfurt am Main: Vittorio Klostermann, 1995.

——. *Gesamtausgabe.* Frankfurt am Main: Vittorio Klostermann, 1977–.

——. "Phänomenologie und Theologie." In *Wegmarken,* vol. 9 of *Gesamtausgabe.* Frankfurt am Main: Vittorio Klostermann, 1976.

——. *Sein und Zeit.* Frankfurt am Main: Vittorio Klostermann, 1977.

——. *Über den Humanismus.* Frankfurt am Main: Vittorio Klostermann, 1949.

——. "Über Nietzsches Wort 'Gott ist tot.'" In *Holzwege,* vol. 5 of *Gesamtausgabe.* Frankfurt am Main: Vittorio Klostermann, 1977.

——. *Unterwegs zur Sprache.* Vol. 12 of *Gesamtausgabe.* Frankfurt am Main: Vittorio Klostermann, 1985.

——. *Wegmarken.* Frankfurt am Main: Vittorio Klostermann, 1967.

——. *Zur Bestimmung der Philosophie.* Vol. 56/57 of *Gesamtausgabe.* Frankfurt am Main: Vittorio Klostermann, 1987.

Heidegger, Martin, and Hannah Arendt. *Briefe 1925 bis 1975.* Edited by Ursula Ludz. Frankfurt am Main: Vittorio Klostermann, 1998.

Heraclitus. *The Fragments of the Work of Heraclitus of Ephesus on Nature.* Translated from the Greek text of Bywater by G. T. W. Patrick. Baltimore: N. Murray, 1889.

Herrmann, Werner. *Der Verkehr des Christen mit Gott (im Anschluss an Luther dargestellt).* 5th/6th ed. Stuttgart: J. G. Cottasche Buchhandlung, 1908.

Hick, John. *The Existence of God.* New York: Macmillan, 1964.

Hitchens, Christopher. *God Is Not Great: How Religion Poisons Everything.* New York: Twelve, 2007.

Horkheimer, Max. *Zur Kritik der instrumentellen Vernunft: Aus den Vorträgen und Aufzeichnungen seit Kriegsende.* Edited by Alfred Schmidt. Frankfurt am Main: Fischer Taschenbuch Verlag, 1997.

Horton, Douglas. "God Lets Loose Karl Barth." *Christian Century,* February 16, 1928.

Hübner, Kurt. *Die Wahrheit des Mythos.* Munich: Beck, 1985.

Hume, David. *Dialogues concerning Natural Religion.* 1779. London: Routledge, 1991.

Ijsseling, Samuel. *Rhetoric and Philosophy in Conflict.* The Hague: Martinus Nijhoff, 1976.

Israel, Jonathan I. *Radical Enlightenment: Philosophy and the Making of Modernity, 1650–1750.* Oxford: Oxford University Press, 2001.

Jachmann, Reinhold Bernhard. *Prüfung der Kantischen Religionsphilosophie in Hinsicht auf die ihr beygelegte Aehnlichkeit mit dem reinen Mystizism.* 1800. Edited by Robert Theis. Hildesheim: Georg Olms Verlag, 1999.

Jacobi, Friedrich Heinrich. *Über die Lehre des Spinoza in Briefen an den Herrn Moses Mendelssohn.* 1785. Hamburg: Felix Meiner Verlag, 2000.

Jaeschke, Walter. *Reason in Religion: The Foundations of Hegel's Philosophy of Religion.* Translated by J. Michael Stewart and Peter C. Hodgson. Berkeley and Los Angeles: University of California Press, 1990.

Jaspers, Karl. *Chiffren der Transzendenz.* Edited by H. Saner. Munich: Piper, 1977.

——. *Der philosophische Glaube.* Munich: Piper, 1985.

——. *Nietzsche und das Christentum.* Hameln: Verlag der Bücherstube Fritz Steifert, 1938.

Jaspers, Karl, and Rudolf Bultmann. *Die Frage der Entmythologisierung.* Munich: R. Piper, 1954.

Jenson, Robert W. *God after God: The God of the Past and the God of the Future, Seen in the Work of Karl Barth.* Indianapolis: Bobbs-Merrill, 1969.

Jonas, Hans. *Philosophische Untersuchungen und metaphysische Vermutungen.* Frankfurt am Main: Insel Verlag, 1992.

Kant, Immanuel. *Briefe von und an Kant.* Vols. 9, 10, and 11 of *Werke.* Berlin: Bruno Cassirer, 1921.

——. *The Conflict of the Faculties (Der Streit der Fakultäten).* Translated by Mary J. Gregor. Lincoln: University of Nebraska Press, 1992.

——. *The Critique of Judgment.* Translated by Werner Pluhar. Indianapolis: Hackett, 1987.

——. *Lectures on Philosophical Theology.* Translated by Allen W. Wood and Gertrude M. Clark. Ithaca, NY: Cornell University Press, 1978.

——. *Religion innerhalb der Grenzen der bloßen Vernunft.* Akademie-Textausgabe Vol. 6. Berlin: Walter de Gruyter, 1968.

——. *Werke.* Akademie-Textausg. Unveränderter photomechanischer Abdruck des Textes der Ausgabe von der Preussischen Akademie der Wissenschaften. 9 vols. Berlin: de Gruyter, 1968.

Kantzenbach, Friedrich Wilhelm. "Idealsitische Religionsphilosophie und Theologie der Aufklärung." In *Idealismus und Aufklärung: Kontinuität und Kritik der Aufklärung in Philosophie und Poesie um 1800,* edited by Christoph Jamme and Gerhard Kurz, 97–114. Stuttgart: Klett-Cotta, 1988.

Kasper, W. *Das Absolute in der Geschichte: Philosophie und Theologie der Geschichte in der Spätphilosophie Schellings.* Mainz: M. Grünewald, 1965.

Kaufmann, Walter. *Critique of Religion and Philosophy.* Princeton, NJ: Princeton University Press, 1958.

Kelber, Wilhelm. *Die Logoslehre von Heraklit bis Origenes.* Stuttgart: Verlag Urachhaus, 1958.

Kierkegaard, Søren. *Fear and Trembling.* Translated by Walter Lowrie. Princeton, NJ: Princeton University Press, 1941.

Knapp, Markus, and Theo Kobusch, eds. *Religion-Metaphysik(kritik)-Theologie im Kontext der Moderne/Postmoderne.* Berlin: Walter de Gruyter, 2001.

Körtner, Ulrich, ed. *Geist und Verstehen: Perspektiven hermeneutische Theologie.* Neukirchen-Vluyn: Neukirchener, 2000.

Koslowski, Peter, ed. *Philosophischer Dialog der Religionen statt Zusammenstoß der Kulturen im Prozeß der Globalisierung.* Munich: Wilhelm Fink Verlag, 2002.

Krokow, Christian Graf von. *Die Entscheidung: Eine Untersuchung über Ernst Jünger, Carl Schmitt, Martin Heidegger.* 1958. Frankfurt: Campus Verlag, 1990.

Kuhn, Thomas S. *The Structure of Scientific Revolutions.* Chicago: University of Chicago Press, 1962.

Küng, Hans. *Existiert Gott? Antwort auf die Gottesfrage der Neuzeit.* 1978. Munich: Deutscher Taschenbuchverlag, 1981.

Kutschera, Franz von. *Vernunft und Glaube.* Berlin: Walter de Gruyter, 1990.

Lambert, César. *Philosophie und Welt beim jungen Heidegger.* Frankfurt am Main: Peter Lang, 2002.

Latour, Bruno. *We Have Never Been Modern.* Translated by Catherine Porter. 1991. Cambridge, MA: Harvard University Press, 1993.

Lawlor, Leonard. *Derrida and Husserl: The Basic Problem of Phenomenology.* Bloomington: Indiana University Press, 2002.

Lazier, Benjamin. *God Interrupted: Heresy and the European Imagination between the World Wars.* Princeton, NJ: Princeton University Press, 2008.

Leibniz, Gottfried Wilhelm. *Discourse on Metaphysics, Correspondence with Arnauld, and Monadology.* Translated by George R. Montgomery. Chicago: Open Court Publishing, 1902.

———. *Kleine Schriften zur Metaphysik.* Edited and translated by Hans Heinz Holz. Frankfurt am Main: Insel-Verlag, 1965.

———. *Philosophical Writings.* Edited by G.H.R. Parkinson. North Clarendon, VT: J.M. Dent (Everyman), 1995.

Leiner, Martin. "Martin Buber und Friedrich Gogarten." *Im Gespräch: Die Zeitschrift der Martin Buber Gesellschaft.* Heft 3, November 2001.

Leiter, Brian. *Nietzsche on Morality.* New York: Routledge, 2002.

Lessing, Gotthold Ephraim. *Philosophical and Theological Writings.* Edited by H.B. Nisbet. Cambridge: Cambridge University Press, 2005.

———. *Theological Writings.* Edited and translated by Henry Chadwick. Stanford: Stanford University Press, 1983.

Leuze, Reinhard. *Die außerchristlichen Religionen bei Hegel.* Göttingen: Vandenhoeck and Ruprecht, 1975.

Lévinas, Emmanuel. *Dieu, la mort et le temps.* Paris: Editions Grasset, 1993.

———. *Gott, der Tod und die Zeit.* Translated by Astrid Nettling and Ulrike Wasel. Vienna: Passagen-Verlag, 1996.

———. *Humanisme de l'autre homme.* Montpellier: Fata Morgana, 1972.

———. "Martin Buber, Gabriel Marcel und die Philosophie." Translated by Yehoshua Amir. In *Martin Buber: Bilanz seines Denkens,* edited by Jochanan Block and Haim Gordon, 319–37. Freiburg: Herder, 1983.

———. *Totalité et infini: Essai sur l'extériorité.* The Hague: Nijhoff, 1961.

———. *Totality and Infinity: An Essay on Exteriority.* Translated by Alphonso Lingis. Pittsburgh: Duquesne University Press, 1969.

Locke, John. *An Essay concerning Human Understanding.* 1689, Oxford: Oxford University Press, 1975.

Löwith, Karl. *Aufsätze und Vorträge 1930–1970.* Stuttgart: Verlag W. Kohlhammer, 1971.

———. *Heidegger: Denker in dürftiger Zeit.* Vol. 8 of *Sämtliche* Schriften. Stuttgart: J.B. Metzlersche Verlagsbuchhandlung, 1984.

———. "Martin Heidegger's Political Decisionism and Friedrich Gogarten's Theological Decisionism." In *Martin Heidegger and European Nihilism,* edited by Richard Wolin, 159–69. New York: Columbia University Press, 1995.

———. *Von Hegel zu Nietzsche: Der revolutionäre Bruch im Denken des neunzehnten Jahrhunderts.* 1939. Stuttgart: W. Kohlhammer Verlag, 1953.

Lubac, Henri de. *The Drama of Atheist Humanism.* Translated by Edith M. Riley. New York: Sheed & Ward, 1950.

Luhmann, Niklas. *Die Religion der Gesellschaft.* Edited by André Kieserling. Frankfurt am Main: Suhrkamp, 2000.

Lukács, Georg. *The Young Hegel: Studies in the Relations between Dialectics and Economics.* Translated by Rodney Livingstone. London: Merlin, 1975.

Luther, Martin. *De servo arbitrio.* In vol. 3 of *Studienausgabe.* Edited by Hans-Ulrich Delius. Berlin: Evangelische Verlangsanstalt, 1983.

———. *Sämtliche Schriften.* Edited by Johann Georg Walch. Vol. 18, *Reformations-Schriften: Dogmatisch-polemische Schriften.* (Includes Erasmus–Luther exchanges.) Groß Oensingen: Verlag der Lutherischen Buchhandlung Heinrich Harms, 1986 (repr. of 1888 St. Louis edition).

———. *Vom unfreien Willen.* Edited and afterword by Friedrich Gogarten. Translated by Justus Jonas. Munich: Chr. Kaiser Verlag, 1924.

Luther, Martin, and Desiderius Erasmus. *Luther and Erasmus: Free Will and Salvation.* Translated and edited by E. Gordon Rupp and P. Watson. Philadelphia: Westminster, 1969.

Lypp, Bernhard. "Über die Wurzeln dialektischer Begriffsbildung in Hegels Kritik an Kants Ethik." In *Seminar: Dialektik in der Philosophie Hegels,* edited by Rolf-Peter Horstmann. Frankfurt am Main: Suhrkamp, 1978.

MacIntyre, Alasdair C., and Paul Ricoeur. *The Religious Significance of Atheism.* New York: Columbia University Press, 1969.

Macquarrie, John. *An Existentialist Theology: A Comparison of Heidegger and Bultmann.* New York: Harper and Row, 1955.

Mariña, Jacqueline, ed. *The Cambridge Companion to Friedrich Schleiermacher.* Cambridge: Cambridge University Press, 2005.

Marion, Jean-Luc. *God without Being (Dieu sans l'être).* Translated by Thomas A. Carlson. Chicago: University of Chicago Press, 1991.

———. "Metaphysics and Phenomenology: A Summary for Theologians." In *The Postmodern God: A Theological Reader,* edited by Graham Ward. Oxford: Blackwell, 1997.

Marsden, George M. *The Outrageous Idea of Christian Scholarship.* Oxford: Oxford University Press, 1997.

———. *The Soul of the American University: From Protestant Establishment to Established Nonbelief.* New York: Oxford University Press, 1994.

Martin, James Alfred. *The New Dialogue between Philosophy and Theology.* London: Adam and Charles Black, 1966.

Martin, Michael. *Atheism: A Philosophical Justification.* Philadelphia: Temple University Press, 1990.

Marx, Karl. "Contribution to a Critique of Hegel's *Philosophy of Right* (Introduction)." In *The Marx-Engels Reader,* edited by Robert C. Tucker, 16–25. New York: W.W. Norton, 1978.

McCullough, Lissa, and Brian Schroeder, eds. *Thinking through the Death of God: A Critical Companion to Thomas J.J. Altizer.* Albany: State University of New York Press, 2005.

Mercer, Christia. *Leibniz's Metaphysics: Its Origins and Development.* Cambridge: Cambridge University Press, 2001.

Meyer, Torsten L. *Franz Rosenzweigs "Stern der Erlösung": Ein Beitrag zur Logik der Philosophie: Transzendentalismus—Kategorienlehre—Sprachphilosophie—Metaphysik.* Frankfurt am Main: Peter Lang (Europäischer Verlag der Wissenschaften), 2001.

Milbank, John. *Theology and Social Theory: Beyond Secular Reason.* Cambridge: Basil Blackwell, 1990.

———. *The Word Made Strange: Theology, Language, Culture.* Oxford: Blackwell, 1997.

Milbank, John, Catherine Pickstock, and Graham Ward, eds. *Radical Orthodoxy: A New Theology.* New York: Routledge, 1999.

Miltenberger, Friedrich. *Geschichte der deutschen evangelischen Theologie im 19. und 20. Jahrhundert.* Stuttgart: Verlag W. Kohlhammer, 1981.

Moltmann, Jürgen, ed. *Anfänge der dialektischen Theologie.* 1963. Part 1: Karl Barth, Heinrich Barth, Emil Brunner; Part 2: Rudolf Bultmann, Friedrich Gogarten, Eduard Thurneysen. Munich: Chr. Kaiser Verlag, 1977.

Neuhaus, Richard John, ed. *Biblical Interpretation in Crisis: The Ratzinger Conference on Bible and Church.* Grand Rapids, MI: William B. Eerdmans, 1989.

Newman, Jane O. "The Word Made Print: Luther's 1522 New Testament in an Age of Mechanical Reproduction." *Representations* 11 (Summer 1985): 95–133.

Niebuhr, H. Richard. *Christ and Culture.* New York: Harper and Row, 1951.

Niebuhr, Reinhold, ed. *Karl Marx and Friedrich Engels on Religion.* New York: Schocken Books, 1964.

———. *The Self and the Dramas of History.* New York: Charles Scribner's Sons, 1955.

Nietzsche, Friedrich. *Also sprach Zarathustra.* Vol. 4 of Kritische Studienausgabe. Edited by Giorgio Colli and Mazzino Moninari. Munich: DTV, 1988.

———. *Aus dem Nachlaß der Achtzigerjahre.* Vol. 3 of *Werke.* Edited by Karl Schlechta. Frankfurt am Main: Ullstein, 1972.

———. *Beyond Good and Evil.* Translated by Walter Kaufmann. New York: Vintage, 1966.

———. *Der Antichrist.* Vol. 6 of Kritische Studienausgabe. Edited by Giorgio Colli and Mazzino Moninari. Munich: DTV, 1988.

———. *Die fröhliche Wissenschaft.* Vol. 3 of Kritische Studienausgabe. Edited by Giorgio Colli and Mazzino Moninari. Munich: DTV, 1988.

——. *The Gay Science*. Translated by Walter Kaufmann. New York: Vintage, 1974.

——. *Jenseits von Gut und Böse*. Vol. 5 of Kritische Studienausgabe. Edited by Giorgio Colli and Mazzino Moninari. Munich: DTV, 1988.

——. *Menschliches, Allzumenschliches. Vol. 2 of Kritische Studienausgabe. Edited by Giorgio Colli and Mazzino Moninari. Munich: DTV, 1988.*

——. *Morgenröte*. Vol. 3 of Kritische Studienausgabe. Edited by Giorgio Colli and Mazzino Moninari. Munich: DTV, 1988.

——. *Nachlass*. Vol. 13 of Großoktav-Ausgabe. Leipzig: Alfred Kroener Verlag, 1901–13.

——. *On the Genealogy of Morals*. Translated by Walter Kaufmann. New York: Vintage, 1989.

——. *The Will to Power*. Translated by Walter Kaufmann and R.J. Hollingdale. New York: Vintage, 1968.

——. *Zur Genealogie der Moral*. Vol. 5 of Kritische Studienausgabe. Edited by Giorgio Colli and Mazzino Moninari. Munich: DTV, 1988.

Nolan, Lawrence. "Descartes' Ontological Argument." *The Stanford Encyclopedia of Philosophy* (Summer 2001). Edited by Edward N. Zalta. http://www.plato. stanford.edu/archives/sum2001/entries/descartes-ontological/.

Novalis [Friedrich von Hardenberg]. "Christenheit oder Europa." In *Werke und Briefe*. Munich: Winkler-Verlag, 1968.

Nowak, Kurt. *Schleiermacher: Leben, Werk und Wirkung*. Göttingen: Vandenhoeck und Ruprecht, 2001.

Oppy, Graham. *Ontological Arguments and Belief in God*. New York: Cambridge University Press, 1995.

Origen. *Commentary on the Gospel of St. John*. New York: C. Scribner's Sons, 1951.

——. *Vier Bücher von den Prinzipien*. Edited and translated by Herwig Görgemanns and Heinrich Karpp. Darmstadt: Wissenschaftliche Buchgesellschaft, 1985.

Otto, Rudolf. *Aufsätze, das Numinose betreffend*. Stuttgart: Verlag Friedrich Andreas Perthes, 1923.

——. *Das Heilige: Über das Irrationale in der Idee des Göttlichen und sein Verhältnis zum Rationalen*. 1917. 12th ed. Gotha: Verlag Friedrich Andreas Perthes, 1924.

Pannenberg, Wolfhart. *Theologie und Philosohie: Ihr Verhältnis im Lichte ihrer gemeinsamen Geschichte*. Göttingen: Vandenhoeck und Ruprecht, 1996.

Pascal, Blaise. *Pensées*. 1669. Translated by Honor Levi. Oxford and New York: Oxford University Press, 1995.

Penelhum, Terence. "Natural Belief and Religious Belief in Hume's Philosophy." *Philosophical Quarterly* 33, no. 131 (April 1983): 166–81.

Peperzak, Adriaan Theodor. *Reason in Faith: On the Relevance of Christianity for Philosophy*. New York: Paulist Press, 1999.

Peterson, Michael, William Hasker, Bruce Reichenbach, and David Basinger, eds. *Philosophy of Religion: Selected Readings*. New York: Oxford University Press, 1996.

Pico della Mirandola, Giovanni. *Oration on the Dignity of Man*. 1486. Translated by A. Robert Gaponigri. Chicago: Regnery Gateway, 1956.

Plantinga, Alvin. *Warranted Christian Belief*. New York: Oxford University Press, 2000.

Pöggeler, Otto. *Heidegger in seiner Zeit*. Munich: Wilhelm Fink Verlag, 1999.

——. *Neue Wege mit Heidegger.* Freiburg: Verlag Karl Alber, 1992.

Prolingheuer, Hans. *Der Fall Karl Barth 1934–1935: Chronographie einer Vertreibung.* Neukirchen-Vluyn: Neukirchener Verlag, 1977.

Rahner, Karl, and Joseph Ratzinger. *"In the Beginning . . . ": A Catholic Understanding of Creation and the Fall.* 1986. Translated by Boniface Ramsey. Grand Rapids, MI: William B. Eerdmans, 1990.

——. *Revelation and Tradition.* 1965. Translated by W.J. O'Hara. New York: Herder and Herder, 1966.

Raines, John, ed. *Marx on Religion.* Philadelphia: Temple University Press, 2002.

Ratzinger, Joseph Cardinal (Pope Benedict XVI). *Church, Ecumenism and Politics: New Essays in Ecclesiology.* 1987. New York: Crossroad, 1988.

——. *The Essential Pope Benedict XVI: His Central Writings and Speeches.* Edited by John F. Thornton and Susan B. Varenne. New York: HarperSanFrancisco, 2007.

——. *The Regensburg Lecture.* Edited by James V. Schall. South Bend, IN: St. Augustine's Press, 2007.

——. *Truth and Tolerance: Christian Belief and World Religions.* Translated by Henry Taylor. San Francisco: Ignatius, 2004.

——. *A Turning Point for Europe? The Church in the Modern World: Assessment and Forecast.* 1991. Translated by Brian McNeil. San Francisco: Ignatius, 1994.

——. *Values in a Time of Upheaval.* 2004. Translated by Brian McNeil. New York: Crossroad, 2006.

Reardon, Bernard M.G. *Hegel's Philosophy of Religion.* London: Macmillan, 1977.

Redeker, Martin. *Friedrich Schleiermacher: Leben und Werk (1768 bis 1834).* Berlin: Walter de Gruyter (Sammlung Göschen), 1968.

Reinhold, Karl Leonhard. *Letters on the Kantian Philosophy.* 1787. Cambridge: Cambridge University Press, 2005.

Religion in Geschichte und Gegenwart: Handwörterbuch für Theologie und Religionswissenschaft. Tübingen: Mohr, 1957–65.

Rocker, Stephen. *Hegel's Rational Religion: The Validity of Hegel's Argument for the Identity in Content of Absolute Religion and Absolute Philosophy.* Madison, NJ: Fairleigh Dickinson University Press, 1995.

Rorty, Richard, and Gianni Vattimo. *The Future of Religion.* Edited by Santiago Zabala. New York: Columbia University Press, 2005.

Rosenzweig, Franz. *Arbeitspapiere zur Verdeutschung der Schrift.* In vol. 4 of *Gesammelte Schriften.* The Hague: Martinus Nijhoff, 1976–84.

——. *Der Stern der Erlösung.* Frankfurt am Main: Suhrkamp, 1990.

——. *Zweistromland: Kleinere Schriften zu Glauben und Denken.* In vol. 4 of *Gesammelte Schriften.* The Hague: Martinus Nijhoff, 1976–84.

Russell, Bertrand. *Why I Am Not a Christian and Other Essays on Religion and Related Subjects.* London: Routledge, 2004.

Saine, Thomas. *The Problem of Being Modern; or, The German Pursuit of Enlightenment from Leibniz to the French Revolution.* Detroit: Wayne State University Press, 1997.

Scheffczyk, Leo, ed. *Rationalität: Ihre Entwicklung und ihre Grenzen.* Freiburg: Verlag Karl Alber, 1989.

Schelling, Friedrich. *The Ages of the World: (Fragment) from the Handwritten Remains, Third Version (1815)*. Translated by Jason M. Worth. Albany: State University of New York Press, 2000.

———. *Philosophical Inquiries into the Nature of Human Freedom*. Translated by James Gutman. New York: Open Court, 2003.

———. *Philosophie der Offenbarung*. Darmstadt: Wissenschaftliche Buchgesellschaft, 1959. (Also in *Sämmtliche Werke*, volume 13 [2. Abteilung, volume 3]. Stuttgart: J.G. Cotta'scher Verlag, 1856.)

———. *Werke*. Vol. 4, *Philosophie und Religion* (1804); *Philosophische Untersuchungen über das Wesen der menschlichen Freiheit und die damit zusammenhängenden Gegenstände* (1809); *Die Weltalter: Bruchstück* (1813); Edited by Manfred Schröter. Munich: C.H. Beck'sche Verlagsbuchhandlung, 1965.

———. *Zur Geschichte der neueren Philosophie*. Edited by Manfred Schröter. Munich: C.H. Beck'sche Verlagsbuchhandlung, 1965.

Schleiermacher, Friedrich Ernst Daniel. *Der christlicher Glaube*. 2 vols. 1830. Edited by Martin Redeker. Berlin: Walter de Gruyter, 1960.

———. *On Religion: Speeches to Its Cultured Despisers*. 1799. Translated by John Oman. With an introduction by Rudolf Otto. New York: Harper and Brothers, 1958.

———. *Schleiermacher-Auswahl*. Edited by Heinz Bolli. With an afterword by Karl Barth. Gütersloh: Verlagshaus Gerd Mohn, 1983.

———. *Werke: Auswahl*. 4 vols. Edited by Otto Braun and Johannes Bauer. Aalen: Scientia Verlag, 1981. Vol. 4, *Über die Religion: Reden an die Gebildeten unter ihren Verächtern* (1799) and *Weihnachtsfeier* (1806).

Schmidt, James, ed. *What Is Enlightenment? Eighteenth-Century Questions and Twentieth-Century Answers*. Berkeley and Los Angeles: University of California Press, 1996.

Schmidt-Biggemann, Wilhelm. "Metaphorphosen der Macht. Die Geschichte des Guten und Bösen bei Nietzsche und Max Weber." In *Das Böse: Eine historische Phänomenologie des Unerklärlichen*, edited by Carsten Colpe and Wilhelm Schmidt-Biggemann. Frankfurt: Suhrkamp Taschenbuch Wissenschaft, 1993.

Schmitt, Carl. *The Crisis of Parliamentary Democracy*. Translated by Ellen Kennedy. Cambridge, MA: MIT Press, 1985.

———. *Political Theology: Four Chapters on the Concept of Sovereignty*. Translated by George Schwab. Cambridge, MA: MIT Press, 1985.

———. *Politische Theologie: Vier Kapitel zur Lehre von der Souveränität*. 1922. Munich: Verlag von Duncker und Humboldt, 1934.

Scholz, Heinrich, ed. *Die Hauptschriften zum Pantheismusstreit zwischen Jacobi und Mendelssohn*. Neudrucke seltener philosophischer Werke. Herausgegeben von der Kantgesellschaft, vol. 6. Berlin: Reuther & Reichard, 1916.

Schopenhauer, Arthur. *Die Welt als Wille und Vorstellung*. 2 vols. In *Werke in fünf Bänden*. Edited by Ludger Lütkehaus. Zurich: Haffmans Verlag, 1999.

———. *Parerga und Paralipomena*. 2 vols. In *Werke in fünf Bänden*. Edited by Ludger Lütkehaus. Zurich: Haffmans Verlag, 1999.

Schrey, Heinz-Horst, ed. *Säkularisierung*. Darmstadt: Wissenschaftliche Buchgesellschaft, 1981.

Schroeder, Brian. *Thinking through the Death of God: A Critical Companion to Thomas J.J. Altizer.* Albany: State University of New York Press, 2004.

Schulz, Walter. *Die Vollendung des deutschen Idealismus in der Spätphilosophie Schellings.* Stuttgart: W. Kohlhammer, 1955.

Schweitzer, Albert. *The Quest for the Historical Jesus: A Critical Study of Its Progress from Reimarus to Wrede.* 1906. Translated by W. Montgomery. London: A. & C. Black, 1936.

Seifert, Josef. *Gott als Gottesbeweis: Eine phänomenologische Neubegründung des ontologischen Arguments.* Heidelberg: Universitätsverlag C. Winter, 2000.

Sikka, Sonia. "Questioning the Sacred: Heidegger and Levinas on the Locus of Divinity." *Modern Theology* 14, no. 3 (1998): 299–323.

Smid, Marikje. *Deutscher Protestantismus und Judentum 1932/33.* Munich: Chr. Kaiser Verlag, 1990.

Smith, James K.A. *Introducing Radical Orthodoxy: Mapping a Post-Secular Theology.* Grand Rapids, MI: Baker Academic, 2004.

Smith, John H. *Dialectics of the Will: Freedom, Power, and Understanding in Modern French and German Thought.* Detroit: Wayne State University Press, 2000.

———. "*Die Gretchenfrage:* Goethe and Philosophies of Religion around 1800." *Goethe Yearbook* 18 (2011): 183–204.

———. "Heretical Thinking Then and Now: Jewish-Christian Dialectics in the Interwar Period." *Franz Rosenzweig Jahrbuch* (forthcoming).

Spinoza, Benedict. *Ethics and Treatise on the Correction of the Intellect.* 1670. Translated by Andrew Boyle. London: J.M. Dent (Everyman), 1997.

———. *Theological-Political Treatise.* 1670. Translated by Michael Silverthorne and Jonathan Israel. Cambridge: Cambridge University Press, 2007.

Taubes, Jacob. *Abendländische Eschatologie.* 1947. Munich: Matthes & Seitz Verlag, 1991.

———. *Die politische Theologie des Paulus.* Edited by Aleida Assmann and Jan Assmann. Munich: Wilhelm Fink Verlag, 1993.

———. *Von Kult zur Kultur: Bausteine zu einer Kritik der historischen Vernunft.* Gesammelte Aufsätze zur Religions- und Geistesgeschichte. Edited by Aleida Assmann, Jan Assmann, Wolf-Daniel Hartwich, and Winfried Menninghaus. Munich: Wilhlem Fink Verlag, 1996.

Taylor, Charles. *A Secular Age.* Cambridge, MA: Harvard University Press, 2007.

Taylor, Mark. *Confidence Games: Money and Markets in a World without Redemption.* Chicago: University of Chicago Press, 2004.

Torrance, Thomas F. *Karl Barth: An Introduction to His Early Theology, 1910–1931.* London: SCM Press, 1962.

Tracy, David. *On Naming the Present: God, Hermeneutics, Church.* Maryknoll, NY: Orbis Books, 1994.

Trinkaus, Charles. "The Problem of Free Will in the Renaissance and the Reformation." *Journal of the History of Ideas* 10, no. 1 (January 1949): 51–62.

Troeltsch, Ernst. *Glaubenslehre (Nach Heidelberger Vorlesungen aus den Jahren 1911 und 1912).* Munich: Verlag von Duncker und Humblot, 1925.

———. *Psychologie und Erkenntnistheorie in der Religionswissenschaft: Eine Untersuchung über die Bedeutung der kantischen Religionslehre für die heutige Religionswissenschaft.* Tübingen, 1905.

Vahanian, Gabriel. *The Death of God: The Culture of Our Post-Christian Era*. New York: George Braziller, 1961.

Vaihinger, Hans. *Die Philosophie des Als Ob: System der theoretischen, praktischen und religiösen Fiktionen der Menschheit auf Grund eines idealistischen Positivismus; Mit einem Anhang über Kant und Nietzsche*. Leipzig: F. Meiner, 1922.

Vallega-Neu, Daniela. *Heidegger's "Contributions to Philosophy": An Introduction*: Bloomington: Indiana University Press, 2003.

Vanhoozer, Kevin J., ed. *The Cambridge Companion to Postmodern Theology*. Cambridge: Cambridge University Press, 2003.

Vattimo, Gianni. *After Christianity*. Translated by Luca D'Isanto. New York: Columbia University Press, 2002.

———. *Belief*. Translated by Luca D'Isanto and David Webb. Stanford: Stanford University Press, 1999.

Vattimo, Gianni, and Richard Rorty. *The Future of Religion*. Edited by Santiago Zabala. Translated by William McCuaig. New York: Columbia University Press, 2004.

Vattimo, Gianni, Richard Schröder, and Ulrich Engel. *Christentum im Zeitalter der Interpretation*. Edited by Thomas Eggensperger. Vienna: Passagen Verlag, 2004.

Verweyen, Hansjürgen. *Philosophie und Theologie: Vom Mythos zum Logos zum Mythos*. Darmstadt: Wissenschaftliche Buchgesellschaft, 2005.

Vetter, Helmuth. "Hermeneutische Phänomenologie und dialektische Theologie: Heidegger und Bultmann." In *Geist und Verstehen: Perspektiven hermeneutischer Theologie*, edited by Ulrich Körtner, 19–38. Neukirchen-Vluyn: Neukirchener, 2000.

von der Luft, Eric, ed. and trans. *Hegel, Hinrichs, and Schleiermacher on Feeling and Reason in Religion: The Texts of Their 1821–22 Debate*. Lewiston, NY: Edwin Mellen Press, 1987.

Vries, Hent de. *Philosophy and the Turn to Religion*. Baltimore: Johns Hopkins University Press, 1990.

Wainwright, William J. *The Oxford Handbook of the Philosophy of Religion*. Oxford: Oxford University Press, 2005.

Waldenfels, Hans. *Kontextuelle Fundamentaltheologie*. Paderborn, 1985.

Wallerstein, Immanuel. *European Universalism: The Rhetoric of Power*. New York: The New Press, 2006.

Weber, Max. *The Protestant Ethic and the Spirit of Capitalism*. Translated by Talcott Parsons. London: Routledge, 1992.

———. "Die protestantische Ethik und der Geist des Kapitalismus." 1920. In *Gesammelte Aufsätze zur Religionssoziologie*, 1:1–206. Tübingen: J.C.B. Mohr (Paul Siebeck), 1988.

———. "Die protestantischen Sekten und der Geist des Kapitalismus." 1920. In *Gesammelte Aufsätze zur Religionssoziologie*, 1:207–36. Tübingen: J.C.B. Mohr (Paul Siebeck), 1988.

Webster, John, ed. *The Cambridge Companion to Karl Barth*. Cambridge: Cambridge University Press, 2000.

Weichelt, Hans. *Zarathustra-Kommentar*. Leipzig: Verlag von Felix Meiner, 1922.

Weischedel, Wilhelm. *Der Gott der Philosophen: Grundlegung einer philosophischen Theologie im Zeitalter des Nihilismus.* 1952. Darmstadt: Wissenschaftliche Buchgesellschaft, 1971.

Welch, Claude. *Protestant Thought in the Nineteenth Century.* Volume 1, *1799–1870.* New Haven, CT: Yale University Press, 1974.

Wilkinson, Elizabeth. "The Theological Basis of Faust's *Credo.*" *German Life and Letters* 10 (1957): 229–39.

Williamson, Raymond Keith. *Introduction to Hegel's Philosophy of Religion.* Albany: State University of New York Press, 1984.

Windelbrand, Wilhelm. "Das Heilige: Skizze zur Religionsphilosophie." In *Präludien*, 2:295–332. Tübingen, 1914.

Wittgenstein, Ludwig. *Tractatus logico-philosophicus.* New York: Routledge, 2001.

Wolfe, Alan. *The Transformation of American Religion: How We Actually Live Our Faith.* Chicago: Chicago University Press, 2005.

Wolin, Richard. *The Heidegger Controversy: A Critical Reader.* New York: Columbia University Press, 1991.

Wolterstorff, Nicholas. *Reason within the Bounds of Religion Alone.* Grand Rapids, MI: W.B. Eerdmans, 1976.

Wrathall, Mark A., ed. *Religion after Metaphysics.* Cambridge: Cambridge University Press, 2003.

Žižek, Slavoj. *The Abyss of Freedom.* Together with Friedrich Schelling, *Ages of the World (1813).* Ann Arbor: University of Michigan Press, 1997.

———. *The Fragile Absolute; or, Why Is the Christian Legacy Worth Fighting For?* London: Verso, 2001.

———. *The Invisible Remainder: An Essay on Schelling and Related Matters.* London: Verso, 1996.

———. *On Belief.* London: Routledge, 2001.

———. *The Puppet and the Dwarf: The Perverse Core of Christianity.* Cambridge, MA: MIT Press, 2003.

Žižek, Slavoj, Eric Santner, and Kenneth Reinhard. *The Neighbor: Three Inquiries in Political Theology.* Chicago: University of Chicago Press, 2006.

❧ INDEX